Colonialism and Nationalism in Asian Cinema

D1234400

Colonialism and Nationalism in Asian Cinema

Edited by Wimal Dissanayake

Indiana University Press

Bloomington and Indianapolis

Manufactured in the United States of America

Library of Congress Cataloging-in-Publication Data

Colonialism and nationalism in Asian cinema / edited by Wimal
Dissanayake.

    p.   cm.
    Includes index.
    Contents: Warring bodies / Patricia Lee Masters — The "peace
dividend" in Japanese cinema / Marie Thorsten — Ideology of the
body in Red sorghum / Yingjin Zhang — A nation t(w/o)o : Chinese
cinema(s) and nationhood(s) / Chris Berry — Korean cinema and the
New realism / Isolde Standish — Melodramas of Korean national
identity : from Mandala to Black republic / Rob Wilson — Vietnamese
cinema / John Charlot — Cinema and nation : dilemmas of
representation in Thailand / Annette Hamilton — National cinema,
national culture : the Indonesian case / Karl G. Heider — The
representation of colonialism in Satyajit Ray's Shatranj-ke-khilari
(The Chess players) / Darius Cooper — Cinema, nationhood and
cultural discourse in Sri Lanka / Wimal Dissanayake — The end of
the National project? : Australian cinema in the 1990s / Graeme
Turner.
    ISBN 0-253-31804-1. — ISBN 0-253-20895-5 (pbk.)
    1. Motion pictures—Asia. 2. Motion pictures—Political aspects—
Asia. I. Dissanayake, Wimal.
PN1993.5.A75C65 1994
302.23'43'095—dc20   93-51497

1 2 3 4 5 00 99 98 97 96 95 94

Contents

Acknowledgments   *vii*

Introduction: Nationhood, History, and Cinema: Reflections on
the Asian Scene   *ix*
    Wimal Dissanayake

1. Warring Bodies: Most Nationalistic Selves   *1*
    Patricia Lee Masters

2. The "Peace Dividend" in Japanese Cinema: Metaphors of
a Demilitarized Nation   *11*
    Marie Thorsten Morimoto

3. Ideology of the Body in *Red Sorghum*: National Allegory,
National Roots, and Third Cinema   *30*
    Yingjin Zhang

4. A Nation T(w/o)o: Chinese Cinema(s) and Nationhood(s)   *42*
    Chris Berry

5. Korean Cinema and the New Realism: Text and Context   *65*
    Isolde Standish

6. Melodramas of Korean National Identity: From *Mandala*
to *Black Republic*   *90*
    Rob Wilson

7. Vietnamese Cinema: First Views   *105*
    John Charlot

8. Cinema and Nation: Dilemmas of Representation in Thailand   *141*
    Annette Hamilton

9. National Cinema, National Culture: The Indonesian Case   *162*
    Karl G. Heider

10. The Representation of Colonialism in Satyajit Ray's
The Chess Players   *174*
    Darius Cooper

11. Cinema, Nationhood, and Cultural Discourse in Sri Lanka   *190*
     Wimal Dissanayake

12. The End of the National Project? Australian Cinema in the 1990s   202
     Graeme Turner

    Contributors   *217*
    Index   *218*

Acknowledgments

This volume is a collaborative effort in the best sense of the term. My first and greatest debt is to the very fine scholars whose writings are included in this book; all of them are deeply committed to the exploration of cultural discourses surrounding Asian cinema. Patricia Mellencamp, who has always shown an interest in my work, encouraged me in this effort as did Andrew Ross and Meaghan Morris. I am grateful to Geoffrey M. White, Director of the Program for Cultural Studies at the East-West Center, for his support. Benjamin Lee, Director of the Center for Transcultural Studies, invited me to present an earlier version of the introduction at one of his seminars, and I benefited greatly from the various suggestions made. In particular, I wish to thank Miriam Hansen and Michael Geyer. John Charlot's essay was initially published in the *Journal of Southeast Asian Studies*, and I appreciate the generosity of the editor, Albert Lau, for granting permission for the essay to be included in this volume. The University of Hawaii kindly granted permission to reprint two Korean poems that are discussed in Rob Wilson's essay. And my wife, Doreen, and daughter Niru helped me with the proofs. I wish to record my gratitude to the staff of Indiana University Press for their guidance and ready cooperation.

INTRODUCTION

Nationhood, History, and Cinema
Reflections on the Asian Scene
Wimal Dissanayake

ASIAN CINEMA IS increasingly attracting the attention of film critics, scholars of cinema, and specialists in cultural studies. Numerous thematizations closely associated with the growth of cinema are being explored from diverse theoretical vantage points. The objective of this collection of essays, dealing with different Asian cinemas and different problematics, is to make a contribution in some small way to this newly emerging interest by exploring the imbricated questions of nationalism and colonialism which are central to the cinematic discourse in Asian countries.

The terms *colonialism* and *nationalism* admit of a plurality of meanings related to such issues as territoriality, power, identity, subjectivity, ideology, symbolization, and narrativity. As Edward Said has observed, imperialism means the practice, the theory, and the attitudes of a dominating metropolitan center ruling a distant territory, while colonialism is almost always a consequence of imperialism and is the implanting of settlements on distant territory. Nationalism signifies a close and emotional identification with the nation and the construction of legitimating and unified narratives linking past, present, and future. However, each of these terms generates a multiplicity of meanings and valences and hence cannot be usefully contained within simple definitions and descriptions. It is important to remind ourselves that colonialism and nationalism are not transhistorical and transdiscursive categories and that historical conjunctures, social formations, and cultural specificities play a crucial role in our understanding of them.

Colonialism is a form of violence and domination, a state of mind, a cultural practice, a multivalent discourse, and an ideology of expansion. The relationship between colonialism and nationalism is complex, ambiguous, and multifaceted. Nationalism, on the other hand, simultaneously extends the range and depth of colonialism, offers the most palpable resistance to it, subverts its imperatives and determinations, and serves to reproduce it in subtle and not so subtle ways. Thus the relationship between colonialism and nationalism is ridden with paradoxes. This relationship is also at the heart of the narrative of cultural modernity in Asian societies. Hence the web of relationships spawned by the interplay of colonialism and nationalism is crucial to our understanding of Asian cultures and their trajectories of development. In this volume of essays we have sought to examine the intersection of the discourses of colonialism and nationalism in terms of two very significant and imbricated thematics, namely, nationhood and history.

The relationship among cinema, nationhood, and history is as complex as it is fascinating. Any investigation into this topic brings us face to face with questions of power, ideology, truth, colonialism, post-colonialism, and so on, and situates us at the center of some of the vital and invigorating debates taking place within the domain of modern cultural studies. Today the world is transforming itself in ways that could hardly have been predicted or imagined only two decades ago. The interlinks among nationalism, globalism, and ethnicity are becoming convoluted, and scholars of diverse persuasions are talking, although mistakenly in my view, about the end of history. The question of collective identity, group belonging, and the historical sense that undergirds it is proving more and more to be intractable. The implications of all these dizzying changes and newer conceptualities are enormous and far-reaching for Asian countries and their cinemas. Events in the modern world are taking place at such a rapid velocity that the political signposts and cognitive markers that in the past enabled us to navigate this troubled terrain of nationhood are proving to be less than helpful today. We have nations without states, and states without nations. States once thought to be united and cohesive are fragmentary; new alliances are being forged; globalization is increasingly gathering momentum; transnational cultural flows are on the rise; new cosmopolitanism is emerging. At the same time nationalism, sub-nationalism, ethnic identities, and religious loyalties have begun to make their presence felt in powerful, and at times, frightening ways. As they find articulation in cinema, all these newly emergent phenomena have deep implications for questions of nationhood and history. They throw into sharp and problematic relief the construction of nationhood, understanding of history, and their representation in filmic texts. The essays contained in this volume seek to examine these and related issues from different geographical and conceptual vantage points.

Benedict Anderson said that nationhood depends on "imagined communities" and emphasized the centrality of the idea that nationhood exists as a system of cultural signification.[1] He also remarked that history is the necessary basis of the national narrative. The consequences of this line of thinking for the study of the ways in which nation his been cinematized are immense and potentially productive. The discourses of nationhood and history and the representational space opened up by films are all vitally connected with modernity and interpenetrate each other in complex ways. The essays gathered in this book seek to illustrate this point.

The dialectic between nation and history—both of which are contested concepts—presents us with a particularly useful point of entry into the understanding of Asian cinema and the mapping of their diverse problematics. History has played a pivotal role in the production of modern nationhood while nationhood has urged a re-definition and re-appropriation of the discourse of history. It is indeed interesting that scholars such as Hayden White who have sought to identify the determining tropes of historical production have failed to recognize what in many ways is a central trope, that of nationhood.[2] As Nicholas B. Dirks observes, "The movement from annals to chronicles to historic narrative is the progression from different forms of kingship to the rationalized reality of the nation-state."[3] Many of the essays collected in this volume aim to reinforce and exemplify this point in terms of the art of cinematography.

Nationhood, as with all other forms of identity, turns on the question of difference—how the uniqueness of one nation differs from the uniqueness of other comparable nations. Nationhood is at the point of intersection with a plurality of discourses related to geography, history, culture, politics, ideology, ethnicity, religion, materiality, economics, and the social. The notion of difference and the incessant interplay between presence and absence are central to the construction of nationhood.

The discourse of nationhood can best be understood in relation to boundedness, continuities and discontinuities, unity in plurality, the authority of the past, and the imperatives of the present. It moves along two interesting axes: space and time. In terms of the space axis, the dominant question is territorial sovereignty; in terms of the time axis, the central question is the velocity of history, the continuity with the past. The way these two axes interact produces results that bear directly and challengingly on the problematic of nationhood. What is important to bear in mind is that the manifold issues related to these axes are man-made and not natural givens. They are human constructs seeking the status of the natural. The privileged narrative of nationhood tends to submerge the local narratives of resistance that attempt to bring into play the historically determined discourses of memory and the challenges to the hegemony of the nationhood. Memory here also includes countermemory in the Foucaldian sense.

Anderson is of the view that nationhood is a cultural artifact of a particular kind. In order to understand its true shape and significance, he advocates the careful investigation of how nationality came into historical being, the diverse ways in which meaning has changed over time, how it has come to command such powerful emotional allegiances and legitimacy today. Anderson defines a nation as an imagined community—both inherently limited and sovereign.[4] It is imagined in view of the fact that the members of even the smallest nation can never get to know most of their fellow members or meet them; yet in the minds of each persists the image of this communion. The nation is imagined as limited because even the largest of them, containing a billion human beings, has finite boundaries. Beyond these boundaries exist other nations; no nation encompasses the whole of humanity. It is imagined as sovereign in view of the fact that the concept came into being at a time when the divinely ordained hierarchical dynastic realms were being rapidly dismantled. Finally, nationality is imagined as community because irrespective of the very real inequities and social exploitations that exist in a nation, it is always seen as deep and horizontal comradeship. In the final analysis, it is the identification with the comradeship that persuades many millions of people to risk death for their imagined communities. One has, of course, to bear in mind the fact that Anderson used the word "imagined" and not "imaginary." Imaginary signifies the absence, or nothingness, while imagined connotes a nice balance between real and not real. Anderson's approach to nationhood can be taken as a useful point of departure for further exploration. However, the critical weakness of his conceptualization is that it pays inadequate attention to the materialities and overlooks discontinuities of history; it also gives short shrift to the political character of nationhood and the role ethnic loyalties and religious affiliations may have played in the construction of nationhood.

Apart from Benedict Anderson, there have been a number of other contemporary thinkers who have influenced our thinking on nationhood, Elie Kedourie,[5] Ernest Gellner,[6] Eric Hobsbawm,[7] Anthony Giddens,[8] and Partha Chatterjee[9] being perhaps the most prominent among them. Elie Kedourie sees nationhood and nationalism as essentially European perceptions that were subsequently spread throughout the world by the power of colonialism and that are obsolete formulations. Gellner perceives a structural link between the idea of nationhood and the requirements of the modern, industrial societies. According to him, the idea of nationhood produces the shared cultural basis and social homogeneity required for the smooth functioning of complexly organized division of labor in modern societies. In order to effectuate productive social arrangements there should be a legitimizing ideology of the polity, and the idea of nationhood, in his view, accomplishes that. Hobsbawm is of the view that nationhood displays a certain cunningness in that it serves to preserve a threatened way of life of the privileged by drawing on the past for historical validation. Anthony Giddens seeks to explain nationalism largely in terms of psychological dimensions as related to the transformations of human experiences initiated by the processes of social modernization. Partha Chatterjee takes a decidedly political attitude to the whole question of nationhood and points out how it is vitally imbricated with epistemology. For him nationalism should give rise to a double decolonization, one ontological and the other epistemological. It is his considered view that political emancipation from colonial bondage by itself, important as it is, does not ensure the inauguration of a new history, a new sense of subjectivity and an assertion of agency. The political emancipation must be accompanied by an epistemological shift which clears a theoretical space in which the much valorized and universalized imperative of the post-Enlightenment could be challenged, Eurocentric subject subverted, and people in former colonies allowed to produce a critically deconstructive knowledge of nationhood and its hegemonic discourse. These diverse formulations and theorizations of nationhood only serve to underline the complex and contested discursive terrain that it undoubtedly is.

National identity, in my judgment, can be most profitably discussed at four interconnected levels: the local, national, regional, and global. Let us for example consider the case of India. The national identity of India is constituted on the basis of a vast geography, of diverse ethnic groups, of various religious affiliations, and multiple sedimentations of history. At the local level, we find different ethnic, linguistic, and religious groups seeking to assert their identity and belongings vis-à-vis the hegemonic discourse of the nation-state and part of the current social unrest in the country is attributable to this phenomenon. At the national level, we see how a unity has been imposed over diverse competing languages, religions, ideologies, and cultural practices and a privileged master narrative constructed that seeks to incorporate the multiple voices with their different stories. This is by no means unique to India and can be seen in most other countries seeking to create a modern nation-state on the basis of past traditions, cultural legacies, and the imperative of modernity. At the regional level, we have the South Asian Association for Regional Cooperation (SAARC) which seeks to work in close cooperation with neighboring countries like Pakistan, Bangladesh, and Sri Lanka. India's identity as an active member of the SAARC is vital to its image both internally and externally. Finally, we have the global level where India forms a part of the global system where questions of economics, trade, information technology, and cultural flows take on a great significance of meaning and urgency. The demands and logic of these four levels are not necessarily compatible; indeed very often they are not. How best to balance and accommodate these conflicting demands emanating from the four levels is centrally connected with the idea of India.

Cinema as a very powerful cultural practice and institution both reflects and intervenes in these discourses. In any examination of the relationship between cinema and nationhood, the question of national cinema becomes extremely important. The concept of national cinema is at the heart of many discussions of popular culture, especially in Asia. This concept privileges ideas of coherence and unity and stable cultural meanings associated with the uniqueness of a given nation. It is imbricated with national myth-making and ideological production and serves to delineate alterities and legitimize selfhood. The concept of national cinema can be analyzed very broadly at two levels: the textual and the industrial. At the textual level we can examine the uniqueness of a given cinema in terms of content, style, and indigenous aesthetics while at the industrial level we can examine the relationship between cinema and industry in terms of production, distribution, and exhibition. Both these levels of analysis which are crucially interlinked should yield fascinating results as is borne out by some of the essays contained in this book.

Nationhood consists of a number of intersecting discourses, and one that is especially germane to the discussions of cinema is one that deals with symbolism, including issues of construction of meaning, consciousness, and problematics of representation. How a nation tells its unifying and legitimizing story to its citizens is exceedingly important in the understanding of nationhood, and in modern times, the role of cinema in this endeavor has come to occupy a central place. Benedict Anderson has pointed out the importance of print capitalism in generating the idea of nationhood and the deep horizontal comradeship it entails, and he remarks that newspapers and nationalistic novels are primarily responsible for the formation of a national consciousness. In social circumstances prior to the establishment of nation-states, print media, and novels, in his view, were able to coordinate time and space in a manner conducive to addressing the imagined community. In the modern world, cinema becomes a dominant mode of communication, and its role in conjuring up the imagined community among both the literate and illiterate segments of the community is enormous. David Harvey has pointed out how cinema works to capture the complex and dynamic relationship between temporality and spatiality in a way that is not possible for other media.[10] Film's role in the maintenance of Anderson's communicative community—an aspect that he himself does not examine in any depth—merits more sustained discussion.

The topos of nationhood is significant in the understanding of cinema and its functioning in social space on another account, too. Cinema in most countries is closely allied to the nation-state due to considerations of economics—production, distribution, and exhibition—and content control. For most Asian countries, which rely on local audiences for their returns on the investments, the assistance and coordination of government becomes imperative. Film corporations, script boards, training institutes, censorship panels, etc., that are commonly found in Asian societies bear testimony to this fact. The demands of the economics of film industries and the demands of the nation-state are intertwined in complex, and at times troublesome, ways.

Cinema is not an indigenous form of entertainment to Asia; however, before long, this imported Western art form was able to sink roots in the national soil and the consciousness of the people to assume the status of a national art. Hence, one should not make too much of its Western roots. Japan and India are two of the most important countries in terms of cinema whose works have generated international attention. Thirty years after the Meiji restoration in 1868 which opened Japan's door to Western influence, the film industry began in Japan. Cinema in Japan, as indeed in most other countries, was originally conceived of as a form of mass entertainment with very little claim to artistic value, and was primarily designed to offer pleasure of a special kind to the movie-going public. From the beginning there was seen an interesting interplay between the authority of the past and the imperatives of the present, resulting in a novel admixture between the inherited art forms and the newly introduced medium of mass entertainment.[11] While the art of cinema was clearly new, the early Japanese filmmakers sought to draw on traditional literature and drama for inspiration. From the very beginning Japanese cinema displayed an interest in two prominent genres: period drama and the modern social drama. The period drama was primarily influenced by the traditional Kabuki theater; the earliest print of a Japanese film that is currently available being *Maple Viewing*, made in 1898. It is the filmed version of a period drama, a Kabuki play with the identical title. Modern social dramas competed with the period dramas for the attention of audiences. This genre took root after 1910 with the successful filming of Shimpa stories, which narrated tragic and sentimental love stories in modern settings. Shimpa stories sought to thematize the misery, sadness, and forlornness of young heroines who were abandoned by their lovers. What we see in Japan, then, is that the imported art of cinema was very quickly transformed into an "indigenous" medium of entertainment capable of representing various facets of the national experience and sensibility.

A similar trend can be discerned in India where the first feature film, *Raja Harishchandra*, was produced in 1913.[12] It was made by D. G. Phalke, who is generally considered to be the father of Indian cinema. This film is based on the venerated Indian epic *The Mahabharata* and was instrumental in giving rise to the genre of mythological film—a genre that continues to flourish even today. The first Indian talkie, *Alam Ara*, was made in 1931 and contained many songs calculated to generate audience interest in the new medium. The musical form took root in the consciousness of the people and became a readily identifiable trait of popular Indian cinema in both the north and the south. As in the classical Indian theater, drama, music, dance, gesture, and spectacle were combined into a multifaceted unity. In 1935, *Devdas*, which had for its theme the rationality and legitimacy of arranged marriages, inaugurated a new genre of social drama. The mythological and the social genres and the music form remain to this day characteristic markers of Indian cinema. Hence as in the case of Japan, in India too, the newly imported art of cinematography became a national form of entertainment before long, having been inscribed with cultural legitimacy.

Broadly speaking one can divide films made in Asia into three categories: popular, artistic, and experimental. In countries like Japan, India, and the Philippines this division is palpably present while in some other countries it exists in more shadowy forms. The popular films which are commercial by nature are designed to appeal to the vast mass of people and to secure maximum profit. The artistic filmmaker, while not totally abandoning commercial imperatives, seeks to explore through willed art facets of indigenous experiences and thought worlds that are amenable to aesthetic treatment. These are the kinds of films that are designated as high art and get shown at international film festivals. The experimental film directors, much smaller in number and much less visible on the film scene, are deeply committed to the construction of a counter cinema where boldness of outlook and opposition to the Establishment are combined with innovativeness. What is interesting from the point of view of nationhood and history is that while popular films by and large seek to reinforce the idea of an essentialized and unitary nation-state and its apparatuses, the artistic cinema endeavors very often to be critical of the nation-state and its diverse social, political, cultural institutions and discourses. For example in a large country like India with its many states, languages, and religions, the artistic films produced in, say, Bengal or Kerala tend to valorize, directly or indirectly, the regional at the expense of the national, thereby opening up certain fissures and fault lines in the nationalist discourse. The experimental filmmakers for their part seek to expose the hegemonic propensities of the nation-state as well as the established vocabularies and strategies of national narration, pointing out the collusions between late capitalism and post-coloniality. Hence the different ways in which different modes of Asian cinema approach questions of nationhood and history are extremely instructive and underline the multivalent nature of the relationship among nationhood, history, and cinema. The artistic and experimental cinemas serve to highlight the ambivalent unities, marginalized voices, and emergent and oppositional discourses that cohabit the national space, thereby setting in motion a de-totalizing dialectic.

In most Asian countries cinema is used strategically to reinforce the myth of the unitary nation and to interpellate the textual subjects as willing members of the nation. To take an example from Indonesia, *The Jade Princess* (*Puteri Giok*), produced in 1981, is a characteristically melodramatic Indonesian film that deals with the need for cultural assimilation in Indonesia and its beneficent consequences. As Heider points out, the opening scene of the film adumbrates the theme and sets the mood as the camera pans across a vast chorus of people dressed in the attire characteristic of each ethnic group and province.[13] However, they all sing the national anthem in harmony, signifying that they have all transcended ethnic and provincial differences to unite in the name of the nation. Similarly, in the Indian film *Ab Dilli Dur Nahin*, the popular filmmaker Raj Kapoor, while pointing out the corruption, brutality, and injustice rampant in society, seeks to inspire hope in the then Prime Minister Jawaharlal Nehru and his leadership. The image of Nehru pervades the film, framing the narrative and inflecting the theme. Referring to Nehru, one of the characters says, "He is everybody's protector. Who else will hear our plea?"[14] Mainstream, commercial cinemas serve to reinforce and strengthen the hegemony of the nation-state in diverse ways. For example, popular Indian films made in Bombay have had the effect of making Hindi an almost pan-Indian language.

The power-wielders in any society strive to enhance their base by making use of all available media of communication at their disposal, and surely film is one of them. Many filmmakers willingly participate in this effort of hegemony. However, there is a constant interplay between centripetal and centrifugal forces taking place within the national-space. Homi Bhabha says, "The scraps, patches, and rags of daily life must be repeatedly turned into the signs of national cinema culture while the very act of narrative performance interpellates a growing circle of national subjects. In the production of nation as narration there is a split between the continuist, accumulative, temporality of the pedagogical and the repetitive, recursive strategy of the performative."[15] He goes on to remark how counter-narrations of the nation that continually seek to evoke and encase its totalizing boundaries de-stabilize those ideological strategies by means of which imagined communities are given essentialist identities. These observations of Bhabha have a pointed relevance to the work of many contemporary Asian filmmakers.

A filmmaker like the late Lino Brocka of the Philippines sought to demonstrate that the facade of a totalizing and consensual nationhood is maintained at the cost of repressing and silencing the dispossessed. In *Bayan Ko: Kapit sa Patalim (My Country: Clutching the Knife)*, Brocka textualizes the numerous economic and social problems encountered by the workers in the context of an authoritarian nationhood. He juxtaposes the private and public agonies of the downtrodden to dramatically underscore how one cannot be understood in isolation from the other. He effectively uses film clips from the people's power revolution taking place in the streets to enforce this point. It is Brocka's intention to bring out into the open the false unity of the nation-state that is enforced through diverse strategies of exclusion and repression.

The homogeneity of the nation-state and its legitimizing metanarratives begin to be fissured when filmmakers seek to give expression to the hopes and experiences and lifeworlds of the minorities whether they be ethnic, linguistic, or religious. Films dealing with the privations of minorities serve to open up a representational space from where the hegemonic discourse of the state can be purposefully challenged and the idea of cultural difference foregrounded. Indeed one discerns a tension between nationhood and cultural identity in almost all Asian countries, and cinema enables us to understand the contours of this phenomenon more clearly. This is a complex interaction which touches centrally on identity and subject positions. Bhabha says that "cultural differences mark the establishment of new forms of meaning and strategies of identification through processes of regulation where no discursive authority can be established without revealing the difference of itself."[16] Questions of cultural difference, assertion of agency, and subjectivity lie at the heart of the more interesting Asian films dealing with minority experiences.

Consequently, one of the ways in which the metaphysics of nationalism, which purports to construct a unitary subject named the people, can be examined is through films which thematize minority experiences whose very semioticization can be read in an oppositional light. In this regard, I would like to refer to four Asian films made in Japan, China, India, and Thailand, respectively, that explore themes of minority lifeworlds. Some of these films are not radical in intent; however, when read against the grain they yield the insight that the boundaries of minority differences are not only about ethnicity, language, and religion, but more importantly about the discourse of power that lies at the heart of the idea of nationhood.

Nagisa Oshima's *Death by Hanging* (*Koshikei*), which in many ways helped to establish his international reputation, was made in 1968 and deals with the plight of the Koreans living in Japan and the discrimination that they are subjected to. The film also interlinks the whole question of capital punishment. It is based on a true story about a Korean student who had a hard time securing a job in Japan owing to widespread discrimination against Koreans. While attending high school he killed two girls after raping them. He was found guilty; his appeals were turned down and he was hanged four years after the alleged crime. Oshima was fascinated by this incident and made a film out of it. However, he changed the plot in order to bring out some of the thematizations that had attracted him. He speculated on the course of events that would have taken place had the student not died by hanging. The film represents a blending of realism and fantasy and poses in strong terms the plight of Koreans in Japanese society. The Japanese flag is the dominant trope in the film and the director uses it to marvelous satiric effect. R is the protagonist of the film, the Korean student. At one point in the film while responding to R's protestations the prosecutor says that it is the nation that wishes to execute him, and he flatly rejects the concept of the nation. There the style of the film is at odds with the normal style of Japanese film-making and Oshima is clearly against both establishments, making the point that they are interlinked in their oppressive designs. *Death by Hanging*, then, opens a discursive space that enables thoughtful viewers to see the politics of erasure that are in place in Japanese society and to recognize the importance of multiple horizons in the understanding of the concept of nationhood.

Sacrificed Youth (*Qingchun Ji*), made in 1985 by the Chinese film director Zhang Nuanxin, is another film that deals with a minority lifeworld although it does not have the same explosive power as Oshima's film. *Sacrificed Youth* narrates the story of Li Chun, a young woman born and bred in the city who is sent to live in a village inhabited by the Dai minority. During the cultural revolution, like many of her classmates, she is sent to the rural areas so that she can learn from the peasants. As she comes to understand and appreciate the lifeways of the Dai, Li Chun begins to develop a deep empathy for them. Their love of nature, beauty, and instinctual life is contrasted with the contrivedness, hypocrisy, and falsity of urban life. It is indeed a learning experience for her and she begins to acquire a greater sense of her own identity; her process of self-discovery takes place against the background and in contrast to the lifeworld of the Dai minority. Although this film contains nothing of the radical nature that characterized *Death by Hanging*, it too in its own way serves to bring into the open the troubled relationship among place, space, identity and the problematics of nationhood, by focusing on the hegemony of the Han majority in Chinese society.

The third film is by the Indian filmmaker Saeed Akhtar Mirza and is called *Don't Cry for Salim the Lame* (*Salim Langde Pe Mat Ro*). The film charts the life course of Salim, a young Muslim, seeking to find his identity in a confused and confusing world. He is poor and lives a life of crime, his heroes being the smugglers and racketeers who have been successful in their materialistic ambitions. This indeed is a world that shows scant respect for moral values, characterized by poverty, gangsterism, hopelessness, misery, and brutality. Salim strives to move in the direction of a more compassionate and fulfilling life, but as the logic of his social ambience and the narrative would have it, this comes to no avail. In this film the director has attempted to focus attention on the Muslim minority in India living in the cities. It situates questions of belonging and identity in modern India against the hegemonic discourse of the unitary nation-state and how the metanarrative of nationhood pays scant attention to local narratives in its haste to obliterate local differences. The idea of space is crucial to *Don't Cry for Salim the Lame*. Nationhood aims to construct a new narrative of space, and the director of this film has sought to subvert it by representing the complex ways in which power relationships are inscribed in it. The "inside" and "outside" are the central tropes that animate the argument of the film, and they serve to refocus attention on identity and difference.

The fourth film that I wish to discuss briefly is the Thai film *Butterfly and Flower* (*Peesua Lae Dokmai*) made by Euthana Mukdasnit in 1985. This film narrates the story of a boy and girl from a Muslim background who live in a preponderantly Buddhist country. *Butterfly and Flower* does not broach the question of the plight of minorities in any significant way. However, when read against the grain, the film opens up a symbolic space in which we could thematize not only the question of the Muslim minority in Thailand but also the reluctance of the film industry to raise such contentious issues.

Butterfly and Flower won the top award at the Hawaii International Film Festival in 1986 and has been well received at a number of international film festivals. It deals with the emotional relationship between two teenagers—Huyan and Mimpi—against a backdrop of social struggle and efforts to rise above poverty. Huyan is a good student and, if allowed to continue with his education, he would have a bright future. However, due to the poverty in which his family is mired, he is forced to look for a job. Before long, he ends up in the rice-smuggling trade across the Malaysian border. His father is seriously injured, and Huyan becomes the sole supporter of his family—his father and younger brother and sister. Rice-smuggling, understandably enough, is a dangerous activity. As he becomes a regular member of a group of young smugglers earning a living in this perilous and unlawful way, he falls in love with a young girl called Mimpi. Seeing the danger that rice-smuggling involves and the tragic fate that befalls some of their comrades, Huyan and Mimpi decide to give up this trade and instead resolve to grow flowers for commercial purposes. The film ends on this hopeful note.

There are a number of interesting points about this film that need to be taken into consideration. First, the story takes place in southern Thailand, which is largely Muslim, in contradistinction to the rest of this country, which is Buddhist. What we find in the background to the action is not the pagodas and saffron-clad monks but the mosque and Muslim calls to prayer. This points out the religious divisions in Thai society. The story of the film takes place against poverty, racial injustice, and crime; however, the story moves along personal lines. This very attempt, through its silences, foregrounds the tension between individuals and the social system. The conflicts engendered in the film are resolved at a personal level: Huyan and Mimpi decide to take up a more honorable trade. The concept of liminality is essential to this film; the protagonist first moves from rice-smuggling to growing flowers, that is, from crime to an honorable occupation. This liminality is intimately connected with questions of dominance and subalternity, power and ideology, but these are only hinted at and never explored in depth. Being a commercial industrial film, naturally, *Butterfly and Flower* had to attract mass audiences; the film serves to achieve this end. And the absence of any serious exploration of issues of ideology and power only serve to highlight the limitations under which talented directors have to work. The way the filmmaker positions the spectator is also interesting; his/her moral imagination is subverted in the sense that, although it is clear that rice-smuggling is an illegal activity punishable by law, our sympathies are with the young men and women who are involved in it. What the discerning critic should look for, I think, in *Butterfly and Flower* is the way in which beyond and beneath the lyrical surface, oppositional viewpoints, values, and ideologies are struggling to find articulation. It is this tension that alerts us to the dangers of accepting the overt ideology that is presented in the film.

The relationship between nationhood and history is complex and is inscribed by ambiguity and contradiction. Although the concept of nation is of recent origin, all nations seek to invoke history as a way of situating it in as distant a past as possible.

What modern metahistorians point out is that historical facts are not found but made. The deeply held and long valorized elements of historical analysis like objectivity, impartiality, and neutrality have proved to be no more than chimeras. History, like cinema, is a discourse, a signifying system constructed by human beings living at a particular time and place, being subjected to the power and ideology inscribed in them. It is asserted that meanings and shapes are not in the events themselves but in the systems of signification and acts of semioticizations that reshape past events into historical facts through the process of writing. It is also pointed out that ideological and institutional affiliations are vital to the production of history. These conceptualizations challenge directly the long held notion of the transparency of historical representation. Michel de Certeau's reminder that history-writing is a displacing operation upon the real past, a limited and limiting endeavor to comprehend the relationship that exists among a place, a discipline, and the production of a text is extremely illuminating in this regard.[17]

We need to focus increasingly on questions of narrative positioning, tropes of narrativization, rhetorical strategies, ideological and institutional affiliations, cultural embeddedness, and problems of representation as ways of understanding the production of history in all its complex polysemy. Equally, questions of plurality of perspective, modalities of inclusion and exclusion, taken-for-granted linearities of historical progression, discontinuities of evolution, and tactics of self-empowerment are being foregrounded. The traditional tropes of "memory" and "gathering" that underpinned theorizations of the historians' project are giving way to tropes of "forgetting," "discontinuity," "exclusion," "marginalizing," "silencing," and "plurality."

Alternative histories of the same event open up multiple horizons and serve to challenge the homogenizing and monological narratives that have been served up as the only real ones, thereby undoing the totalizing proclivities reflected in traditional history-making. The presence of diverse voices with their diverse stories is being increasingly recognized as important to the construction of history. Just as much as the discourse of nationhood is challenged, pluralized, subverted, and deconstructed so is the discourse of history being subjected to the same anti-hegemonic and centrifugal forces.

The relationship between nationhood and history, as we have seen, is multifaceted. Similarly, the relationship between history and cinema occupies a number of different levels: the representation of history in cinema, the history of cinema in different cultures, cinema as history, and cinema as a metaphor for understanding the nature of historical inquiry are four such perspectives.

History finds expression in cinema in many and interesting ways. Let us, for example, consider Satyajit Ray's *The Home and the World* (*Ghare Baire*, 1984), which is by no means a historical film. The story takes place nearly nine decades ago, during the British Raj, when a conscious policy of divide and rule was pursued. The viceroy of India at the time, Lord Curzon, proposed the division of Bengal into two distinct administrative units. This proposal drove a wedge between the Hindus and Muslims who formed the population of the state, generating much controversy and ill-will, particularly among the middle classes.

A leader of the group antipathetic to the policy of Lord Curzon is Sandip Mukerji. He arrives at the country estate that belongs to his friend Nikhilesh in order to win more support for his cause. Nikhilesh is a man with a liberal outlook who has absorbed the best of Western civilizations. In his considered judgment, his wife, Bimala, who has been brought up in accordance with traditional Indian values, should attempt to adapt to a more modern life-style. For her part, she is quite content with her way of life. Bimala meets Sandip and is completely taken with his affable personality. Sandip, too, is attracted to her; he decides to conduct his political campaign as a house guest of Nikhilesh. Despite the fact that Sandip and Nikhilesh are united in their opposition to their viceroy, they have differences regarding tactics. Meanwhile Nikhilesh realizes that both his emotional and social lives are getting more and more complicated. The political crisis deepens. He comes to the realization that his wife has fallen in love with Sandip. Nikhilesh is also increasingly convinced that Sandip is more an opportunistic politician than a true patriot. As he becomes progressively estranged from his wife, Nikhilesh's only hope is that Biimala will be able to see through Sandip's disingenuousness. As the film closes, Bimala realizes that she has committed an error of judgment and goes back to Nikhilesh. Both have been irrevocably affected by the troubling experience.

The Home and the World is essentially about three characters; the tensions, conflicts, and attractions among them constitute the human drama. However, although this is not a historical film, we are also made vividly aware of the fact that history is a central player in this human drama. The attitudes and behavior of the characters as well as the symbols of communication bear the unmistakable imprint of history. This is indeed a trait that is discernible in most artistic films.

Let us consider a different type of film—Chen Kaige's *King of the Children* (*Haizi wang*, 1987). This film shows us how contemporary history can be explored allegorically to great effect. The "king of children," Lao Gar, is sent to a school in Yunnan province, where the majority of students are poor and lead miserable lives. He is a dedicated teacher; he sees the futility of learning by rote and encourages the creative and critical faculties of the students. His unorthodox ways of teaching do not sit well with the local power elite, and Lao Gar is fired. Chen Kaige has expanded this story visually into a powerful and allegorical indictment of the Cultural Revolution that caused irreparable damage to Chinese society. The self-destructive educational system depicted in the film becomes a metonym for the Cultural Revolution. As director Chen Kaige has said, "I did not directly depict the violent social confrontation that took place during the Cultural Revolution. Instead, I chose to use the language of film to create the atmosphere of the era. The forest, the fog, and the sound of trees being chopped down are all reflections of China during that period of time."[18]

The third Asian film that reveals the complex relationship that exists between cinema and history is Kumai Kei's *The Sea and Poison* (*Umi to dokuyaku*, 1986). This film is based on actual incidents, hideous in their lack of humanism, that took place in 1945 toward the end of the Pacific War. Two medical students are compelled to be accomplices to brutal surgery that is to take place in the prestigious Kyushu Hospital. Prisoners of war were used as human guinea pigs in high-risk operations. The film not only recounts a forgotten incident during that war in all its horror but also foregrounds the animosities, misunderstanding, and visciousness associated with wars. *The Sea and Poison* recreates a brutal event from the Pacific War to memorialize it for a long time to come, and by that means it converts the incident into a remarkable trope of the inhumanity of war.

In these three films, we see how history becomes a character, how the cinematic allegorization of history takes place, and how aspects of history likely to be forgotten can be kept alive and invested with a tropological force. The spate of films dealing with the Vietnam experience open up a different terrain related to cinema and history; namely, the reexperiencing and recreating of history. The Vietnam War, which is the only war Americans lost, was the most divisive in American history. How to assess it has always been a problem for historians, and now with more and more films being made about that experience, that reevaluation is taking place at the level of popular consciousness. There have been a number of American films made about the Vietnam War and its effects, ranging from *Rambo, Missing in Action, Uncommon Valor,* and *First Blood II,* to *Platoon, Coming Home, The Deer Hunter, Apocalypse Now, Full Metal Jacket,* and *Born on the Fourth of July.* These films, in their widely divergent ways, have sought to recapture history as a way of making sense of it. Questions of guilt, misjudgment, scapegoating, remorse, anger, valor, bitterness, and despair surface again and again as filmmakers bring the spectators face to face with history and thereby extend its discursive boundaries. Some of the more important films, such as *Apocalypse Now, Platoon,* and *Full Metal Jacket,* achieve their effects through mythologizing and moral inquiry; still we find little deep political exploration. On the other hand, Hollywood's willingness to support Vietnam films is reflective of the specularization and commodification of that history. The films dealing with the Vietnam War, with their diverse thematics and discursivities, shows us the way in which cinema becomes the terrain for historical reconstruction and contestation of historical meaning. These movies vividly illustrate how the changing imperatives of the present take on the authority of the past.

The whole notion of counter-memory is central to historical understanding and representation. Here, too, cinema can prove to be extremely valuable. Counter-memory underlines the fact that history is a multivoiced and multileveled narration and that normally the single voice and single level are privileged depending on the preferences of the author. The idea of counter-memory problematizes this easy writing of history; it opens up the locked doors, allowing for the marginalized and silenced voices to be heard. As a recent commentator has observed, counter-memory looks to the past for the hidden histories excluded from dominant narratives. But unlike myths that seek to detach events and actions from the fabric of any larger history, counter-memory forces revisions of existing histories by supplying new perspectives about the past. Films, mainly representatives of the avant-garde and Third Cinema, can be extremely illuminating in this regard.

Cinema can be extremely effective in persuading us to deconstruct the putatively unified narrative of nationhood by focusing on the diverse elements that go to form it as well as by urging us to take a second look at certain well-accepted positionalities. For example, the Indian film *Hot Winds* (*Garam Hava*) by M. S. Sathu deals with the collective violence directed against the Muslims during the partitioning of India, and this is shown through its impact on the lives of a single family. Salim Mirza is a shoe manufacturer whose family has lived in Agra for many generations. With the partitioning of India in 1947, Mirza, like a large number of other Muslims, was confronted with the cruel choice of either leaving India for the newly created nation-state of Pakistan or staying back and risking the collective wrath of the Hindu majority. Halim, his elder brother, who is a cunning politician, elects to leave India; Mirza refuses to follow his lead. He feels that India is his country and is determined to remain and continue with his family business. To make matters more complicated, Salim Mirza's daughter, Amina, is engaged to Kazim, Halim's son. As the border between India and Pakistan is closed Kazim cannot come back to meet his bride. At last he succeeds in crossing the border illegally; preparations for the wedding are made in haste; however, before the completion of the wedding, the police show up and take Kazim away. The miseries and privations flowing from the partitioning begin to have an impact on Mirza's life in numerous ways, including the loss of his business and the death of his daughter by his own hands. The film textualizes honestly and movingly all his troubles and disappointments. At last Mirza accepts the inevitable and decides with his son to leave India. As they make their way to the railway station, they find themselves caught up in a procession of protesters of diverse ethnic, racial, and religious groups, all representatives of the oppressed. Mirza joins them, giving up his plans to leave the country, in the hope that their voices will be heard and things will improve.

In this film, Sathu has focused on the plight of the Muslims in India, and he has done so with a great measure of humanity. His effort is all the more praiseworthy considering the fact that he himself is a Hindu. *Hot Winds* serves to uncover the pluralisms embedded in the national sign, reminding us of the fact that the interplay between indentity and differences is at the heart of the discourse of nationhood.

Masahiro Shinoda's *MacArthur's Children* (*Setouchi Shonen Yaku Dan*), made in 1984, shows us by focusing on a group of school children how the inhabitants of a small town in an island come to terms with the transformations ushered in by the defeat in the war. The story takes place in the island of Awaji after World War II. A group of sixth-grade school children are being taught how to edit their textbooks in keeping with the orders from higher-ups in the administration. Two of the children, as a way of protesting the loss of their motherland, run away from school. Mune, the daughter of a captain of the navy who is considered to be a war criminal by the Allied forces, is a newcomer to class. Komako, the teacher in charge of the class, is a young widow. Her husband was killed during the war. When the American forces arrive, the American culture begins to influence the school children in a very big way. Some of the boys meet a wounded one-legged soldier hiding on the island and it turns out that he is Komako's husband who was assumed dead. It is against interactions like these that Shinoda takes a hard and satirical look at post-war Japan, and the impact of American culture. In terms of the question of nationhood, the film opens up the multilayered representational space of the nation by pointing out its different sedimentations.

The third film that I wish to call attention to is the Taiwanese film *A City of Sadness* by Hou Xiaoxian. Allen Chun says that the culture industry in Taiwan has sought to construct a total ideology of culture as a means of creating national identity, ensuring conformity to the existing political order and regulating the norms of day-to-day behavior.[19] A film like *A City of Sadness* calls into question this ideology of imposed unity by dramatizing alternative narratives of nationhood and history, and by opening up a symbolic space wherein other perspectives may be brought into the discourse.

The film deals with four important years in the evolution of the nation-state of Taiwan from the end of Japanese colonization in 1945 to the ascent of communist power in China and Chiang Kai-shek's setting up his Kuomintang government in exile in Taipei in 1949. Understandably enough, this was a period of tumultuous change in Taiwan, and the director explores some facets of these changes through the fortunes of one family consisting of an elderly widower, Ah-lu, and his four sons. Li Wen-heung, the eldest son, is a black-marketeer, a nightclub owner, and a gangster who dies through violence. He is in a sense attuned to the social realities of the emerging nation-state. Lin Wen-ching, the youngest son, is deaf and mute and stays somewhat aloof from the crises in the life of his family. Lin Wen-sun, the second son, was recruited into the Japanese army to serve as a doctor in the Philippines and has not come back. Lin Wen-leung, the third son, was also recruited by the Japanese army as a translator, and his bitter experiences have left him mentally deranged.

Through the interplay of these characters, the film focuses on an episode that is brushed under the carpet by official historians, namely, the massacre on February 28, 1947, of the supporters of the Taiwan independence movement by some of those who supported the KMT troops. This is an extremely sensitive area, and director Hou Xiaoxian was fully aware of the controversies that his film was likely to trigger. He is on record as saying that he made this film, "not for the sake of opening up old wounds, but because it's vital that we face up to this incident if we are to understand where we come from and who we are as Taiwanese. The Chinese way has always been to cover over domestic scandals, to pretend they never happened, but I am not at all persuaded that that's a good thing. My own feeling is that problems must be acknowledged and discussed if we are ever to resolve them in our minds."[20] *A City of Sadness* represents the ambivalences and the fractured signs that inevitably occupy the national space.

What is clear, then, is that the idea of nationhood aims to present itself as a transcendental domain of identity which occludes the diverse elements of difference that we have discussed above. Nationhood also presents itself, as we have already seen, as legitimizing the importance of the state as the historical articulation of a basic unity of peoplehood living within its borders ignoring the local narratives of difference. What cinema can do most productively, and as certain innovative and experimental film directors in Asia are indicating, is to offer contestatory narratives of nationhood and history, thereby reemphasizing the point that nationhood is not a transhistorical, supra-ideological, and self-identical category. Cinema has the power and the obligation to represent the multiple and incompatible differences that are folded into the privileged and monological narrative of nationhood. Filmmakers like Hou Xiaoxian, Hara Kazuo, and Saeed Mirza have demonstrated the potentiality of cinema to incarnate the contradictory and pluralistic discourses occupying the national space. Similarly, as many Asian filmmakers are beginning to point out, cinema has the capacity to foreground the lifeworlds of the subalterns, to give them voice and salvage them from what the progressive historian E. P. Thompson has called the "enormous condescension of history."

Another area in which film excels is in the signification of the vital relationship that exists among space, time, and identity. People are brought together in a physical space that is political, topographical, representational, juridical, and symbolic. It is indeed this space that is responsible for the conscription of subjectivity. A filmmaker like Satyajit Ray who may not have displayed the radical nature of some of his younger contemporaries nevertheless succeeded marvelously in textualizing the interlinkage among space, time, and identity through carefully and economically chosen images. And to understand the complex interactions among space, time, and identity is to move closer to an understanding of discursive production of nationhood and history.

Aspects of nationhood and history that social theorists discuss at a high level of abstraction are given specificity and concreteness—a human face as it were—in cinema. For example, the Indian historian Gyanendra Pandey makes the point that the grand narratives produced by historians, sociologists, and political scientists deal largely with the context and are about the larger forces of history. According to him this is a kind of sanitized history that seeks to avoid violence, suffering, and pain of ordinary human beings.[21] It is here that cinema can play a vital role by textualizing the experience of human suffering with its attendant psychic economies.

The essays that follow, in their different accents and from their distinct vantage points of enunciation, address these and related issues. The first essays deal with Japan. The essay, by Patricia Lee Masters, looks at memory and nationalism in the realm of the senses. Through a reading of two films, *Fires on the Plain* (*Nobi*) and *The Emperor's Naked Army Marches On* (*Yuki Yukite Shingun*), she explores the ways in which nationalism is refigured and relocated discursively. In this essay Masters has sought to foreground the intertextualities of war, cinema, and nationalism in terms of the trope of food. Marie Thorsten Morimoto's essay describes the complex metaphors of a demilitarized nation. This chapter is concerned with metaphors of national identity in Japanese cinema that represent the growing points of Japanese transition from a defeated military power to a successful economic power. These essays, then, are devoted to investigations of important and interlocking discourses related to nationhood and history in Asian cinema.

From Japanese cinema we move on to Chinese cinema. Yingjin Zhang explores the ideological implications of the body in contemporary Chinese culture. He has chosen for his reading the widely acclaimed film *Red Sorghum* by Zhang Yimou. Here he discusses the issues of sexuality and politics from a comparative perspective, drawing on the theories of Bakhtin, Nietzsche, and Jameson. In the next chapter, Chris Berry describes the (mis)fit between China and the concept of the nation as manifested in the cinema. He discusses films from the mainland and Taiwan that attempt to signify China as a nation, and films that move beyond this toward post-colonial, fractured, dynamic representation of what Homi Bhabha has called "DissemiNation."

The next three chapters in this volume deal with the cinema of two other important Asian countries, South Korea and Vietnam. Isolde Standish explains the texts and contexts related to Korean cinema and the new realism. In 1988, there was a relaxation of the political censorship laws in South Korea. The objective of Standish's chapter is to situate the films of the Korean "New Wave" produced as a result of this relaxation within their social and political context. In the following chapter Rob Wilson engages in a reading of national allegory and motif and a sensibility for melodrama as manifested in Korean cinema. He explores the problematic of selfhood and national ideology from a cross-cultural perspective. From South Korea we proceed to Vietnam. John Charlot presents us with a historical sketch of Vietnamese cinema along with a definition of the industry in 1987–1988. In this chapter, major directors, films, and themes are discussed and the special aesthetic characteristics and determinants delineated.

The cinema of Southeast Asian countries has begun to attract increasing attention as a result of the work of such directors as Lino Brocka, Ishmael Bernal, Euthana Mukdasnit, and Eros Djarot. In this volume, we highlight the cinematic traditions of three countries, Vietnam, Thailand and Indonesia. Annette Hamilton focuses on the dilemmas that arise for local Thai filmmakers who wish to improve the quality of their films and develop "realist" approaches, but face a popular taste which will not accept their projects and a state that seeks to exert close control over all forms of media. The consequence of this is that certain "worthy" films enter the global art cinema market and as the representatives of Thai cinema, while popular Thai films are devalorized by the educated Thai elite who vastly prefer American movies. In his chapter, Karl G. Heider considers the cultural issues connected to the construction of a national Indonesian culture in terms of cinema. He points out how there is an emergent national Indonesian culture that is being imagined, modeled, and developed in the national cinema.

The next two chapters are devoted to an examination of questions of nationhood and history in relation to South Asian cinema. Darius Cooper, in his essay on Satyajit Ray's film *The Chess Players*, seeks to examine the diverse narrative discourses through which Ray critically examines facets of Indian history and the complex nature of Indian nationalism. In his chapter on Sri Lankan cinema, Wimal Dissanayake probes into the question of nationhood in relation to certain social formations and cultural discourses articulated in a number of significant filmic texts.

The last chapter addresses Australian cinema. Strictly speaking, Australia is not an Asian country. However, given its geographical proximity to Asia and in view of the fact that Asia, particularly Japan, has begun to have an impact on the economy and social fabric in significant ways, I decided to include this essay. In this chapter, titled "The End of the National Project? Australian Cinema in the 1990s," Graeme Turner explores the question of the apparent disarticulateness of the Australian film industry from the project of nation formation over the last decade.

Notes

1. Benedict Anderson, *Imagined Communities: Reflections on the Origin and Spread of Nationalism* (London: Verso, 1983).
2. Hayden White, *Tropics of Discourse: Essays in Cultural Criticism* (Baltimore: Johns Hopkins University Press, 1978).

3. Nicholas B. Dirks, "History As a Sign of the Modern," *Public Culture* (Spring 1990) 25–33.

4. Anderson.

5. Elie Kedourie, *Nationalism* (London: Hutchinson, 1960).

6. Ernest Gellner, *Nations and Nationalism* (Oxford: Basil Blackwell, 1983).

7. E. J. Hobsbawm, *Nations and Nationalism since 1780: Program, Myth, Reality* (Cambridge: Cambridge University Press, 1990).

8. Anthony Giddens, *The Nation-State and Violence* (Cambridge: Cambridge University Press, 1985).

9. Partha Chatterjee, *Nationalist Thought and the Colonial World: A Derivative Discourse* (London: Zed Books, 1986).

10. David Harvey, *The Condition of Post-Modernity* (London: Basil Blackwell, 1989).

11. Wimal Dissanayake, *Cinema and Cultural Identity: Reflections on Films from Japan, India, and China* (Lanham: University Press of America, 1988).

12. Wimal Dissanayake and Malti Sahai, *Sholay—A Cultural Reading* (New Delhi: Wiley Eastern, 1991).

13. Karl Heider, *Indonesian Cinema* (Honolulu: University of Hawaii Press, 1991).

14. Wimal Dissanayake and Malti Sahai, *Raj Kapoor's Films: Harmony of Discourse* (New Delhi: Sikas Publishers, 1988).

15. Homi Bhabha, *Nation and Narration* (London: Routledge, 1990) 297.

16. Bhabha, 312.

17. Michel de Certeau, *The Writing of History* (New York: Columbia University Press, 1988).

18. Wimal Dissanayake, *Viewers Guide: The Tenth Hawaii International Film Festival* (1990).

19. Allen Chun, "An Oriental Orientalism: The Logic of Cultural Construction in the Formation of a Modern Chinese Nation-State." Typescript.

20. Tony Rayns, *Viewers Guide: The Ninth Hawaii International Film Festival* (1989).

21. Gyanendra Pandey, "In Defense of the Fragment: Writing about Hindu-Muslim Riots in India Today," *Representations* (Winter 1992): 27–51.

Colonialism and Nationalism in Asian Cinema

1 | Warring Bodies
Most Nationalistic Selves
Patricia Lee Masters

Memory is bound up in the creation of nationalism, just as nationalism itself is constructed from particular memories, beliefs, and images. The cementing of nationalism occurs most profoundly in times of war and, not surprisingly, can receive its most vibrant questioning and critique at that time as well.

The power of nationalism is obvious in moments of war. When rulers and ruled bind together to fight an Other in the name of Self—national and otherwise—questions of loyalty, meaning, and nation arise. In war, when ideology overshadows life and there emerges a hostile imagination which allows for the killing of those designated, for the moment, as enemy, nationalism becomes the focus and the reason.

It is surprising to think how war, particularly the Second World War, has shaped, displayed, and configured national politics and nationalism in most of the world today. With the fiftieth anniversary of the attack on Pearl Harbor having just passed, we are presented directly with how war signals feelings of a nationalistic kind, and how memory holds on to such feelings as if they had occurred just yesterday.

In this chapter, the focus is the Japanese at war, specifically the Pacific War—exploring how nationalism was advanced and made sacred, and then how, after the war, such nationalism was openly critiqued and questioned. The two filmic texts that I have chosen to look at in this regard are *Fires on the Plain* (*Nobi*) and *The Emperor's Naked Army Marches on* (*Yuki Yukite Shingun*). It is my desire to show how nationalism is figured and critiqued—obliquely and directly—in these two films and to explore the intertextuality of war, film, nationalism, and food.

Paul Virilio tells us that there are several kinds of war films and that the whole relationship between war and film was exploded in the Second World War. Films made during the warring period were primarily used to promote and support the war effort and nationalism, and films made after the war to glorify, critique, or comment upon the events and meanings of conflict. In Japan, films critical of the war made during war time were never shown. In fact, it became impossible for such films to be made. As the surveillant forces of the Ministry of Home Affairs and the Media Section of the Imperial Army invaded the film world, particularly after the Motion Picture Act was passed in 1939, not only were film makers censured, but entire film companies were forced out of business. Actors were fired and blacklisted, and every film underwent screening by authorities before release and was subject to pre-production script censorship. Such censorship nearly silenced all but the most creative film makers who subtly used angling of camera shots and analogous symbols to get their meanings across without being censored. Most retreated into making period films or not making films at all. Many were silenced for the duration of the war, and some never returned to making films after. Some succumbed to making *kokusaku* or "National Policy" propaganda films.

Tadao Sato, one of Japan's leading film critics, suggests that Japanese war films can be characterized in the following way: they contain a minimum of rhetoric about why Japan was at war, a vagueness of the image of the enemy, little reference to the emperor, and heroes who were innocent. The enemy was either not shown at all or at a great distance. There was rarely a close encounter of any kind with the enemy Other as there was in American wartime films. The concentration was, rather, on the human side of Japanese soldiers as in the classic *The Story of Tank Commander Nishizumi* (Kozaburo Yoshimura, *Nishizumi Senshacho Den*). In this film, the commander is shown speaking of his children, taking care of his men, and finally being ambushed and killed. Such films were overwhelming successes in that they represented the nature of the hero in Japanese war.

An additional characteristic of Japanese war films was the treating of war as a kind of spiritual training. This kind of cinematic propaganda elicited feelings of sacrifice but greater returns in terms of spiritual strengthening. Many wartime films utilized this theme to incite young men and to induce them to join in the war effort.

Postwar films in Japan about the war, however, offer quite different images. Immediately after the war, there was what Sato calls a period of "conversion" among film makers. Those who had cooperated with the war effort complied once more with the wishes of the Occupation forces. They not only focused on democracy as their themes, but they denied the nationalistic thoughts to which they had rallied during the war. Questioning of the meanings of war, the nation, and nationalism came much later, and then only obliquely. Direct critiques did not do well at the box office and so were lost.

The two films that I would like to look at use an interesting device in order to critique the war and the nationalistic tendency in Japan. They employ the metaphor of food in order to say something about the mindlessness of battle and about the sacrifices in the name of nation. I began thinking about this theme while still living in Japan.

In the middle of May, the double cherry blossoms begin their flowering in Kyoto. My friend and I had gone to the place considered most perfect for viewing them and had packed the appropriate supplies for *hanami* (flower viewing): *onigiri, tsukemono, sake.*

As we walked along the path under the flowering trees, Nagai-san pointed to a large root that she said was edible. I walked over to retrieve it for our picnic and she implored me not to take it as she could not stomach its sight. It had been, she said, one of the main things she had to eat during the war and she could not bear to look at it now.

"What else," I inquired, "did you eat at that time?" And being a close friend, she did not seem to mind the impertinence of my question. She began: "Rice gruel, very little rice and a lot of gruel, potatoes and pumpkins." She began to detail the lack of food and how families would cook their small amount of rice together, making a milky-white porridge, thinned almost into water. She said that her family was lucky and that many went without even that. I began to think about these remembrances and how unpalatable the war must have literally been and how indelible the memories of that culinary past must be.

Many people are reminded of war through their memories of food. What deprivations, what extremes people went to and were forced into, and what people ate during times of war are easily recollected and have a profound impact on their memories. Wartime memories of privation are among the most vivid and yet, the improbable analogy of eating and memory are not usually accorded serious treatment or thought. How we remember and are brought back to the events of war is often in terms of the carnal and the culinary. In Studs Terkel's *The Good War*, one Japanese woman recalls how scarce food was during wartime:

> "My younger brother began to look like one of those starving Indian children: skinny, toothpick legs, and large, distended stomach. The only people who had food were farmers. Nothing was available in the stores. Food meant potatoes and plants, nothing else. The farmers would not accept money because it was regarded as worthless. So my mother started exchanging her beautiful silk kimonos for third-grade rice and a few potatoes.
>
> In the Fall of 1945, American soldiers showed up. . . . It took a long time for the food to arrive. Until then, we were always hungry. When the white rice came, it was bartered like gold. When the Americans gave us dark bread, we couldn't swallow it; most of us had only known white rice. We had no sugar, no sweets for a long, long time. And then, one day Cuban sugar arrived—that's what we called the brown crystals. We made puffed caramels. Oh, I was in heaven."

How vividly, forty-five years later, these things are remembered. The memory of food eaten or not eaten, as well as its symbolic worth is astounding. This is not particular to the Japanese nor is it particular to moments of war. Food has import everywhere not only as sustenance for the body but as an important signifier of the religious, the familial, and the social. Claude Lévi-Strauss found that some tribes of people designate food as "good to think" or "bad to think." We talk of some foods as "brain food" and some as sensuous or aphrodisiac. Food has an intimate relationship with creation, fertility, and sex, being created by the sex of plants or animals, and we find it in the realm of the senses. It is used in ritual, as reward, for seduction. In times of little food, its importance mushrooms. It is those hungry moments nearest our death that glisten in our memories. Recalling hunger is almost a physical sensation, so close is it to the source of our being. Food and its meanings have great impact upon us and consume much of our waking thoughts. Its place in war is even more acute.

In the film *Fires on the Plain*, such emphasis on the culinary is evident. The first scene opens with an interaction between a Private Tamura and his commanding officer in Leyte Island of Luzon, Philippines during the Pacific War. In this grueling scene, Tamura who, ironically, has "consumption" has returned to his company after being rejected for care at the field hospital nearby. He is reprimanded by his squad leader for not having fought to stay in the hospital and is told that the squad has no food to spare for him because he is no longer able to "pull his weight" and help the squad. Food is the overwhelming issue in this scene and, in fact, throughout the entire film. The squad leader orders him to go, and Tamura responds:

> "Yes, sir," I said, my eyes fixed on the squad leader's humid lips, "I understand perfectly. I am to report back to the hospital. And if I am not admitted, I am to kill myself."
> Normally the squad leader would have objected to the suggestion of individual judgment implied in the words "I understand perfectly," a terse repetition of orders being considered adequate; this time he chose to overlook the peccadillo.
> "That's right. And look here, Private Tamura. Try to cheer up! Remember— it's all for the Fatherland. To the very end I expect you to act like a true soldier of the Emperor."
> "Yes, sir, I will."[1]

Private Tamura's interaction with the squad leader dramatizes the the main theme of the film—eating—the lack of, the need to, the search for, the desperate ends one will go to for. It also indicates the analogic dimension of food—as critique of war and nation. This film is a story of struggle not just for personal survival but for a survival of Japanese spirit and human feeling. It is also a work of memory, for it is written from a mental ward six years after the war, after a long period of amnesia about escape, surrender, and survival. It is a story that exemplifies the struggle of many in Japan to remember and forget the Pacific War and its miseries.

As the film progresses, we find Private Tamura spending time among the other hospital "rejects"—Japanese imperial soldiers barred from entrance to the hospital because they have no more currency as killers or patients due to a lack of rations—and Tamura experiences an overwhelming display of feelings among these comrades. As they huddle some distance from the hospital, marking time by the meals served within, and exchanging critiques of war, of Japan, and of the Emperor, some relationships of care are also established. These too, surround food more often than not. The more disabled or ill are aided by those less sick; some who are hoarding food are goaded for not sharing and are cast out; some make deals with their portions, while others plan how to scavenge or steal more food.

After an attack by American fighter planes, the "group" scatters, and the story follows Tamura pillaging, foraging, and scrounging his way to a sea port where he might escape to Japan. Throughout Tamura's journey, we are constantly brought back to food and its overwhelming presence and absence. However, there is more to the food than just its consumption in this story. Ooka uses food to display many other things—critique of the war through the mouths of the "starving" soldiers (not to be taken too seriously because of their delirium); critique of the military and its unfair treatment (only the officers have food in the story); and critique of the country, as when Tamura is finally cast out by his company with six potatoes and he ponders:

> "As I put the potatoes into my haversack, my hands were trembling. Six small potatoes—to this extent and no further was my country prepared to guarantee my survival: the country to which I belonged and to which I was offering my life. There was a terrifying mathematical exactness about this number six."[2]

Food becomes a signifier for struggle. It represents possibility, not only of physical sustenance but of Tamura's struggle for humanity as well. Food becomes an overriding concern when the enemy is sighted and when fellow soldiers approach. Tamura kills two Filipino farmers for their food, and is plagued by this savagery throughout the rest of the film. Later, when he is being rescued by a unit of Japanese soldiers and contemplates hiding his cache of salt, taken from those dead Filipinos, he determines that he needs the companionship almost as much as he desires the salt. He decides to share the salt in exchange for safer passage to the coast and for being allowed to join the wayward unit on their own quest for escape and survival. Food becomes Tamura's bargaining tool, his weapon, with which his life is measured. When his supply begins to dwindle, he panics, not only because of the possibility of starving but because it is his currency, his worth to the company he keeps. As he struggles to live, his vision becomes acute. Not only is he able to literally see possibilities of food in the landscape he has come to know but in addition he is able to see the ravagings of war in a new light. Critique of the deeds done and legitimized as sacred through the Emperor's name arises as the story moves closer to the end and to Tamura's "escape." His allegiance to a Japan that asks him to die willingly "for the Empire" becomes questionable and Tamura interrogates himself about meaning and duty. He wonders about the reasons for dying in a foreign land and for a little understood cause. He calls on the Emperor to explain what it is that Japanese soldiers are dying for. In his delirium, more and more clarity comes to him. He surveys the landscape and upon seeing the remains of enemy soldiers and Japanese alike, he cries:

> "Here are the feet and hands of Japanese soldiers, dead on a foreign battlefield. For what did they die? For what did they lose those limbs on these plains? Wars may be advantageous to the small group of men who direct them, and I therefore leave them aside; what baffles me is all the other men and women who seem anxious to be deluded by these leaders. Perhaps they will not understand until they have gone through experiences like these I have had in the Philippine mountains. But even then, will they?"

Chance becomes his explanation for everything from escape to his not having been eaten by his fellows or by the enemy Other. He comforts himself by remembering that he did not engage directly in the cannibalism that he saw all around him and eschews those who did. He recalls a dream in which he sees dead people approaching him through the grasses in a field:

> "The dead people are laughing. If this is indeed celestial laughter, how awesome a thing it is!
> At this moment a painful joy enters my body from above. Like a long nail, it slowly pierces my skull and reaches to the base of my brain.
> Suddenly I understand. I know now why they are laughing. It is because I have not eaten them. I have killed them, to be sure, but I have not eaten them. I killed them because of war, the Emperor, chance—forces outside myself; but it was assuredly because of my own will that I did not eat them. This is why in their company I can now gaze at that dark sun in this country of the dead."[3]

His saving grace in the end is the fact that he did not literally consume his comrades or the enemy either. Since much of the film concerns itself with graphic detailing of cutting up bodies for food, surviving by consuming that which is usually inedible, and distorting the already perverse nature of war, Tamura's revelation relieves and saves him. Undoubtedly, he is driven mad by his remembrances of bodies with buttocks cut out for their sumptuousness as a meal, but he is also redeemed, in his own mind, for not having partaken in the feast. The ravages of war are displayed through these bodies and what men will do out of "hunger," and for nation, and although Tamura understands that he has in fact been a cannibal of sorts just by his participating in the war, he finds his comfort in the fact that, in the end, his humanity was saved by his not having eaten his fellow men.

The ending of the story is a stunning indictment of Japan's ruling elite and men of the military who led the Japanese people into a disastrous defeat. "How little we know" Tamura cries, condemning both the Japanese military for their silence about how Japan was faring in the war, and the more general lack of wisdom we all exhibit in war. His recollections and reflections of memories too unpalatable to recall until he is institutionalized and drugged exaggerate the hideous appetite for killing, war, and the idea of nation. How memories of traumatic moments, especially in war, come to be forgotten or hidden, are continuously returned to in Tamura's diary, and he searches hopelessly for some place to let those memories rest. They rest in his body, he tells us, and there is no erasure possible until that body no longer lives. His "madness" allows him to voice his condemnation of war, nationalism, and the Emperor. He speaks to the lack of humanity that emerges in the time of war and of what it says of the appetites and lack in man.

In another film, a similar deficiency and appetite is displayed. Perhaps the most extreme example of the dietary lack of World War II for the Japanese appears in the film *The Emperor's Naked Army Marches On* (*Yuki Yukite Shingun*). This semi-documentary, five years in the making, took the life of the protagonist's wife and left two others badly injured. It portrays the almost obsessive hunger for truth by an aging soldier named Okazaki Kenzo. The story is an astounding one, not only for its outcome but for the energy and vitality this 68 year old man exhibits in his undying quest for meaning. He seeks to tear away the years, trample the taboos of speaking out about the war, and to hold up the skeletons of Imperial Japan for all to see.

Okazaki is one of about 30 survivors from the 36th Engineering Corps, a regiment of over a thousand which was all but annihilated in the vicious fighting and treacherous conditions of New Guinea at the end of the war. When the war ended, Okazaki, who saw out its ending in a P. O. W. camp, returned to Japan to discover how the people there had been systematically brainwashed; how the nobility of the Emperor's War had been a shabby pretence; how millions had died in the name of quasi-religious mumbo-jumbo. The shock of the truth turned him into an anarchist, dedicated to exposing Hirohito and eradicating corruption of all sorts. In January of 1969, he attempted to attack Hirohito while the Emperor was greeting New Year's wellwishers by firing on him with four pachinko balls in a slingshot. As he fired off each ball, he screamed the names of comrades killed in the war. He did a year in prison for the attack. He did ten years after that for murdering a notorious *yakuza* who was engaging in crooked real estate schemes which victimized many elderly people.

When we meet Okazaki in the film he is obsessed by his major life crusade: to find out how and why two privates in his unit in New Guinea were executed three weeks after the war ended in 1945. We travel with him across Japan, tracking down nine officers from that unit, who he interrogates for their involvement in the executions of these young men. The soldiers are old men, some frail, some invalid, living in their countryside homes, who are visibly disturbed on camera by Okazaki's unexpected and unwelcome visits.

Okazaki grills these men about their roles in the executions and asks: Were you in the firing squad? What were the charges and the crimes? Who gave the orders to kill the privates? The old soldiers lie. Some claim they cannot remember whether they shot the two young men or not—such a long time ago you know—or some say that they weren't there at the time of the killing at all. Okazaki pieces the stories of the nine officers together and quickly spots the lies and discrepancies. In one scene, he cannot contain his rage and jumps on one of the officers, punching him and yelling at him to tell the truth. We witness him wrestling with the old man and watch as the police are called in. Director Hara Kazuo, who doubles as cameraman, catches all of this on film until forced to stop by the police officers.

Okazaki, the protagonist, establishes by the end of the film that the 36th Independent Engineering Corps had been reduced to cannibalism, eating their own comrades because of dire conditions suffered at the time. It is pointed out, however, that the New Guinean natives were considered "black meat" and therefore, inferior and not palatable to the Japanese soldiers. Okazaki discovers that "white pig" was consumed by the officers and later we learn that "white pig" was American and allied soldiers. Okazaki finally determines that the two Japanese privates, lowest on the military "pecking order," had been sacrificed because of a lack of supplies to the troops, and that in the confessions of one of the officers he interrogates, "there was nothing else that could be done." Okazaki goes to the house of the commanding officer, Captain Koshimizu, and after detailing the execution as he has heard it, asks him whether he gave the orders for the killings. Koshimizu tells him that he had merely passed the orders on from a superior and that he wasn't even present at the execution.

Unconvinced, Okazaki continues his investigations and finds a man who confesses to having been in the firing squad. Sitting at a *kotatsu* with this man, a former corporal, Okazaki reconstructs the execution, using tangerines to represent the five men in the squad, all of whom he can now name, and the two victims, Privates Yoshizawa and Nomura. He then picks up a tangerine to represent Captain Koshimizu. "Was he standing here at the back?" he queries. "No," says the man and places the tangerine just next to the firing squad. "He was here. When the squad fired, the men didn't die right away, so Captain Koshimizu finished them off with his own gun. One shot each."

This is the pivotal moment in the film. The big lie is exposed. Koshimizu is revealed as the villain but, in Okazaki's words, is merely a "messenger" for the evil Empire. The real villain is the Emperor, himself, and Okazaki shouts, "It is not the soldiers who committed those sins who should be punished, but Emperor Hirohito who was, after all, the Supreme Commander of the Japanese Army."

The film ends with a long gaze into the face of Captain Koshimizu and a quick shot of the Emperor. Then, flashed up on the screen are newspapers whose headlines tell the rest of the story: that Okazaki went to Captain Koshimizu's house with a gun, looking to kill him; that Koshimizu was not at home, and Okazaki, in his rage, decides to shoot Koshimizu's son who is protecting his father and his whereabouts; that the son is seriously wounded and Okazaki is arrested and sentenced to twelve years for attempted murder; and that Okazaki's wife has died of cancer while her husband is serving out his prison sentence. As unsympathetic a character as Okazaki is in this film, we feel the anxiety and dismay that he feels throughout his search and for the entirety of the film. And in a way, we can be somewhat more objective about the film because of our ambivalence about him.

What the film reveals is more than cannibalism and the unpalatable nature of war. It speaks of a society gone mad. While *Yuki Yukite Shingun* has been highly praised and widely acclaimed by several critics outside of Japan, many within Japan recreate that madness and still express their outrage at Okazaki's actions. They question his methods and also the ethics of the film's director, Hara Kazuo, who filmed the real unstaged acts of violence without intervening. They suspend the horror of what the film is saying and ask for protection of the Imperial name. In post-war Japan, where the outrages of war have been assiduously covered up and the implications have been carefully avoided, such a demonstration as Okazaki's is rare. Instead, things go on as usual or as before. In 1957, Kishi Nobusuke, who had been a leading member in the Tojo cabinet and in charge of the subjugation of Manchuria, became Prime Minister of Japan. Even more recently, the election of Koiichi Miyazaki, who was involved in the famed Recruit Scandal, as Prime Minister, further amplifies this ability to assuage and forget the past. One western journalist has compared this kind of activity to Goebbels or Himmler becoming Chancellor of Germany.[4]

The fact is that even today in Japanese political circles and in the business world there are many who cultivated Emperor-worship and imperialism in the prewar years, and who cheered as the army set off for New Guinea and the Philippines and other Asian fronts. There are those who participated directly and returned to Japan as future leaders and decision-makers. Their cravings for silence and for digesting the war past in particular ways have been roasted by Okazaki and his exposé. *The Emperor's Naked Army* is shown in barest forms: soldiers eating their own bodies or, rather, the bodies they commanded to do the Emperor's bidding. The official line, that Hirohito had no control over the military or the militarists in the Cabinet, is offered and Okazaki rails against this. In fact, the contention that Hirohito finally overruled the Cabinet to bring about the surrender, is still widely believed in Japan, and rarely discussed.

One of the major critiques of Okazaki, and of Hara Kazuo's agreement to do this film, surrounds the exposure of the Emperor as villain. The eating of Japanese soldiers becomes foregrounded only momentarily in these critiques and fades quickly into the dark as the critics focus on the need to protect the Imperial name. The fact is that Japan needs its Okazakis. It needs outrageous extremists who obsessively seek for meaning. The calm repose so carefully staged in Japan needs to be unsettled to allow the space for dialogue to begin on the horrors of the war and the madness of nationalism. The unwillingness to expose such wartime stories leaves a past that is as yet, undigested. It also makes the Japanese "unpalatable" to many in the West and in Asia who suffered at the wartime hands of the Japanese militarists. There is still a hunger for some reflection to come out of Japan, not just in the apology for things past but for some willingness on the part of Japanese officials to look at Japan's participation in the devastations of war, to increase public knowledge of that war, and to acknowledge the atrocities of war and those victimized by it.

Notes

This chapter is taken from "Tastes of War and Other Unpalatable Memories" which appears as part of my Ph.D. dissertation. The dissertation concerns the politics of memory in post-war Japan—how memory is constructed, who gets to remember, what is silenced, what is forgotten, what becomes part of social memory—and this particular chapter concerns itself with how war is remembered and refigured in the narrative of nation.

1. Ooka, Shohei. *Fires on the Plain* (London: Secker and Warburg, 1957), 7–9.
2. Ibid., 10.
3. Ibid., 210.
4. Tom Gill in *Ampo, Japan-Asia Quarterly Review*, vol. 20, no. 3, 1989, 28.

2 | The "Peace Dividend" in Japanese Cinema
Metaphors of a Demilitarized Nation

Marie Thorsten Morimoto

... the nation is a family, the government the parents, the people the children, and the police their nursemaids.

—Kawaji Toshiyoshi, founder of Japanese police, 1876

J APAN, THE LAND of miniaturization—of haiku poetry, dwarfed plants, and pictographic language. With its ubiquitous mirrors and myths of self-identity, Japan often seems to savor the symbol and personification of its cultural self-portrait. In its history, Japan did not even exist as a modern "nation" until the founding of new images: in particular, the "family-state" (*kazoku kokka*) and its variation, the "household" (*ie*), metaphors which were propagandized to consolidate the Japanese people under the banners of militarism.

A nation's metaphors converse with its politics. Hence, with the dismantling of the Japanese Empire at the close of the Second World War, the images which shaped the garrison state also became, in a sense, "demilitarized." Like the guns and missiles they supported, war metaphors were "left over," waiting to be reinvested into peacetime Japan.

I borrow the expression "peace dividend," now frequently discussed in American politics. It means that what is divested from the war budget becomes reinvested in the "peace" budget. If it can mean converting guns to butter, it should also refer to the psychological reinvestment of the various images so inextricably linked to war. In this chapter, I consider the reinvestment of Japan's metaphors, from war to peace, in one of the most important conduits for cultural representations, the Japanese cinema.

I will identify four films which utilize personifications of the demilitarized Japanese nation—afterimages, we might imagine, of the family-state leitmotif—but the "family" or group unit in each of these cases has been torn apart. The emphasis is thus on reconciliation and reconstuction, toward economic rather than military objectives. The films portray Japan in youth (Shinoda Masahiro's

Takeshi: Childhood Days, 1990); Japan as an abandoned mother (Kinoshita Kei-suke's *A Japanese Tragedy*, 1953); Japan as a lonely soldier (Kurosawa Akira's *Yo-jimbo*, 1961); and finally, Japan dismembered as a family unit (Oguri Kohei's *The Sting of Death*, 1990).

The making of these films overlaps several decades. But each, with either hindsight or foresight, conveys or anticipates the problems which would beset Japan in the first two decades of the postwar era. The settings also diverge in timing. Kinoshita's and Oguri's films concern the immediate aftermath of the war; Shinoda's film takes place in the final year of the war but foreshadows the demilitarized Japan which would emerge. Kurosawa's timely classic, in this ren-dering, represents a displacement of then-contemporary ideas onto the lives of fictional characters of an era long ago, and becomes, whether accidental or in-tentional, an apt metaphor of Japan in the Cold War.

Nation and Cinema

Japan's film industry got started nearly one hundred years ago, with the importation of several Edison Kinetoscopes. This was in 1896, only two years after the first Kinetoscope was introduced in New York. It was twenty-eight years following the Meiji Restoration, which marked the entry of the Japanese archipelago into the world of modern states.

A vastly new technology, the cinema joined all of its viewers in an "imag-ined community" as a nation, to borrow Benedict Anderson's apt depiction: the nation is "imagined" because through the absorption of common images, indi-viduals who would never have a chance to meet face-to-face are instantly brought into communion and empathy with one another (1983: 15). At the same time, the film industry projected images of other nations to this new commu-nity of film-goers, individuals who previously had few means, perhaps even little motivation, to imagine the world outside of them so vividly.

Thus, the Japanese people who had shunned foreigners for several centu-ries began watching *Mary Queen of Scots* and *The Spirit of Saint Louis* with great eagerness and enthusiasm. By 1898 they could see their own Japanese-made films as well (Anderson and Richie 1982: 22–26). Interest in things foreign boomed thereafter, but for several decades, the film industry in Japan was fa-mously resistant to establishing a "generic" product which would be viewed in the same way to all audiences. This was because as long as the films were silent, a lecturer, called a *benshi*, interpreted the film to his private audience members, using their own regional dialect and local humor. If the *benshi* held more sway than either the actors or the producers of the film, perhaps it was because people needed the mediating link to ease them into the centripetal pull of the nation.

The story of the homogenization of the cinematic image is thus the story

of the homogenization of the Japanese nation: linguistically, culturally, and politically. In Japan as elsewhere, media images alone facilitated such a consolidation partially irrespective of influence "from above." Given the political climate of Japan in the 1920s and 1930s, however, the militaristic government
stepped in to accelerate and direct the process. The pictures which were acceptable to the nascent form of nationalism were gradually pulled in, while those
which were unacceptable were held back.

Nation and Metaphor

Often described as the most important bilateral relationship in the world,
both Japan and the United States—that is, Japanese people and American people—speak of each other's nation as possessing the qualities of individual human beings. Both nations speak, feel, believe, understand, misunderstand. They
get tired, angry, frustrated, and upset. The nation is personified; likewise the
person is nationalized. An aging member of Japan's parliament makes a crude
remark; his American counterpart retaliates at "Japan," not at the individual
politician.

I introduce my inquiry into nation and cinema with this in mind—the
metaphoric "conversation" between nation and person. The relationship should
not be considered *reductive*; metaphors are not arbitrary puzzles designed to occupy the passive imagination. Rather, they are *productive* devices which *structure*
the imagination, since "we draw inferences, set goals, make commitments, and
execute plans, all on the basis of how we in part structure our experience, con-
sciously and unconsciously, by means of metaphor" (Lakoff and Johnson 1980:
158).

A bumper sticker slogan comes to mind: "the personal is political." The personal day-to-day actions with friends, family, and co-workers not only *resemble*
the actions of politicians, and vice versa—but also, the two realms, personal and
political (a word which in its old-fashioned sense, refers only to governments),
overlap. They converse with one another; they borrow each other's metaphors,
and what one does affects the other. Therefore, a film representing the family
as a metaphor of nation does not *simplify* the narrative; rather, it makes it all the
more *complex* and compelling.

Maruyama Masao's explanation of "dialogue" in Japanese texts depicts the
sort of metaphoric conversation to which I refer (1963: 245):

> . . . [the dialogue] exists as a recognized literary genre for the exploration of
> new ideas that have not been fully developed. Writers who do not have the time
> for a thorough examination of every stimulating idea that occurs to them will
> tentatively pursue a particular insight by means of a loosely constructed col-
> loquy. There is no intent to preach, or to press upon the reader, some well-

rounded theory. Nor is there any pretense at sifting out internal inconsistencies. Ideas [like metaphors] are submitted as they come to mind, for whatever they are worth, in the hope that the reader [or the viewer] may carry the analysis one step further and gain some new insights for himself.

Thus, the nation and person conceived in the cinematic embryo arrive for a dialogue. They begin talking, converging, and diverging, sometimes even changing representations as the narrative proceeds. It happens much more like a dream than a neat formula where viewers can easily predict where they will end up. In an effective film, as in a prescient dream, this dialogue is enabling: viewers gain insights and direction in the murky ground between personal and political.

Fitting this essay into the New World "Order of Things,"—to adapt the Anglicized concept of Michel Foucault—the stories we tell, the "orders" of our images, are always vulnerable and amenable to political circumstances. For example, America of the "new world order" is a slow-motion version of demilitarized Japan in the aftermath of the Second World War. In a recent metaphor of popular fiction (Crichton 1992), the United States has now become a masochistic prostitute, secretly enjoying its rape by Japan—a reversal of Japan's own metaphor of fifty years ago. Japan, on the other hand, began a new wave of assertion at the start of its Heisei Era (1989–) with the publication of Ishihara Shintaro's *The Japan That Can Say No.*

Without pitting Us against Them, therefore, it should be a matter of *mutual* concern to assess these images of transition between war and peace, tentatively questioning along the way what really lies beyond the era of militarism. In addition, as has been already suggested, we should be attentive to the gendering of these concepts, war and peace, and how that gendering figures in with national identity.

Nation and Gender: Japan's "Trans-Sexual" Identity

Discourses of war and metaphoric "war" are often distinctly gendered. Gender codes structure the way people think of war because they construct relations of dominance and submission, superiority and inferiority, rapaciousness and victimization. This can be seen not only in war but in all aspects of the imagery of international relations, a point elucidated by Edward Said.

What Said calls *Orientalism* is the accumulated product of centuries of textual production through which the West could assume postures of superiority—vantage points from which it could create and control an entire consciousness known as the "Orient." Orientalism, hence, is "a praxis of the same sort as male gender dominance, or patriarchy":

... the Orient was routinely described as feminine, its riches as fertile, its main symbols the sensual woman, the harem and the despotic but curiously attractive ruler. Moreover, Orientals, like housewives, were confined to silence and to unlimited enriching production (1985: 12; 1978).

Japan's position in international politics has long been an ambivalent one, but it was especially so during the "peak" periods of Orientalism, the nineteenth and early twentieth centuries. Though never colonized by Western powers, Japan—as "Orient"—keenly perceived its vulnerability to the West; at the same time, it began its own aggressive campaign of colonization in Asia. Vulnerable victim, aggressive attacker, the Japanese national metaphors of self were likewise "trans-sexual": both "feminized" and "virilized."

In his landmark thesis, *War Without Mercy*, which concerns the production of national stereotypes and images during World War Two, John Dower notes the pervasiveness of the slogans "virile national mentality" and "racial virility" heard in wartime Japan (1986: 230). These were likely the slogans most appropriate when dealing with Japan's "lesser" neighbors in Asia. For example, Dower cites one medical doctor, also an official in the Ministry of Health and Welfare, as saying: "[No] nation in this part of the Orient can stand comparison with Japan in point of racial virility and organizational ability. The racial vigor of Japan is the most potent factor that has enabled it to attain its present distinguished position in the polity of nations" (1986: 276).

The "virile mentality" often becomes sterilized, however, in one of Japan's most "potent" cultural media: the popular film. For example, perhaps the most conspicuous mystery concerning Japanese wartime cinema is the absence of images of violence and aggression. Certainly in other forms of propaganda, Dower remarks, "the Japanese did dehumanize the enemy and call for their extermination," but " ... for whatever reason, [the] Japanese cinema message was softer" (1987: 5). An example is Mizoguchi Kenji's *Genroku Chushingura*, that most loyal tale of Japanese filmlore—having been produced over 100 times by the present date—concerning the classic tale of the loyal 47 ronin. While it may hardly seem possible that a narrative about *bushido* (samurai spirit) could be called "feminine," it was just that: a counter-image to the slogan of "racial virility."

Women rarely appear in *any* version of *Chushingura*, and in Mizoguchi's, their introduction is brief, but significant. In fact, in her encyclopedic volume on Japanese cinema, Joan Mellen locates Mizoguchi's *Chushingura* in the chapter, "The Japanese Woman" (1976: 32–43). Often labeled a "feminist" or "woman's director," Mizoguchi adds a segment which is identified by Mellen as his special signature on this otherwise "party line" propagand*ish* film (though the authorities, it seems, were pleased with it). Just before the captive ronin are about to receive permission to commit honorable *seppuku*, an erstwhile fiancée of one warrior appears, begging to speak to the warrior who betrayed her. Now that she's found out that the reason he left her was for such a noble cause (to avenge his lord, the basic plot of *Chushingura*), all she wants to know is whether he truly loved her.

A frivolous request for these stoic soldiers—but thanks to the woman's persistence it gets taken seriously after considerable deliberation, i.e., camera movement. The former betrothed meet, their conversation anticipating a similar pattern to be seen in *The Sting of Death* (Oguri Kohei, 1990): the female presses for *honne*, the true "interior" realm of meaning, while the male offers *tatemae*, the superficial but safe "exterior" response. He answers that he doesn't love her—the rejoinder of a dedicated samurai. Secretly, however, he reveals he kept a small memento of their relationship, a piece of her koto. He obliquely confesses, "Tell your father I am still his son-in-law."

Besides this specific incident, *Genroku Chushingura* is a "feminized" narrative because it overstates victimization while vastly understating the impulses of aggression. To any viewer's surprise, the famous climactic point of this tale of vengeance is totally withdrawn from the viewer: the storm on Lord Kira's castle, when the 47 behead their late master's enemy. In place, we have more protracted scenes on the suffering and victimization of the ronin themselves. The mass ritual suicide of the 47 ronin is hidden from our view; instead we witness only the suicide of the foresaken fiancée.

It may be the case that the essence of *bushido* purity, with its emphasis on suffering and sacrifice, were more readily conveyed in the feminine persona, or that militarists believed the brutality of the battlefield needed no exposition. In any case, the effect was to produce a narrative totally in line with government propaganda. "The overriding image that any viewer of these films will retain," Dower explains, "is one of the Japanese as an innocent, suffering, self-sacrificing people. It is the image, in the end, of the Japanese as eternal victims—victims of war, of fate, of noble commitments, of vague enemies, of misguided antagonists, of whatever one might choose to imagine" (1987: 9).

The national self-portrait of Japan as eternal victim is the diametric opposite of that portrayed in the Cold War pop films of the seventies in America, with the likes of cool, cocky John Waynes or James Bonds, who made political colonization and womanizing the same project. The latter hero "whips out his revolver and his cock, and though there is no known connection between the skills of a gun-fighter and love-making, pacifism seems suspiciously effeminate" (cited in Herman 1984: 21). If, as Herman says, the U.S. has been a "rape culture," (1984) Japan has certainly been a "rape victim culture."

Yet there is some equivalent of "perniciousness" and "perversity" in this "effeminate" nature of Japan's war-mongering, however. As Dower puts it, "[the victim image] is devoid of any sense whatsoever of individual or collective responsibility for war, or of any recognition that, at every level, the Japanese also victimized others" (1987: 9).

Japan's "masculinized" metaphor, thus, would occur not through the glorification of violence, but through the "family state." Speaking of the various slogans Japan used to instill a sense of bonding with its Asian neighbors in creating the "Greater East Asia Co-Prosperity Sphere," Dower writes that the family metaphor was introduced as "the most benign metaphors of inequality" (1986: 279). The family system promoted in textbooks and the media was clearly a *patriarchal* one, based on the samurai elite wherein each individual knew his or her "proper place," and accepted the authority of the patriarch without question.

Director Ozu Yasujirô is best known for his filmic depictions of every day Japanese home life, depictions which are said to be representative of traditions in Japan. In that sense, opposite of Mizoguchi, Ozu's everyday home dramas metaphorize the masculine side of Japanese national identity. During the war, Ozu made two prominent films concerning the theme of patriarchy and national identity, *Brothers and Sisters of the Toda Family*, and *There was a Father*. But Ozu would likely not call himself, nor be called, a propagandist. Mellen writes that "Ozu evoked traditional ideas not because the militarists forced him to, but because he believed in them" (1976: 152). Loathing both militarism and capitalism, his metaphors may have been his own escape journeys, his own contemplations about the fate of the nation which used the symbolism of the patriarchal family.

Thus, besides aiming for a consolidation of identity, the cinematic representations which emerged during Japan's military period had the following characteristics: they alternated in portraying Japan in "feminine" (viz., victimized by western powers) and "masculine" identities (viz., consolidating Japanese citizens and Asian neighbors under the patriarchal family-state metaphor); they utilized what Dower has called a "phantom foe" (unnamed, absent) to represent Japan's enemies (1987: 6), and they rarely used any sort of war imagery or violence.

In the postwar period, the following situations occur in some of Japan's cinematic metaphors. First, "feminine" representations seem to prevail, while "masculine" images are de-emphasized; second, the "phantom foe" still applies (unlike America, Japan does not need to name its enemies), and finally, the portrayal of the family as nation focuses on its disintegration rather than its consolidation, aiming at the same time for reconstruction, or at least, acceptance of the circumstances which caused such disintegration.

Japan in Youth: Growing Pains of the Peace Dividend

Shinoda Masahiro, Takeshi: Childhood Days (Shōnen Jidai, *1990*)

Japan's "peace dividend" was its metamorphosis from a military superpower to an economic, "information age" superpower. The transition was also one from a society threatened by the scarcity of food, where physical resources translated into physical strength, to a society hungry for knowledge, where young people began competing with their wits in a new game of "human capitalism." This is the subject of Shinoda Masahiro, *Takeshi: Childhood Days (Shōnen Jidai)*. Produced in 1990, the film is a wartime tale narrated with a hindsight intimately acquainted with Japan's peacetime conversion.

The setting is a mountain village in the final year of the Second World War, where a fifth-grade boy is brought to live with his relatives in anticipation of the bombing of his hometown of Tokyo. While the war rages outside their surroundings, the boys of this village construct their own allegory of Japanese history through their school fights and gang rivalries. Yet their allegorical "war" resembles the struggle which would take place *after* Japan's surrender. It is the struggle between an old, traditional Japan where strength was measured by brutality—like military hardware—versus a new Japan where strength would be measured by knowledge—like information age software. This would be the "peacetime" Japan which these young boys would inherit.

Shinji, the diminutive but scholarly evacuee, plays the intermediary of this transition from "war" to "peace." When he first arrives, the village bully-cum-class leader is Takeshi, a farmer's son, and an apt signifier of prewar Japan. Besides being stronger, tougher, and taller than the other boys, Takeshi is also poor, sensitive, intelligent, and hard-working. Though well-intentioned in private, he is inclined toward raucous behavior in the presence of the group.

As the film progresses, Takeshi's power is undercut by a signifier of postwar Japan: a boy who is physically debilitated, but wealthy in knowledge. The smaller boy's home is decidedly Westernized, and his family owns a large collection of books enclosed in a glass-doored bookcase. This boy comes back to his class after being away for a year due to his illness. Though weak, lacking in humor, and insensitive to others, he works his way into the position of class leader/town bully, entirely through his mental acuity.

In this power struggle from brawn to brain, Shinji, with his storehouse of Tokyo education, becomes the resource which all the village boys begin to tap into, in order to compete with their new leader. Rather than scrambling for a few morsels of rice or potatoes as most children did during the war, these country boys wage fights for access to Takeshi's stories and books. None is more ravenous for his supply of information than the village fat boy.

Thus, though small, weak, and possessing an air of the city boy himself, Shinji manages to emerge unscathed in the midst of these country boy bullies. He steers his way through Takeshi's episodes of split personality, and through competing loyalties to the city boys and the village boys.

Here we see the transition of power from the physically strong, kind-hearted, but poor, ignorant, and given to outbursts of temper—to the Japan which is rich and knowledgeable, but physically debilitated and ambitious to the point of being asocial. The longing to remember the things that were good and honorable in the old Japan, however cruel it had once been, is expressed in the metaphor of Takeshi. Likewise, the figure of the smart, new bully signifies all that is dubious in Japan's new era of demilitarized "peace."

Feminine Japan: The World's Oldest Metaphor

Kinoshita Keisuke, A Japanese Tragedy (Nihon no Higeki, *1953)*

The theoretical perspective taken to understand what creates images of a "peace dividend" might begin by working backward from what creates images of war. Perhaps the most conspicuous metaphors of war are those of masculinism, a theory which was operationalized under the psychoanalytic theory of Sigmund Freud. Consistent with the Freudian notion that violence and war are sublimations of the aggressive urges of the phallus (for the uncultivated men who were not fortunate enough to learn to control those urges at an early stage; Elshtain 1987), a common motif in representations of demilitarization is that of "de-virilization." Removing a nation's identification with military muscle is metaphorically conveyed as impotence, a profound feeling of the loss of a masculine identity or principle.[1]

Immediately following Japan's surrender, there were so many films made portraying the demasculinized Japanese family state—in the form of a family *sans* patriarch—that a new genre was coined: the *hahamono*, or "mother matters." These films usually depict a strong, self-sacrificing mother who seems to bear the suffering of the Japanese nation all on her own yoke.

Perhaps the most emblematic of the suffering mothers, Kinoshita's heroine of *A Japanese Tragedy* also becomes another ageless female symbol of suffering: the prostitute. Along with her daughter, a rape victim, these female characters portray an analogy of a fallen Japan at the behest of Western powers.

An antecedent to their fate can be found in Mizoguchi's *The Sisters of Gion* (1936), concerning a geisha who plays her own game of business inside the boundaries of the patriarchal society. She proves herself remarkably adept at cajoling and manipulating men to get what she wants: a little bit of money, fun, vengeance, and a feeling of self-worth for her and her sister. But her tactics backfire when one of her suitors kidnaps her with the intention of "teaching her a lesson." Plunging from the backseat of the moving car, she chooses thus to injure herself rather than be injured. Critically wounded, she still vows to continue her struggle against circumstances, acknowledging, "If we're sharp in business, we're criticized. What are we supposed to do?"

If prostitution, broadly conceptualized as the selling of one's own human dignity for self-survival, is the world's oldest profession, perhaps it is the world's oldest metaphor. Haruko, the suffering widow in *Japanese Tragedy* must sell herself to feed her children in order to survive the war years. But this dire necessity also becomes a "leftover" metaphor—one which is passed on to her children, who process it to fit their needs in peacetime Japan.

Utako, Haruko's daughter, and Seiichi, her son, choose to forget their mother's sacrifices, but not to forgive. But despite the shame they feel for her desperation and debauchery, each child becomes his and her own kind of "prostitute." Utako offers herself to a married man for his protection. Seiichi, though nearly full-grown, has himself adopted into a wealthy family in need of an heir so that he can attend medical school. With this complete annihilation of her family, Haruko has no choice but to end her life.

Kinoshita's classic allegory of Japan's peacetime transition is presented with fast-paced newsreel clips and flashbacks. A noble experiment for a Japanese director, yet much to Kinoshita's credit, neither the documentary "political" story nor the specific "personal" story get in the way of one another. The metaphoric overlap is also represented in the title: *Nihon no Higeki*, alternatively translated in English as "*A* Japanese Tragedy" and "*The* Japanese Tragedy." As Burch agrees, the Japanese title renders both meanings: "*a* tragedy *in* Japan, and *the* tragedy *of* Japan" (1979: 284n; emphasis mine).

Masculine Japan: The Lonely Soldier in the Cold War

Kurosawa Akira, Yojimbo, *1961*

> Aspiring sincerely to an international peace based on justice and order, the Japanese people forever renounce war as a sovereign right of the nation and the threat or use of force as means of settling international disputes. . . . The right of belligerency of the state will not be recognized.
>
> Article IX, Japanese Constitution

Joan Mellen briefly touches on the idea that the period drama, the *jidai-geki*, was used as a "surrogate for modern Japan" in the postwar era, just as it surely had been in the pre-militaristic period (i.e., the twenties). She calls the sixties *jidai-geki* a "protest film in disguise." But unfortunately, Mellen doesn't develop this theme much, except to say that no one is fooled by the film's suggestion that the social problems it explores are set in the distant past (1976: 85).

Kurosawa's comic, nihilistic *Yojimbo* proves an excellent metaphor for the correspondence between the transition from militarism to mercantilism in Japan's *feudal* past, and the transition from Japan as a military power to Japan as an economic power in the *recent* past. In its own transition, Japan stood caught between the competing forces of Communism and capitalism in the world, in what came to be known as the Cold War. Japan demilitarized, while the Cold War between the Soviet Union and the United States escalated.

Three paradoxes of the Cold War, often mentioned, were extremely relevant to Japan, even though it seemed to stand in the sidelines: first was the idea that "peace" was the same thing as war in a suspended state of animation; second, that any incremental increase in arms to match that of the opponent still amounted to the same thing—mutual assured destruction (MAD); and third, that total detachment from the war amounted to the same thing as total involvement.

Kurosawa's hero, the bodyguard Yojimbo, experiences such paradoxes in this accidental allegory. Yojimbo is a "masterless samurai" (*ronin*) caught between two opposing factions in a "civil war" of a provincial town. His simultaneous involvement and detachment in the civil war mirrors that of Japan in the Cold War. Though he is armed with nothing but "his wit and his sword," it is the former which proves far more advantageous, dangerous, and lucrative. As in the film *Takeshi*, reason triumphs over weaponry. Even the escalation of weapons in the film, such as the introduction of the gun, is made to look cumbersome and ridiculous against the destructive powers of information and knowledge.

As for *Yojimbo*'s popular narrative: the year, we are told, is 1860. Somewhere, Japan. The warrior class has dissolved with the rise of the merchant class. A *ronin* wanders aimlessly, until at random chance he comes upon his fantasy land, a provincial town involved in a little civil warfare, where both sides are brainless boneheads about to exterminate each other. The sage samurai draws his sword, casually killing two men, maybe three. The local coffin maker can barely begin pounding nails fast enough before the leaders of both factions put up their bargaining chips. They want to buy the services of this savior samurai who never surrenders his weapon: he just learns to sell it, and profit handsomely. Yojimbo is no altruist, he makes off with a "fistful of yen" for himself. (Three years following the release of *Yojimbo*, Italian director Sergio Leone made a virtual copy of the film along the lines of the "Western" (cowboy) genre, calling it *A Fistful of Dollars*. The "spaghetti Western" launched actor Clint Eastwood into international stardom.)

When *Yojimbo* was released in 1961, the point of view of Japan looking at the world might have appeared like that of this *ronin*. When he is perched up on the tower, viewing both sides of the conflict, the rogues on both sides appear equally as dim-witted and defenseless. Five years earlier, political theorist Maruyama Masao remarked: "It is ironical that with intensification of the Cold War both the United States and the Soviet Union have come more and more to resemble each other as they turn their internal organizations into 'garrison states' " (1969: 179; from an essay published in 1956).

The lone warrior struggling against all odds may seem, at first blush, un-

Japanese. Yet, on the contrary, the representation is *distinctively* Japanese, if we are talking about the use of the *jidai-geki* as a metaphor of Japan as *nation*. Dominant themes in Japanese cultural self-representations have long been those of uniqueness, isolation, and victimization—hence, of a lone nation struggling against all odds.

Furthermore, if anyone was in a position to understand the isolation, it was Kurosawa himself. An eclectic auteur with no fixed "master" in either Japanese or Western traditions, hence, a *ronin* in his own way, Kurosawa eventually had to "peddle" his camera in different countries just to obtain funding.

Yojimbo was made fairly early in his career, however, and it earned tremendous success in Japan. Kurosawa has only faintly alluded to this film's role as a political metaphor; the famed international director, however, is notorious for denying his own politics, even while directing and screenwriting some of the most politically relevant films ever produced in Japanese cinema. Of *Yojimbo*, whose screenplay he co-wrote (along with Kikushima Ryuzo), the director has stated (cited in Richie 1984: 147):

> The story is so ideally interesting that it's surprising no one else ever thought of it. The idea is about rivalry on both sides, and both sides are equally bad. We all know what that is like. Here we are, weakly caught in the middle, and it is impossible to choose between evils. Myself, I've always wanted to somehow or other stop these senseless battles of bad against bad, but we're all more or less weak—I've never been able to. and that is why the hero of this picture is different from us. He is able to stand squarely in the middle, and stop the fight. and it is this—him—that I thought of first.

Kurosawa wittingly portrayed the comic aspects of this tragi-comedy. Yojimbo is confronted with two choices: to leave town, and be uninvolved, or to stay, get involved, and thus kill everyone. He chooses the latter, but manages to save, in the process, a nuclear family, whom he helps to re-unite and escape. This reuniting of the social bond corresponds with one of the most startling metaphors used in the film—that of a mangy dog carrying away a human hand in its teeth—perhaps a rendering of the "dismembered" family-state.

The year is now 1992. The Cold War has ended. Of the role of Japan, David Sanger writes (*New York Times*, May 5, 1992, p. 1):

> No country prospered more during the cold war than Japan, and perhaps no country is more wistful for that era's comforting certainties. While the United States and Europe were preoccupied with throw weights and satellite photographs, Japan was able to focus almost entirely on building an economy that became the envy of the world, largely undistracted by, and often profiting from, the superpower rivalry.

Thus, hiding under the military umbrella of the United States, Japan played the part of the *yojimbo*, the *ronin* bodyguard, carrying on with its own economic plan—even playing one superpower off against the other—often as if it were entirely independent from the situation, a *ronin* in the world of nation-states.

Japan as the Dismembered Family Politic: The Homeless *Honne*

Oguri Kohei, The Sting of Death (Shi no Toge, *1990*)

The supreme irony of the family-state metaphor which was used to consolidate the Japanese empire was that it was the Japanese empire which destroyed the family. As in all wars, many fathers never returned home to their families; those who did were sometimes not welcomed. Thus the imperialist designs of the Japanese military were like a mistress who distracts a husband from his family. As a consequence of his betrayal, they may never take him back again.

This is how the war and its aftermath are portrayed in the representation of the Shimao family, the subject of *Sting of Death*, a film by Oguri Kohei, based on a novel by the film's protagonist, Shimao Toshio. Toshio severs ties with his mistress, vowing in all earnestness to reconstruct his household. But the foundations of the house have been shaken irreparably, causing the walls outside eventually to give in, too.

The foundations and the walls of the household (*ie*) are personified in Miho, the wife, and Toshio. Miho continuously pushes for the "truth" of detail after detail concerning her husband's betrayal. Because Toshio "lied" to her about the affair before, she thinks he can never be trusted again. The concepts of "falsehood" and "truth" overlap roughly with the Japanese concepts of *tatemae* and *honne*. I consider that correspondence an integral part of the film's narrative.

The nuanced concepts which the Japanese most often use to convey the "politics" in their lives, whether public or private, are *tatemae* and *honne*, whose etymological roots, respectively, mean "surface structure" and "true tone." They are usually rendered in English in terms such as "surface appearance" and "true feelings."

Tatemae and *honne* are not dualisms in the Western sense; they co-exist whether in harmony or ambiguity. A politician may be accused of *tatemae*, of acting superficially and against his true feelings, of putting up a façade—but the accusation may not necessarily be a condemning one. Sometimes it is; but the Japanese may regard a *tatemae* statement as being as innocuous as a white lie, *or* as a statement which is not a "lie" or "political" ploy at all but a socially *expected* and *accepted* statement of *policy*, that is, of public *structure*. The etymology, again, consists of two characters, "structure" and "front." *Tatemae* plays a constructive role in society; it holds things together.

Kyôgoku Jun'ichi, a political scientist, explains how the concept of *tatemae* originally referred to a ceremony which marked the construction of the wooden framework of a house. It developed into the meaning of "an official or officially professed principle or doctrine that will serve as the goal or target of the collectivity, and provide guidance for its members in managing it." Its opposite, *honne*, refers to a "true voice" which is also a volatile voice and one which can shake the valued framework of the house. *Honne* thus is a silent voice and *tatemae* is an expressed voice. In a more policy-oriented definition, "*tatemae* refers to the communal and public facets of the common interest of the members of the collectivity as articulated by the leadership," and "*honne* refers to the fulfillment of the desires of the individuals that are not in accord with the official line, at least in the eyes of and, perhaps, in the interest of the leaders" (1987: 59–60).

A former lieutenant returning home after the war, the sedate, poker-faced, mild-mannered Toshio thus signifies *tatemae*, the socially presentable exterior of his household. But when the more expressive Miho, signifying *honne*, relentlessly struggles to break down Toshio's wall (and she literally hits herself against the wall in places), she develops mental illness.

In general, there is nothing wrong with *tatemae* in Japanese culture; nor is there anything sacred about *honne*. What is culturally impermissible is the inability to discriminate, to have *kejime*, to know in which situation to use which sort of self. Telling a lie can be just as bad as telling the truth too much when the situation doesn't warrant it.

A *tatemae*, however, is not necessarily a false exterior. Sometimes it is a "white lie," or just something less than the truth. It is something like a public statement pronounced by an official: an American might say, "That's political"; a Japanese might say, "That's *tatemae*." Often it is, however, a kind of legitimate lie, a false exterior to protect a volatile truth from rocking the boat. Uttering true intentions are just that—volatile and dangerous—and that's why *honne* is certainly no worse than *tatemae*.

Thus, using the metaphor of the house (the physical structure as well as the family) as nation, *Sting of Death* concerns the conflict between truth and falsehood (which is a more appropriate rendition of the Japanese word *uso* than the more narrowly conceived "lie"), past and present, wife and husband, parents and children, surface and depth—all conflicts which are in some way representative of Japan's rise to economic power in the immediate aftermath of the Second World War.

As for the film's household, it is typically cramped, piled high with books and papers, its doors smeared with paint and crayons. It's usually nightfall when husband and wife, Toshio and Miho, engage in stilted quarrels. Sometimes their two children are awakened and absorb the incessant tension which will force the family to move and try to reconstruct their lives elsewhere.

Tatemae and *honne* intend to complement each other in Japanese culture, as long as one practices the right *kejime*. But the paradox of this film is that when Toshio tries to compromise with Miho by bargaining: "I won't lie if you'll stop digging into the past," the concepts cancel each other out, likewise canceling out memory altogether. Toshio only lies about the past, so if Miho never discusses the past, certainly he will never lie. The old wall will be dismantled, but only if the sequestered past is not allowed to be seen. It is a kind of mutual self-destruction, corresponding to the way the quarreling couple competes to see who will commit suicide first. The only answer is to build the household over again from scratch, to move.

Now a struggling writer and a history teacher in night school, Toshio has periodic flashbacks to the war. But his memories are of halcyon days, of crystal waters and sunlit bucolic pastures. The soldiers salute him; children gather to hear his stories and neighbors call him "the kind Lt. Shimao."

In contrast, the dark present is his hell, Miho reminds him. Desperately struggling to regain the stability of his family, Toshio will endure almost anything. This means letting his wife dominate and assume "male" roles, while he becomes docile and domestic, both "feminized" and "infantilized."

In the opening scene, for example, Miho accuses Toshio of not treating her like a wife. But she requests that he address her as "*anata-sama*" rather than "*omae*," hardly a generic way for a Japanese man to address a wife. "*Omae*" is a somewhat vulgar pronoun, but it is often used between men; and some men use it to speak to women or children condescendingly (though some would argue, indulgently). In *Sting*, "*omae*" is translated as "hey," the English language lacking any equivalent. "*Anata sama*" is rendered as "dear," though it should really be "your highness," since one could not expect an expression this formal to be used between spouses—unless uttered by the wife of a distinguished samurai or aristocrat during the shogun days.

Toshio never calls Miho "*anata sama*," but he does begin calling her by name. He helps her shop, obsequiously holding the shopping bag, and in another scene helps her with her shoes—all to the dismay of neighbors and relatives. The most telling reversal of gender codes occurs when Kuniko brings a gift of money to Toshio after the family has moved. Miho attacks her erstwhile rival, screaming out *otoko no kotoba* (men's language) and mounting her as if in a position of a male rapist—even entreating Toshio to remove her underwear. Yet all the while, Toshio stands on the sideline, an expressionless, motionless stone.

Only in two instances does Toshio change his monotone demeanor. Once, while Miho is having one of her headache fits, he pours water over her, assuming a militarist pose as this were an act of ritual ablution and thunders: "Lt. Shimao . . . !" In another situation, resisting one of Miho's inquisitions, he lets out a deafening cry in the middle of the street and crawls to the train tracks as if to await his death. Weeping afterward when Miho takes him home, he behaves like a sickly, spoilt child.

At the beginning of the film, Toshio apologizes to Miho for passing his "weakness" on to her. This "weakness" can be interpreted as his breach of the marital contract, and likewise, as his own impotence as a husband, father, struggling writer, and useless soldier. In a flashback, he is pulling something through a tunnel—a trite sexual metaphor, perhaps—but the thing he's pulling is a boat, which never reaches the water. This, then, is the weakness, the impotence he "transfers" to Miho and to some extent, his children. Miho finds a diary where he's referred to her as an "impotent wife," and later, the whole family has a picnic in a boat on a dried-up lake—like postwar Japan forcing itself to pull together as a nation even while still in a delirious state of desiccation.

At the personal level, Kuniko helps Toshio recover his manhood. This becomes more representational when Miho hums a ballad about a man who leaves his woman never to return again: the lyrics seem to narrate a story of betrayal in love, but instead they turn into a patriotic ballad about a man who goes off to war. Hearing the song, Toshio reverts to one of his reveries of the war. But he severs ties with his mistress, like Japan's unconditional surrender, transforming himself into a man who will do anything to rebuild his torn household.

Miho wants every bit of his hypocrisy turned inside out, however, so she asks, "If you loved her so much, why do you ignore her now?" This is not at all unlike the hypocrisy of Japan toward its Asian neighbors. Japan represented itself as the paternalistic caretaker of China and Korea during the construction of the "Greater East Asia Co-Prosperity Sphere," then quickly withdrew the premise after the dissolution of the empire.

As noted, the "Other" in Japanese cultural self-representations is often a vague "phantom foe" (see p. 17), what Kuniko may represent in this film. With her offer of money, a collection taken up among her colleagues to assist the Toshio family's recovery, Kuniko becomes like a Western Other, America and its allies who conducted the Occupation of Japan, which ended in 1953, the year before the setting of *The Sting of Death*. (C.f., "The twist in propaganda films, where actual Westerners rarely appear," Dower observes, "is to portray weak and dissolute Asians as Westernized individuals" [1987: 7].)

The impotent soldier likewise extends metaphorically to the image of a family cut off from the rest of society—like the way Japan was cut off from the world. In his flashbacks, Toshio is on the other side of the water while his comrades salute him. While kite-flying on New Year's, a siren is heard and all the other families run toward the vehicle producing it, leaving the Toshio family behind. Miho is put into an asylum twice; the second time Toshio joins her and their children are taken away by the grandparents. Nurses in the second asylum install opaque curtains, telling the couple to take some "sleeping therapy."

Toshio, qua *tatemae*, tries to move the family into a new house—a new exterior—away in the country, with a newly built fence. Again, however, Miho, as *honne*, bores into the new dwelling, finding hidden in the storage cabinets of the old house medical instruments used for tuberculosis. This place will be no good for the children, she admonishes.

What keeps husband and wife from destroying one another is the presence of the children, their project for the reconstruction of the family. The children sleep beside their parents and are ever-present throughout the family quarrels, as Oguri's portrayal of the Toshio family is located in the Asian concept of holism, in which the family is a single unit, sharing the same life-blood and health patterns, mental as well as physical; hence, parents do not try to hide their faults from the children. Toshio and Miho often refer to the day when their kids will be in school as a time for a new beginning. At last, by the end of the film, the children are taken away to school by their grandparents, while the parents remain behind the dark curtains of the asylum.

Here, *The Sting of Death* is consistent with another third-generational war movie, Kurosawa Akira's *Rhapsody in August,* and to a lesser extent, Imai Tadashi's *War and Youth* (both produced the following year, 1991, but far less sophisticated than Oguri's film). The common thread of all three films it that it is the middle generation which is truly left in a state of "disease" following the war. In Kurosawa's film, like Oguri's, the older grandparents help the younger children escape the "disease" of their parents (in *Rhapsody*'s case, greediness and amnesia).

Sting offers a brief "foreshadow" of what will happen if the disease of the parents is passed on to the children. (I continue with the word "disease" because Asian holism is closely tied to the medical metaphor.) While Miho is hospitalized for the first time, the daughter Maya hides her overcoat—her own *tatemae.* She tells a string of lies to her father as to the whereabouts of the coat, leading him on a wild goose chase and affording her the chance to run away. Like her father, she thus establishes a false *tatemae*; like her mother she forces her father to dig in places where he doesn't want to go, e.g., in rubbish cans.

Aside from Maya's excursion, the children seem remarkably normal and optimistic, given their surroundings. The morning after the worst of the parents' sessions, when they both try to hang themselves and collapse in exhaustion, sunlight comes into the room and the boy, Shinichi, wakes up, announcing to his parents: "Hey, it's morning. The people are already going to the factory."

The average age of workers in Japan's major corporations at the time of this film's production (1990) would have been about the age of Shinichi (6) in the year this film was set (1954). It was largely owing to this sort of energy drive, the ability to ignore the devastation around them and just say, "It's morning, get up and go to work," that Japan became the economic success story it is today. How surrealistic this must appear from the standpoint of the Heisei era (1989–). Indeed, it would appear to us of the late twentieth century as odd a picture as taking a boat out on a dried up lake.

To reassess this inventory of the postwar family metaphors in the era of Japan's "peace," we have seen Japan as a young boy thinking about a new role model of leadership and strength, one which was bookish rather than brutal (*Takeshi*); Japan as a victimized prostitute turning over her trade to a new generation which would sever ties with her altogether for the sake of economic security (*A Japanese Tragedy*); Japan as a kind of male prostitute—a mercenary soldier—who fantasizes of a situation in which he can use his weapon as well as his wallet in the best of both worlds (*Yojimbo*); and finally, Japan again as a family unit, *ie*, coming to grips with its own collapse and opting for a process of reconstruction with its children (*Sting of Death*). Yet, in all the representations, "peace" is a dubious achievement, often "suspiciously effeminate," and emphasizes wartime victimization more than postwar economic victory. What sorts of new metaphors will attach to the reinvigorated "Japan Which Can Say No" remain to be seen.

Note

1. However, scholars whose research concerns this phenomenon of masculinism and militarism strongly admonish against this highly simplified explanation of war. "Although women do not do the actual killing [in war], they are part of the structure of oppositions that encourages and requires it," writes Jean Bethke Elshtain, whose thesis debunks the common assumption that women are generically pacifist, and men likewise militarist (1987: 201).

The author would like to acknowledge Prof. D. William Davis for his valuable support of this paper.

Bibliography

Anderson, Benedict. 1983. *Imagined Communities: Reflections on the Origin and Spread of Nationalism*. London: Verso.

Anderson, Joseph L., and Donald Richie. 1982. *The Japanese Film: Art and Industry*. Princeton: Princeton University Press.

Burch, Noël. 1979. *To the Distant Observer; Form and Meaning in Japanese Cinema*. Rev. and Ed. Annette Michelson. Berkeley: University of California Press.

Crichton, Michael. 1992. *Rising Sun*. New York: Knopf.

Davis, D. William. 1989. "Back to Japan: Militarism and Monumentalism in Prewar Japanese Cinema." *Wide Angle* 11, no. 3: 16–25.

Desser, David. 1988. *Eros Plus Massacre: An Introduction to the Japanese New Wave Cinema*. Bloomington: Indiana University Press.

Douglas, Mary. 1982. *Natural Symbols: Explorations in Cosmology*. New York: Pantheon Books.

Dower, John W. 1987. "Japanese Cinema Goes to War." *Japan Society Newsletter* (July): 2–9.

———. 1986. *War without Mercy: Race and Power in the Pacific War*. New York: Pantheon Books.

Elshtain, Jean Bethke. 1990. "The Problem with Peace." In *Women, Militarism and War: Essays in History, Politics and Social Theory*. Ed. Jean Bethke Elshtain and Sheila Tobias. Savage: Rowman and Littlefield: 255–66.

———. 1987. *Women and War*. New York: Basic Books.

Foucault, Michel. 1973. *The Order of Things: An Archeology of the Human Sciences*. New York: Vintage Books.

Gluck, Carol. 1985. *Japan's Modern Myths: Ideology in the Late Meiji Period*. Princeton: Princeton University Press.

Haraway, Donna. 1989. *Primate Visions: Gender, Race and Nature in the World of Modern Science*. New York: Routledge.

Herman, Dianne. 1984. "The Rape Culture." In *Women: A Feminist Perspective*. Ed. Jo Freeman. Palo Alto: Mayfield Publishing Co.: 20–38.

Ishihara Shintaro. 1989. *The Japan That Can Say No: Why Japan Will Be First Among Equals*. Ed. and trans. Frank Baldwin. New York: Simon and Schuster.

Kyôgoku Jun'ichi. 1987. *The Political Dynamics of Japan*. Trans. Ike Nobutaka (original 1983). Tokyo: University of Tokyo Press.

Lock, Margaret. 1980. *East Asian Medicine in Urban Japan: Varieties of Medical Experience*. Berkeley: University of California Press.

Lyotard, Jean-François. 1989. *The Postmodern Condition: A Report on Knowledge*. Trans. Geoff Bennington and Brian Massumi (original 1979). Minneapolis: University of Minnesota Press.

Maruyama Masao. 1963. *Thought and Behaviour in Japanese Politics*. Ed. Ivan Morris. Trans. Ivan Morris et al. London: Oxford University Press.

Mellen, Joan. 1976. *The Waves at Genji's Door: Japan Through Its Cinema*. New York: Pantheon Books.

Richie, Donald. 1984. *The Films of Akira Kurosawa*. With revisions by Joan Mellen. Berkeley: University of California Press.

Said, Edward W. 1985. "Orientalism Reconsidered." *Race & Class* 27, no. 2: 1–15.

———. 1978. *Orientalism*. New York: Vintage Books.

3 | Ideology of the Body in *Red Sorghum*
National Allegory, National Roots, and Third Cinema

Yingjin Zhang

In his famous essay "World Literature in an Age of Multinational Capitalism," Fredric Jameson postulates his theory of "national allegory." The primacy of national allegory is, according to him, a remarkable feature apparently common to all Third World cultural productions and radically distinguishable from analogous cultural forms in the First World. As he forcefully argues:

> Those [Third World] texts, even those narratives which are seemingly private and invested with a properly libidinal dynamic, necessarily project a political dimension in the form of national allegory: the story of the private individual destiny is always an allegory of the embattled situation of the public Third World culture and society.[1]

Jameson's theory, to be exact, is based on his observation of "a radical split between the private and the public, between the poetic and the political" (or "Freud versus Marx") that characterizes much of capitalist culture, "the culture of the western realist and modernist novel."[2] Third World culture, on the contrary, is "necessarily" allegorical in that "the telling of the individual story and the individual experience cannot but ultimately involve the whole laborious telling of the experience of the collectivity itself."[3]

Given his mapping of Third World cultural "totality" (in complement with another mapping of the present-day Western, postmodern world),[4] Jameson's theory of "national allegory" has obvious relevancy to our study of Third World literature and cinema—even though the theory itself does not go without an immediate intellectual challenge.[5] The purpose of this chapter is, however, not to reflect on the hypothetical nature of Jameson's theory, but rather to see how its theoretical components, such as the concepts of the private and the public, the poetic and the political, can better inform our reading of Third World texts.

The chosen text is a Chinese film, *Red Sorghum*,[6] and this chapter will necessarily take into account the problem of "national roots," partly because the film itself is incorporated into Director Zhang Yimou's broader project to search for the distinctive nature of Chinese people and Chinese culture. The fact that *Red Sorghum* won the Golden Bear at the 1988 Berlin Film Festival,[7] the highest honor a Chinese film had ever achieved until then, will also lead us to consider the film in its international, or cross-cultural context, specifically in relation to a Western film discourse, the "Third Cinema."[8]

Violence and Obscenity: Images of the Body

What immediately impresses the audience in *Red Sorghum* is the exuberance of its initial celebratory mood. The opening sedan-chair dance is, without any doubt, typically Chinese: against a setting of barren yellow land, eight bare-shouldered sedan carriers are dancing with a red sedan-chair, chanting in their hoarse voices a song full of vulgar and obscene words, and shaking the bride who is helplessly confined in the sedan. For about ten minutes, the audience is delighted by such a sheer cinematographic display of color and action, accompanied by exotic music, and punctuated with obscene, sexist remarks ("to rock urine out of the bride"). The audience is only later reminded of the impending fate of the young bride, who is forced by her father to marry a fifty-year-old leprous owner of a sorghum wine distillery in exchange for a small mule.

A number of shots repeated in this initial scene deserve our closer attention: From within the sedan, the bride, profoundly upset, at times anxiously peeks through the curtains. Her vision, again and again, is blocked by the strong muscles of the sedan carriers, covered as they are with sweat and dirt. To the bride confined in the sedan, the presence of the muscles is posed here as a fascinating threat—fascinating because by comparison lack of muscles (and lack of sexuality) is even more threatening in her leper "husband." This idea of fascination is further enhanced in the same scene when the robust sedan carriers overpower a masked highwayman who has kidnapped the bride with his fake pistol.

In terms of this "repressed" fascination with muscles, or more precisely, with *the human body*, the bride's willing submission in a subsequent scene to a violent act of abduction and "rape" (Vincent Canby's word) by the strongest of the sedan carriers is perhaps more understandable to the Western audience. As a matter of fact, the "rape" (or rather, "love-making") scene is poeticized and enthusiastically celebrated in the film. After running through the thickets of wild sorghum, the sedan carrier stamps out a space in the field, a round circle much like a sacred place for sacrifice. The bride lies motionless on the ground, her eyes closed, while the man kneels down, his face up toward the empty sky. Obviously, this is a sacred moment in the film: a moment of *deification*, a moment of returning the human to its natural elements, and a moment of desperate triumph of the primitive "body," with all its undaunted violence and vitality, over the repressive tradition of the Chinese (patriarchal) society.[9]

Another celebratory scene, with equal emphasis on the human body, is set in the wine distillery after the mysterious murder of the leprous owner (who actually makes no appearance in the entire film). The male workers, bare-shouldered as in the film's first scene, sweat by the heated wine distiller. The bride, now the sole owner of the distillery, is invited to see the conclusion of winery work—the pouring out of new wine. All partake in the moment of joy and fulfillment as they taste the newly brewed wine in turn.

The festive mood, however, is abruptly destroyed by the arrival of the sedan carrier. He was previously driven out of the winery when in his drunkenness he had insulted the bride-owner with obscene references to their love-making in the wild sorghum fields. This time, however, he is sober and looks very determined. He shows off his strength by carrying big pots of new wine, placing them in a row, and urinating right into each of them. In spite of such a blasphemous affront (which later turns out to be a "blessing" act because the wine proves better than before), the sheer presence of muscles overwhelms the workers and, significantly, "intoxicates" the bride-owner into a semi-(un)conscious state. With a triumphant air, the sedan carrier carries the "bride" on his shoulder and walks right into the privacy of the bride-owner's room. They live together thereafter and have a son before long.

From the violence, vulgarities, indecencies, and abusive language highlighted in the above two scenes—all of them linked to the human body—we can see clearly that in *Red Sorghum* the image of the human body is deliberately exaggerated, primitivized, and so projected onto the screen as to fulfill a special ideological function. It becomes part of the carnivalesque.

Carnival: The Private (Re-)Turned to the Public

In his brilliant study *Rabelais and His World*, Bakhtin offers an exhaustive examination of what he calls the "popular-festive forms" (e.g., eating, drinking, cursing, abusing) and "the grotesque images of the body" (e.g., sex, defecation, pregnancy, birth, and death). To him, all forms of "degradation" in carnival are not just entertainments in the negative sense of the word; rather, "with all its images, indecencies, and curses," carnival "affirms the people's immortal, indestructible character."[10]

This positive view of carnival is arrived at in a dialectic way by Bakhtin through his recognition of the original (and by now almost "lost") meaning of the human body. In the Middle Ages and up to the Renaissance, there was little question as to the unifying forces within the human body. According to Bakhtin, two characteristic tendencies existed in the Renaissance philosophers:

> First is the tendency to find in man the entire universe with all its elements and forces, with its higher and lower stratum; second is the tendency to think of the human body as drawing together the most remote phenomena and forces of the cosmos.[11]

The human body, seen in this light, is a unity of heaven and earth, of the public and the private, and even of death and rebirth.

This primordial unity, however, was lost in the subsequent development of human (especially bourgeois) societies. As Bakhtin puts it, "in the modern image of the individual body, sexual life, eating, drinking, and defecation have radically changed their meaning: they have been transferred to the private and psychological level. . . . "[12] In other words, the public features of the human body have since been transformed and confined exclusively in a private, psychologized space. From this observation, we can realize that Bakhtin's theory of carnival carries with it an important historical mission—to return the human body from its now private and psychological status to its original public domain.

Red Sorghum can also be viewed as such an attempt. In the film, the private space has always been transgressed and/or destroyed (the bride's closed sedanchair at the beginning of the film is just one instance; her "wedding" room which is later violently "shared" by the sedan carrier is another). Private, intimate acts (such as urinating and sweating) are performed before the eye of the public. The implication of these private-turned-public moments, arguably, is to emphasize the interconnectiveness of all human bodies. In Bakhtin's apt words:

> The individual feels that he is an indissoluble part of the collectivity, a member of the people's mass body. In this whole the individual body ceases to a certain extent to be itself; it is possible, so to say, to exchange bodies, to be renewed. . . . At the same time the people become aware of their sensual, material bodily unity and community.[13]

Given the original, material unity within the human body, the dominance of the bodily images in *Red Sorghum* is actually a signal toward a reunion of the private to the public. The process of such a reunion is interestingly demonstrated in the configuration of the central object of the film, the red wine.

Red Wine: A Poetic Spirit Shared by the Public

In terms of the carnivalesque nature of *Red Sorghum* where the bodily images dominate the screen, red sorghum wine, as a specifically symbolic object, invites interpretations at various levels.

On a popular level, red wine perfectly fits festive images and is readily consumed in a celebration of life or death on a largely collective scale. It is both the product of collective labor and the crowning glory for the workers. Drinking wine, to quote Bakhtin's observation, is therefore "not a biological, animal act but a social event."[14] In *Red Sorghum*, the winery workers' drinking and chanting prayers in front of the Wine God is a good example. In the film's two praying scenes, drinking is not only done as a social event, but virtually performed as a serious *ritual*, thus acquiring a mythic dimension which outweighs any isolated individualistic aspect of configuration.

On another, less obvious level, wine (red or otherwise) is a poetic imagery deeply rooted in Chinese culture. It is, for one thing, a frequent means for a solitary poet to escape his/her immediate realities; it is, for another, a spirit that inspires a poet's individual vision (e.g., Li Bai's solitary drinking to the moon and to his own dancing shadow), and further sustains his/her independent, often secluded life. Red wine, seen in this tradition, symbolizes a (wild) passion for an intoxicated, ecstatic life (rather than a mediocre, repressed one)—a passion, that is, for a unique vision of *life* in the true sense of the word (vitality, productivity, and creativity).

On a more specific level, red wine in *Red Sorghum* refers to a special type of sorghum wine that is brewed by collective labor (led by the experienced foreman Luohan), "finished up" magically by the sedan carrier's urine, given a name ("red over a thousand miles") by the bride-owner, devoured by workers in the aforementioned ritual scenes, and finally deployed as the dynamite to destroy a truckload of Japanese soldiers. It is not difficult to identify several individual elements in the wine—which is a strange mixture of, among other things, the sedan carrier's urine, the bride-owner's inspiration and her power of naming; nor is it surprising to see that it becomes in the end an object of the collective memory of an individual, Luohan, who leaves the winery in the middle of the film to join the Communist armies and is later captured and skinned alive by the Japanese soldiers. This specific red wine, as a locus of the unified private and public, encompasses the whole cycle of life, death and rebirth (we see the son running on-screen and hear the grandson speaking offscreen), serving as a witness to the glory of collective work and the tragedy of lost freedom and independence in the wake of the Japanese invasion.

Red wine, then, can be regarded in *Red Sorghum* as a spirit characterized by its powerful unifying force. As such, it immediately evokes another image in the Western tradition—that of Nietzsche's Dionysos (the Greek god of wine). In *Red Sorghum*, we are often touched—or "intoxicated"—by the scenes similar to what Nietzsche so enthusiastically celebrates in his *Birth of Tragedy*:

> Not only does the bond between man and man come to be forged once more by the magic of the Dionysiac rite, but nature itself, long alienated or subjugated, rises again to celebrate the reconciliation with her prodigal son, man.[15]

The love-making scene in the sorghum fields is a good example of such a "magic" moment; so are the scenes of two wine praying rituals. As if all are intoxicated by the "Dionysiac" spirit, the individuals in *Red Sorghum* often express themselves, in Nietzsche's words, "through song and dance as the member[s] of a higher community," and their collective power is manifest "to the glorious satisfaction of the primordial One"—an ultimate unity.[16]

To further illustrate how an individual "loses" him/herself in the public (community), we observe two points here: First, the red wine, from its initial production to its ultimate destruction, is closely associated with the bride-owner; second, the bride-owner is virtually the only one in the film who consistently claims a real vision. At the beginning of *Red Sorghum*, she feels (and thus lets the audience feel) the fascination of the muscles; in the middle, she realizes the importance of collective work and thus leads the winery to a blooming success; in the end, she senses the responsibility to avenge the death of Luohan and thus brings the whole story to a tragic, yet heroic conclusion. If we confine our view to this particular angle (red wine), *Red Sorghum* can well be seen as a story of the bride-owner—a story about her individual poetic vision shared and realized by the public.

Such an idea is effectively visualized in the final ritual scene. Before they set out for combat, the male workers line up in a row in front of a portrayal of the Wine God, performing their ritual prayers while drinking the red wine. "Drinking our wine," they chant, "you won't kow-tow to the Emperor." The idea of fighting is originated by the bride-owner, but when she airs it, it is readily picked up by the collective without any questioning. Ironically, the bride-owner sees the significance of fighting not in terms of the dominant Communist ideology, but simply in terms of the loyalty an individual should demonstrate to his own folks in the community. Their ritual sacrifice, in other words, is performed exclusively by and *for themselves*, not for any abstract concept such as "anti-imperialism." There is an evident absence of a canonical ideology in the protagonists of the film.

An Innocent Narrator: Politics of De-Politicized Narration

The final scene of *Red Sorghum* is a projection of the sedan carrier and his nine-year-old son standing in the thickets of the rummaged sorghum field, the body of the bride-owner by their feet, stained with blood and red wine. The music of a folk song fills the soundtrack, presumably sung by the son. It is at this moment that the narrator (i.e., the grandson) speaks about his father's "red" vision, and this voice-over, which has been heard on and off throughout the film, finally pulls the audience back to the present and brings the film to a close.

A contrast, then, exists in *Red Sorghum* between the visual narration (synchronic to the events in the film) and the verbal narration (more like a number of added commentaries). Whereas we actually see the visual, poetic presentation of the winery people's "epic" life, we only listen to the "phantom voice" that has unsuccessfully attempted to encode that life in a more overtly political terminology (e.g., "Uncle Luohan" tried to "mobilize local armed bandits into anti-Japanese forces,"—a knowledge simply beyond the comprehension of the winery workers in the film). Such a contrast amounts to a confession that the "innocent" narrator knows very little of the richness of the narrated story—a consequence which obviously results from his limited perspective of a fully politicized present, and which yet evokes an ever-increasing yearning for the "lost" meaning of a primitive life.

From the narrative point of view, therefore, we are confronted in *Red Sorghum* with a strange ideological phenomenon: the whole story is presented in such a way as to reduce its political overtones to a minimum. This deliberately *depoliticized narration* is "strange" and non-canonical in the overall cultural-political contexts of contemporary China where the Communist Party dictates that literature and art must serve politics.[17] Nonetheless, this phenomenon is not so strange if we take into account the recent Chinese literary tendency toward a de-politicization in narration (exemplified, in cinema, by the so-called "Fifth Generation Directors"—including the director of *Red Sorghum*, Zhang Yimou—and, in literature, by the "avant-garde writers"—including, not surprisingly, the original author of "Red Sorghum," Mo Yan).[18]

The film *Red Sorghum*, it may be quite clear by now, belongs outside of Chinese mainstream literary ideology. The marginality of the film can be demonstrated sufficiently by observing a number of obvious absences in the text: First, the setting of the story in a remote winery distillery indicates a deliberate absence of the historically typical mode of production in Chinese society—what Jameson calls "the great bureaucratic imperial systems."[19] Its celebratory presentation of another mode of production, that of "primitive, or tribal society" (Jameson's term), with all its backwardness, vulgarism and blasphemy, places the film in opposition to traditional Chinese values of culture and civilization.

Secondly, the depoliticized narration of *Red Sorghum* results in a complete absence of class distinctions and political consciousness (e.g., self-conscious "patriotism") in the film. The only character with a political vision, Luohan, is given little function in the film; perhaps even worse, he is portrayed as a helpless victim of the invaders' cold-blooded brutality (being skinned alive in public).

Thirdly, the primitive life-style poeticized in the film displays a challenging disregard of traditional moral values. Instead of exemplary virtuous women (we see too many of them in Chinese mainstream films), *Red Sorghum* valorizes the wild passion of "my grandpa," the sedan carrier, and "my grandma," the bride-owner. (I have insisted on using the term "bride-owner" because, lacking a proper name for "my grandma,"[20] the woman protagonist is more meaningfully regarded as a bride than a "widow," the latter being a legal term imbued with "civilized" values.) Such a wild passion, invigorated by red wine and regenerated by wild sorghum fields, gives a poetic expression to an ideology of the body in the film.

The strategic absences in *Red Sorghum*'s depoliticized narration thus testify fully to the subversive nature of its marginality. The film's positioning of itself outside the mainstream of Chinese filmmaking and the canonical Communist ideology enables (and actually invites) the audience to reflect critically on larger social and cultural issues in contemporary China.

Ideology of the Body: Search for National Roots

The depoliticized narration in *Red Sorghum* is achieved by a process of "degradation" of what used to be the gentle (in human behavior), decent (in human speech), moral (in human relations), and honorable (in social interaction). "The purpose of degradation," as Bakhtin points out, is "the lowering of all that is high, spiritual, ideal, abstract."[21] The civilized becomes uncivilized; the indecent glorified; and the blasphemous blessed. The result of such a degradation, unavoidably, is a re-structuring of the existing (concepts of) world orders.

That is exactly what Bakhtin has enthusiastically embraced in his notion of carnival:

> [Carnival] is outside of and contrary to all existing forms of the coercive socioeconomic and political organization, which is suspended for the time of the festivity.
>
> Carnival was the true feast of time, the feast of becoming, change and renewal. It was hostile to all that was immortalized and completed.
>
> Carnival celebrates the destruction of the old and the birth of the new world.
>
> During carnival time life is subject only to its laws, that is, the laws of its freedom.[22]

As the subversive and destructive force is true and real in the theory of carnival, so is it in an ideology of the body—an ideology boldly articulated in *Red Sorghum* and ascertainable to varying degrees in recent Chinese cinema, literature, and literary theory.

The essential principle of the ideology of the body is to return the body to its "primitive" origin. The image of the body can be a human body, thus returning it to its most basic biological needs (i.e., eating, drinking, defecating, making love, raising children—the themes that are also explored in recent films such as *Horse Thief* and *Old Well*). The image of the body can also be the body, in an abstract sense, of one's ontological status, thus returning the long-forbidden topic "*subjectivity*" to Chinese intellectual milieux (the best example in this connection is Liu Zaifu's aesthetic projects of subjectivity).[23] The image of the body can yet be further extended even to that of the whole nation, thus returning Chinese culture to its original cradle, the Loess Plateau (as is clearly the case in the film *Yellow Earth*). A recent Chinese cultural phenomenon—a search for national roots, which means both a search for national characteristics of Chinese people, and for literary styles to capture that characteristic Chineseness[24]—can thus meaningfully be discussed in terms of the emerging ideology of the body.

As in the case of an ideology of the body, the search for national roots in

China entails a conceptually downward movement, a movement exploring the most fundamental elements of human life. What are considered most "national," not surprisingly, are often (re)discovered in rituals (like rain prayers in *Yellow Earth*, or chess games in Ah Cheng's story, "The Chess Master"),[25] in folk customs (most frequently marriage and funeral proceedings, as in *Old Well*), and in religious ceremonies (like those in *Horse Thief*)—all invariably and significantly set in locales remote from China's contemporary cultural-political centers. The search for roots, therefore, is frequently executed in the form of myth (with all its emphases on legends, rituals, even superstitions). What Nietzsche says in the end of *The Birth of Tragedy* is very illuminating in this connection:

> Man today, stripped of myth, stands famished among all his pasts and must dig frantically for roots, be it among the most remote antiquities.[26]

It is as if "modern men," having lost their vital tie with history and nature, can only move backward and downward to search for their lost origin—the mythic home and/or the mythic womb. In the context of contemporary China, it is as if only by moving away from the interfering forces of the dominant political dogmas and doctrines (a movement yet exemplifying the "politics" of absence and marginality) could a new ideology be fully established, a ideology that embodies the high and the low, the far and the near, all in a truly material, tangible, and hence comprehensible self—the body.

One message in *Red Sorghum* is quite clear by now: it eulogizes the life of a nameless couple whose unabashed confrontation with their own bodies brings home to us a realization of *a new ideology of the body*. The body in question, to borrow Bakhtin's brilliant expression, is not "the biological body, which merely repeats itself in the new generations, but precisely the historic, progressive body of mankind."[27] From here we can proclaim, by following Bakhtin further, that an ideology of the body is "not abstract thought about the future but the living sense that each man belongs to the immortal people who create history."[28] Indeed, it is the body of people, not dogmas and doctrines, that can ever be immortal; and it is this immortality of the body that the Director Zhang Yimou celebrates so enthusiastically in *Red Sorghum*.[29]

Liberation: Third Cinema and National Allegory

The final tragic scene in *Red Sorghum* conforms, in a sense, to what Jameson calls the Third World's "life-and-death struggle" with First World imperialism.[30] Such a struggle, by its very definition, must be a political struggle.

Jameson's insistence on the political nature of the allegory form in Third World culture may find support in the recent discussion of the "Third Cinema" in the West. Initially proposed by Fernando Solanas and Octavio Getino in a manifesto in 1969, the "Third Cinema" now refers to, in Teshome Gabriel's words, "a cinema of decolonization and for liberation."[31] Given the political agenda built into the proposition of the Third Cinema, it is no surprise that its style must be very subversive and revolutionary, "full of the imagery of guerrilla combat," as Roy Armes describes it.[32]

Judging from this political criterion, *Red Sorghum* (like some other Chinese films in the 80s, such as *Yellow Earth* and *Horse Thief*) does not perfectly fit in the category of Third Cinema. While there is no denying that these recent Chinese films also make use of "the major themes in third cinema"—class, culture, religion, sexism, armed struggle[33]—to varying degrees, the concept of Third Cinema may be more usefully applied, as Chris Berry proposes, to a study of Chinese Leftist films in the 30s, marked by their heavy ideological emphases on anti-colonization and anti-imperialism.[34]

The apparent discrepancy between the revolutionary politics explicit in Third Cinema and the seemingly depoliticized narration of *Red Sorghum*, to be sure, does not rule out all possible grounds for comparison. The central tenet of liberation is still eminently evident in *Red Sorghum*. What need to be differentiated at this point are the various levels at which the concept of liberation is applied. At the nationhood level, the liberation of the country from the Japanese imperialists is overtly set as the background of the story. At the individual level, the liberation of women from the patriarchal oppression is touched on. Yet these two kinds of liberation only constitute a small proportion of the entirety of the film. *Red Sorghum* pronounces through its consistent and colorful visual images a total liberation and desperate triumph of the body.

It is this ideology of the body that undermines other political concerns in the film. By valorizing the "primitive" way of living and the simple nature of Chinese people—intact as they seem to be from any form of political indoctrination—*Red Sorghum* aspires to *a liberation of the human body*, a liberation that hopefully will return Chinese people from their now uniform life-style and sterile way of thinking, to their nurturing, regenerating origins. According to Director Zhang Yimou, the fast-moving pace and the celebratory mood in *Red Sorghum* are to awaken and return Chinese people to their lost vitality, thus rejuvenating (the body of) the whole nation.

The story of *Red Sorghum* is not a story of any individual (be it "my grandpa" or "my grandma" or two together); its poeticized narration, no matter how depoliticized it appears, is *ultimately political in nature*. The aspiration to liberate people's thoughts from political indoctrination, to subvert the seemingly insurmountable authority of the dominant ideologies, and, in short, to advocate a new ideology of the body in contemporary China, is, and must be, a political aspiration.

It is in this sense that Jameson's theory of "national allegory" can be meaningfully applied to *Red Sorghum*. The individual experience of "my grandpa and grandma," narrated as it is in a seemingly depolitized way, is ultimately an allegory of China, an allegory involving the experience of the whole Chinese nation—the experience, this time, not of liberating the country from colonialization or imperialist invasion, but of liberating its own body, or more precisely, *liberating itself.* Given the contemporary Chinese situation, the present task of liberation, as assumed by the ideology of the body, is as political as the first one in nature.

Notes

1. In *The Current in Criticism: Essays on the Present and Future of Literary Theory*, ed. Clayton Koelb and Virgil Locke (West Lafayette, Indiana: Purdue University Press, 1987), 142.

2. Ibid., 141.

3. Ibid., 158.

4. Fredric Jameson, "Postmodernism, or The Cultural Logic of Late Capitalism," *New Left Review* 146 (July-Aug. 1984): 53–92. He clearly presents both essays as his attempts to map the totality of the cultural scenes in the first as well as the Third World.

5. See, for example, Aijaz Ahmad, "Jameson's Rhetoric of Otherness and the 'National Allegory,' " *Social Texts* 17 (Fall 1987): 3–25; see also Jameson's reply in the same issue.

6. For reviews of the film in English, see Vincent Canby in *The New York Times* (9 Oct. 1988); Stanley Kauffmann in *New Republic* (17 Oct. 1988); and Zhang Jia-Xuan in *Film Quarterly* XLII, 3 (Spring 1989): 41–45.

7. For reports of the Berlin International Film Festival, see David Stratton in *Variety* 330 (2 March 1988): 5; and Richard Roud in *Sight and Sound* 57 (Summer 1988): 152.

8. For the definition of the "Third Cinema," see Fernando Solanas and Octavio Getino, "Toward a Third Cinema," in *Movies and Methods*, vol. 1, ed. Bill Nichols (Berkeley: University of California Press, 1976), 44–64; also Teshome Gabriel, *Third Cinema in the Third World: The Aesthetics of Liberation* (Ann Arbor: University of Michigan Press, 1982), especially 121–22.

9. In an article comparing the film with its original story, Zhong Chengxiang asserts that the "love-making" scene is a celebration of "man's freedom" and as such is "a classic shot" in Chinese film history. See his "Honggaoliang: xinde dianying gaibian guanglian" (Red Sorghum: A New Concept of Film Adaptation), *Wenxue Pinglun* 4 (1988): 44–50.

10. M. M. Bakhtin, *Rabelais and His World*, trans. Hélène Iswolsky (Bloomington: Indiana University Press, 1984), 256.

11. Ibid., 365.

12. Ibid., 321.

13. Ibid., 255.

14. Ibid., 281.

15. Friedrich Nietzsche, "The Birth of Tragedy from the Spirit of Music," quoted from *Critical Theory Since Plato*, ed. Hazard Adams (New York: Harcourt Brace Jovanovich, 1971), 637.

16. Ibid., 638.

17. This Party line was originally laid down by Mao Zedong and has been kept quite consistent in the past forty-six years in China, though the present version—literature and art must serve socialism—is comparatively "mild" in tone. See Bonnie McDougall, *Mao*

Zedong's Talks at the Yan'an Conference on Literature and Art: A Translation of the 1943 Text with Commentary (Ann Arbor: Center for Chinese Studies, University of Michigan, 1980).

18. For Chinese "Fifth Generation Directors" and their films, see Tong Rayns, "The Fifth Generation," *Monthly Film Bulletin* 53, 633 (Oct. 1986): 296–98; also Ma Ning, "Notes on the New Filmmakers," in *Chinese Film: The State of the Art in the People's Republic*, ed. George S. Semsel (New York: Praeger, 1987), 63–93. As for Chinese "avant-garde writers," see Li Tuo, Zhang Ling and Wang Bin, "1987–1988: Beizhuang de nuli" (Heroic Efforts), *Dushu* 1 (1989): 52–58.

19. Jameson, in *The Current in Criticism*, 140.

20. The woman protagonist does at one point in the film ask the winery workers to call her "Jiu'er," but that is a nickname (literally, "the ninth birth"), lacking any value of identity. It can be argued that by denying its major protagonists their proper names, *Red Sorghum* aspires to a mythic representation of the "primitive" life where the private and the public always converge.

21. *Rabelais and His World*, 19.

22. Ibid., 255, 10, 410, and 7 respectively.

23. See, especially, Liu Zaifu, "Lun wenxue de zhutixing" (The Subjectivity of Literature), *Wenxue Pinglun*, 6 (1985): 11–26, & 1 (1986): 1–15. Also see his *Xingge zuhe lun* (On the Construction of Characters), Shanghai: Shanghai wenyi chuban she, 1986.

24. A recent cultural phenomenon in China is the so-called "search for roots." For a preliminary study, see Ji Hongzheng, "Wenhua 'xungen' yu dangdai wenxue" (Searching Cultural Roots and Contemporary Literature) *Wenyi Yanjiu* 2 (1989): 69–74.

25. See Ah Cheng, "The Chess Master," trans. W. J. F. Jenner, *Chinese Literature* (Summer 1985): 84–131.

26. Nietzsche, quoted from *Critical Theory Since Plato*, 641.

27. *Rabelais and His World*, 367.

28. Ibid.

29. Zhang Yimou's enthusiasm is critically acclaimed in China, so much so that one critic even hails him as "the Dionysos of today's China." See Chen Xiaoxin, "Lun Honggaoliang de wenhua jiazhi" (On *Red Sorghum*'s Cultural Values), *Dianying yishu* 2 (1989): 29–35.

30. In *The Current in Criticism*, 140.

31. *Third Cinema in the Third World: The Aesthetics of Liberation* (Ann Arbor: University of Michigan Press, 1982), 1.

32. *Third World Film Making & the West* (Berkeley: University of California Press, 1987), 99.

33. These are subtitles in Gabriel's book, 15–20. As a matter of fact, common knowledge can easily tell that these themes are by no means confined to a revolutionary treatment in Third Cinema; literature of all times and all schools has tackled these themes in one way or another.

34. See his discussion of Third Cinema and Chinese film in "Poisonous Weeds or National Treasures: Chinese Left Films in the 30s," *Jump Cut* 34 (March 1989): 87–94.

4 | A Nation T(w/o)o

Chinese Cinema(s) and Nationhood(s)

Chris Berry

> I heard a feminist ask: "How should we read what is going on in China in terms of gender?" My immediate response to that question was, and is: "We do not, because at the moment of shock Chinese people are degendered and become simply Chinese." (Chow, 1991, 82)

THE "SHOCK" REY CHOW refers to here is the 1989 Tiananmen Square Massacre or "incident," as the Beijing regime would prefer us to call it. The article the quote is drawn from includes many interesting observations about the complex politics of Chinese identity today, but when I was asked to write this chapter, it was this remark that came to mind. I had not paid special attention to it before. If one takes the article as a response to the white liberal feminisms that overlook race and national identity as easily as many other discourses overlook gender, it can slip by quite smoothly.[1] However, within the frame of nationhood, I find myself tripping up on the phrase "simply Chinese," especially in light of what Chow has to say immediately after the above remark:

> To ask how we can use gender to "read" a political crisis such as the present one is to insist on the universal and timeless sufficiency of an analytical category, and to forget the historicity that accompanies all categorical explanatory power.

What does it mean to be or become "simply Chinese"? In the context of Chow's remark, the modifier "simply" renders being "Chinese" ambiguous to the point of reversibility. On the one hand, at the same time as Chow insists on the ineradicability of one sort of difference in her article, this phrase can seem to erase many other sorts in its insistence that "at the moment of shock, Chinese people . . . become simply Chinese." Such a reading of the remark depends on "simply" defining "Chinese" as a universal and timeless identity along the lines of a collective version of the Cartesian subject; a national (or ethnic? or cultural?) identity consisting of a unified, coherent, and transcendent whole.

But on the other hand, maybe "simply" does not presume Chineseness as a unified, coherent subjectivity. Maybe "simply" points to the very opposite; maybe it suggests that the massacre provokes a shattering crisis around Chineseness that is overriding and blots out all other considerations. In this sense of "simply," a simple unity of the Chinese people is precisely what the Tiananmen Square Massacre renders impossible. At Tiananmen in 1989, as many commentators pointed out at the time, the People's Liberation Army (was) turned on some of the people. The "people" are, at least rhetorically, the subject of the nation-state known as "The People's Republic of China" and the army. However, at Tiananmen, that unity among the people, the People's Republic, and the People's Liberation Army was violently broken. At and after this moment of shock, it is not possible to be simply one of the Chinese people, and that collective noun is shattered into a series of positions produced in relation to the massacre.[2]

In realizing the reversibility of the phrase "simply Chinese," it is not my aim to find a single, correct understanding, nor do I intend to descend into the circles of authorial intentionality in an effort to do so. Rather, I want to start this tracing of the interplay between Chinese cinema and nationhood by simultaneously pointing to being "Chinese" and fracturing and undermining any simple understanding of that term. In other words, I do not wish to "simply" trace how the cinema signifies Chinese national identity (or what the elements composing that identity are), nor do I "simply" wish to attack the idea of a unified Chinese national identity, suggesting that Chinese nationhood does or does not exist in a transcendental sense. Rather, I hope both to acknowledge and trace the circulation of a something labelled as Chinese national identity, and at the same time show how that something Chinese is inherently unstable and bracketed in its very enunciation, and therefore both in need of constant reinforcement and subject to destabilization. As Homi Bhabha puts it:

> Cultures are never unitary in themselves, nor simply dualistic in relation of Self to Other. . . . The reason a cultural text or system of meaning cannot be sufficient unto itself is that the act of cultural enunciation—the *place of utterance*—is crossed by the *différance* of writing or *écriture*. (1989, 128)

More Mao Than Ever

Certainly, the response of the Chinese government to the Tiananmen Massacre indicates that it, too, is acutely aware of the fragility that its action has brought to the fore. Among the steps it has taken to prop up the unified national space in whose name it rules are at least three forms of discursive response: denial, simulation, and hysterical compensation. To pursue the morphological homology between the (Western, bourgeois) individual, psychoanalytic subject and the collective national subject, it is interesting to note that all these discursive responses can be read as permutations of disavowal and fetishization.

Denial has appeared in the claims of the Chinese government that no students were killed in Tiananmen Square, a claim which may possibly be literally true, but which ignores the many gunned down and crushed in the streets surrounding the square itself. These claims have been accompanied by videotapes of the occasion that allegedly prove the case, and which were sent to Chinese embassies and consulates to be shown to Chinese nationals outside the country in the months following the massacre.[3]

Second, the government has responded with simulation by attempting to recreate a (mythical) happy time long, long ago when there was no conflict and fragmentation among the people of the People's Republic. An example of this is the revival of the Lei Feng campaign. Mass political movements and campaigns (*yundong*) were a major feature of life in the People's Republic before the "cultural revolution," but that event made them unpopular and they had been largely abandoned during the eighties.[4] Indeed, the film *Hibiscus Town* (*Furongzhen*, Xie Jin, Shanghai Film Studio, 1987) ends after the end of the "cultural revolution" with a mad ultraleftist proclaiming another movement, and we know he is mad because, of course, such a thing could not happen. However, it has now, and the country has been swept by a new campaign to "Learn from Lei Feng" over the last two years. Lei was a soldier who died saving his comrades in an accident. In 1962, the first emulation campaign was launched around this model of self-sacrifice when Mao Zedong wrote an essay calling on the people to learn from him, and other campaigns have followed periodically.

The film industry has played a role in the "Learn from Lei Feng" campaigns, making one film about Lei in 1964 (*Lei Feng*, Dong Zhaoqi, August First Film Studio), and another in 1979 (*The Song of Lei Feng* [*Lei Feng zhige*], Wang Shaoyan, August First Film Studio). Both are catalogs of saintly acts. It is interesting to note that the date of the second film, 1979, marks a revival of the Lei Feng myth in the wake of the "cultural revolution." Presumably, the film makers were trying to patch over the conflicts of the "cultural revolution" (1966–76), often referred to in China as "the decade of chaos," by invoking a past when the People's Republic was (allegedly) whole and unfragmented. Their actions thus form a precedent for the current Lei Feng campaign.

However, the return to Lei Feng has been much more intense this time than it was in 1979. Presumably, this is because Lei's status as both a PLA soldier and a member of the ordinary working people of China has a particular appeal for the government at a time when the unity of those two has been jeopardized. The intensity of the current Lei Feng campaign also fits the third type of effort to reinforce the unity of the People's Republic that I have suggested: hysterical compensation. However, an even better example of this response is the large number of revolutionary history films that have been made in the last few years.

This glut of revolutionary history films is partly motivated by the fortieth birthday of the People's Republic in October 1989 and the seventieth birthday of the Party in July 1991, and partly the result of a policy shift after the Tiananmen massacre. In a speech to film workers in October 1989, Li Ruihuan, head of the Central Propaganda Department of the Central Committee of the Communist Party of China since the massacre and therefore the most powerful figure in the film industry today, announced a cutback in production to ensure greater Party control, and that from that date on sixty percent of films should be of the *"leitmotif"* (*zhuxuanlu*) variety. The Party has called for a stress to be put on the *"leitmotif"* in all cultural production. This odd use of a musical term turns out to mean a return to putting educational and propaganda aims above all commercial or other considerations (A C, 1991).

Li has also announced a return to selected state subsidies, with a donation of what in China is the very considerable sum of ten million *yuan* to help with the production of ten films to congratulate the Party on its seventieth birthday (A C, 1991). In practice, this has resulted in the production of films that return to the military achievements of the years preceding the establishment of the People's Republic in 1949. Titles include *The Birth of New China* (*Kaiguo dadian*, Li Qiankuan and Xiao Guiyun, Changchun Film Studio, 1989), *The Kunlun Column* (*Weiwei kunlun*, Hao Guang and Jing Mukui, August First Film Studio, 1989), *The Baise Uprising* (*Baise Qifa*, Chen Jialin, Guangxi Film Studio, 1989), *Long Yun and Chiang Kai-Shek* (*Long Yun he Jiang Jieshi*, Ren Pengyuan, August First Film Studio, 1990), *The Creation of A World* (*Kaitian pidi*, Li Xiepu, Shanghai Film Studio, 1991), *Zhou Enlai* (Ding Yinnan, Guangxi Film Studio, 1991), and many others (Zhang Xiaotian, 1989, Ni Zhen, 1991, Huang Tingyi, 1991). This return to revolutionary history is an attempt to reunite precisely those fragments I have suggested the People's Republic is shattered into by the shock of Tiananmen. The People's Liberation Army that appears in these films is not composed of soldiers who fire on the people, but instead soldiers who work together with the people and on their behalf to build the People's Republic itself.

These war films are over-the-top in more ways than one, and their excess is what makes their compensation hysterical. This response is similar to that examined by Susan Jeffords in her study of post-Vietnam American culture (Jeffords, 1989). Hysteria is not only a matter of the greatly increased proportion of annual output given over to these films or the prestige accorded them, but is also inscribed in the texts themselves. In China, these films are known as "epic films" (*jupian*). They are comparatively long (at least three hours), and have (in Chinese terms) massive budgets, casts of thousands and all the military hardware and explosions the army can provide.

Perhaps the most extreme example of this type of film is the film series, *The Decisive Engagements* (*Dajuezhan*, August First Film Studio, 1991). This epic, which promises to tell us everything we never wanted to know about the Civil War between 1946 and 1949, is beginning to rival the *Rocky* series. To date, it has already generated three two-part films, each over three hours long, at an overall cost of 60 million *yuan* (approximately AUS $15 million) (Preston, 1991, 47). The series itself has an overall director (*zongdaoyan*, Li Jun), and each part has a separate chief director (*shouxi daoyan*), plus four additional ordinary directors. Each individual film features long battle sequences with helicopter shots of winding columns of troops and tanks, extensive entrenchments, and lots of explosions. Almost every actor's first appearance is marked by a subtitle identifying the historical character he or she is portraying. This parade of look-alikes has become such a prevalent feature of current mainland Chinese filmmaking that China's most popular star, Liu Xiaoqing, has complained that she cannot get roles because she does not look like Chairman Mao (Preston, 1991, 47–48).

The revolutionary war films currently produced in such large numbers in mainland China do more than attempt to patch up the People's Republic by representing a fundamental unity of the people and those acting in their name. As well as binding the inhabitants of a space, in their reference to history, these films also attempt to mark out, bind, and stabilize in time the whole that is the People's Republic. However, this rhetorical strategy can be shown to be as inherently unstable as the attempt to signify unity between people and PLA which, in the very materiality of those two signifiers, undercuts the unity they claim to signify: if people and PLA were really unified, why would we have two separate signifiers? In the temporal dimension, a similar but historical double-bind arises from a contradictory double need. On the one hand, there is the need to mark out the nation as founded at a particular time in the struggle against other forms of socio-political entity. On the other hand, there is a need to resist the implication that if the nation had a beginning it is historically bound and might have an end by eternalizing it and claiming a link with a mythical, ever-receding, unified, and therefore transhistorical past:

> It is through this syntax of forgetting . . . that the problematic identification of a national people becomes visible . . . the identity of part and whole, past and present, is cut across by the "obligation to forget," or forgetting to remember. (Bhabha, 1990a, 310)

How Many Chinas Does It Take?

In the case of the People's Republic, even before Tiananmen, before the "cultural revolution," one of the things that had to be forgotten was the existence of another national entity that called itself China; the Republic of China on Taiwan. The People's Republic of China was established in 1949 precisely as a result of the battles covered in *The Decisive Engagements*, and the rump of the Republic of China persists on the island of Taiwan, where it claims to be temporarily ensconced pending the recovery of the mainland. Both states claim to be the Chinese nation and both claim the indivisibility of the Chinese nation. Of course, they differ on the question of which of them is the true China. To pursue the psychoanalytic metaphor again, if hysterics suffer from reminiscences according to Freud and are provoked by a certain inability to quite make it through one or other of Lacan's famous two doors, it might be said that the continued existence of both the People's Republic and the Republic of China reminds the other of that originary choice that has still not been satisfactorily resolved.

In these circumstances, it is not surprising that the pre-credit scene that opens *The Decisive Engagements* strains to claim the legitimacy of the People's Republic as the (one and only) Chinese nation in the voice-over and works to forget the Republic altogether, displacing it and replacing it with a foreign-identified individual. An authoritative male voice speaks of the struggle between the people, working to produce the People's Republic with the help of the PLA, and Chiang Kai-shek, led in his actions by the United States. According to this rhetoric, the struggle we are about to see is not between two quasi- or proto-national entities. Rather, on the one hand, we have a national subject (the Chinese people), a nation (the People's Republic), and its agent (the People's Liberation Army), and on the other hand, we have a traitorous individual (Chiang Kai-shek) and his foreign master (the USA).

At the same time as the claims of other socio-political entities to be "China" are actively forgotten in this voice-over, the images that accompany it work to eternalize the People's Republic. Mao Zedong is shown walking alone in the hills of Hebei province, overlooking the frozen Yellow River. As the river ice begins to melt and move to the accompaniment of sonorous cracks and crunches, the relentless progress of history is symbolized. However, the Yellow River is also the mythical birthplace of Chinese civilization, and in these shots, the film creates an association between Mao as representative of the nascent People's Republic and a much older, mythical, and transcendent culture. In this contradictory manner, the film encourages us to forget to remember that there was something else called "China" before the very nation that it is about to rewrite the creation myth of.

This contradictory movement toward the erasure of both spatial and temporal difference while simultaneously marking out the boundaries of the nation is not confined to the anxious post-Tiananmen period. Far from it; just as the individual subject must be repeatedly inscribed and the enunciatory act of inscription erased in order to maintain that subject, so the collective, national subject must trace and retrace its spatial and temporal boundaries and the identity of part and whole and past and present in order to maintain itself in circulation. Indeed, the shots of Mao overlooking the Yellow River echo and are quite possibly modelled on what is probably Mao's most famous poem, *Snow*, written in 1936 and known to nearly every mainland Chinese (Engle and Engle, 1972, 56–57). Thus, the beginning of *The Decisive Engagements* is only one small example of a persistent and long-standing tendency in mainland Chinese cinema.

In an article that traces some deployments of the term "race" (*minzu*) in Chinese film criticism, I have already examined some aspects of the pre-Tiananmen process of forgetting to remember (Berry, 1992). This term appears in various combinations, such as "race color" (*minzu cesai*), "race characteristics" (*minzu tedian*), and "race form" (*minzu xingshi*). It is used as a signifier of some parcel of transhistorical, distinctively Chinese signifieds that can allegedly be found in Chinese literature and art, including the cinema, and which distinguish them as national forms. By finding these alleged characteristics in mainland Chinese cinema, critics participate in the effort to eternalize the People's Republic in the same way as the opening scene of *The Decisive Engagements* operates. Furthermore, as I have tried to outline in more detail in my other article (Berry, 1992), this reified concept of "race" has become useful to deeply conservative cultural forces in China; they attack all change they do not support on the ground that if it is different from those works that have been identified as having "race characteristics," then it must lack "race characteristics" and be tainted by foreign influence.

The discourse of "race" in Chinese film criticism is only one of many operations that helps to unify and identify past and present and part and whole. For example, in films from the fifties through to the present day, the majority of narratives are driven by an opposition between those identified as the agents of the people and the enemies of the people, with the former working to locate and erase the latter. However, I would like to point out one particular factor: the role of certain characteristics of the Chinese language(s). These peculiar characteristics are often proclaimed as part of that parcel of uniquely Chinese characteristics discussed above. However, they have simultaneously caused particular problems for the efforts of the Chinese cinema to participate in the signification of the identity of part and whole, although certain policies have been pursued in regard to language in the cinema to overcome this obstacle.

Unlike the alphabetic languages, as we all know, written Chinese is an ideographic, non-phonetic language. While different areas of other linguistically linked communities may be distinguished by accent or even dialect, in the case of those communities using Chinese characters, pronunciation of these written forms can vary much more drastically. As a result, although it can be claimed China is united in its use of Chinese characters, it is simultaneously divided into an enormous number of mutually unintelligible spoken languages.[5] However, in both the People's Republic and the Republic, the same single spoken Chinese language has been designated as the dominant form. This dominant form is known in English as Mandarin. Unsurprisingly, the People's Republic and the Republic use different terms. On Taiwan, this language is referred to as *guoyu*, which literally means "national language." On the mainland, the same language is called "*putonghua*," which means "common speech." Both terms signify the universal, nation-building function and claims attached to the language.

As a result, it is not surprising to discover that in the cinemas of both the

Republic and the People's Republic, Mandarin has been privileged, regardless of whether the regional setting within China justifies this or not, and that this has been encouraged and enforced by the agents of the state. Just as until recently, all class and regional accents were ironed out and everyone spoke "BBC English" on the radio in the U.K., so everyone appearing in most mainland Chinese films speaks in perfect Mandarin. Characters who allegedly represent Fujianese peasants speak Mandarin, not Hokkienese. The movie version of Guangdong traders also speak Mandarin, not Cantonese. In the case of Taiwan, a form of Hokkienese called Minnanhua is the most common language on the island itself, and before 1945 there was a thriving local language cinema industry on the island.[6] This industry continued to exist alongside a Mandarin cinema, but the KMT government privileged the development of the Mandarin cinema, for example by excluding non-Mandarin films from participation in the annual government-sponsored Golden Horse awards. As a result, local language films declined and almost disappeared in the sixties and seventies, and a Mandarin cinema in which local characters whose ancestors come from Fujian speak in incongruously perfect Mandarin thrived, as in the People's Republic. In both of the states claiming to be the Chinese nation, this linguistic violence is an example of a more generalized denial of other specificities and differences in the process of identifying part and whole as a homogeneous Chinese "nation."

From ImagiNation to DissemiNation

So far, most of the examples of the interaction between the cinema and the construction of nationhood that I have traced have been conservative: denying difference and blocking change. As such, they tie into the wider issue of how the nation and nationalism should be judged politically. Various recent events have recast this question and made it pertinent again on a general level, and not just within the context of post-Tiananmen China. For many years after World War Two, nationalism was judged by Western leftist critics according to where it occurred; many commentators were understandably uncomfortable about nationalism in Europe, but tended to see "Third World" nationalism as positive because it was anti-colonial.

Recent events, however, have undermined this geographic principle and demand a reexamination of how we are understanding and judging nationalist movements. On the one hand, uneasy though we may feel about some of the tendencies associated with the nationalisms that have participated in the collapse of the Soviet empire, including the "fraternal" socialist satellites in Eastern Europe, we are forced to acknowledge that those alternative centers for identification have played powerful roles in breaking the post-war log jam and opening up new possibilities in Europe. On the other hand, the nationalist response to Tiananmen and other events in many post-colonial "Third World" countries including the Khmer Rouge atrocities in Cambodia and revelations coming out of various post-colonial African nation-states have undermined the assumption that nationalism is inherently a force for good in the "Third World."

The old geographically based judgments arise to some extent from how the nation itself is conceptualized. Much of the discourse around "Third World" nationalism is that of revolution and liberation; it assumes that the nation is a pre-existing given, waiting to be liberated from the yoke of foreign oppression. However, much of the recent writing that I have been calling upon in this chapter so far has shifted away from this approach and toward an understanding that theorizes the nation as a contingent and discursive object. This contingency marks the nation not as a given, waiting in the case of a colony to be liberated, but as a constructed, cultural entity, and in the case of colonialism, an entity constructed as part of the process of resistance. Just as many nations are unravelling now, there was a time before the nation and a time in which the nation was conceived and built. The cinematic operations I have traced so far in this chapter are part of the work involved in the construction and maintenance of the nation known as the People's Republic of China, and the nation known as the Republic of China, too—two states which agree only in their claim to be one nation.

Although the idea of the nation as contingent rather than given has been brought to the fore again in recent work, it is not a new idea. It goes back at least to Ernest Renan's address "What is a nation?" in 1882, which has recently been reprinted as part of the current reassessment of the nation. In this address, Renan knocks down each of the various claims for nations as natural entities from linguistic unity to natural frontiers and racial unity, in order to claim that nations are an act of the will (1990). The question that Renan does not answer adequately is: whose will? Renan allows the idea of the will of the people to persist unexamined, as do most of those who talk about "the people" being oppressed, or, as in the case of the narrator of *The Decisive Engagements*, "the people" making revolution.

It is often said of religion that if God did not exist, "man" would have had to invent "Him." The collective subject called "the people" is as necessary to nationalists as God is to religious believers. Benedict Anderson's remarkable 1983 book, *Imagined Communities: Reflections on the Origin and Spread of Nationalism*, has moved beyond Renan's stance by laying the groundwork for the deconstruction not only of the nation but also the people in whose name it is built (Anderson, 1983). Anderson points out that, as a type of imagined community, the beginnings of the nation are closely linked to the struggle of certain interests against other types of imagined community operated by other interests (17–41). He outlines two other major forms: the religious empire and the monarchical or imperial dynasty. In their different ways, both these types of imagined community are marked out from the nation by being vertical and defined by a center; they are hierarchical, with the apex of those hierarchies in either a sacred city or the site of the throne. Nations, on the other hand, are horizontal and defined by boundaries; they claim a people composed of equal citizens who share a space in which measures such as equality before the law, equal access to universal education, universal suffrage, and so forth are applied to construct their homogeneity.

In tracing the struggle between nationalists and the supporters of earlier forms of imagined community, Anderson effectively lays the ground for a discursive displacement away from a rhetoric of revolutionary movements liberating the people and the nation from oppression to an examination of the groups and individuals who deploy that rhetoric as part of their self-interested struggle. For example, he discusses the invention of printing as a seed for large-scale capitalist marketing tied to European language communities as one of the seeds of bourgeois nationalism there (Anderson, 41–50).

However, Anderson also notes the emergence of some of the earliest self-conscious nation-states in the Americas in the late eighteenth and early nineteenth centuries, and points out that the impetus there came from the discrimination those born in Spain's American colonies experienced in the imperial bureaucracy. Regardless of parentage, wealth, education, or talent, if they were not born in Spain itself, although they could climb quite high in the imperial bureaucracy, they were confined to provincial or colonial territories and could not reach the center of the empire. This and other forms of institutionalized provincialism helped to form proto-national consciousness, not only in Latin, but also in North America (Anderson, 50–65).

Anderson's work here is complemented by that of the post-colonial and subaltern studies scholars who have distanced themselves simultaneously from both imperialism and nationalism in colonized areas, seeing the latter as often a self-interested movement initiated by Westernized locals thwarted by the well-documented racism of imperialisms and standing to benefit from the establishment of the nation-state. Chakrabarty (1991) details much work by Indian scholars on nationalist movements there that supports this analysis. As such, the move toward the establishment of nation-states in colonized areas (including China) cannot be accepted in the terms of its own rhetoric as an attempt by the people to throw off the yoke of the oppressor and restore the nation to some mythical pristine condition. This is not least the case because the nation itself as a form of imagined community is a European export. Instead, it may be useful to consider the formation of nations in the drive against colonialism as a process of resistance along the lines of Bhabha's mimicry, a process whereby the discourse is taken over by a different enunciator, whose very difference then changes the discourse mimicked (Bhabha, 1984).

This post-colonialist understanding of nationalism entails a different way of judging nationalisms. Instead of a mechanical geographical reductionism whereby European nationalisms are bad and Third World nationalisms are good, we have to shift to a precise, case-by-case analysis of the forces involved and their deployment of nationalism. Neither the nation nor nationalism can be seen as simply and inherently good or bad, but rather they are to be judged on the basis of the uses they are put to. From this perspective, nationalism can simultaneously be seen as positive in its fragmentation of the Soviet monolith and negative in China and other countries where it is propping up exploitative and oppressive ruling interests. It also becomes possible to see a nationalism as useful in its anti-colonial phase, but then as becoming conservative once the nation-state is established as the organ of a now dominant grouping whose power it helps to maintain at the expense of other elements of the "people" in whose name it claims to rule.

However, this common tendency of nation-states to become conservative, even oppressive, forms raises a considerable problem. Although Spivak has spoken of nationalism as a possible form of "strategic essentialism," neither she nor anyone else I know of has suggested a way to prevent the tendency of such strategic essentialisms to become entrenched and conservative without further anti-nationalist struggle (McRobbie, 1985, 7). In these circumstances, the struggle becomes one of breaking down nations and nationalisms. As Homi Bhabha has pointed out in his discussion of the uses of theory, finding a way to speak about and conceive of such a process is both integral to and part of enacting it (Bhabha, 1989).

To this end, and following his own ideas about mimicry, Bhabha has adopted and adapted Derrida to suggest that much of the world today is undergoing what he calls "DissemiNation" (Bhabha, 1984, 1990a). He argues that European nation-states are being subverted from within by a multiplication of other imagined communities, themselves built on mimicry of the model of the nation. This seems to be a sort of postmodern hyper-nationalism, where the unitary, eternal collective subject is fragmented into a kaleidoscopic array of fleeting quasi-national sites for collective identification to match the fragmented postmodern individual subject. The result is a dynamic hybrid space, tending toward a new type of entity, even a new type of imagined community which we have no name for and cannot yet describe in positive terms. In regard to these developments, Bhabha not only cites Fanon to discuss racial minorities resulting from migration into the USA, Canada, and Western Europe as nations, but also Kristeva's use of the nation in her conception of contemporary women (Bhabha, 1990a, 302–305). One might also cite the more recent prominence of the militant American gay and lesbian group interestingly called Queer Nation. No doubt the list could go on.

Borderline Problems

Bhabha's work and the work he cites attend mostly to DissemiNation in the metropolitan centers of European culture. However, given the difficult history of nationalism in post-colonial spaces, it becomes imperative to consider whether and how DissemiNation and the move toward new post-national imagined communities also operates in these other places. In the case of China, it is tempting to suggest that the split between the People's Republic and the Republic of China (not to mention the existence of Hong Kong and Singapore), already constitutes DissemiNation. However, this fails to understand that neither DissemiNation nor post-national imagined communities can exist in and of themselves; they have to be rendered in some process of writing, of *écriture*, and, as I have indicated already in my discussion of Chinese cinema, the rulers of both nation-states have expended much energy in encouraging the people within their boundaries to imagine themselves as citizens of a single nation only.

At the moment, we have no concept of or even term for a concept of a new post-national, DissemiNatory imagined community of the type Bhabha traces in Europe or in colonies and post-colonial nations. Given the relatively tight control of the film industries in both mainland China and Taiwan, it would be unrealistic to expect any great outpouring of DissemiNatory films that might begin the work of imagining such a new form of community, even though the bifurcated condition of China may seem to provide fertile ground for such work. If anything, this bifurcated condition may have only added to the vigilance protecting the "nation" in both cinemas. Certainly, since Tiananmen, there has been nothing that I am aware of that could be construed as DissemiNatory from the People's Republic.

However, it can be argued that, in their own way, the films associated with the Fifth Generation of mainland Chinese filmmakers, produced in that small window of opportunity between 1984 and 1989, move to break down the monolithic unity of the People's Republic, even if they do not self-consciously move it toward some sort of hybrid space. Their variety alone could be understood in this way, as could their emphasis on the individual and individual difference in a society that stresses (almost hysterically) collectivity and homogeneity. This period witnessed the appearance of a group of highly subjective films directed by women filmmakers (Berry, 1989), as well as films like *Black Cannon Incident* (*Heipao shijian*, Huang Jianxin, Xi'an Film Studio, 1985), *King of the Children* (*Haizi wang*, Chen Kaige, Xi'an Film Studio, 1987), *Horse Thief* (*Daoma zei*, Tian Zhuangzhuang, Xi'an Film Studio, 1986), and many others, all of which revolved around misfit individuals.[7]

In this context, it is also interesting to note the tendency of these directors to move toward both the temporal and spatial edges of the People's Republic. *Black Cannon Incident* is unusual among Fifth Generation films in its contemporary setting in a Chinese metropolitan center. From *Yellow Earth* (*Huang tudi*, Chen Kaige, Guangxi Film Studio, 1984) onward, a more marginal setting is usual. That film is set in a remote village in the late thirties, the early period of the revolution before the establishment of the People's Republic. *Horse Thief* is set in Tibet, and Tian Zhuangzhuang's earlier film *On The Hunting Ground* (*Liechang zhasa*, Inner Mongolia Film Studio, 1984), takes place among the Mongols on the steppes. *King of the Children* is set in the most remote Southwestern borderlands of Yunnan province, as is *Sacrificed Youth* (*Qingchun Ji*, Zhang Nuanxin, Youth Film Studio, 1985), which features the Dai minority nationality.

I have discussed the DissemiNatory qualities of these and other Fifth Generation films in further detail elsewhere (Berry, 1992), but to return to the uses of the Chinese language mentioned earlier, *Sacrificed Youth* is also unusual in its breach of the insistence on the cinematic ubiquity of Mandarin. The old Dai Grandma, played by a local woman, speaks the Dai language in the film. Most of the other characters speak Mandarin. Both of Tian Zhuangzhuang's films also negotiate this linguistic difference, straining at the unity imposed by Mandarin. *On The Hunting Ground* features a double soundtrack, presumably largely for reasons of economy, on which the Mongolian speech of the characters is drowned under a Mandarin translation read out by a single male narrator. For *Horse Thief*, Tian made a Tibetan language version which features only Tibetan characters and is set before the Chinese invasion in 1959.[8] However, to the best of my knowledge, this version was never released and, in the release print, the Tibetan characters have been postdubbed and speak perfect Mandarin.

Nonetheless, in going out to the very margins of the People's Republic and its history, it seems the Fifth Generation were straining the unity of past and present and of part and whole that constitutes a nation. In doing so, I presume their aim was to question what China is and attempt to signal difference within the People's Republic and, in this act of unfreezing unity, open up the possibility of change. However, whether this was intended to or can be used to move toward hybrid space and other new disseminated forms of imagined community or whether this is only useful for a reorganization of the qualities that compose the national form is another question. Not least among the reasons for this concern is the fact that this straining at the borders often depends for its very signification of difference upon groups already labelled as other: non-Han Chinese, minority nationalities within the People's Republic. This blurs the division between hybrid cultural difference within one disseminated space and pluralistic cultural diversity:

> Cultural diversity is also the representation of a radical rhetoric of the separation of totalised cultures that live unsullied by the intertextuality of their his-

torical locations, safe in the Utopianism of a mythic memory of a unique collective identity. (Bhabha, 1989, 127)

With a little adjustment, this quote could be a critique of the socialism-in-one-country doctrine that has legitimated the welding together of socialism, nationalism, and isolationism in China and elsewhere. At the moment, in the wake of Tiananmen, those doctrines are being reinforced more harshly than ever, and so it seems unlikely that much cultural difference is going to be found in mainland Chinese cinema at the moment. In these circumstances, it seems more useful to direct attention toward the Chinese periphery, to the spaces of the Chinese diaspora, rather than to concentrate on the frozen heartlands. Unlike the European imperial powers, where the metropolitan areas seem to contain the greatest tendency toward hybrid space and DissemiNation, it seems that in the case of the colonized, it is the margins and the littoral cities that bear the greatest mark of cultural difference, and also as a direct result of colonialism itself. Within the People's Republic, the colonial port of Shanghai is infinitely more hybrid than the ancient inland capital, Xi'an. However, even more hybrid today are the spaces of Hong Kong and Taiwan.

There is no room in this chapter to discuss all the qualities of Hong Kong and the Hong Kong cinema that constitute it as a hybrid space, and as a self-consciously hybrid space, too. Furthermore, I think many of the elements that work to construct this consciousness, such as the use of foreign locations and the crisis of identity articulated through contradictory ways of being Chinese, are self-evident to even the most casual viewer of Hong Kong cinema. However, hybrid space alone is not enough. The DissemiNatory quest is for a hybrid space that is also an imagined community, that has a simultaneous sense of collective and fragmented selfhood. Although I think the hybrid qualities of Hong Kong cinema are relatively evident, I see fewer elements signifying this as a self-identity. Maybe this is unsurprising, given Hong Kong's status as poised between colony and component of the People's Republic.

However, an exception to this lack of self-identification can be found by returning again to the Chinese language in the cinema and a recent change that has occurred in the Hong Kong cinema. Hong Kong films have gone through different periods of using either the Mandarin or Cantonese language, although for the last decade and more Cantonese has been almost universal. Although they are made in Hong Kong, where the most common first language is Cantonese, these films have a market which is far wider, consisting of the international Chinese diaspora, and for some of these people, Mandarin is more appropriate. Either way, regardless of the language spoken on the soundtrack, Hong Kong films have always carried both Chinese character and English language subtitles in an effort to maximize audience. Recently, however, there has been a tendency to move away from the standard Chinese character subtitles and replace them with a Cantonese variant on Chinese characters. These Hong Kong characters, as I will term them, provide a written form of the Cantonese language totally unintelligible to Mandarin speakers or speakers of other dialects. To date, these subtitles tend to be found only on lower-budget films, although I am not sure why. However, they do begin to mark out a local self-consciousness in the same way that political developments such as the agitation for greater democracy also do.[9]

Taipei or Not Taipei?

Significant though these Hong Kong characters are in marking a certain resistant self-consciousness, it must be noted that they also tend to construct a quasi-national unity among the Hong Kong language community. In so doing, this act of mimicry works against hybridity, rather than moving simultaneously toward collectivity and/in a specific fragmentation. For a fuller signification of hybrid space as a point of collective identity itself and as a different, post-national imagined community, the most fruitful films are those of Taiwan, and in particular director Hou Xiaoxian.[10] Hou's films, in particular *City of Sadness* (*Beiqing chengshi*, Central Motion Picture Corporation, 1989), deploy the Chinese language to provide the grounds for simultaneously imagining Taiwan as a community in its own right, as a collective self, and for that selfhood as being constituted by the very hybrid space that the films construct.

That Taiwan should provide a fruitful ground for the construction of a hybrid imagined community is no surprise when one considers its complex history. The island has been traversed by so many colonizing powers at different times in its history that it is almost impossible to integrate it credibly into any sort of eternalized national entity, although one must acknowledge that the present government has worked very hard to do so. Of course, plenty of colonizing powers have also tried to, and, ironically, there are both Japanese and Chinese creation myths for Taiwan, each of which securely identifies it as part of that entity's claimed heritage. Both powers also lay claim to being the original source of the "aboriginal" Taiwanese (*shandiren*), who have been there far longer than most of the island's inhabitants, and who now live in the mountainous central areas of the island. Taiwan was also a Dutch colony between 1624 and 1662, and a Japanese colony between 1895 and 1945. It derives its other name, Formosa, from Portuguese explorers, and today it is home to the nationalist government of the Republic of China, which proclaims Taipei (Taibei) its temporary capital until it returns to Nanjing (Long, 1991, 1–33).

Despite this remarkable hybridization, the same regime that maintains that its presence in Taipei is temporary has worked hard to ignore that history of difference, and to deny that that history marks Taiwan out from the mainland in any way. They, like the communist mainland government they refuse to acknowledge, insist that Taiwan is integrated completely into the identity of past and present and part and whole that, for both of them, is the Chinese nation. However, possibly more than any other films, Hou Hsiao-Hsien's mark the difference they deny (albeit probably in the name of realism).

In Hou's 1987 film *A Time to Live and a Time to Die* (*Tongnian wangshi*, Central Motion Picture Corporation), the hybrid space of Taiwan is signified in the linguistic diversity of the characters' speech. As mentioned earlier, after the retreat to Taiwan in 1949, the Kuomintang Nationalist government discouraged the production of non-Mandarin language films and maintained a strict separation between the two. This separation is maintained to this day on television, for example, where, on the one hand, there are news services in Mandarin that purport to serve the entire Republic of China (including the mainland), and which include weather forecasts for the whole of the mainland, and, on the other hand, there are local "provincial" news services in the Hokkienese Minnanhua dialect most common on the island. In the cinema, however, this strict separation between languages has begun to break down since the early 1980s with the emergence of the Taiwanese New Cinema associated with "nativist" (*xiangtu*) literature and younger directors who grew up on the island. Among other things, these directors are dedicated to describing the experience of living in contemporary Taiwan in a realistic and credible manner, and as a result they tend toward a mix of spoken languages as one might hear on the streets of Taipei.

Hou's *A Time to Live and a Time to Die* is a relatively highly developed example of this tendency. This largely autobiographical film follows the story of a family of mainland migrants from Guangdong province through the voice-over memories of the eldest son, Ah-Ha. Although Ah-Ha's voiceover is in Mandarin, it is not pure, but rather the southern-accented Mandarin of a speaker for whom it is a second language. Unlike him, his younger siblings would have grown up almost entirely on Taiwan, and so they speak a somewhat purer Mandarin, as would have been taught them in school. The older generations, including his mother and grandmother, speak a Cantonese dialect, which the children clearly understand, but do not speak themselves. Most of the other people in the village speak a Hokkienese dialect.

With this linguistic diversity, Hou marks out Taiwan as a space criss-crossed by a specific and intricate network of nuanced and subtle differences. It is noteworthy that pure Mandarin is associated most strongly in the film with the voice of the radio announcer, who is the agent of the nation-state bringing news about national day celebrations and so forth. In this way, the nation and the discourse of the nation are positioned as another space connected to but outside that of the main characters in the film, and usually the source of bad news or at least worry. More humorously, the film also marks the impact of neo-colonialism in its deployment of language. There is a brief scene in which the youngest son is shown memorizing the romanized alphabet as part of his English lessons. The rhyme he uses to help himself repeats the phrase "one dollar."

The hybridization of Taiwan marked in *A Time to Live and a Time to Die* is increased considerably in *City of Sadness*, which was a major success in Taiwan. Here, the central family of the film is not composed of refugees from the mainland, but is a "local" family who speak a Hokkienese dialect. The film is set in the period of the KMT nationalist takeover of Taiwan from Japan after World War Two. Among the friends of one of the four brothers in the family is a Japanese brother and sister. The Japanese man first appears speaking Mandarin to introduce some of his Han Chinese friends to the Han Chinese brother. Interestingly, he introduces a character called Lin who is a teacher not as *"Lin laoshi"* or *"Lin xiansheng"* as might be the standard form of introduction in Mandarin, but as *"Lin-san,"* the standard Japanese form. In the hospital where his sister works, another language learning lesson is shown in progress. Unlike the English lesson of *A Time to Live and a Time to Die*, the staff of the hospital is being taught in Japanese various salient Mandarin Chinese phrases in preparation for the arrival of the next wave of colonials. Whether the staff is entirely Japanese, or whether the language of the hospital is Japanese is not made clear. However, the phrase they seem to repeat most often is the very resonant "Where does it hurt?"

The Japanese brother and sister are to be repatriated. They are shown to be sad to leave, and their interactions with their local friends show them to be an integrated, although different part of the hybrid community of the island. Apart from Japanese and Hokkienese dialects, there are also the two languages associated with the mainlanders who take over from the Japanese (returning the island to the bosom of Chinese rule, or perhaps as a new colonizing power). First, there is Shanghainese. This is spoken by a bunch of gangsters and racketeers with whom the third brother in the main family gets involved. The other language is Mandarin, the "national language." As in *A Time to Live and a Time to Die*, Mandarin is mostly associated with a space elsewhere: a space outside the diegesis of the film and associated with the source of official communications such as the radio news which work to signify and construct the nation. The unstable integration of the locals into this national space is signified in an amusing dinner scene in which they recount their difficulties over changing the flag from the Japanese flag to the Nationalist Chinese flag. One of the characters explains that no one in the village knew which way up the new flag should go, and various humorous anecdotes follow deriving from the anxieties of the leading citizens. Furthermore, we hear there was the question of what to do with the old Japanese flags—no one could bear to waste the material, so they were sewn into shorts and trousers, leaving everyone with red bottoms where the formerly rising sun had set. So much for Taiwanese inclusion among the "people" of the liberated nation-state.

This humorous moment turns out to be ominous, for *City of Sadness* marks out Taiwan as hybrid not only in the breakdown of any identity of part and whole, but also in the undermining of the identity of past and present proclaimed in the Nationalist rhetoric of the takeover as a decolonizing return to Chinese rule. The central event in the film is a suppressed incident in Taiwanese history, known as the February 28th Incident, when, in 1947, local Taiwanese rebelled against the mainlanders and were bloodily suppressed. This incident, which, in retrospect, might be said to be Taiwan's Tiananmen Square, has been suppressed for many years and, although most Taiwanese are all too aware of it, its circulation in Taiwanese popular discourses such as the cinema has been marginalized and suppressed until recently. This is an excellent example of the active forgetting, or forgetting to remember, that both Bhabha and Renan argue is important to the foundation of the nation-state. However, in centering on this event, the film insists on the inclusion of violent cultural difference as a founding act for modern Taiwan as a hybrid imagined community.

Interestingly, the enunciation of the film also reinforces this idea of a Taiwanese collective selfhood that is founded in its very hybridization. Although the film is not exactly one man's story—it has an enormous cast—there is a character in the film who stands as a relay of enunciation. This is one of the brothers. His job as a photographer places him as a stand-in for the filmmakers and, with his camera, he is witness to much of what goes on. Ever since a childhood accident, he has been a mute and, as a result, he is a sidelined bystander to most events. Hou's camerawork in this film, as in most of his films, mimes this position, choosing long shots and minimal camera movement over any interventionist stylistic gestures such as the close-up or the shot-reverse-shot sequence. The linguistic neutered quality of muteness resulting from injury mimes the impact of the suppressed February 28th Incident. Together with the restrained camerawork, it moves this enunciatory character outside unambiguous membership of any of the particular language groups that contest the space of the film, although he is a local and sympathetic to them. In this combination then, we have a collective self that is hybridized and riven with difference, a subject that cannot speak, and at least the shadow of a post-national imagined community founded on hybrid space.

In the last two or three years since the enormous box office success of *City of Sadness*, linguistic hybridity has taken over the mainstream Mandarin cinema to an extent undreamed of a few years ago. Even the most ordinary films mix spoken languages freely. For example, this year's big melodrama is *Rouge* (*Yanzhi*, Wan Ren, 1991), a film which traces the relationships between three generations of mothers and daughters in contemporary Taipei. The eldest of the women originates from Shanghai, and the film slides effortlessly back and forth between Mandarin and Shanghainese. Another interesting instance is *Wawa* (Ke Yizheng, 1991), a children's film about a young girl from the aboriginal dominated mountain areas who comes to live in Taipei when her parents die. Although she speaks Mandarin in the film, the pet pig she brings with her has an aboriginal name, "Bala." As there are no Chinese characters for this name, it appears throughout the subtitles in the film in the Chinese phonetic alphabet.

This hybridization is also found in two more significant films. *A Brighter Summer Day* (*Gulingjie shaonian sharen shijian*, Edward Yang [Yang Dechang], 1991), and *Man from Island West* (*Xibu lai de ren*, Huang Mingchuan, 1990) may be triangulated with *City of Sadness*'s local Chinese Taiwanese perspective to cover Taiwan's hybrid identity from the mainlander and aboriginal point of view, respectively. *A Brighter Summer Day* is in many ways Yang's answer to *City of Sadness*. Also featuring a large cast and a restrained, distant camera style, the film also returns to a historical act of communal violence to examine the problems of adjustment to exile for mainland Chinese and their families. In this case, the incident featured in the film is a killing among the gangs of mainland children growing up in Taiwan in the fifties and early sixties. Although punctuated with romantic American ballads from the period, including the Presley hit from which the English title is taken, any sense of a nostalgic return to the days of Yang's own childhood is undermined. First, there are the continual frictions among the gangs of teenagers, often divided according to the geographic loyalties, and second, the possibilities of their parents' generation forgetting the past and establishing a new life on Taiwan are constantly threatened by the paranoia of the KMT government, manifested in the film by the rumbling tanks on night manoeuvers and the interrogation of the father in the central family in the film, who is suspected of politically unacceptable contacts with the communist mainland.[11]

Man from Island West is an independent film made by a Chinese Taiwanese and is particularly significant as one of the first attempts to depict the impact of colonization on aboriginals from the an aboriginal perspective. Previous films have sometimes been sympathetic to the aboriginal experience, but they have taken a Chinese perspective, depicted aboriginal culture in folkloric manner, and tended to stress assimilation. *Man from Island West*, on the other hand, traces the return journey from Taipei of a man who has attempted assimilation but failed, and contrasts his desperation to return with the desire of the young men still in the aboriginal areas to depart. The exotic, folkloric elements of other films are strikingly absent and, in their place, the film depicts a brutalized, poverty-stricken people stripped of much of their previous culture and with little to replace it. However, they retain the contemporary form of their particular aboriginal language, which, significantly, has absorbed many Japanese words as a mark of difference from the latest Chinese wave of colonization.[12]

Writing from Australia, another site which has plenty of potential to be a post-colonial hybrid space outside the metropolitan centers of Europe, I find the possibilities of the contemporary Taiwanese cinema and especially Hou Hsiao-

Hsien's films very pertinent. However, the older, predominantly Anglo-Saxon colonial classes of Australia have only in the last two or three decades begun to adopt the language of nationalism to mark themselves out from the "mother country," something that their equivalents in South Africa did over a century ago. Furthermore, other waves of migration from all over the globe have already made that move toward constructing Australia as an old-style national space difficult if not redundant. In these circumstances, I am reminded that an imagined community that is hybridized in its very collective identity requires enunciation as well as material potential, and this makes films such as those I have been discussing here significant beyond Taiwan itself.

However, while affirming the positive challenge this Taiwanese cinematic development poses for verbal language, which as yet lacks the means to communicate the same collective identity in hybridity, I will risk closing on a negative note by pointing to two continued uses of nationalist rhetoric in verbal (as opposed to cinematic) language. First, there is the rhetoric of the DPP, the Taiwanese opposition party. The members of this party use the local non-Mandarin Hokkienese dialect, which they call *taiyu* or "Taiwanese," a terminology which nationalizes the dialect. They have also declared themselves in favor of dropping the idea of reunification with the motherland and declaring Taiwan an independent nation in its own right. Their rhetoric tends toward a local nationalist resistance to the mainland-derived government, which is (understandably) positioned as colonial. On the other hand, there is the equally nationalist position of the Communist government on the mainland, as communicated in this quote from Hu Yaobang, ironically the man in the commemoration of whose name the Democracy Movement I began this chapter with was launched:

> In the present and in the future we seek the peaceful unification of the motherland. We will not easily abandon this wish. But if this wish cannot be realised for a protracted period, and if it is clear that some elements in Taiwan are opposing unification with foreign encouragement, then we should re-examine the situation. . . . Unification is the last frontier for China. (Harrison, 1986, cited in Long, 1991)

Notes

1. The complication of feminist discourses by ethnicity has been a major intervention in the field in the last few years with works by Trinh (1989), Spivak (1987), and Mohanty, Torres, and Lourdes (1991), as well as Yvonne Rainer's film *Privilege*. Various journals have also devoted special issues or large parts of issues to the topic, including *Discourse* 11:2 (Spring-Summer 1989, edited by Trinh T. Minh-ha), and, partially, *Screen* 29:4 (Autumn 1988).

2. It might be useful to remind ourselves at this point that the fit between the "people" and the "nation" has always been problematic in mainland China. This is manifested in the proliferation of signifiers referring whose signifieds are unstably distin-

guished, including "people" (*renmin*), "masses" (*qunzhong*) and "worker-soldier-peasant" (*gongnongbing*) on the one hand, and "nation" (*guojia*), "culture" (*wenhua*), "civilization" (*wenming*), "People's Republic of China" (*zhonghua renmin gongheguo*), and "Republic of China" (*zhonghua minguo*), not to mention Singapore and Hong Kong, on the other.

3. When the Chinese embassy in Canberra attempted to have these tapes shown in Brisbane, where I was living at the time of the massacre, this provoked Chinese students there to protest and demonstrate. Embassy officials explained that this tape was intended to be viewed by all Chinese nationals outside China at the time of the massacre, so that they might learn the "truth" of what had (not) happened.

4. For example, after the "cultural revolution" many of the production figure claims associated with campaigns to have those involved with agriculture learn from the Dazhai commune and those involved with industry to learn from the Daqing oilfield were publically discredited (Tsou, Blecher, and Meisner, 1981).

5. Even this explanation can be deconstructed further. It is not merely a matter of differing pronunciations, because the grammatical forms of many of the spoken languages of China also vary considerably from the grammar used in the written form of the dominant Mandarin Chinese language.

6. Ray Jiing, director of the National Film Archive in Taipei, told me in a conversation on November 20, 1991, that over 2,000 films have been made in the local language, but that unfortunately very few of these survive today.

7. Peter Dale's discussion of the political function of individuality as a response to the collective homogeneity stressed by the discourse of Japanese nationalism makes an interesting comparison (Dale, 1988).

8. I saw and subtitled a print of this version for export during my 1985–88 stay in Beijing.

9. I have suggested that the written characters used in the written form of Chinese are universal. This is in fact slightly misleading, since simplified forms of the traditional characters are used in the mainland and not in Hong Kong, Singapore or on Taiwan. However, most readers can make their way through texts in either simplified or traditional form, whereas these Cantonese characters are only intelligible to Cantonese speakers. A La Trobe University student, Seekam Tan, is currently investigating the implications of this development in Hong Kong cinema in more detail.

10. "Hou Hsiao-Hsien" in the Wade-Giles romanization system preferred on Taiwan, just to further break down and hybridize the unity of the Chinese language.

11. For further details on this film, two useful books may be consulted: Yang's notebook (Yang, 1991), and the script (Wu Danru, 1991).

12. This point was made by director Huang Mingchuan in an after-film discussion at the Hawaii International Film Festival, December 1991. For further details on the film, see Huang's account of the making of the film (Huang Mingchuan, 1990).

Bibliography

A C (pseud.).

　　1991　　"Letter from China," *Metro* 87 (Spring 1991), 3–6.

Anderson, Benedict.

　　1983　　*Imagined Communities: Reflections on the Origin and Spread of Nationalism* (London: Verso).

Berry, Chris.

1989   "China's New 'Women's Cinema,' " *Camera Obscura* 18, 8–19.

Berry, Chris.

1992   " 'Race' (*Minzu*): Chinese Film and the Politics of Nationalism," *Cinema Journal* (Winter 1992), 45–59.

Bhabha, Homi.

1984   "Of Mimicry and Man: The Ambivalence of Colonial Discourse," *October* 28, 125–33.

Bhabha, Homi.

1989   "The Commitment to Theory," in Pines and Willemen (1989), 111–32.

Bhabha, Homi.

1990a   "DissemiNation: Time, Narrative and the Margins of the Modern Nation," in Bhabha (1990b), 291–322.

Bhabha, Homi, ed.

1990b   *Nation and Narration* (London: Routledge).

Chakrabarty, Dipesh.

1991   "Subaltern Studies and Critique of History," *Arena* 96, 105–20.

Chow, Rey.

1991   "Violence in the Other Country: China as Crisis, Spectacle, and Woman," in Mohanty, Russo, and Torres (1991), 81–100.

Dale, Peter.

1988   *The Myth of Japanese Uniqueness* (London: Routledge).

Engle, Hua-ling Nieh, and Paul Engle.

1972   *The Poetry of Mao Tse-tung* (London: Wildwood House).

Harrison, Selig.

1986   Interview with Hu Yaobang, *Far Eastern Economic Review*, 26 July 1986, cited in Long, xv.

Huang Mingchuan.

1990   *Duli zhipian zai Taiwan* (*Producing an Independent Film In Taiwan*, Taipei [Taibei]: Qianjie Publishing House [*Qianjie chubanshe*]).

Huang Tingyi.

1991   "Perfect Acting Both in Figure and Expression—About Wang Tiecheng in *Zhou Enlai*," *China Screen*, 1991:3, 16–17.

Jeffords, Susan.

1989   *The Remasculinization of America: Gender and the Vietnam War* (Bloomington: Indiana University Press).

Long, Simon.

1991   *Taiwan: China's Last Frontier*, (London: Macmillan).

64 | Colonialism and Nationalism in Asian Cinema

McRobbie, Angela.

1985 "Strategies of Vigilance: An Interview with Gayatri Chakravorti Spivak," _Block_ 10, 5–9.

Mohanty, Chandra Talpade, Ann Russo, and Lourdes Torres, eds.

1991 _Third World Women and the Politics of Feminism_ (Bloomington: Indiana University Press).

Ni Zhen.

1991 "An Interview with Ding Yinnan, the Director of _Zhou Enlai_," _China Screen_, 1991:3, 14–15.

Pines, Jim and Paul Willemen, eds.

1989 _Questions of Third Cinema_ (London: British Film Institute).

Preston, Yvonne.

1991 "Box-Office Empress," _Good Weekend—The Age Magazine_, September 28, 1991, 44–49.

Renan, Ernest.

1990 "What Is a Nation?" in Bhabha (1990b), 8–22.

Spivak, Gayatri Chakravorty.

1987 _In Other Worlds_ (New York: Methuen).

Trinh T. Minh-ha.

1989 _Woman, Native, Other: Writing Postcoloniality and Feminism_ (Bloomington: Indiana University Press).

Tsou, Tang, Marc Blecher, and Mitch Meisner.

1981 "Policy Change at the National Summit and Policy Change at the Local Level: The Case of Tachai and Hsiyang in the Post-Mao Era," in Tsou (1981), 249–392.

Tsou, Tang, ed.

1981 _Select Papers from the Center for Far East Asian Studies_ (Chicago: University of Chicago).

Wu Danru.

1991 _Gulingjie shaonian sharen shijian_ (_A Brighter Summer Day_, Taipei [Taibei]: Lianliu Publishing Company [_Lianliu chuban gongsi_]).

Yang, Edward (Yang Dechang).

1991 _Yang Dechang dianying biji_ (_Notebook on My New Film_, Taipei [Taibei]: Times Cultural Publications Enterprise Company Limited [_Shibao wenhua chuban qiye youxian gongsi_]).

Zhang Xiaotian.

1989 "A Flourishing Family Concern—Directors Li Qiankuan and Xiao Guiyun," _China Screen_ 1989:3, 23.

5 | Korean Cinema and the New Realism

Text and Context

Isolde Standish

In KOREA THROUGHOUT the 1980s, there was a gradual easing of the laws governing the production and the release of films. When Roh Tae Woo (No T'ae-u) succeeded Chun Doo Hwan (Chon Tu-hwan) as president of the Republic of Korea in 1988, this process reached a peak with the enactment of a new constitution which, among other things, established the right to artistic freedom. The accompanying relaxation of the political censorship laws brought about a rebirth of films which attempt to address and interpret social realities through serious representations of the working-class experience. These films represent the shift into mainstream popular culture of the formerly suppressed underground philosophies of the *Minjung* Movement.[1] It is to these films, which were produced after the 1988 reforms, that I want to address the bulk of this chapter, and to demonstrate how a new wave of realism in contemporary Korean film production became possible as a direct result of the relaxation of the censorship laws.

The aim of this chapter is to investigate how these films handle contemporary social realities, and what interpretations of social reality they are seen to be encouraging; also, the question of how successful these films are in tackling the issues and problems presented. In order to do this, I have adopted a particular form of critical approach which David Bordwell sets out in his latest book *Making Meaning* as an alternative to interpretation—an "historical poetics of cinema." This he defines as "the study of how, in determinate circumstances, films are put together, serve specific functions, and achieve specific effects" (1989: 266–67). The discussion will include an assessment of the significance of these films in relation to the society of which they are a part. In this respect, I am concerned to emphasize how an understanding of the society from which these films came can tell us more about the films and the nature of their representations than can purely analytical structuralist interpretations of their content. This does not mean that I intend to rule out all analytical interpretation, but rather that I intend to subordinate it within a holistic approach.

It has been argued that films "reflect society." However, they do much more than just reflect; they also actively explain and interpret the way in which the world is perceived and understood. Accordingly, in a society with deep political divisions and fragmented by class, sex, etc., access to the means of film production is limited to certain groups. Therefore, the positions of a minority adopted by film representations often come to be seen as the "natural" or "normal." Thus what films tell us about a given society has to be interpreted in terms of the groups and viewpoints from which they are derived and connected. By adopting a multi-disciplinary approach including the historical, social, and economic contexts of film production and reception, I intend to consider not only how adequately the issues raised in these films are dealt with, but also what perspectives and attitudes have been adopted in the films, and how these films appear to encourage particular ways of interpreting the world.

Korean Society 1960–1991, from the Minjung Perspective[2]

A key to an understanding of Korean politics and society since the Korean War resides in the interaction of two factors: one, economic development which led to a degree of affluence; and two, the gradual suppression of political freedoms. The degree of economic affluence grew out of a policy of industrialization which was predicated on low wages and the suppression of labor. Closely tied to economic development was the trend to urbanization, similar to that which occurred in Japan after World War Two. Economic growth was also in part responsible for the gradual dissolving of the old agrarian-based class structures and the creation of new social groups.

Between 1945 and 1960, the proportion of South Koreans living in cities more than doubled to 30 percent of the total population. This increased during the 1960s with as many as 500 people a day arriving in Seoul. A similar move in rural population occurred in other urban areas. The attraction and opportunities of employment in the cities in conjunction with the pressure of rural overpopulation drew villagers in large numbers to the urban areas. This trend grew as the nation changed to a cash economy. There was an accompanying boom in education: the literacy rate in 1960 was over 70 percent of the population and between 1948 and 1960, the number of tertiary institutions had doubled. The circulation figures for the *Tonga Ilbo* newspaper rose from 20,000 after the war to 400,000 by 1963 (Eckert 1990:353). The newspapers were, moreover, critical of the American-imposed government of Syngman Rhee (Yi Sŭng-man) and helped to stimulate an already existing urban discontent. This discontent increased because as many as 60 percent of students graduating from university found it almost impossible to get a job. If they did find work, it was often unrelated to their fields of study and therefore unsatisfactory.

Students were at the heart of Korea's new urban discontent. By 1960, student protest had a long and heroic tradition. As Carter J. Eckert explains:

Students saw themselves in good Confucian fashion as guardians of state virtue, and they identified that virtue in 1960 with many of the ideas of constitutional democracy that they had been taught since 1945, but had never been
practiced by their governments. (1990:353)

It was the students who acted as the vanguard that brought down the Rhee government in the spring of 1960. After Rhee's resignation, there was a freeing of
the press and the restraints on political activity were removed. This precipitated
the publication of a profusion of new newspapers and magazines. However, this
was short lived. In less than a year after the second republic's inauguration, a
military coup d'état brought Major General Park Chung Hee (Pak Chŏng-hŭi)
to power on May 16, 1961.

Park's first act after assuming control was to establish an Economic Planning Board which would put Korea on the road to capitalism and a hoped-for
equality with Western industrialized nations. Shortly after the Economic Planning Board was established, a five-year plan was implemented which would begin the process of overcoming Korea's poverty. Park's systematic approach to
this problem of industrialization succeeded. Each year the GNP grew by an average 8.6 percent; between 1963 and 1972, per capita income increased from $80
to $225, and unemployment also declined. This new economic growth helped
Koreans once again to feel a certain pride in their country. In the 1963 presidential election campaign, Park spoke of the need for "pride in one's country and
one's self" and of how the Korean people "had to work together to build their
nation and be dependent upon no one" (Ogle 1990:14). In those early days, he
was appealing to the nation's sense of *han*,[3] which the internationally imposed
division of Korea into north and south had intensified. This sense of *han*
stemmed from the Japanese occupation of 1910–1945 and appears to have precipitated a generalized cultural anxiety around questions of male identity.

This anxiety has manifested itself in popular culture as attacks against "ef-
feminacy" in general and violence against women in particular. One example
is the film version of *Ch'un hyang-chŏn* (The Story of Ch'un hyang) directed by
Lee Kyu-hwan, which opened at the Kukdo Theatre in Seoul on January 16,
1955. The film was a huge box-office success; in the first two months, 200,000
people saw it and this was more than 10 percent of the population of Seoul at
that time. Ch'un hyang is a classic Chosŏn dynasty (1392–1910) Confucian morality tale about a beautiful daughter of a *kisaeng* (*geisha*) who promises to marry
a nobleman. He, however, is sent off to the capital and leaves the hapless Ch'un
hyang behind. The local governor/magistrate tries to force her to become his
concubine, but Ch'un hyang refuses, whereupon he throws her in jail and subjects her to unimaginable tortures daily until she almost dies. The nobleman
eventually returns as a secret government inspector and saves her. The subtext
of this narrative has been interpreted variously at different historical periods,

the most recent being that the rape of Korea by foreign powers is depicted symbolically in Ch'un hyang's torture.

This film precipitated the birth of a major genre in Korean cinema that takes female rape as its theme. A more recent series is *Ppong*, in which the heroine is raped by Korean officials of the Japanese occupation government. Another recent development of the theme includes attacks on homosexuals and male prostitutes who are seen to have been contaminated (raped) by foreigners, e.g., *In'gan sijang 2* (The Human Market 2, 1989) and *Namja sijang* (The Male Market, 1990). Korean cinema has been dominated by heroic images of a tough virile masculinity which is a reaction to a sense of national impotency, the final humiliation of a nation no longer in charge of its manhood.[4] Park, through his promise of an "economic miracle" offered a chance to alleviate this *han*, something his successor Chun Doo Hwan was unable to do.

In reality, Park's economic development plan was based to a large extent on low wages and the suppression of labor through both physical force and an elaborately oppressive legal structure. On October 17, 1972 Park declared a state of emergency under the pretext of a communist threat from the north. All democratic rights and civil liberties were suspended and in their place he imposed a new social order which he called *Yusin*. *Yusin* usually translates into English as "restoration," but Park preferred "revitalizing reforms."

Under the *yusin* system, Park established himself as a dictator. The National Assembly became a mere rubber stamp; unions, universities, churches, and the media were put under surveillance by the Korean CIA, the riot police were used to control the students, and a network of spies infiltrated the population to control public opinion. However, these draconian measures only served to strengthen the already strong public opposition to Park and his policies. Students took to the streets in anti-*yusin* demonstrations.

By the mid-1970s, labor union membership was increasing at a fast rate, reaching 1 million by 1978. Park could not completely ban labor unions because of Korea's relationship with the USA, which mitigated against such direct action. Workers in the 1970s, supported by students, intellectuals, and Christian groups, were becoming increasingly assertive.

In the 1963 presidential election campaign, Park had created a myth of affluence that aimed to give the working class a stake in a future industrialized, strong Korea, binding the new urban classes to the hegemonic order. Government and management propaganda constantly reinforced this myth, appealing to patriotism and spurring workers to even greater heights of production. In the 1970s, this myth was blown wide open; economic inequalities had not been eroded and the realities of continuing inequalities were only too apparent.

Because of the opposition to the *yusin* policies and the failure of eight earlier emergency decrees to quell the unrest, Park was forced to announce the implementation of Emergency Measure No. 9 in May 1975. This law made criticism of the president, or of the measure itself, a criminal act. There followed a profusion of arbitrary arrests, prolonged detentions, forced confessions taken under torture, sham trials, and executions. It was in this period when the *Minjung* Movement became firmly established as an underground political and cultural opposition to the dominant ruling hegemony. The victims of Park's *yusin* policy became part of its pantheon of heroes and martyrs. As Carter J. Eckert has observed:

> By 1979, the movement had begun to assume the character of an underground institution in South Korean society, with its own extensive organisation, heroes and martyrs, patois and culture. Works by dissident musicians, writers and other artists, together with the artists themselves, became icons of the new subculture and gave it both emotional strength and intellectual substance. (1990:368)

Yŏgong: Factory Girls

One of the effects of rapid industrial growth and the need for cheap labor was the emergence of a new urban group, the *yŏgong* (factory girls). In the 1960s, *yŏgong* aged between fourteen and twenty-four made up some 30 percent of the workforce, and by 1980, the figure had risen to 40 percent. Most were, and still are, employed in textile-related industries and some are in mining and manufacturing. They came from rural backgrounds and were housed in overcrowded dormitories, a practice that still continues today. The average worker has two days off a month and frequently is obliged to send a large proportion of her wages back to her family in the country. The money that she earns often goes toward the university education of male siblings.[5]

Women's positions in the factories are very weak, due to the inferior social standing of women in traditional Korean society, where their main function is biological, in providing a male successor for their husband's family. Sexual harassment from male supervisors is a real threat. Violence, characteristic of many marital relationships, often extends into the workplace, where male supervisors feel that they have a moral right to physically and verbally chastise female employees. Despite Korea's rapid industrial growth, attitudes and behavior toward women have lagged sorely behind, though there are now some signs that change is occurring, albeit slowly. This has been reflected in the film industry from the mid-1950s with the development of a new genre targeted at a predominantly female audience.

This development attests not only to the film industry's acknowledgment of a growing degree of economic independence on the part of women, but also, through the narrative content of the films, a growing awareness of the renegotiation of women's roles within society.

The films all follow a tight narrative framework in which an affluent married heroine, neglected by her husband, falls in love with a handsome, more attentive man. The first film to be released dealing with this theme was *Chayu puin* (The Free Woman, 1956), directed by Han Hyong-mo. In 1981, Park Ho-tae directed a sequel which, like its predecessor, was a huge box-office success. The success of these films prompted the production of a number of films taking similar themes; some more recent examples include *Onŭl yŏja* (Today's Woman, 1989), *Che i sŏng* (The Second Sex, 1989), and *Chayu puin 90* (1990). A further recent thematic variation has grown out of this genre with the production of films like *Mul-wirŭl kinnŭn yŏja* (1991), which deals with friendships between women and the conflicts of career and family. Male/female relationships in this film take a secondary place, reflecting Korean women's growing concerns with careers and opportunities outside the marital home.

From the 1970s, women workers began to assert themselves and responded to the harsh conditions of employment imposed on them rather more frequently than their male counterparts. All instances of work stoppages in this period were strikes by women, and most of the disputes registered were by women. In the mid 1980s, women employed in the Kuro-dong district of Seoul took sweeping industrial action in a wave of demonstrations which became the theme for one of the first films to come out of the 1988 reforms, *Kuro arirang* (1989).

Kwangju: The Turning Point

Park was assassinated on October 26, 1979, after which General Chun Doo Hwan, through various measures, eventually took control of the government. One of the first things he did after gaining control of the government was to put down, in a particularly brutal fashion, a demonstration by students at Chŏnnam National University, Kwangju. The students had been demanding the release of Kim Dae Jung, one of the leaders of the opposition who had been imprisoned for political activities. Shocked by the brutality of the attack, ordinary people joined the students, but the black-bereted paratroopers killed indiscriminately. By May 21, 1980, angry Kwangju citizens began seizing arms from police stations and army stockpiles and succeeded in driving the army out of Kwangju. For five days, the citizens controlled the city. However, on May 27, Chun sent in the 20th Army Division which invaded the city. Again there were indiscriminate killings. The official number of dead was given at 200, but witnesses to the tragedy claim a much higher number, usually around 2,000. The *1986 Asia Watch Report* noted that the city's death statistics for May 1980 were 2,300 over the monthly average.

The Kwangju incident became the focus for subsequent anti-American sentiments, as the 20th Army Division had been brought in from the DMZ (the Demilitarized Zone between North and South Korea), where it was under the command of General John Wickham, US Army. It was assumed that General Wickham knew of Chun's intentions when he released the division and therefore was an accomplice in the plan.

The Kwangju incident also served to strengthen the anti-Chun atmosphere. This mood was intensified by the government's refusal to accept responsibility or to compensate victims of the incident. As Carter J. Eckert has observed: "The Kwangju Incident continued to haunt Chun throughout the Fifth Republic and, more than any other factor, denied him the legitimacy he sought" (1990:378).

Students' Opposition

The students of the 1980s appeared to have undergone an ideological shift to the left or at least toward a *minjung*-based Christianity. Unlike their parents, who had grown up during the Korean War and had been influenced by it and a state-provoked fear of communism, these students had grown up under General Park's *yusin* policy and had been influenced by the Kwangju incident. The 1980s saw the emergence of a generational consciousness among students who saw the threat coming not, as their parents had done, from the north, but from their own government and the imperialistic policies of the USA. The students believed that the USA had played a major role when Chun seized power by force in 1979–1980, and that the USA was equally responsible for the Kwangju massacre. Their suspicions were confirmed when President Reagan invited Chun to the White House in February 1981. This period saw a shift in the appropriation of blame for Korea's problems, as Carter J. Eckert confirms:

> The students regarded South Korea's major political and social ills, including the national division, as structural problems embedded in the country's sociopolitical system or in its 'neocolonialist' relationship with the United States— impervious, in either case, to reform at the top. The logical task from the students' perspective, was revolution against these two evils, usually seen as interconnected. (1990:379)

It is from this generation of 1980s students that some of Korea's most influential contemporary film directors have emerged. For example, Pak Kwang-su, Yi Myŏng-se, and P'ae Yong-kyun are all in their thirties now and their films reflect the political and social issues that dominated this period.

In 1986, there was a spate of student suicide protests, and massive violent confrontations broke out between the police and demonstrators, by this time a mixture of students and workers. In the early 1980s, Chun had increased the security forces by tens of thousands of young conscripts who trained as riot police. This intimidated not only the students, but also the average citizens and "suggested a country under seige by its own government" (Eckert 1990:378).

Many students left the universities and went to work in factories to create an alliance between students and workers for political change. It is estimated that as many as three thousand students became factory hands during this period. According to police records in 1985–86, they claim to have arrested 671 student-"agitators" working in factories.

In January 1987, the death by torture of Pak Chong-chŏl, a Seoul National University student, became known publicly. It was the first time that the Chun government had admitted to torturing its suspects. Two policemen were prosecuted, and the Home Affairs Minister was dismissed along with the head of the National Police. However, public opinion had turned against the Chun government and after continuing strikes and demonstrations, Roh Tae Woo, the Democratic Justice Party's next presidential candidate, announced on June 29, 1987, his eight-point program of reforms that began with an endorsement of direct presidential elections and included the restoration of civil rights for Kim Dae Jung and other political prisoners, protection of human rights, the lifting of press restrictions, the encouragement of local and campus autonomy, the promotion of political parties, and a call for "bold social reforms."

Roh Tae Woo was inaugurated as president on February 25, 1988, after having won the election with 37 percent of the vote. He was able to win largely due to the divisions in the opposition parties; Kim Dae Jung had won 27 percent of the vote and Kim Young Sam 28 percent.

It might be suggested the the the Sixth Republic offers greater hope for the establishment of a quasi-democratic political system. At this stage, it is too early to say. The students, who have always been at the cutting edge of political change, continue to demonstrate, and in the spring of 1991 there was another spate of six student self-immolations as protest against the death of a student who was beaten by police with an iron rod. Amnesty International continues to publicize the cases of three young artists held under the National Security Law. However, there has been a considerable freeing of the press which has prompted the publications of new newspapers, journals, and books. In addition, the restrictions on the film industry have been eased.

The Film Industry

After the Korean War, in the late 1950s, the Korean film industry experienced a minor boom period generated by the extraordinary success of *Ch'un hyang-chŏn* (The Story of Ch'un hyang, 1955). However, that period was short lived. After General Park seized power in May 1961, he enacted the Motion Picture Law of January 1962. This was the first law pertaining to film to be decreed by a Korean government.

Its purpose was to push out independent film producers, forcing the industry into a Hollywood style studio system that was more amenable to central control. Stephen Neale (1987) has shown how the film industry can regulate spectator "desire" and "memory" at the point where spectator expectations, regarding film narrative (generic) conventions, meet the industry's need to provide novelty in films. This results from the peculiar nature of film itself. Audiences do not buy a product in the conventional sense, they pay money at the box-office in the expectation of receiving some form of pleasure. In order to attract audiences, the industry has to maintain a balance in film production between spectator expectations of generic conventions and a degree of novelty. Through this law, Park sought to limit access to the means of film production and thereby to ensure that the ideological positions of the ruling minority came to be seen as the "natural" and "normal." This he did by requiring all production companies to be licensed and to fulfill the following conditions:

    (i) the company had to provide studio space of not less than two hundred *p'yŏng* (approximately 800 sq. yards);

    (ii) they had to possess adequate sound recording and laboratory facilities;

    (iii) they were required to have an elaborate lighting system;

    (iv) they had to own not less than three 35mm cameras; and

    (v) they had to employ at least two full-time directors and several full-time actors and actresses.

Each company had to produce a minimum of fifteen films a year. In order to secure finance, each film production company licensed under the new law was given a special quota for the importation of foreign films.

This law effectively reduced the number of licensed film production companies from seventy-one to sixteen, forcing many established film-makers out of the industry. Under the law, the minimum requirement of film productions proved to be unrealistic and only four companies managed to meet their quotas in the first year of their license. This led to the first revision of the Motion Picture Law in March 1963. Despite this revision, there was still great dissatisfaction within the industry and a committee was formed in 1964 in an attempt to have the law repealed. The government compromised and agreed to a further revision which was enacted in August 1966.

During the 1960s, the number of film productions did increase. This was due mainly to a provision in the law that linked the quotas for importation of lucrative foreign film to domestic production at a one to three ratio. This gave rise to the production of many cheap second-rate domestic films known as "quota quickies" in the latter half of the 1960s and the early 1970s. The foreign film import quota system had been established to help to protect domestic production by limiting the number of foreign films that could be screened in Korea, and as a means of providing funds for making domestic films. However, in reality it had the opposite effect, reducing the quality of domestic films produced. The quota system stipulated that foreign films could be exhibited for up to 245 days a year. This meant that domestic films were given only very short runs. Cinemas did not want to give more time to domestic films at the expense of the more lucrative foreign films which generally accounted for about half their annual box-office takings. Despite the poor quality of domestic films being produced, in 1969 attendance figures were a record 173,043,272, but by 1979 this figure had dropped to 65,518,581.

The main cause of this rapid decline is attributed to two factors. The first reason is the decline in the quality of domestic films brought about by the foreign import quotas mentioned above. This was exacerbated by the fourth amendment to the film law in February 1973 which placed far greater political censorship burdens on the industry. In keeping with Park's *yusin* policy, this fourth amendment required film companies to produce films directly related to government policies. These films became known as "formality films." The second reason for the decline in cinema attendance has been attributed to the increase in television ownership in the 1970s. This figure rose from just over one million in 1973 to nearly six million in 1979.

The 1980s saw a slight relaxation in government policy rendered necessary perhaps by the democratic image required in order to be able to host the 1988 Olympic Games. This was reflected in the film industry, as greater emphasis was placed on the promotion of films as art, a reaction against the "quota quickies" and the "formality films." In July 1985, a further amendment was made to the Motion Picture Law, again brought about by the agitation from within the industry. Article Four changed the laws concerning the establishment of film companies from a license system to a registration system, greatly reducing the original requirements laid out in the 1962 law. This meant that virtually any Korean citizen who could fill in the forms and demonstrate sufficient funds could start up a film production company. It was also added that independent film-makers could make one film a year without registering if they were Korean nationals, and if they notified the government of their intention. Equally important was the separation of film production companies from import companies, effectively breaking the link that had tied import quotas to domestic production. By June 1987, sixty-two film production companies and fifteen independent producers had registered under this new law. A further sixty foreign film importation companies had also registered.

The law included a "screen code" which was designed to protect domestic films. The number of days on which Korean films must be exhibited in cinemas was set at 146 (two-fifths of the year). The reform to the laws relating to the importation of foreign films brought about a tremendous increase in the number of imported films exhibited. This can in part be attributed to the great pressure the United States government had exercised on the Korean government to liberalize its importation laws to allow American companies to open agencies for the direct distribution of American films in Korea. This they achieved in July 1987. It is predicted that Korea is likely to become Asia's second largest American film market by 1992, second only to Japan. In 1989, foreign films accounted for US $44.2 million of total box-office takings—a total of 79.8 percent.

Moreover, the percentage of people going to foreign films showed an increase of 3.1 percent on the 1988 figures.

These latest reforms to the Motion Picture Law have brought about mixed results as the analysis of the 1989 box-office takings clearly indicates. Koreans are continuing to go to foreign films rather than to their own domestic productions. However, the liberalization of the studio licensing system has meant that the means of film production have again been opened up to a variety of different independent producers and groups. Also, the new constitution of February 1988 included Article 22, which clearly states "the right to artistic freedom," a right incorporated into the revised Motion Picture Law of May 1988. At this time all government agencies were removed from the censorship board.

The following three factors have led to the demise of the "quota quickie": first, the diversification of the means of production; secondly, the removal of the obstacle of political censorship on film content; and thirdly, the separation of domestic film production and foreign film importation. Generally speaking, there has been a rise in the standard of contemporary Korean films characterized by the growth of a "new realism." For the first time since the late 1950s, film-makers have been free to choose their own subject matter and, judging from recent audience rating figures, there would appear to be a swing back to the popularity of certain domestically produced films. However, this is not at the expense of foreign films, but hopefully, it is sufficient to ensure a continued growth in the domestic industry.

Realism and Narrative

When reading Korean film journals on contemporary cinema, one is struck by the number of times the term "new realism" (*nyu riŏllijŭm*) appears describing films produced in the late 1980s and early 1990s. I want to discuss in theoretical terms the relationship between realism and narrative before going onto a discussion of some of the films of the new wave.

As stated earlier, the film industry attracts audiences by providing a balance between cinematic conventions based on spectator expectations and a degree of novelty. One of the central expectations is that a film should tell a story, and allied to this is a demand for realism. An audience should be able to think of the story a film is telling them as if it were a real event.

> The audience expects to operate a particular suspension of disbelief in which the mimesis of the photographic image reinforces the circumstantial and psychological 'realism' of the events those images contain. (R. Maltby 1983:187)

It is perhaps these two factors, narrative and realism, which are paramount in our definition of a good film.

I maintain that these conventions of narrative and realism are not neutral conductors of meaning, but that they, just like the economic and political structures within which films are produced, encourage the development of certain types of meaning while discouraging others. Freed from political censorship, the films of the Korean new wave have taken over as their subject matter the social and political problems which had until recently only found expression in the underground *Minjung* Movement. In keeping with the philosophies of the *Minjung* Movement, these films have placed the working man/woman at the center of the narrative, hence the use of the term "new realism" in describing them. However, these films of the Korean new wave express attitudes and ideas not only through their subject matter, but also through the very form in which that subject matter is placed. Spectator expectations of narrative convention constrain and structure a film's subject matter. Obviously these conventions of film narrative still allow for a great degree of flexibility, but there are certain general implicit tendencies inherent in these conventions which affect the way certain subject matter is portrayed.

Tzvetan Todorov in the *Poetics of Prose* sets out the basic structure of narrative:

> An "ideal" narrative begins with a stable situation which is disturbed by some power or force. There results a state of disequilibrium; by the action of a force directed in the opposite direction, the equilibrium is re-established; the second equilibrium is similar to the first, but the two are never identical. (1977:111)

Built into the re-establishment of equilibrium in this structure of narrative is the idea of solution, a return to order. This presumption of solution affects the way a film can treat subject matter related to social and political problems. An attitude toward the subject matter is already taken by the very structure of the narrative form which requires a solution. The stress which the narrative structure places on the resolution of the problem raised in the film implies that the problem can be solved without any great change to the existing social and political structures of the society. This is further reinforced by the narrative's tendency to put stress on individuals as agents of causality. The actions or ambitions of characters, rather than more general social or political relations, precipitate the plot. A stress on private, personal dramas is implicit in the conventions of narrative. Therefore, these contemporary Korean films dealing with social and political problems tend not to treat them as social or political problems (that is, problems of the social and political structure), but as personal problems (that is, personal qualities, attributes, etc.). The emphasis is on interpersonal drama rather than on the interaction of social and political forces.

Raymond Williams has stated that "realism" in the artistic sense is an emphasis on the "real world" as against the characteristic presentation of the world in romance and myth. In European society it came about as a result of a "revolt" against previous conventions. He goes on to state that realism in

> eighteenth century bourgeois drama . . . made three innovations: that the actions of drama should be contemporary (almost all earlier drama, by convention, had been set in historical or legendary past); that the actions and resolutions of the drama should be secular (conceived and worked through in solely human terms, without reference to a supernatural or metaphysical dimension); and that the actions of drama should move beyond their conventional social exclusions (tragedy as confined to princes) and include the lives of all men. . . . (*Exploration in Film Theory* 1991:122)

Just like eighteenth-century drama, contemporary Korean film is now "making a break towards realism" characterized by the three innovations to subject matter set out by Williams above. The Korean new wave has come about as a "revolt" against traditional conventions imposed by a stringent system of political censorship. The Korean new wave is characterized by new content: new characters (the working classes, radical students), new settings (the factory, slum houses) and new problems (the north/south division, urbanization, industrial unrest, and family breakdown). Thereby, these films have appropriated the established conventions of realism. Williams has demonstrated that realism is dependent on conventions just as much as any other artistic expression. However, in the case of realism these conventions have successfully achieved the status of being accepted as realistic.

The subject matter of contemporary Korean cinema has changed but the conventions of the narrative form remain the same, reducing the subject matter to personal solvable dramas. It is possible to show in film how the poor live, but it is difficult for Korean directors to stay within film conventions of narrative and show how such poverty is the result of a particular sociopolitical economic structure.

The Films

One of the most striking characteristics of the Korean cinema toward the end of the 1980s was its increasing concern with contemporary social issues and its commitment to realism. As stated above, the 1980s saw the emergence of a generational consciousness among students who saw the threat to their society coming from their own government as well as from the imperialistic policies of the USA. These students represented a new breed of restless youth produced by increased opportunities in education and influenced by Park's oppressive *yusin* policies and Chun's excesses during the Kwangju massacre. By combining with the working class (*minjung*) whom they saw as representatives of the true Korea, untainted by corruption and foreign connections, they became the center of political and social change in the 1980s.

It is from this generation that some of Korea's most prominent contemporary film-makers have come. They have sought to differentiate their films from earlier periods by their apparent determination to confront "real situations" and important social issues, and in so doing, to make a positive contribution to society. They seek to go beyond mere entertainment by extending cinema's subject matter to include the industrial working classes (the *minjung*). In this way, they are seeking to oppose the traditional marginalization of such social groups, representatives of the lowest levels in the Confucian social hierarchy, and previously excluded by the former state-controlled cinema. These new wave directors represent a group who, for the first time since the late 1950s, have been able to choose freely their material. By placing working-class people in working-class settings on the screen, they express an authorial style that is committed to humane values.

One of the first films to come out of this "break toward realism" was Pak Chong-wŏn's *Kuro arirang* (1989), based on a short story by Yi Mun-yŏl and first screened in the west at the Berlin Film Festival of 1990. The narrative evolves around a group of young female workers (*yŏgong*), who gradually get drawn into industrial action as a result of the harsh conditions under which they are expected to work and live. The Kuro-dong textile factories had been at the center of the wave of industrial action which had helped to bring about the political demise of Chun in the latter half of the 1980s. This film takes up the central concerns of the women workers at that time on two levels. Firstly, the factory-related external issues are exposed—the long hours of work, the addiction to "timing" pills (a drug taken by the workers to keep awake), the mistreatment by male supervisors and the overcrowding of the company dormitories and the lack of amenities. Secondly, at the emotional and psychological level, the film deals with the failures of the women's personal relationships and in some cases, the disintegration of their sense of morality.

The film begins with a group of new recruits commencing work at the factory. Chŏng-mi (played by Ok So-ri) is a slightly senior girl, and it is largely from her perspective through subjective camera work that the events of the narrative unfold. At first, she strongly resists all attempts by would-be union organizers to draw her into the plan to establish a union in the factory. However, through the course of the film she is gradually converted, not by the words of the union organizers, but through a series of incidents that include the injury by electric shock of a male worker through the negligence of one of the supervisors, and later the death of a female worker due to a dependence on "timing" drugs. The death of this girl carries with it all the symbolism of the martyrs of the *minjung* subculture. Her death becomes a catalyst for action. In the final scene, the workers and riot police clash over the body of the dead girl. The authorities, in taking the body from the women during the funeral procession, acknowledge its potential power as an icon of the opposition movement.

Chŏng-mi's character is treated with great sympathy in the depiction of her devotion to her family through her relationship with her younger brother. She works at the factory in order to pay for his university education and is thereby denied the opportunity to marry and to lead a "normal" life. At all times she remains within a Confucian morality which places a woman's loyalty to her family very high on its list of female virtues. Unlike some of the other girls, she never weakens. When she finally does take action, it is not seen as deviant; the film from the beginning sought to legitimate her actions in this final scene.

The narrative is tightly contained within the opening shots of the roofs of Kuro-dong's factories and the final scene in which the camera pans back along the street in front of the factory as the workers and riot police clash. The narrative conforms exactly to Todorov's basic structure, built into which is an ideology of individualism. The film exploits this ideology in its attempt to express worker alienation and the breaking down of traditional Korean group orientated morality. Individuals, whose desires and motivations structure the film's forward flow, are the agents of causality. The treacherous action of Chin-sŏk (played by Choe Minshik), one of the male workers who betrays his friends after Chŏng-mi refuses to marry him, is directly blamed for the hardships the women endure. He is also held accountable for the injury suffered by a male worker and the subsequent deal made with the injured worker's wife to defraud her of any financial compensation to which she may have been entitled. The film exploits this sense of individualism to create an atmosphere of vulnerability and isolation. The workers are ultimately powerless, and there is a Buddhist sense of fate pervading the film. This is reinforced by the few scenes in which the manager of the factory watches his workers from a window high above the factory forecourt. The camera is placed just behind his head and we, the spectators, look down onto the small ant-like workers from his god-like point of view. He is inextricably linked to the power that controls the anonymous gas-masked riot police who threaten the women whenever they hold a meeting. The very title, *Kuro arirang*, alludes to the ascribed status of Korean women's *han*. The folksong *Arirang* is symbolic of the suffering of women under a Confucian social order which discriminates against them. It has come to represent the futility of their situation.

Chin-sŏk's betrayal of his friends is linked to his failed relationship with Chŏng-mi who asks him, "How can I marry when I have my younger brother's education to provide for?" The industrialization of Korea is inadvertently being held responsible for Chŏng-mi's inability to marry. Women in the industrial age must sell themselves to support their male relatives, increasing the general cultural anxiety around definitions of masculinity. Chin-sŏk is weak and needs a strong woman and the support of his family to keep him from transgression.

His character is contrasted in the film with his senior supervisor who is depicted as corrupt from the beginning. Chin-sŏk's progression to betrayal is a gradual process that continues throughout the first half of the film.

The use of location in the new wave films has taken on a new meaning in Korean cinema as a realist innovation. As I have demonstrated above, realism is a construction and not an unmediated reflection of the external world. Raymond Williams has shown that the factors which identify a realist innovation are not really connected to its relationship with an external referent, but to its place in the history of artistic conventions. Realistic innovations uncover reality by exposing the artificiality of the realist conventions that had gone before. Traditionally in Korean narrative cinema, location has been transferred into a setting that is a site for the action of the drama. However, in *Kuro arirang* it is often the factory or the dormitory sites, rather than the action of the characters, which demand spectator attention. In *Kuro arirang* there are several shots that delay the fixing of a place as a locale for action by extending the number of establishing shots involved in the introduction of a scene, thereby establishing the reality of the Seoul industrial suburb of Kuro-dong. Roland Barthes has suggested that the function of objects not directly related to the narrative process in fiction is to signify reality, to furnish the effect of the real. In this way the factory and the dormitory in *Kuro arirang* are accredited with an autonomy of their own outside the narrative, authenticating the film's claim to realism.

By giving locations a degree of autonomy, the film acknowledges the fact that work is a crucial determinant of how the characters' personal lives are expressed. By confining the action almost completely to the factory and the dormitory, the film emphasizes the dominance of work in shaping the physical and emotional existence of the employees. There is an emphasis on noise and a sense of imprisonment; the women are caught behind their sewing machines unable to leave for even a minute. Numerous shots of the closed factory gates and the riot police lined up outside help to create a claustrophobic atmosphere of confinement and a sense of siege. These shots are bound into the actions of individuals as the camera pans from one worker to another. The film successfully makes a strong connection between the characters and their work, but the emphasis is always on the individual and interpersonal drama. It is only in the last few scenes that a group is really brought together through the death of a colleague. Throughout most of the film, the group is fragmented, reduced to its individual members. As stated earlier, this increases the sense of isolation of the characters and a foreboding sense of fate which dissolves into a general sense of *han*, appealing to an empathetic and not an analytical mode of spectator reception. It is at this point that Todorov's narrative structure adopted by the filmmakers fails its subject matter. The company and the socio-economic structures that caused the situation that developed in the Kuro-dong in the 1980s escape being censured in the film. The political issues of exploitation and alienation are reduced to individual conspiracies. The dynamics of the industrial actions taken by the women are reduced to simple manipulation and the characters in the film become representations of a general human condition rather than a concrete social situation.

Pak Kwang-su's films also take up questions of working-class alienation resulting from the period of rapid industrialization symbolized by Park's *yusin* policy. *Ch'il-su wa Man-su* (1988), Pak Kwang-su's first film, follows the day-to-day tribulations of two young men, symbols of the *minjung*, who have been cut off from their families and society due to a breakdown in traditional Korean social values and morality. They are victims of a society which encouraged, or in some cases forced, their parents to go against traditional codes of behavior. As a result, they are shunned and misunderstood as social outcasts. This theme, of people living on the economic edge of Korean society, is taken up again in Pak Kwang-su's later film *Kŭdŭlto urich'ŏrŏm* (Black Republic, 1990).

In *Ch'il-su wa Man-su*, Ch'il-su, age 22 (played by Pak Chung-hun), was born near an American army base. His mother died when he was young and his stepmother and sister became prostitutes for the American soldiers. This accounts for his ability to speak some English. Eventually, his sister went off to America, promising to send for him when she was settled. He has fallen for the American dream, so his flight of imagination superimposed over the video screen in an amusement arcade informs the viewer in the opening sequence of the film. He and his sister have been contaminated by American cultural imperialism. It is significant that when he goes to the cinema, it is *Rocky IV* that he sees. In this film, Rocky fights and wins against the super-human Russian boxer, a celebration of the ultimate American dream. Ch'il-su wants to escape the oppressiveness of Seoul and go to the Miami of his dreams. Of course, the letter from his sister never arrives. As his drunken father tells him, once his sister went to America, it was as if she had died.

Man-su, age 27 (played by An Sŏng-ki), also harbored a dream. He applied for a passport to work in the Middle East, but was refused on the grounds of his father's political activities and subsequent imprisonment. Both Ch'il-su and Man-su had dreams of escape which would have freed them from the trap of their everyday lives. Both have relatives, but neither have families—the divisions have become too deep. Man-su cannot understand his father's refusal of a three-day pass from prison to come home and celebrate his sixtieth birthday. The gap between them is too wide. This sense of division is implicit in the opening shots of Seoul, still and deserted because of the air-raid drill practice, a constant reminder to all South Koreans of the division of their country. American imperialism is inadvertently blamed for the divisions in Ch'il-su's family, while the emergence of a new bourgeois class consciousness is alluded to as the cause of his failure to establish a relationship with Gina, a young middle-class Korean girl. It is this theme which provides the black humor which pervades the film, a humor based on the inability of people to communicate with each other. They talk, but only in platitudes.

Pak Kwang-su uses location in much the same way as does Pak Chong-wŏn in *Kuro arirang*. In one scene early in the film, an open deserted place under a railway line is shot from a high angle. Ch'il-su and Man-su emerge from a vinyl tent which serves as the local bar. They walk slowly, half drunk, across the emptiness and out of the screen, small insignificant objects in a desolate industrial wasteland. Once again it is place rather than action which assumes importance—it is the insignificant actions of Ch'il-su and Man-su walking across the screen that provide the pretext for a visual display of space. As members of the lowest social level, their job as advertising billboard painters on high-rise buildings is paradoxical, reinforcing the lack of communication theme, as people shout to them from the ground.

In the final scene, Ch'il-su and Man-su at last reach a point where they are being honest with each other and the facade is dropped. They look out onto the streets of Seoul from their position on top of the billboard, high up on the Kangnam-do bus terminal building. They shout out to the people of Seoul, but no one can hear them. This scene becomes the ultimate representation of non-communication as the people of Seoul misinterpret their antics as a suicide attempt. The police are brought in and the whole incident escalates until Man-su, no longer able to cope with this inability to communicate with people, jumps. His attempted suicide had been alluded to earlier in the film through a television news broadcast which ran a report on a man who committed suicide by jumping off an apartment building. Man-su's life was always perilous, hanging from tall buildings, and his attempted suicide becomes his ultimate escape from a repressive society. Ch'il-su is then taken by the police and pushed into a police car, his face framed in the final shot by the rear window of the police car as he looks back, helpless.

Pak Kwang-su's films are characterized by the desolate locations in which he places his characters. In *Black Republic* the hero Han T'ae-hun (played by Kim Ki-yŏng) is placed in a bleak mining town. The starkness of the all-pervading slag heaps around the town almost reduces the film to black and white. The landscape emphasizes T'ae-hun's isolation as a student activist who is wanted by the police. Yi Song-ch'ŏl (played by Pak Chung-hun) is the wealthy estranged son of the coal pit owner. He jealously guards a watch with a picture of his mother, his only emotional link with his family. His father took a second wife and abandoned his mother and sister when Yi Song-ch'ŏl was young, the reason given in the film for his wild James Dean-like behavior as he rides recklessly through the town on his motorbike. All the characters in the film are cut off from their families, concealing their pasts, and in so doing fail to communicate with those around them. The mining town is cut off from the outside world and provides a microcosm of Korean society, made up of individuals who are outcasts, each existing in his/her own isolation. Money is not the answer. Song-ch'ŏl is wealthy, since his father tried to buy his affections, but he is shown to be just as lonely as the incidental character Tae-shik who works at the briquette factory. Tae-shik's father is in prison because of his union activities and his mother works in Seoul as a housekeeper. This family, too, has been divided by industrialization. T'ae-hun, the student activist, is the only person able to communicate with these characters in an honest way. Both Tae-shik and Yong-suk, the local prostitute, are able to open up to him. He is seen to have a moral authority, based on his Confucian student role as moral guardian of the state. The final scene of the film does, however, provide hope for the future. T'ae-hun escapes once again from the police and as his train pulls out of the station, he says to himself: " . . . the change has already begun. . . . To some people today's darkness is despair, but to those of us who dream of a brilliant tomorrow, today's darkness is called hope."

Once again Pak Kwang-su's films conform to a narrative structure which reduces socio-economic and political issues to individual drama. Man-su suffers because of the actions of his father. Song-ch'ŏl likewise has been denied the maternal affection that would have made him into a "normal" man and not a rebellious lout. The characters in Pak Kwang-su's films all suffer for their parents' past actions, but at no time do the films successfully examine the forces that prompted their parents to act as they did. This stress on individualism in the films has led one Korean critic, Kim Kyŏng-uk, to reduce these films to the rantings of a young director out of touch with the realities of the previous generation. That is, the critic's own generation, as Kim Kyŏng-uk is sixty-five. His critique of the films clearly demonstrates the inability of the conventional narrative structure to deal adequately with this subject matter.

In Pak Kwang-su's films, the problem is located in the individual. It is portrayed as a problem for society rather than a problem of society. The films invariably end with the reestablishment of order through the corrective action of legal restraint or punishment. Man-su and Song-ch'ŏl are rushed to the hospital and will probably die; Ch'il-su and Yong-suk are taken off by the police. Despite Pak Kwang-su's commitment to represent the plight of working-class Koreans, his films, through their adoption of conventional narrativity and realism, reduce the whole question of industrial urbanization and its effects on the family to an accentuated individualism that can only appeal to a shared sense of *han* in the spectator. These films provide an hermetic critique of the events of the narrative that fails to recognize the political and economic structures which caused the situation in which the characters are placed.

The films discussed so far all share a common concern with social control reflected in an implicit nostalgia for a past Confucian patriarchal order which placed the extended family in the center of society, where women were contained and manageable within a family group. Industrialization and the resultant urbanization has led to a breakup of rural communities and a move toward nuclear family units. This process has put great pressure on traditional male roles, thus aggravating a growing cultural anxiety about the male image in general. The increasing number of women in the workplace and their increasing financial independence has further precipitated anxieties about masculinity, family stability, and the decline in moral standards. These are all implicit concerns in the films already discussed. However, in films like *Umukpaemi ŭi sarang* (Love in Umukpaemi, 1990) and *Sut'ak* (The Rooster, 1990), they become the main theme.

The narrative of *Umukpaemi ŭi sarang* evolves around a young textile worker who has an extra-marital affair with a young married woman working in the same sweat shop. The film is characterized by its preoccupation with the control and stabilization of sexuality within the regime of marriage. The characters are punished for their expressions of sexuality outside marriage and are rehabilitated back into the family and marital norm. The narrative is told predominantly in the form of a reminiscence from the young man's (played by Pak Chunghun) point of view, with the use of voice-over and flashbacks. It is only when he leaves his wife and transgresses Confucian morality that the perspective of the narrative changes. (A Confucian morality tolerates male dalliance outside marriage as long as the institution of marriage itself remains unthreatened.) We are given a subjective view of his wife which includes flashbacks to their first meeting when she was a prostitute. This revelation is softened by further flashbacks showing her cruel poverty-stricken childhood in the country and her escape to the city. When she does track her husband down after his abandonment of her, she drags him back in a most humiliating physical fashion, a metaphorical castration, through the town to his parents' house. There he experiences the full humiliation of traditional group censure. His wife and Miss Min, his lover, are juxtaposed. His wife represents the modern Korean woman who has known an economic freedom which has given her strength to stand up against her husband who is physically afraid of her. She is a threat to his masculinity and by implication to the patriarchy. Miss Min, on the other hand, becomes even more threatening as at first she is gentle with him and is seen to represent traditional passive female virtues. Her transgression is justified by her husband's brutality toward her. However, as a modern working woman, she still poses a threat to traditional male authority as she is not content to bear the abuses of her husband, but enters into a relationship with another man. Also, it is she who finally ends the illicit relationship with the young textile worker and leaves him in the final scene crying like a child in a winter landscape. If an excess of sexuality outside marriage represents a "problem" in the film, so too does a deficiency within marriage. The unfulfilled woman is also problematic.

In *Sut'ak*, the unfulfilled woman becomes the source of the hero's problems, the locus of his discontent. The strength and economic competence of his wife in the day-to-day running of their chicken farm has, over the years, reduced him to sexual impotence. His wife frequently humiliates him in sudden outbursts of rage in front of the whole family. His inadequacies are well known to those around him. It is only when, by accident, he visits a barber shop and is given extra service that his masculinity is restored. Again a strong economically competent woman threatens male authority. A fear of the socially disruptive potential of sexual desire is evident in both films. However, this fear does not manifest itself in violence against the women who threaten male authority. Unlike contemporary American films that have stemmed from "male paranoia" about the new woman, Korean female characters in this genre do not appear to be killed off, an interesting point of cultural divergence.

The assumption of a sexual norm and a corresponding concern with its regulation within traditional marriage relations is the central concern of these two films. However, they tend to conceal or detract from the socially structured determinants of the issues related to changing gender roles in industrial Korea. As a result, the responsibility for the social problems that are dealt with in the narrative are shifted onto isolated individuals. It is for this reason that these films, despite the issues they raise, seem to end up confirming rather than questioning a Confucian based consensual world view.

Conclusion

> Texts and contexts are individually interrelated . . . and to conceptualise them as discrete is to render full analysis impossible. (A. Medhurst, *Screen*, 1984:35)

The aim of this chapter has been to provide an analysis of selected film texts relating to the Korean realist films of the new wave, in relation to the social and economic context of their production. The emphasis has been on the interconnection between film and ideology, in that the narrative content of these films grew out of ideas and ideologies of the underground *Minjung* Movement of the 1970s and early 1980s. Filmmakers like Pak Kwang-su, who belong to the 1980s student generation, have attempted to make a connection in their films between, on the one hand, the division of Korea, US imperialism and the repressive regimes of successive Korean military/civil dictatorships; and on the other hand, the sufferings (*han*) of working-class Koreans. This chapter has attempted to provide explanations of why films assumed the ideological position of the *Minjung* Movement and of how these films were shaped and influenced by the socio-economic context in which they were produced.

This chapter has also touched on questions of how the films could be effective in shaping and influencing ideological attitudes and perceptions of contemporary Korean society. This area has only been touched on in this study and requires much more work in the future. However, I have attempted to demonstrate how these films themselves are active in the construction of meaning. This is not to suggest that the meanings which these films produce are autonomous, but that they work in conjunction with many other social and cultural factors to produce meaning. Finally, this chapter has argued that despite the innovations and a shift in attitudes evident in the films, permitted by the relaxation in political censorship, they still remain constricted and constrained within conventional narrative structures and therefore are limited in the world view which they construct.

Notes

I would like to thank Martina Deuchler and J. Ross King for their comments on an earlier draft of this chapter.

1. *Minjung*, as defined in the *New World Dictionary* 1979, means quite simply the "mass of the people." However, it has in recent times taken on new connotations when used in relation to culture and politics. One Korean theologian has stated that

> the *minjung* are those who are oppressed politically, exploited economically, alienated sociologically, and kept under-educated in culture and intellectual matters. (Quoted in *Minjung Theology* 1983:xvii)

Sasse argues that the word *minjung* started to take on political connotations some fifteen or twenty years ago. He links *minjung*, quite correctly in my view, to

> a growing self-awareness and self-respect on the part of Koreans coupled to the psychological recovery from Japanese occupation, the destructive and divisive Korean war and the almost absolute dependence on help from outside which followed the war. (1991:31)

I would argue that, as the first definition implies, this concept has its roots in a working-class culture, but that the word *minjung* has, in recent times, through the *Minjung* Cultural Movement become linked to another Korean word, *minjok*, which is related to concepts of racial homogeneity and nationhood, and that it is from this blurring of the boundaries between these concepts that Sasse's "process of psychological healing" stems from. This process of psychological healing is reflected in nationalistic attempts to establish notions of Korean "uniqueness." Concomitant with this is the establishment of the "otherness" of non-Koreans, with particular emphasis on the Japanese and the Americans. It also explains in part the current interest of bourgeois artists and intellectuals in the movement.

2. In the introduction to a book called *Minjung Ŭi Yŏksa* (The *Minjung* History), the authors state their aim in writing it. They say that they have tried to place the workers at the center of history and that they tried to interpret historical events from the perspective of the common people. They argue that this perspective is central to an understanding of the whole *Minjung* Movement (1989:7). It is from this perspective that I have approached the following discussion of Korean society from 1960 to 1991.

3. *Han* is defined variously in the dictionary as a "bitter feeling," "hatred," and "un-

satisfied desire." Sasse attempts to describe the sensation of *han*: "The basic meaning of *han* is the kind of feeling one develops based on an unfulfilled wish or longing" (1991:31). Shapiro, on the other hand, is concerned with the causes of *han* when he defines it as

> the result of injustices perpetrated by, among other, parents, friends, siblings, a colonial ruler, an occupying army, past governments, the present government, and those who in crucial moments failed to display sincerity. (1990:11)

The counterpart of *han* is *chŏng*. *Chŏng* is defined in the dictionary as "tender feelings," "emotion," or "affection." However, I believe that *chŏng* transcends English language concepts of affection. It is a bond, an unspoken understanding which connects people forever. *Chŏng* is particularly strong between members of the same sex, starting at school, and develops as people grow into adulthood. *Han* and *chŏng* are inextricably bound together (Shapiro 1990:18). In Japanese society the *on* (favor)/*giri* (obligation) dyad brings about relations of interdependence between people. In Korean society, it is the *han*/*chŏng* dyadic relationship which binds people together. In other words, *chŏng* is the emotion which binds people who suffer from the same *han*.

Suh Nam-dong lists the fourfold *han* of the Korean people:

(1) Koreans have suffered numerous invasions by surrounding powerful nations so that the very existence of the Korean nation has come to be understood as *han*.

(2) Koreans have continually suffered the tyranny of the rulers so they think of their existence as *baeksong* [*paeksŏng*] (common people).

(3) Also under Confucianism's strict imposition of laws and customs discriminating against women, the existence of women was *han* itself.

(4) At a certain point in Korean history, about half the population were registered as hereditary slaves and were treated as property rather than as people of the nation. These thought of their lives as *han*. (*Minjung Theology* 1983:58)

4. The hero of *In'gan sijang 1* and *In'gan sijang 89* is a Christ-like Jackie Chan student who *tae-kwon-do*'s his way through brothels and night clubs etc., taking on American soldiers and corrupting Koreans in an attempt to restore a moral code. This he does while intermittently holding conversations with God. The film *In'gan sijang 1* was adapted from a best-selling novel that came out in the 1970s. The film seems to have had a similar success as it was re-released on video in May 1989, to correspond with the opening of the sequel *In'gan sijang 89* in the cinemas.

5. The theme of women selling themselves in various forms to support their male relatives is a common one in Korean films. A particularly good example is Im Kwon-Taek's *Tik'et* (Ticket, 1986).

Filmography

Ch'il-su and Man-su (1988), director Pak Kwang-su.
Kŭdŭlto urich'ŏrŏm (Black Republic, 1990), director Pak Kwang-su.
Kuro arirang (1989), director Pak Chong-wŏn.
Sut'ak (The Rooster, video release February 1, 1991), director Sin Sŭng-su.
Umukpaemi ŭi sarang (Love in Umukpaemi, video release August 10, 1990), director Chang Sŏn-u.

Bibliography

Korean Texts

Hanguk Yŏnghwa 70 Nyŏn: Tyaep'yojak 200 Sŏn.   Yŏnghwa Chinhŏng Kongsa, 1989, Seoul.

Kim Kyŏng-uk.   "Nassŏmgwa Syaerum Ŭi Ch'ai: Pak Kwang-su, Yi Myŏng-se, Pyae Yong-kyun Chakpumi Ŭimihanŭn Kot," *Han'gil Yŏnghwa*, Summer 1991, no. 2, pp. 52–65.

Ko Chŏng-uk.   "Hyŏnshil Panyŏngŭrosŏ Yŏnghwa," *Yŏnghwa Yesul*, March 1991, pp. 160–65.

Minjok Yŏnghwa 1.   Minjok Yŏnghwa Yŏn'guso Ch'in'gu, 1989, Seoul.

Minjok Yŏnghwa 2.   Minjok Yŏnghwa Yŏn'guso Ch'in'gu, 1990, Seoul.

Pak Suk-hŭi.   "Han'gil Yŏnghwaga Kwŏnhanŭn Pidio Yŏnghwa 10 Pyŏn," *Han'gil Yŏnghwa*, Spring 1991, no. 1, pp. 129–32.

"Sigŭphan Chŏnmun Pangsongp'ŭrodŏksyŏn Hwalsŏnghwa—Hyŏnchaeŭi Pangsongje-donŭn Kaesŏndoeŏya Handa." *Yŏnghwa Yesul*, February 1991, pp. 112–13.

Yi Sŏng-kwang.   *Minjung Ŭi Yŏksa*, Yŏl Saram, Seoul 1989, parts 1 and 2.

Yi Young-kyu.   "Kŏlp'ŭ Chŏnjaenggwa Demowa Yŏnghwa Hanguk Yŏnghwa Yŏ Saeropke Pinnara," *Yŏnghwa Yesul*, June 1991, pp. 134–35.

Yŏnghwa P'yŏngron.   Che 2 Ho 1990, Seoul.

Yonsei Taehakkyo Hangukŏ Haktang 89 Kaŭl Hakki T'ŭkkang (notes from) "Haepangi-hu Hyŏndae Hanguk Chŏnjiŭi Yŏksachŏk Chŏngae."

Japanese Text

Lee Young-il and Sato Tadao.   *Kankoku Eiga Nyŭmon*, Tokyo, 1990.

Texts in English

Boff, L. and Boff, C.   *Introducing Liberation Theology*, Burns & Oates, London, 1987.

Bordwell, D.   *Making Meaning: Inference and Rhetoric in the Interpretation of Cinema*, Harvard University Press, Cambridge, Massachusetts, 1989.

Buruma, I.   "Korea: Shame and Chauvinism," *New York Review of Books*, vol. xxxiv, no. 1, January 29, 1987.

Eckert, C. J.   "Authoritarianism and Protest, 1948–1990," *Korea Old and*

New: A History, Korea Institute, Harvard University, Il-chokak Publishers, Seoul, 1990.

Kim Won-key. "Haunted by 'Ghost' but Resolved to 'Die Harder'," *Business Korea*, March 1991, pp. 70–72.

Lee Young-il. *The History of Korean Cinema: Main Current of Korean Cinema*, translated by R. L. Greever, Saehan Printing Company, Seoul 1988.

Lost Victory: An Overview of the Korean People's Struggle for Democracy in 1987. Edited by the Christian Institute for the Study of Justice and Development, Minjungsa, 1988, Seoul.

Lovell, T. *Pictures of Reality: Aesthetics, Politics and Pleasure*, British Film Institute, London, 1983.

McCormack, G. and Gittings, J. (eds.). *Crisis in Korea*, Spokesman Books, London, 1977.

Maltby, R. *Harmless Entertainment: Narrative Structure in Fiction and Film*, Cornell University Press, Ithaca, 1980.

Medhurst, A. "Victim: Text as Context," *Screen*, vol. 25, nos. 4/5, July-October 1984.

Minjung Theology: People as the Subjects of History. Edited by the Commission on Theological Concerns of the Christian Conference of Asia, C. C. A., 1981, Zed Press, London.

Neale, S. *Genre*, British Film Institute, London, 1987.

Ogle, G. E. *South Korea: Dissent within the Economic Miracle*, Zed Press, London, 1990.

Sasse, W. "*Minjung* Theology and Culture", *Papers of the British Association for Korean Studies*, 1991, vol. 1, pp. 29–43.

Shapiro, M. *The Shadow in the Sun: A Korean Year of Love and Sorrow*, Atlantic Monthly Press, New York, 1990.

"South Korean Films." *The Economist*, July 13–19, 1985, vol. 296, no. 7402, pp. 79–87.

Spencer, R. F. *Yŏgong: Factory Girl*, Royal Asiatic Society, Korea Branch, Seoul Computer Press, 1988.

Todorov, T. *The Poetics of Prose*, Basil Blackwell, Oxford, 1977.

Wade, J. "The Cinema in Korea: A Robust Invalid," *Korea Journal*, vol. 9, no. 3, March 1969, pp. 5–12.

Williams, R. "Realism, Naturalism and Their Alternatives," *Explorations in Film Theory*, ed. R. Burnett. Indiana University Press, Bloomington, 1991.

6 | Melodramas of Korean National Identity

From *Mandala* to *Black Republic*

Rob Wilson

> To the others, these accounts are about (one more) distant land, like (any other) distant land, without any discernable features in the narrative, (all the same) distant like any other.
>
> —Theresa Hak Kyung Cha, *Dictee*

As THE REPUBLIC of South Korea enters kicking and screaming into the text-and-missile thick culture of the postmodern New World Order, films by Korean directors of the 1980s and 1990s can be experienced, even by cultural outsiders such as myself, as one of the crucial mediums by which the costs and gains of contemporary social transformations of country, city, location, and cultural identity can be measured. Although historically remote in thrust of political allegory or melodramatic in cinematic style and structures of feeling, such South Korean films are, like many films these days, staunchly about the will to national identity and express the class and gender struggles of the present age. Films by Im Kwon-Taek, Lee Doo-Yong, and Pak Kwang-su seek to articulate conflicts of contemporary history/modernity in some culture-specific sense as the vast Korean past (with its complex grip of Buddhist tradition and Confucian piety) haunts the Korean self and the future (interpreted as an ongoing process of "democratization") beckons with both unforeseen terrors (the nuclear threat and specter of socialism to the North) and pragmatic possibilities (the South as model of hightech export-driven economies across the Pacific Rim).

Despite a history of colonization, war, economic recovery, and the labor of three generations of area-studies experts in oriental knowledge, *Korea* remains a blank and unimagined space for most American readers, a vacancy or exotic name shore of specific history or cultural concern. "To the others, these accounts are about (one more) distant land, like (any other) distant land, without any discernible features in the narrative, (all the same) distant like any other" is how Theresa Hak Kyung Cha captures this disheartening sense of the First World's reduction of Korea to an exotic, oriental, and irrelevant vacancy when she published *Dictee* in 1982.[1]

Given a telematic world wherein the Berlin Wall has been dismantled and models of autocratic modernization and state-run socialism discredited, the post-Cold War fate of remaining a *divided* North/South Korea has weighed heavily upon the sensibility and style of emergent directors of this "New Seoul." I am speaking here of directors like Lee Doo-Yong, Im Kwon-Taek, Bae Chang-Ho, and Pak Kwang-su. These directors (just to name some of the more prominent) of what has been theorized as a "Third Golden Age" of Korean cinema struggle to remain unflinching in social imagination, finished in aesthetic style, if engagingly raw and vulgar in content. Whatever the lure of post-feminist cyborgs in Hollywood or spectacles of transnational sublimity in *Blade Runner, Terminator,* or *Robocop,* the future is something local Korean cinema helps to imagine forth and redeem in specific, unflinchingly social detail and national scope.[2]

It seems hard to deny that this fate of being a divided, two-nation, rivalry-ridden, and self-divided Korea from 1953 onward has played a part in the emergence of filmic visionaries of this new social order. Clinging, by necessity, to local artifacts and cultural icons of some "Korean" essence/difference to ward off neo-colonial pressures from Japan, China, the Soviet Union, or the United States (not to mention "self-reliant" pressures from the communist regime to the North), Korean directors beneath the DMZ have moved beyond pained isolation, cultural inferiority, or a lingering sense of international resentment to measure, in uncanny imagistic narratives, the brutality of patriarchal repression and social injustice at home if not to express, as well, a longing for national unity and global respect. Such desires for the "Korean" subject pervade spaces of domestic privacy and aesthetic creation, in film as in literature.

Indirectly about the political turmoil of this South Korean present, *Mandala* (1980) is a central Korean film by which to approach, in terms of narrative simplicity and iconic directness, this landscape of pained modernity. It is an uncanny Buddhist allegory of vast Asian vistas and all but cinematic perfection. I have seen Im Kwon-Taek's film four or five times at the International Film Festival at the East-West Center in Honolulu, where it is considered one of the most popular and intelligent films from contemporary East Asia ever to be shown there. The film follows the ascetic journey of Pobun, a young monk disillusioned with the worldliness of Seoul and even disgusted with the love of his own mother, as he journeys across Korea and meets the wizened Jeesan, a roguish monk of utterly worldly spiritual conviction. Im Kwon-Taek has managed to transform a novel of Buddhist life into an unforgettable allegory of contemporary Korean life with one moral imperative: to engage with or to reject the all-too-worldly world of sex, greed, ambition, desire, and conflict as a site of social redemption. Influenced more by Kurosawa than Hollywood, as he confided to me in an interview in Honolulu in 1987, Im Kwon-Taek has managed to achieve a masterwork of national focus, bleak urbanity, and troubled conscience that, I am sure, will have a wide and lasting circulation. This is one Korean film that may haunt and challenge viewers to the ends of our Late Capital earth, especially if Korean films are given more global video circulation in English translation (which regrettably, at this moment, they are not).

Pak Kwang-su represents this next, still-emerging generation of postmodern Korean directors. A film director whose career will be one to follow, especially as local Korean production goes global in distribution and importance, Park started his vocation by joining a film club and theater group when he was a student of art at Seoul National University. He helped to launch Korea's independent cinema movement when he co-founded the Seoul Film Collective in 1983 and, later, went on to study postmodern cinematography in France, Turkey, and Switzerland. He returned to Korea and worked as assistant director to Lee Jang-ho on such popular films as *A Baseball Team of Strangers* and *The Man with Three Coffins*.

In *The Black Republic* (1990), a film grounded in Korean cultural politics and the linkages between the student intellectual class and the working class struggle, Pak Kwang-su depicts the gritty journey of an urban runaway who, caught up in the student labor movement and subject to arrest under the authoritarian rule of the 1980s, seeks refuge in a coal mining village. Employed as a coal-brick factory worker, the alien Kim Ki-young meets a girl who labors in a coffee shop, but whose main job (due to relentless poverty) is prostitution. This girlfriend of the village gangster boss is soon attracted to our intellectual outsider, this sensitive soul. Still, the class struggle continues here, whatever the attractions of steamy sex and romantic evasion. In *The Black Republic* Pak Kwang-su deftly portrays the harsh reality of contemporary life in such mills and villages, such hemmed-in lives as that of Song Young-sook and the rural poor for whom Seoul offers little option or, alas, any redemption from their vulgar dreams. The film is bleak, but the imagery remains haunting, fresh, grounded in the late capitalist deformation of Korea.

Producing films of singular imagination and global/local engagement such as *Ch'il-su wa Man-su* (1988), which deals with the impossible class rebellion of two whiskey-sign painters high over the demo-ridden streets of Seoul,[3] Park suggests that South Korean film can now move in more open, if not defiantly romantic directions that will come to terms with the post-Cold War present.

During the 1970s and early 1980s, the production of Korean film—increasingly one of the dominant genres of cultural self-imagining within postmodern societies—has not been slow to register these psychic shocks and pressures of modernization upon its characters, plots, thematic polarities, and available store of techniques, as the films of Lee Doo-Yong, Pak Kwang-su, and Im Kwon-Taek testify. As a social apparatus assuming all-but-unconscious control over public consciousness through shifting images and narratives of political subjectivity, film can be scrutinized in local and global contexts and decoded as a multivoiced genre of national self-reflection.

First, a large-scale disclaimer on my part: my comments on South Korean film only apply to a limited time-frame and only to a core of internationally distributed Korean films. My comments will be fractured as well by the trans-cultural poetics of a first-world North American whose sublimated market-dynamics and transnational capitalogic at all points would contest the emergence of countries of the Asia/Pacific into the New World Order of shopping mall co-prosperity and the liberating free-world dynamics of commodified desire. From 1982, when I went to live and teach in Korea for some two years, until 1987, the year a retrospective on Korean films was held at the East-West Center and a new president was elected in Korea, this is the time-frame of my analysis. This period roughly corresponds to the consolidating reign of President Chun Doo-won (now doing penance in a Buddhist monastery for oppressive and financial wrongs against the South Korean people), whose Korean Performing Arts Ethics committee, for example, included a Cinema Censorship Board composed of four KCIA members and other aesthetic-minded government officials.

To delimit such an analysis at the outset, I would cite a personal anecdote that, while about poetic/cultural interpretation, may tell us something larger about the Korean approach to coding/interpreting films as negotiations of national identity. In the fall of 1984, while teaching a graduate course in American literature at Korea University in Seoul, I turned from a close textual reading of Robert Frost's poem "For Once, Then, Something," about a metaphor-making New Englander looking into a well to see a self-glorified image of himself and, beyond that, to puzzle out the Emersonian connections between nature and God, to a poem called "Self-Portrait" by Yun Tong-ju (1917–1945). This Korean nature poem also contained a well and tracked the spectatorial dynamics of a puzzled male self in it—or so I thought. The Korean poem reads, in English translation by Peter Lee, the poet-scholar who first connected me to the cultural poetics of Korea:

> I go round the foot of the mountain seeking a lone well by
>   the field, to look into it without words.
> In the well the moon is bright, clouds flow, sky spreads
>   open, a blue wind blows, and there is autumn.
> Also, a young man is in the well. Hating him I turn away.
>   But as I go on I come to pity him.
> When I return and look into the well again, that young man
>   is still there. I start to hate him again and turn
>   away. But as I go on, I come to long for him.

In the well the moon is bright, clouds flow, sky spreads
   open, the blue wind blows, autumn reigns, a young man
   stands there.[4]

Making cross-cultural analogies to the transcendental metaphysics of Robert Frost, whom Korean students know through translations in their high school anthologies, I theorized Yun's temporal progression beyond self-division toward identity and self-wholeness—a post-Hegelian plot of the soul. The Korean students grinned immediately and weren't at all buying it. One of the older students chimed in, "But, professor, every Korean knows that this poem is not about Yun Tong-ju, really, it's about the fate of Korea during the time of the Japanese occupation." The mingled self-hatred and self-division the poet expressed were, I came to see, signs of Korea's historical division and colonial torment: the self of the poet was used to stage an implied geopolitical allegory of colonization and (displaced) historical resitance—a Korean strategy I will return to in an analysis of films by director Lee Doo-Yong.

   The Korean plight of nation-state modernization and state control is memorably portrayed, to invoke another literary example, in Hwang Chiu's contemporary poem, "Even the Birds Are Leaving the World":[5]

Before the film begins
We all stand up for our national anthem.
On Ŭlsuk Island
In the "Splendid Land of Three Thousand *Ri*,"
A flock of white birds
Leaving the field of reeds
Fly in one, two, three files,
Honking, giggling,
Carrying their own world,
Separating their world from ours,
To some place beyond this world.
I wish we could fly off too,
Giggling, crackling,
Forming a file,
Carrying our world
To some place beyond this world.
But with "preserve forever the integrity of Korea to Koreans"
We sit down,
Sinking into our seats.

Shorn of Korean social context, Chiu's poem would appear insular, self-absorbed, remote. The poem articulates a politicized landscape of engagement and withdrawal, as staged during President Chun's reign in 1983, which might seem weirdly other, at first, to readers chastened to formality or beholden to First-World narratives of lyric redemption.

Tastes are shifting both locally and globally, however, in effect recontextualizing the way we experience the literature and culture of (post)modernity. "As Korea approaches the end of the century," literary critic Peter Lee urges, "the continued production of a literature of engagement and relevance attests to the resilience, strength, and tenacity of modern Korean writers" within a fast-changing postmodern world.[6] Chiu's poem measures the ironies, and costs, of existential claims to survive as a culture within a nation of rival economies and polities, a nation divided by the very Cold War binary of domination/freedom we seemingly cannot move beyond.

Embracing culture-specific landscapes and a history of displacement, Korean culture needs to be situated as a conjunction of local, national, and global forces. If "Korean writing in the twentieth century has been obsessively political," as U-chang Kim has outlined in "Art and Politics in Korea,"[7] these very pressures of Cold War geopolitics (experienced as the demonized binary of communism and capitalism, for example) are felt by poets and film makers to pervade the local cinema, as the pathos or metaphysics of nature "carrying [its] own world," while the national anthem gets used (here by President Chun in the South) to interpellate cultural difference, not to mention routine gestures and submissive desires of a rural audience "sinking into our seats." There abides no other world in which Korea can be preserved, except within the tormented world of geopolitics this little country of Ŭlsuk Island is caught up in. Worldly even in its other-worldliness, South Korean culture might well long for what U-chang Kim would project as a release from Korea's "ideological overload" just as American postmodernity, for decades lost in mirrors of domesticated subjectivity, lyric solipsism, and nature-worship, might well want to seek its long-delayed politicization.

By most measures, post-war South Korea has given way to a "New Seoul," which is more than just a sprawling complex of dense high-rises and kalbi houses south of the Han River. The impact of rapid industrialization and glitzy Western lifestyles has created large-scale disturbances upon older, more agrarian-based ways of life and value in South Korea as well as upon modes of aesthetic representation. (The sign of this on tv melodramas is typically a woman smoking in a nightclub, say, Wine & Roses, to suggest all kinds of potential freedoms and Western degenerations.) As Hagen Koo, Professor of Sociology at the University of Hawaii, claimed in a recent study of the expanding middle-class lifestyle, "It's not simply a success story. It (economic growth) created many problems, a lot of social tensions, social conflicts."[8]

In 1985, Lee Doo-Yong's graphic portrayal in *Spinning Wheel* (*Mulleya Mulleya* [1984]) of a woman's subjugated life during the Yi Dynasty created a storm of controversy at the Fifth International Film Festival of Honolulu even before it was shown. A Screening Committee at the East-West Center found the work objectionable on sexist grounds, as if Lee's depiction of the heroine Gilrye's rape by a Confucian scholar was not only sensationalist but also potentially offensive to mild-mannered American filmgoers. (Sensationalism, visceral excess, or at least a deep-rooted sentimentality for the reign of moral opposites seems to afflict Korean films at the core, as the major Korean film critic Ahn Byung-Sup has admitted.[9])

Yet as one flabbergasted defender in the Honolulu Varsity Theatre audience pointed out in a public discussion with Director Lee afterwards, "I find it amazing that an American audience so used to enjoying violent and sex-crazed movies like *Rambo* or *To Live and Die in LA* can be offended by this Korean film, which in my opinion shows such an extraordinary empathy to women that at first I thought it was made by a woman!" Bluntly put, was the Korean movie director endorsing the male gaze of patriarchal domination or empathizing, through the characterization of Gilrye, with the subjugated viewpoint of a muted, violated woman's critique?

Even after the South Korean film was shown, its imagery of feminine subjugation during the Confucian patriarchy of daily life polarized the audience into viewers who felt that Lee's grasp of injustices large and small shows an incredible sensitivity to women and, more obliquely, speaks to the ongoing condition of the South Korean woman today. But detractors of the film objected that its portrayal was shocking, vulgar, extreme, a kind of sensationalist indulgence in stock imagery of sex and violence, from which Gilrye's suicide comes, finally, as a merciful release. In Im Kwon-Taek's *Come, Come, Come Upward* (*Aje aje bara aje* [1989]), not one but two Buddhist nuns are raped as they trek forth magnanimously into the fallen world of *samsara*, making a series of Korean males (from a disturbed coal miner to a hospital medic, a student, and a lone monk) look like selfish, brutal, disturbed, lost souls, whom not even the love of indestructible women can save from destruction. At a certain point in the movie, as a Buddhist nun recounts her tale of attempts to save a series of mindless and legless men, the audience both gasped and moaned, and some applauded with relief as the medic dropped dead after an all-night sex session.

Such polarized responses can be read not only as signs of generic melodrama, with scapegoated innocence working finally to reinforce a patriarchal culture's moral binaries. Such responses also serve as after-effects of the way *Spinning Wheel* is compelled to resort to a code that *allegorizes* back into a space of past history to speak to a present which, given the less than open condition of Korean censorship, is often shackled from direct expression. Working within a quasi-repressive national discourse, this allegorization of remote-but-present history has become a major cultural technique in South Korean fiction and literature, as well as in its developing film industry. Esther C. M. Yau has called attention to the way contemporary Chinese films like Chen Kaige's *Yellow Earth* (1985) and *The Black Cannon Incident* (1985) present "powerful, and often displaced, critiques" of Chinese culture and state ideology as a way of circumventing the Film Bureau's censorship rather then fantasmatically bypassing some Freudian censor—that is, the Western libido and family reified into generic universality; and this phenomenon of allegorical displacement and political coding needs to be taken into consideration, I think, when assessing contemporary South Korean films.[10]

The larger claim that Third World literature, as it emerges from global processes of industrial modernization into the more hybrid and polyvocal waters of the postindustrial/postmodern, will typically code into its imagery of emerging strong selfhood/imagined community an *allegory* of national identity-formation has been worked out within a world-system framework of domination/liberation by Fredric Jameson.[11] Jameson's examples are drawn from China, Cuba, and Africa and though he makes no mention of South Korea, his master narrative of domination and resistance is often very much—if implicitly—at work in various Korean films, poems, and novels which do seem scarcely concerned with orgasmic quests for "self." As Ahn Byung-Sup, author of *History of Korean Cinema*, summarizes the 1980s as represented by the films of Lee and Im Kwon-Taek, "Strong nationalism and a sense of identity dominated cultural activities, and there were strong efforts in every field to preserve the old and discover cultural roots."[12] Nation-making provided an abiding subtext.

To point to just one of Lee's invocations of social allegory, the portrayal of the corrupt and brutal *yangban*, as a Confucian scholar who rapes the married Gilrye and drinks himself silly while reading moral scriptures, satirizes cultural mores in a radical way, as happened in traditional *p'ansori* ("one-man opera") melodramas.[13] In effect, the film undermines that all-too-Korean code of venerability whereby, even today, Korean teachers (*paksanim*) are afforded the automatic cultural respect of bowing and deference, based upon a class distinction which assumes intrinsic moral purity on the part of the elder or the socially superior. The underside of such enforced piety is pugnacious brutality, a lifelong resentment (*han*) clamoring to be heard—or at the very least, *displaced*. Yet, in the 1980s, even post-Mao China turned to "New Seoul" to serve as modernization model for technocratic emergence as well as a culture of pious silence best administered, top-down, with white kid-gloves. More openness has to emerge simultaneously, as it were, on the melodramatic quietness of the postmodern screen.

A no less brutal, melodramatic, and shocking example of the Korean will to national identity is shown in Bae Chang-Ho's *Deep Blue Night* (1985), which uses Green Card-seeking Korean emigrants to a weirdly hyper-decadent Southern California to allegorize—rather luridly, I think—deep-rooted racist/nationalist tendencies that are emerging in Seoul within a volatile climate of "anti-Americanism." Will the influx of postmodern culture disrupt existing myths and forces of nationalism; or, on a more strictly aesthetic level, disturb reactionary currents of cultural chauvinism? Some have claimed, for example, that Bae Chang-Ho has already become a kind of Woody Allen depicting romantic sentiments and male/female career-quests afflicting consumers of the "New Seoul"; in other words, that Bae has turned from the tenderly liberal politics of *People in a Slum* (1982) to articulate the hedonistic, banal, largely harmless college-boy sentiments of *Our Sweet Days of Youth* (1987).[14]

Hardly evasive, Lee's filmic imagery implies a commentary on bland cultural assumptions, suggesting that the pure scholar (Confucian father-figure) is part of a sanctimonious profession which is (like corporate leaders today) quietly responsible for the patriarchal subjection of women. Confronting such a patriarchy, Gilrye's only free act is in the choice of her own suicide, not by the Fidelity Knife but by her own mode of hanging, in the film's haunting final image. The melodrama of Gilrye, in other words, implies the drama of Korean women in New Seoul, displaced, coded with tears, cicadas, and the silence of historical distance and national critique.

In *First Son* (*Changnam* [1984]), Lee depicts the problem of a contemporary family's eviction from the once pastoral countryside, and shows to disturbing effect the fast-paced, indifferent, routinized, and atomizing life of apartments in New Seoul has upon father and mother, as well as upon sons who can no longer live up to traditional expectations. (Why the family had moved into the city was hard to understand in the English version of the film, which mysteriously omitted to translate the crucial detail that the government was putting in a dam and displacing the family from its native village, adding to their sense of bewildered disorientation.) The final scene in which the father's casket is lowered down by pulleys from the "first son's" claustrophobic apartment and bangs against the wall and almost drops, passes a mute malediction on the architecture—and blithe inhumanity—of Seoul's modernization from country community to urban solitude.

As I learned from conversations with Mr. Lee on his visit to Hawaii in 1985 for the showing of *Spinning Wheel*, Lee carefully researchs indigenous filmic symbols—its shaman tree, its fidelity knife, its white clothing, its stratified village architecture—so that *Spinning Wheel* manifests a seamless sheen of landscape and village beauty which is played off against the moral horrors the plot and characterization reveal. As in *The Mulberry Leaves* (*Pong* [1986]), set during the Japanese occupation and affirming both love and resistance, Lee has other films of Korea that fall into this genre of historical allegory which comment on the contemporary through images of the ancient. At that time, Lee was working on a movie partly set at Schoffield Army Base in Honolulu, which we drove around in sleepy Wahiawa, as if through a time warp movie set remaining from

From Here To Eternity, with its little Korean bars, Seoul Inns, and spunky women often brutalized by American military husbands who get angered at the Dumbo muteness of their "Oriental blossoms."

The Honolulu response when a Chinese film (*Yellow Earth*) was afforded first prize and the Korean film was ignored was not politically unexpected, given the emergent alliance between post-socialist China and the Republican master narrative of the State Department. But it was atypical of the international response. The film has garnered international prizes at Cannes and at Chicago. A friend who enjoyed *Yellow Earth* said that the Chinese film, while striking in cinematography, did not confront the theme of women's sexual maturation or gender oppression in Asia, which by contrast *Spinning Wheel* confronts head on in a way that even cauterized American filmgoers can find shocking as rape follows upon rape, blow upon blow, complaint upon complaint.

As perennial fans of the East-West Center's International Film Festival have realized, Korea has a resource in the filmic imagination of Lee Doo-Yong, who threatens (with Im Kwon-Taek of *Mandala* fame) to become the Korean Kurowsawa of indigenous thematics and an international style: an artist who can make it on the international scene and bring global respect to the developing Korean film industry. I would not want to see the government hinder this symbolic resource. If the film industry of post-Chun Korea can give such cultural workers in film enough money, time, relative *autonomy* (that journalistic code word for "freedom of speech"), South Korea will have narratives representing its past and speaking to its democratizing present.

Registering the shocks of daily life in films like *First Son* and the pain of Cold War division in *Kilsottum,* cultural arts such as film and poetry, as much as the industrial works and megachips of Daewoo Industry, play an important part in shaping the sensibility and values of a more pragmatic, open, less tradition-obssessed "New Seoul."

What about the cultural construction of national melodrama within Korean films? Does it emerge from within the Hollywood paradigm of ego-identity as formed within family conflicts, a basically oedipal framework of melodrama—what Roland Barthes has termed the subjective "dialectic of tenderness and hatred"?[15] Or must more culture-specific, indigenous factors be taken into consideration to grasp the visceral excess and emotive indulgence of Korean films?

Arguing that "in Korean cinema, sentimentalism is more prevalent than humor" (90), Ahn Byung-Sup traces this deep-rooted melodramatic tendency to two indigenous factors: (a) what might be called the *han* factor, that is, a sensibility of resentment, longing, envy, spite, or "a frame of mind characterized by a sorrowful lament" and sense of tragic resignation that has long been associated with the Korean national character by Koreans themselves; and (b), what might be here called the *colonial* factor, the polarized emotion, eternal sense of political victimization, and moral simplification resulting from a subaltern history of "experiencing pessimism, frustration, and resignation caused by the Japanese occupation" (95). A powerful expression of this culturally rooted sense of *han* takes place, for example, at the conclusion of Pak Kwang-su's *Chilsu and Mansu* (*Ch'il-su wa Man-su* [1988]) as the romantic and class resentments of Chilsu (who dreams of marrying a college girlfriend, despite his low status, and taking his artistic talents to America) mingle with the political and class resentments of Mansu, whose father remains a political prisoner. They stage a dadaesque protest of drunken rage and grief high over Seoul, having painted a billboard for Glamour Whiskey. Chilsu may dream of going to America and procuring a fast, new life in Miami Beach, but America is already in South Korea as the lifestyle of the commodified breasts he paints to make a living suggests.

This will to express melodramas of national identity and traumas of national community grows out of conflicts of Korean history as much as out of nativist sensibility or the formal traits of an international cinematic genre like "melodrama." Formalist, or more strictly cine-psychoanalytical analysis, will take us only so far into understanding national melodrama, which needs to be situated within culture-specific historical contexts that make the local speak to the global rather than the reverse.[16]

Even in the everyday practice of looking into a well, a South Korean may not see just himself—or, of course, *herself*—but some aspect of Korea, imagined into emergence, coded with sentiment if not displaced from the tech-thick future (postmodernity) into an enchanted past (the mystique of a precapitalist space when Koreans were still unified and as one).[17]

Postmodern culture as it goes transnational threatens to become a promiscuously hybrid collage of cultures, styles, voices, and narratives shorn of affect, local placement, or historical depth. As cultural narratives free themselves from claims to history, turn fictive and undermine fundamental claims to truth-status, this avant-gardist death (if not hyper-production) of narrative may be symptomatic less of generic exhaustion and more of a larger social crisis of mimetic contagion. The soft imposition of commodity-logic and technologies of irreality on a triumphantly global scale at times makes critique or resistance seemed doomed to capitulation, or at best to recapitulation of Late Capital's cultural logic and market processes. But the local remains a space of resistance and possibility.

My own take on the intertextual terrain of postmodern crosscultural poetics, *Waking In Seoul* (1988), was pitched to be a work of romantic pilgrimage, in Edward Said's cautionary sense of this hyper-textual Western cultural genre, wherein orientalist constructions of "Korea" are evoked, foregrounded, collaged, embodied, and undermined by active encounter and dialogue with a polity and culture that are absent from the foci of American poetics. As a miscellany comprising "lyric reportage," the poetic travelog aimed to evoke a surplus or *excess* of ordinary and poetic language that would, at times anyway, elude the reductions and stereotypes of "orientalist discourse" while at other times the self/other would be subjected to these prior sets of Western distortions, cliches, images, half-truths, and exotic myths that maintain power imbalances and ideological mystifications of East/West. Such languages would evoke the myriad interactions (politicized, imaginary, private, arbitrary, idealized, unofficial and so on) taking place between the asymmetrical cultures of President Chun's "Korea" and President Reagan's "America."[18] Poetry warps power games.

What melodramas remain at the end of history, so to speak, when the Third World has all but dissolved into the capitalogic and specular theories of the First? What strategies of local/national resistance can be circulated when a Marxian cultural critic like Aijaz Ahmad can only marshall the socialism of Second World Pakistan and nonaligned tactics of multicultural India to do counter-hegemonic battle against the first-world postmodernity model itself, seen as a totalizing "cultural logic of late capital" disseminated by First World theorists no longer nostalgic for a narrative of national emergence or linked, in any palpable way, to working-class resistance?[19] Furthermore, residual institutions of orientalist knowledge, transformed into policies and tactics of area-studies management during the postwar era of American hegemony, may still subtend the idealism of any such "American Orientalist" engagement, however idealized and good willed.[20]

Contemporary South Korean films, in the grittiness of their local struggles and complications of their national situation of emulation and isolation, would suggest local ways for contemporary film culture to keep emerging on the full and by now global terrain of *difference*. Korean films allow viewers from outside cultures to get a deeper historical look into the Korean soul and its torments: torn as it seemingly is by subaltern history, geopolitical forces, if not factions of class resentment (*han*) emerging, dialectically, from passional regions within the divided country that remains "Korea" North and South.

Notes

1. Theresa Hak Kyung Cha, *Dictee* (New York: Tanam, 1982), p. 33.

2. On American cyborg spectacles and the Hollywood manipulation of local spaces and times of the transnational Pacific Rim, see Rob Wilson, "Cyborg America: Policing the Social Sublime in *Robocop I* and *II*," in Richard Burt, ed., *The Administration of Aesthetics: Censorship, Political Criticism, and the Public Sphere* (Minneapolis: University of Minnesota Press, 1994).

3. For a more sustained reading of class resentments and romantic longings in this rather amazing film and the way films by Lee Doo-Yong confront, by historical displacement, struggles of contemporary South Korea, see Rob Wilson, "Filming the 'New Seoul': Reflections on Lee Doo-Yong's *Spinning Wheel & First Son*," *Korean Culture* 11 (Fall 1990): 36–41, which builds upon the Korean film criticism of Ahn Byung-Sup, Ha-il Kim, Roan Williams, Bae Chang-Ho, and Walter Lew, as well as postmodern film theorists such as Gilles Deleuze and Fredric Jameson. Also see *East-West Film Journal* for diverse essays on South Korean film in its full global/local emergence, a problematic idealistically touched

upon by Ahn Byung-Sup in "Globalism is Humanism—Localism and Globalism in Korean Cinema," talk presented at the East-West Center in Honolulu at the 1992 International Film Festival.

4. Peter H. Lee, ed., *Silence of Love: Twentieth-Century Korean Poetry* (Honolulu: University of Hawaii Press, 1980), p. 81.

5. *Modern Korean Literature: An Anthology*, Peter H. Lee, ed. (Honolulu: University of Hawaii Press, 1990), p. 308.

6. Ibid., p. xxii.

7. *Manoa* 2 (Fall, 1990): 41–47. On the Korean geopolitical situation, also see Paik Nak-chung's interview with Fredric Jameson in *Global/Local: Cultural Production in the Transnational Imaginary* (forthcoming, Duke University Press), ed. Rob Wilson and Wimal Dissanayake.

8. Hagen Koo, "The Emerging Class Order and Social Conflict in South Korea," *Pacific Focus* 2 (1987): 95–112. Tactics by which this "New Seoul" has been melodramatically inflected in Korean films are traced by the Korean film maker, Bae Chang-Ho, in "Seoul in Korean Cinema: A Brief Survey," *East-West Film Journal* 3 (1988): 97–104. On the tendency, within industrializing countries, to allegorize the rural-urban opposition in stark, moralistic terms, as in Lee Doo-Yong's *First Son*, see Raymond Williams, *The Country and the City* (New York: Oxford University Press, 1973), Chapter 19, "Cities of Darkness and Light."

9. See the cultural generalizations and all but essentializing characterizations of Korean national identity by the South Korean film critic, Ahn Byung-Sup, on "Humor in Korean Film," *East-West Film Journal* 2 (1987): 90–98.

10. For an analysis of allegorical displacements in Asian film, see Esther C. M. Yau, "Cultural and Economic Dislocations: Filmic Phantasies of Chinese Women in the 1980's," *Wide Angle* 11 (1989): 6–21, especially p. 10; and Fredric Jameson's decoding of magical realism in the Filipino film *The Perfumed Nightmare* (1977) by Kidlat Tahimak as an allegory of neocolonial oppression: "allegory seems to depend on just such indirection and systematic displacement from one level to another. In the present instance, the allegorical 'substitute' is in fact American imperialism (itself the cause and origin of the Marcos regime), inscribed mythically," *The Geopolitical Aesthetic: Cinema and Space in the World System* (London: BFI Publishing, 1992), p. 191. Allegory works especially well under state regimes of film production, if not under the more sublimated capitalogic apparatus of Hollywood-generated film codes and cultural norms.

11. Fredric Jameson, "Third-World Literature in the Era of Multinational Capitalism," *Social Text* 15 (1986): 65–88.

12. Ahn Byung-Sup, "Humor in Korean Cinema," pp. 93–94.

13. On melodramatic structures of feeling and formulaic traits of Korean *p'ansori*, an indigenous form of opera central to Korean folk culture and influential on Korean sensibility, I am indebted to Marshall R. Pihl, "P'ansori: The Korean Oral Narrative," paper presented at Conference on Korean Literary History, University of Hawaii, 1981. On tactics of mimetic emulation and colonial mimicry of foreign subjectivity, see Homi K. Bhabha, "Location, Intervention, Incommensurability: A Conversation," *Emergences* 1 (Fall 1989): 63–88.

14. See Roan Williams's reading of Bae's *Our Sweet Days of Youth* (1987), "The Best of the Hawai'i International Film Festival" catalogue, 1987, p. 5. On aesthetic traits by which "the legacy of historical sorrow is present in [Korean] melancholy and fatalism," see Walter Lew, "Desire and Melancholia: Unobscure in Seoul Cinema," *Bridge: Asian American Perspectives* (Summer 1983): 36–38. On tactics of displacement in Korean-American filmmaker and novelist-poet Theresa Hak Kyung Cha, see her collection *Apparatus: Cinematographic Apparatus, Selected Writings* (New York: Tanam, 1980); Walter K. Lew,

Dikte for 'Dictee' (Seoul: Yeul Eum Pub. Co., 1992); and Rob Wilson, "Falling Into the Korean Uncanny: On Reading Teresa Hak Kyung Cha's *Dictee*," *Korean Culture* 12 (Fall 1991): 33–37.

15. On refigurings of this oedipal genre into the pathos of feminist critiques, see Robert Lang, *American Film Melodrama: Griffith, Vidor, Minnelli* (Princeton: Princeton University Press, 1989), p. 70. Barthes's comment is from *The Pleasure of the Text*, trans. Richard Miller (New York: Hill and Wang, 1975), p. 47, and reads in full: "If there is no longer a Father, why tell stories? Doesn't every narrative lead back to Oedipus? Isn't storytelling always a way of searching for one's origin, speaking one's conflicts with the Law, entering into the dialectic of tenderness and hatred?" Without understanding "the unconscious of different cultures as it might pertain to the level of the imaginary," however, must we oedipalize Asian films in order to interpret them? See E. Ann Kaplan, "Problematizing Cross-Cultural Analysis: The Case of Women in the Recent Chinese Cinema," *Wide Angle* 11 (1989): 40–50; and Esther C. M. Yau, "*Yellow Earth*: Western Analysis and a Non-western Text," *Film Quarterly* 41 (1987–88): 22–33 for related critiques.

16. Given mounting anti-American sentiments if not the transnational globalization of "the ideology of consumer-culture," as outlined in Leslie Sklair, *Sociology of the Global System* (Baltimore: Johns Hopkins University Press, 1991), one must wonder whether Americans will not increasingly play the role of postmodern neo-colonial 'villain' in future Korean melodramas. This happens in Bae Chang-Ho's daemonization of blacks and business people from Los Angeles (if not the whole USA) in *Deep Blue Night*. For an analysis of this geopolitical shift away from American models towards the love/hate of Japanese cultural and economic models, see Jinwung Kim, "Recent Anti-Americanism in South Korea: The Causes," *Asian Survey* 29 (1989): 749–63.

17. On the geopolitics of American/South Korean border crossings and symbolic imbalances in cross-cultural dialogue, see Rob Wilson, "Theory's Imaginal Other: American Encounters with South Korea and Japan," *boundary 2* 18 (1991): 220–41, which aims to shift the Eurocentric focus of American poetics toward representing this repressed Korean terrain where the United States, as a government, military state, and globalizing economy had been involved since World War II as Cold War superpower. New genres of cultural politics are needed.

18. Rob Wilson, *Waking In Seoul* (Seoul: Mineumsa Press; Honolulu, University of Hawaii Press, 1988).

19. See the trenchantly situated critiques of global-postmodernity models like Jameson's offered for Third World emulation in Aijaz Ahmad, *In Theory: Classes, Nations, Literatures* (New York: Verso, 1992), especially chapters 1 through 3; as well as the complexly articulated cultural politics of filmic emergence, given a contemporary situation where the local increasingly inflects and challenges the global, theorized in *Questions of Third Cinema*, Jim Pines and Paul Willemen, eds. (London: British Film Institute, 1989) and *Public Culture* on global/local disjunctions.

20. See Edward Said, *Orientalism* (New York: Random House, 1978), pp. 166–97, on British and French literary experiments to represent the Orient as "less a place than a *topos*, a set of references, a congeries of characteristics that seems to have its origin in a quotation, or a fragment of a text, or a citation from someone's work on the Orient, or some bit of previous imagining, or an amalgam of all of these."

Concerning the social-science orientation and missionary unconscious of postwar "American Orientalism" Said would remind us: "Genealogically speaking, American Orientalism derives from such things as the army language schools established during and after the war, sudden government and corporate interest in the non-Western world during the postwar period, Cold War competition with the Soviet Union, and a residual missionary attitude towards Orientals who are considered ripe for reform and reeducation" (291).

In this era of the Asian/Pacific knowledge boom and a hypercapitalist turn toward Pacific Rim area studies, Americans need to be reminded of this Cold War frame which may linger and deform the postmodern era: see Arif Dirlik and Rob Wilson, eds., "Asia/Pacific as Space of Cultural Production," special issue of *boundary* 2 21 (Spring 1994) for essays that would move beyond the disciplinary frames of Cold War knowledge, especially Christopher Connery, "Pacific Rim Discourse: The U.S. Global Imaginary in the Late Cold War Years"; and Arif Dirlik, ed., *What Is in a Rim?: The Pacific Region Idea* (Boulder, Colorado: Westview Press, 1993).

7 | Vietnamese Cinema
First Views
John Charlot

Vietnamese cinema has only recently become known outside of the East Bloc countries.[1] The first public showing of a Vietnamese feature film in the United States was that of *When the Tenth Month Comes* at the 1985 Hawaii International Film Festival in Honolulu.[2] At the 1987 Festival, a consortium of American film institutions was formed with Nguyen Thu, General Director of the Vietnam Cinema Department, to organize the Vietnam Film Project—the first attempt to introduce an entire new film industry to America.[3] The purpose of this chapter is to provide a brief description of Vietnamese cinema along with an appreciation of its major characteristics and themes. I base my views on my two visits to the Vietnam Cinema Department in Hanoi—for one week in 1987 and two in 1988—on behalf of the Hawaii International Film Festival. During those visits, I was able to view a large number of documentaries and feature films and to discuss Vietnamese cinema with a number of department staff members. I was able to obtain more interviews during the visits of Vietnamese to the Hawaii International Film Festival in Honolulu.[4] This chapter cannot claim to be an adequate introduction to the history of Vietnamese cinema, a task I hope will be undertaken with the aid of my informants and the sources I list as completely as possible. I am able to provide a sketch of Vietnamese cinema at the end of the 1980s, a particularly important period for the industry as well as for the nation. The people I met were at the cutting edge of Vietnamese *glasnost*, using their prestigious positions as artists to win greater freedom of expression and to support a nationwide rethinking of history and society. That process continues today, and the trends I describe toward openness and critical independence have reportedly intensified over the last years. My chapter reflects generally the view that the Vietnamese gave me of themselves and their work, a view supported by the films they showed me and the general impressions I received.

For many of the Vietnamese I met, I was their "first American." I had never been to Vietnam, but the country was naturally filled with emotional associations for me. Almost immediately, my hosts and I began to communicate with unusual directness and intensity. I felt they were people who had experienced so much that they no longer had time for pretence and maneuvering. They on their side were anxious for me to be perfectly frank with them because they had so few opportunities to hear foreign evaluations of their work. By the end of my first visit, we had formed friendships that have continued despite the distance between us. We had also established a stimulating intellectual relationship. At the end of my first visit to Hanoi, my hosts asked me to speak to the Cinema Department about their work; the entire presentation with discussion took over two hours. Since then, we have exchanged writings and mutual criticisms, which we have been free to accept or reject. For instance, the director Dang Nhat Minh told me that my view of the alienation theme in *The Lamp in the Dream* is excessively Western; I countered that he did not see the full originality of that work.

An adequate evaluation of Vietnamese cinema will need to be based on a larger program of research. This chapter is a first look by a Westerner, an American, who was provided with a special opportunity to experience Vietnamese cinema at a key moment in its history.

The Vietnam Cinema Department

Cinema was introduced to Vietnam in 1910 by the French colonists, and films from France, the United States, and Hong Kong were distributed mostly in the urban areas. Documentary footage of Vietnam was taken by various individuals and organizations, and a number of feature films were made starting in the 1920s with local French and Chinese capital. Some Vietnamese made short films with a nationalist thrust, but Vietnamese film historians currently trace their cinema back to a newsreel of Ho Chi Minh's declaration of independence on September 2, 1945, filmed by a French amateur (incorporated into the 1975 documentary *Independence Day 1945*). A number of documentaries were subsequently produced, some of which were screened abroad. The State Enterprise for Photography and Motion Picture was established on March 15, 1953, by a decree signed by Ho Chi Minh. Several short documentaries were released that year, followed in 1954 by the major, five-reel *Dien Bien Phu*.[5] The first feature film, *On the Same River*, was released in 1959. Production was naturally sparse during the war years, but now averages twenty feature films a year.

The Vietnam Cinema Department was founded in 1956 and placed under the Ministry of Culture. Its main institutions are the two feature film studios in Hanoi and Ho Chi Minh City and the Documentary and Scientific Films Studio in Hanoi. Recently, a third feature film studio has been founded under Hoan Tich Chi. The department also manages an animated cartoon studio, technical enterprises, film distribution, and import and export. Its Vietnam Cinema School was merged with the Hanoi College of Dramatic Art and Cinema at the University of Hanoi, also under the Ministry of Culture. The Vietnam Film Archives are also placed under that Ministry. Three other film units are outside the Ministry.[6]

The department has undergone a number of changes over the years. I will describe its procedures, as I observed them in Hanoi. The salient problem is its lack of funds.[7] Vietnam is one of the five poorest countries in the world, and staffers have been told by foreign filmmakers that they are laboring under perhaps the worst conditions anywhere. The department is housed in some converted brick buildings. Equipment is antiquated and scarce. At one point, sound mixing was being done in a car. This naturally limits the types of films that can be made. Battle footage, for instance, is big-budget. For one movie, since airplane models were too expensive, cameramen were sent out to film real air battles! The greater part of a feature film budget is spent on materials, which must be paid for in precious foreign currency.[8] So little film stock is available that the shooting ratio can be as low as one to two-and-a-half, although it rises occasionally to six or seven. The overuse of the zoom lens in some movies may be due to the fact that it is one of the very few effects available. The high technical quality of Vietnamese films is remarkable in view of the limitations to be surmounted. Hai Ninh, Director of the Feature Film Studio in Hanoi, stated in an interview, "We can't make poor films because we're poor. We have to achieve international standards."

Salaries are low as they are throughout Vietnam. A major star can receive up to the equivalent of US $1,200.00 per picture. Tra Giang, the top female star in Vietnam, leaves work on the back of a friend's bicycle. Staff can but need not belong to the Vietnam Cinematography Association, which reportedly is most active in establishing relations with colleagues in East Bloc countries. The highest officials of the department are reportedly members of the Communist Party, but no pressure is apparently applied to others to join. One prominent director joined only after the current liberalization had begun. All those I have met, however, are fervent Vietnamese nationalists, whatever their criticisms of aspects of the current regime.

The number of theatres in Vietnam has grown from two hundred forty-two theatres in 1983 to eight hundred halls and twelve hundred open-air venues, serviced by over 2,000 cinematographic units, the majority mobile. Low prices encourage attendance. "70% of the films screened are from abroad, mainly from the Socialist countries."[9] For rare screenings of American films, tickets could fetch high prices on the black market. Recently strong competition has begun to be felt from television, especially official and unofficial (now illegal) VCR theatres at which pirated or illegally imported videotapes are often shown.[10] The government has had little success in regulating the private and even public circulation and use of videotapes. A recent trend, reported by Neil Gibson, is to show them at small, dimly lit *gia khat* "refreshment cafes," which cater mainly to young couples.

Government and Filmmakers

Filmmaking in Vietnam is clearly a government enterprise, but the impact this exercises on the films themselves is variable and not easily defined. Government influence has not had the oppressive and retardative effect found before the recent, pre-crackdown period in the People's Republic of China.[11] The major reason for this seems to be that all the directors of the pertinent government agencies are themselves artists. The Vice Minister in charge of culture and the arts is Dr. Nguyen Dinh Quang, theatre director, writer, and professor of drama. The top management of the Vietnam Cinema Department is composed without exception of filmmakers.

In fact, the filmmakers at lower levels seem to feel they are being *protected* by their bosses from possible outside interference. For example, Dang Nhat Minh's *When the Tenth Month Comes* was criticized for the scenes in which the village god appears to the heroine and in which the dead meet the living on the Day of Buddha's Forgiveness. Some government officials felt that he was making propaganda for religion. Minh argued that the scenes were perfectly understandable in the context: "If any woman says she sees her dead husband because of this film, I'll withdraw it." Dinh Quang, chairman of the censorship board, approved the film with the words, "An artistic style that shows the metaphysical side of life is legal in Vietnam." Nevertheless, the scenes remain remarkable as products of a Communist film industry. I have heard that the actors did not believe at the time that the scenes would be allowed to be shown in public. In my discussions with some of the people involved, I felt that the word "metaphysical" was being used as a substitute for "religious" or "spiritual"; that is, an effort was being made by Minh's colleagues to render the scenes ideologically innocuous in order to save them because they were successful and expressive. But the motivation was probably deeper even than the aesthetic. Vietnamese folk religion is an important expression of nationalism, and the Vietnamese remain, whatever ideology they profess, innately religious. The scenes were authentically Vietnamese in content and therefore important for the development of a national cinema.

This quasi-independence of filmmakers is reinforced by the prestige accorded the arts in Vietnamese culture (many of the major politicians are published poets), by an antiauthoritarian streak in the Vietnamese personality, and by a certain humorous and personal approach. That is, there is concern not about the constitutional question—whether government interference is legal— but about the individual government official in charge of one's department. If he is good, his subordinates feel he is a help rather than a hindrance, even if he in fact possesses the power of interference. As Dang Nhat Minh once said, "Why are Americans worried about government control of our films? For me, who *is* the government? It's Mr. Thu!" Similarly, when Dinh Quang told me he had just directed a play satirizing Vietnamese society and I asked him whether he had submitted it to the censors, he said, "I was the censor. I was both judge and jury!"

The fact that the Vietnam Cinema Department is controlled by artists explains the aesthetic emphasis in the Vietnamese film industry. Directors are given artistic control of their films. Films are rated for their aesthetic quality on a five-point system that is operated independently of any other criteria. As a result, a director will receive a bonus for high aesthetic achievement even if his film is a financial failure. Moreover, he will receive preferential treatment for his next film. Dang Nhat Minh feels that this policy frees the artist's mind from worries about financial success or popularity. In fact, the aesthetic emphasis of the department seems to be shared by the audience; films that are highly rated aesthetically are often commercial successes as well. The Vice Director of the Vietnam Feature Film Studio in Hanoi, Tran Dac, told me, "We know that our poetic films are not only better, but more popular." The general taste may however be deteriorating with the importation of *kung fu* thrillers from Hong Kong.

This variable relation between government and artists can be seen in censorship. Descriptions of the procedures used vary, and I suspect that a good deal of informality and personal communication is involved.[12] In general, one can say that until recently, scripts and projects had to receive prior approval from a board composed of representatives of the Ministry of Culture (Dinh Quang) and the department. This responsibility has now been given to the department as part of a general government movement to decentralize itself and confer authority on the responsible parties. Approval to begin production is now given by Deputy General Director Bui Dinh Hac and the director of the studio involved. A final check is made and final approval given before sound is added; by then, of course, the studio has already made a major investment in the project. If there is a controversy about or objections to a film that has been released, the old board can be reconstituted to examine the question. For instance, after the release of Dang Nhat Minh's *The Young Woman on the Perfumed River* in 1987, objections were raised to its sex scenes and to the fact that the foil of the faithless Communist official is a South Vietnamese Army veteran who marries the heroine, a former prostitute. Minh compromised by cutting one of the sex scenes, but saved the role of the veteran, which he considered more important. An indication of the department's new authority was that it successfully supported Minh against certain officials in the Ministry of Culture.

There are obviously limits to what a Vietnamese filmmaker can do. I was told that no film would be allowed that attacked "the very principle" of the government. But contrary to what one might expect, the very strong criticisms of party officials seen in several films have not been a target of censorship. There is a long tradition of such antiauthoritarian criticism in Vietnamese culture, and no government official apparently wants to be seen as defending the bad characteristics attacked. Moreover, autocriticism is encouraged in socialist societies. As a result, Vietnamese movies can be as scathing about officialdom as any libertarian would require. The outer limits of such criticism were explored by Tran Van Thuy's *Hanoi Through Whose Eyes* (1983) and *Report on Humaneness* (1986), described below, which indeed provoked a negative response among government officials. But Nguyen Van Linh, the General Secretary of the Vietnamese Communist Party, ordered the films to be released. They did a booming business and became two of the pioneering works of Vietnamese *glasnost*.[13]

Vietnamese filmmakers seem to feel that censorship is just another of the problems that any artist has to face. "No one makes films in a vacuum," says Dang Nhat Minh. Filmmakers are given the opportunity to defend their work and argue their points and seem to have sufficient confidence in those making the final decisions. In fact some prefer to deal with a board than with a single studio head. American filmmakers are themselves limited, they argue, by financial considerations, which are in effect just another form of censorship. "We go before our board of censors," Minh says. "You go before your board of financiers." Although Vietnamese filmmakers could always use more freedom and support, they do not feel at this time that the involvement of their government in filmmaking compromises their artistic integrity. Hai Ninh states, "We filmmakers need freedom and independence. My life is a trip on the road to that purpose." Neil Gibson reports an ever-increasing openness in the last three years.

Nguyen Thu

The importance of personal influence in Vietnamese filmmaking is illustrated by the role of the General Director of the department, Nguyen Thu.[14] Thu brought considerable prestige and authority to his post as well as exceptional energy and decisiveness. He is able to cut through red tape and bring his forces into line to reach his goals—always difficult in as bureaucratic an environment as Vietnam. Moreover, Thu is extremely broad-minded. In my work with him on the Vietnam Cinema Project, I saw time and again how his thinking would expand immediately to the greatest potential of a possible decision.

Thu's subordinates give him the major credit for encouraging high standards and new directions. The director Nguyen Xuan Son told me that there was much resistance in a department meeting to his script for his first film, *The Last Distance Between Us*, because it was "so sad." Thu signed off on the script with the words, "War is sad." Dang Nhat Minh went to Thu's sickbed with his first ideas for *When the Tenth Month Comes* and was greatly encouraged by his enthusiasm for the project. Thu says, "I told him he absolutely *had* to make that film!" Thu encourages a stronger dramatic sense in scripts. *The Last Crime* now ends with a shoot-out between gangsters on a beach, whereas the original script had them being arrested by the police, in fact a more socially uplifting ending. "Can you imagine how flat that would have been?" Thu asked me.

Thu's major emphasis is, however, on the distinctive national character of

Vietnamese cinema. "Why make something that exists already? If every artist did the same thing, why do it? I dislike films that borrow from other cinemas, that express unreal people." Authentic Vietnamese cinema arises from a study of society. For instance, the "metaphysical" scenes in *When the Tenth Month Comes* are true to Vietnamese culture and personality. Moreover, that national character should be "in every scene." There are some rules of scene construction common to world artists, but the special Vietnamese art tradition—with its vivid expression of the humanity, philosophy, and feelings of the Vietnamese—should be made visible.

Education and Influences

The first Vietnamese filmmakers "learned on the job, read books and prac-tised their skills by making newsreels and documentaries."[15] The Vietnam Cin-ema School was established in 1959 to train staff in all aspects of production. It offered a three-year course for directors taught mostly by East Bloc artists such as Ajdai Ibraghimov, an Azerbaijanian from the Soviet Union (East Bloc artists have periodically provided training and lectures in Vietnam). In the first gradu-ating class of 1962 were the directors Tran Vu, whose excellent student work *The Golden Bird* is considered an early classic, Hai Ninh, now director of the Feature Film Studio in Hanoi, and Bach Diep, the most important woman director. In 1980, the cinematographic section of the school was joined to the School of Dra-matic Art to form the Hanoi College of Dramatic Art and Cinema at the Uni-versity of Hanoi.[16] The school is well respected and is given much of the credit for the good work done by its graduates. Many artists and staff members have studied in East Bloc countries and China, and a few have studied in France.[17] A further source of training has been collaboration with East Bloc filmmakers, notably with Roman Karmen on his documentary on Dien Bien Phu.[18]

Nguyen Thu is actively seeking collaborative projects—either coproduc-tions or the provision of services and facilities to foreign companies—which would provide further opportunities for training. Secofilm, "Service and Coop-eration Film Company," has been established under the direction of Luu Xuan Thu, former director of the Central Studios of Documentary and Scientific Films, to coordinate this enterprise (*seco* means "will have" so the name is an expression of hope). Three French films are currently in production, including a high-budget film coordinated by the great director Pierre Schoendoerffer on the battle of Dien Bien Phu. A multinational production was in progress, and a British one is being planned.

Exposure to world cinema is uneven. Diem reports that by 1959 "hundreds of classical and modern films" were available from Socialist countries as well as "a few progressive films from capitalist."[19] Eisenstein is much admired as are

112 I *Colonialism and Nationalism in Asian Cinema*

such later Russian films as *The Cranes are Flying*. Vietnamese in Europe have had the opportunity to view a wider range of films, and the French embassy in Hanoi has occasionally made available modern French productions. There seems to be some acquaintance with classic American films, such as *Citizen Kane* and Chaplin's work. Francis Ford Coppola presented the department with a 35-mm. copy of *Apocalypse Now*, which has been viewed by many. *Platoon* has been shown in video theatres and is generally appreciated. Many Vietnamese find *Coming Home* similar to Vietnamese films in its concentration on the effects of war, rather than on the war itself. *Rambo*, shown privately on video, is considered ridiculous. Dang Nhat Minh stated, "you can look at all the films in Vietnam, and you'll never see a 'Rambo.' Jamais. Jamais."[20] Filmmakers would welcome more exposure to American films, a possibility now limited by the U.S. trade embargo on Vietnam. Among the now available videocassettes, *kung fu* and American adventure films seem particularly popular.

Some influence of foreign films can be noticed. Hai Ninh's large facial close-ups shot from down up, as in *The 17th Parallel—Day and Night*, may derive from Eisenstein and his successors. Sections of *The Abandoned Field* reminded some American viewers of Russian films of the 1930s. Large masses of peasants charging up smoke-filled hills seem similarly inspired. A curiosity is the scene of this type in *When the Tenth Month Comes*, which represents the heroine's unrealistic, media-influenced imagining of battle. An anonymous reader of this chapter suggested the existence of Chinese influence in the 1960s, but I did not see or hear of such. I did see influence from French films—particularly those of the 1950s—in the common 90-minute length (films tend to be longer in other Asian nations), the international style of narration, and the expressive black-and-white photography. Dang Nhat Minh writes that Alain Resnais made "the deepest impression" on him as a youth.[21]

The better Vietnamese films could not, however, be described as derivative. I found that directors consistently took an informed and critical stance toward non-Vietnamese films. Hai Ninh was asked by a Russian director if he had based the demonstration scene in *First Love* on *Strike*. Hai Ninh replied that he had not seen that particular film. Similarly, an Algerian asked Ninh whether he had graduated from a U.S. school. Ninh expressed his position very clearly: he does not take a xenophobic stance but adapts good elements from East and West; foreigners can, of course, recognize influences.

Vietnamese self-assurance in the face of foreign influences is in fact characteristic of the culture, a result of millennia of contact with both larger and smaller nations. Their solid appreciation of their own culture enables them to enjoy unproblematically their wide interests—both scholarly and creative—in others. Despite all their conflicts with China and France, the Vietnamese continue to feel a deep cultural sympathy with both and learn from them without losing their identity.

Documentary and Scientific Films

Documentaries are unusually important in Vietnamese cinema history and current practice. The decision to create a government film agency was based on the perceived need to record the momentous events of the war of independence, and the production of war documentaries has continued up to today.[22] In sheer numbers, more documentaries are produced in Vietnam than any other type of film. Moreover, most of the directors of feature films—notably Pham Ky Nam, Hai Ninh, Hong Sen, and Dang Nhat Minh—began their careers in documentaries, and that work exercises a continuing influence.[23] For instance, Hai Ninh made *City at Dawn*, the first department documentary on Saigon, in 1975, and immediately afterwards began his feature *First Love*, using some of the same locales and subjects: prostitutes, drug addicts, and night life. The romantic feature *When the Birds Return* follows two documentaries, including *Dong Ho Painting Village*, on the area in which the story is located. Indeed in many early features, such as Tran Vu's *We Will Meet Again*, the documentary-type sections are much more assured than the dramatic.

Documentaries are not considered merely informative, but are recognized as essential products of the general aesthetic quest of Vietnamese filmmakers. For instance, Diem writes: "The poetic touch in the national character was presented in every film even in the midst of the fighting"; *The Electric Line to the Song Da Construction Site* "was essentially a cinema poem, short, concise. . . . "[24] Completely without dialogue or commentary, the film is a beautifully photographed and involving one-reel documentary on the construction of an electric line by workers using mostly low-tech means. The contrast between their tools and methods and their results reveals much about development in third-world countries.[25] Similarly carried by its beautiful photography is *1/50th of a Second in a Lifetime*, a one-reel documentary on Vo An Ninh, Vietnam's most famous photographer. Other aspects of documentary making can be equally aesthetic. *Nguyen Ai Quoc—Ho Chi Minh* is a masterful, if hagiographic, narrative of Ho Chi Minh's life up to 1945, in which archival materials, photographs, interviews, and modern footage of the sites discussed are expertly integrated by one of Vietnam's major directors, Pham Ky Nam.[26]

The aesthetic interest of the Vietnamese documentary makers is evident in their numerous films on specifically artistic subjects. Particularly successful are those on traditional Vietnamese music. Two famous examples have been filmed of *cheo* village opera, an art form predating the tenth century: *The Goddess Quan Am* and *Luu Binh and Duong Le. Cheo* opera is extremely popular in North Vietnam among all sections of society—and of great interest to Western scholars, who have not yet been able to study it adequately. Filmed in color with rather poor sound, the films communicate with appreciation and enthusiasm the excitement of the form: striking costumes, lively music, vivid characterizations, and much humor and action. *Love Duets of Bac Ninh*, 1987, is about a traditional village song festival, the setting for the 1974 feature film *We Will Meet Again*. Young people, divided into male and female choirs, serenade each other with traditional songs, which often allude to places and events in the neighborhood. The documentary provides a good deal of background information on the customs of the festival and on the songs, which are performed at the very sites mentioned. The viewer is thus able to appreciate the social, historical, and artistic dimensions of this extraordinary music.

The effort to place a subject in its historical, social, and also ideological setting is characteristic of Vietnamese documentaries and scientific films. For instance, *The Red Cochineal* describes the natural environment of the insect, its varied industrial uses along with their economics, and also the ethnic minorities that live in the area and exploit this resource. Similarly, *The Forest of Cuc Phuong* describes, along with the flora, fauna, and ethnic minorities, the archaeology and history of the forest, efforts to preserve it, and the possible uses of some of the plants. This concern to establish a context for a subject is especially evident in documentaries on historical subjects. Most often, as in *Independence Day 1945*, historical footage is supplemented by foreign materials, photographs, interviews, and so on, in order to place the object of discussion.

This method can be illustrated by a sequence of films on the 1972 Christmas bombings of Hanoi and Haiphong. The earliest, *The Evil and the Punishment*, was being shown in Europe two weeks after the event and consists of almost raw footage of bombs and antiaircraft shells exploding, planes falling in flames, American flyers being brought in through the darkness by soldiers and civilians, people being rescued from the rubble, foreign observers taking photographs, and so on. The horror of the event is communicated very directly. The later films on the same subject, *Hanoi, an Epic Poem* (produced by the Vietnam People's Army Film Studio) and *Unforgotten Days and Nights*, enlarge the focus: they are portraits of the fullness of life of the city at that moment in its history. The historical background is given, various sectors of the city's population are shown (including foreign visitors), the operations of the antiaircraft units are described, the attack is narrated from its beginning to its results, and the foreign reaction is emphasized. Aesthetic devices are used, such as symbolism: shots of dead flowers are juxtaposed with those of dead people. As in many Vietnamese documentaries on the war, the point is emphasized that life must go on—every effort is made to continue the normalcy of living. Young students play classical music; babies are born during the bombing that has killed other babies; newspapers and books continue being published underground. Similarly, the work of reconstruction begins immediately as bulldozers start clearing the rubble.[27]

Some of the immediacy of the battle footage can be lost in this later contextualization. In fact, Vietnamese filmmakers generally prefer the shorter 1954 documentary *Dien Bien Phu* to the longer version made in 1964, *Victory at Dien Bien Phu*, as "closer to the facts."[28] Nevertheless, the war documentaries considered most successful—such as *On the Crest of the Waves, Facing the Storm* and *The Citadel Vinh Linh*—are those that show the community as a whole simultaneously confronting the crisis of the war and making every effort to continue its functions.

This long background in documentaries explains perhaps why two of the most imaginative and daring modern Vietnamese films are in that genre. *Hanoi Through Whose Eyes* by Tran Van Thuy is in fact an editorial in the guise of a travelog of Hanoi—the city that symbolizes more than any other the national identity. Thuy shows how people are forgetting the history of Hanoi because of their preoccupation with modern creature comforts. He uses his visits to the royal tombs to quote the sayings of kings and nobles about the necessity of treating the people well; thus admonishing the current revolutionary government in a particularly galling but unassailable way. *Report on Humaneness* is even more unusual. Members of the Documentary and Scientific Film Studio meet at a friend and colleague's grave on the anniversary of his death. The film cuts back to his burial at the site. It cuts back again to the friend on his deathbed, ordering them to make this film: "If you don't, I'll come back to take you with me!" Emboldened they set out into their contemporary society to ask the question, "What is humaneness?" Their fellow citizens are only too eager to provide answers. Thuy's two films are among the most important pieces of evidence of the new openness of Vietnamese society, an openness being pioneered by Vietnamese filmmakers. In view of the place of documentaries in Vietnamese cinema history, it is characteristic that the way would be led by a documentary maker.

Characteristics of Vietnamese Cinema

I have already mentioned several characteristics of Vietnamese cinema, and a more extended discussion would be useful before examining feature films. This section should, however, be read in conjunction with the following one, in which the films I mention are placed in their historical context.

Vietnamese filmmakers and historians are frank about the propaganda purpose of many of their early works and blame it for the shortcomings of their results: "the formalist and simplistic manner"; "Routine, formalism, lengthy commentary and monotonous imagery. . . . "[29] When a bricklayer in *Report on Humaneness* asks the film crew why they make such boring documentaries, footage of heroic, happy peasants working on a community project is cut in. Hai Ninh stated:

During the war, we concentrated on war films. Now we have turned to other subjects, comedy, sport, and so on. Recently our government and party recognized that the role of culture and cinema is very important, that they contribute to the building of the country as other fields do. So the most important task of films now is to express the humanity of man in society. Our newest films concentrate on humanity and moral character.

This echoes the remarks of many Vietnamese filmmakers that their works do not show the war as a subject in itself, but rather its impact on human beings. (On the other hand, scenes that might seem propagandist to Westerners may be perfectly realistic; for instance, the flag waving in the last scene of *When the Tenth Month Comes* is normal on the first day of school.) Such remarks should not be understood as denying the importance of nationalism in Vietnamese films, as seen from the remarks of Nguyen Thu reported above. In fact, Diem lists among the three characteristics of Vietnamese feature films—along with film being a *"Weapon of revolutionary struggle"*, employing "the *methods of creation of socialist realism"*: "Each film has a *national character*, reflects the joys and sorrows, concerns and hopes, aspirations and will of the people, and the soul and way of life of the nation."[30]

The Vietnamese are an extremely nationalistic people, with a patriotism forged through millennia of resisting powerful neighbors. Vietnam is holy ground, and they have a sacred duty to protect it. This relation to the land is emphasized in *The Abandoned Field*, in which the male protagonist spends a good deal of time contemplating the beauty of the terrain around him, which the camera sees through his eyes—this is the land he is fighting for and these the emotions he brings to the struggle.

In their remarks, Nguyen Thu and Diem place the emphasis on content—as exemplified by the specifically Vietnamese cultural elements in *When the Tenth Month Comes* and *Bom the Bumpkin*. Indeed, a full appreciation of Vietnamese cinema is impossible without a close comparison with literature, both ancient and modern. But Vietnamese character is expressed also in certain elements of style.

Poetry is at the center of Vietnamese culture and sensibilities, and cinema cannot be divorced from it.[31] This poetic sense separates their creations clearly from conventional socialist realism. Poetry and musical lyrics are in fact often central elements in plots and scenes. The heroine of *When the Tenth Month Comes* breaks down while singing a role in a village opera that mirrors her own situation. The young girl in *Fairy Tale for 17-Year Olds* reveals her feelings while reciting a poem in class.

Symbols are unusually important in Vietnamese films. Traditional Vietnamese icons are used, such as the woman and her baby who turned to stone waiting for her husband—referred to in such films as *City Under the Fist, Fairy Tale for 17-Year Olds,* and *Legend of a Mother*. Filmmakers regularly create symbols as a means of expression. In Hong Sen's *The Abandoned Field*, the liaison family lives in a hut on stilts in the delta. As the water rises, they must raise the level of the floor, leaving them less room between it and the ceiling. At the same time, the Americans are "escalating" the war and closing in on the couple. The helicopters that attack the family are seen from down up, their broad undersections forming a sort of ceiling that lowers down upon the fleeing targets. (These exceptionally powerful scenes were inspired by the director's own frightening experiences of helicopter attacks during the war; in filming the scenes, he cooperated closely with a pilot friend of his to create the exact effects he sought.)

Vietnamese tend to understand foreign films in symbolic terms. Dang Nhat Minh was struck by the scene in Peter Markle's *Bat 21*, in which a downed American enters a peasant's hut and takes food. The peasant returns and asks indignantly (unfortunately without subtitles), "What are you doing in my house?" In that situation and question, the whole meaning of the war seemed to be symbolized for Minh.

Similarly, quite realistic characters can be understood as exemplary. In war films, the suffering of women is depicted as the most powerful means of presenting that of the people as a whole (in fact, women occupy central roles in *all* the Vietnamese features I have seen, an indication of their recognized place in culture and society). In several films of the post-war situation, the prostitute is a key case for Vietnamese reconciliation and reconstruction. The problems of the veteran in *Brothers and Relations* reveal those of the society, as do those of the adolescent in *The Lamp in the Dream*.

Also poetic is the creation of multiple layers of meaning. For instance, in *When the Tenth Month Comes*, a woman, wanting to spare her sickly father-in-law, asks a village schoolteacher to write letters as if they came from her dead soldier husband. This complex event is seen in different ways throughout the film. There is the surface appearance: the understanding between the principals. There is misinterpretation: the villagers think the woman is carrying on an affair with the teacher. There is a deeper emotional level at which the teacher is indeed falling in love with her. Their story is placed in the context of the war, and that war in turn is placed in the context of the thousands of years of Vietnamese resistance. Similarly, in *Fairy Tale for 17-Year Olds*, a girl escapes into fantasies about a young soldier at the front, while her family and friends urge her to face reality. The soldier is killed, but his last letter expresses his gratitude for her love for him, the last beautiful thing in his life, and thus acutely real for him as for her. Multiple levels of meaning can be present in films in surprising and interesting ways. In *The Last Distance Between Us*, many of the statements and actions of the father have a double meaning because he is an underground agent.

Much Vietnamese poetry is lyric, indeed, love poetry, and this fact encourages the worldwide tendency to include romantic interest in movies. In the most "socialist realist" film I have seen, *The River of Aspiration*, a rather cursory, but potentially interesting, love interest was included. Eroticism, a major part of the traditional literature, has become the subject of controversy. Generally suppressed in socialist countries, it makes its presence felt under the surface of a number of films, and in several—such as *Shipwreck Beach* and *The Young Woman on the Perfumed River*—has become overt and an occasion for debating questions of realism and artistic freedom. Hai Ninh argues that in both films, nudity and sexuality were necessary to describe accurately and dramatically the life of prostitution that provides the impetus for the plots. Interestingly, lyric love poetry, long de-emphasized as not socially constructive, is being reintroduced into the curriculum.

Related to this romanticism is the emphasis in Vietnamese films on tenderness. The American director Richard Sykes found the films he saw a combination of "sophistication and gentleness." A "war film" like *The Abandoned Field* seems to spend an inordinate amount of time showing the young parents playing with their baby and each other. Children play together at length in *When Mother Is Away*. The mother consoles her son in *When Grandmother Is Away*, as does the young university student console the veteran in *Brothers and Relations*. The Vietnamese obviously derive a good deal of emotional satisfaction from watching people being nice to each other.

This tenderness is very much part of Vietnamese humor, which tends to teasing and jollity and is a frequent mood in conversation. All the characters of *A Quiet Little Town* have something to recommend them, no matter how much they can make us laugh. Moreover, just as romance can become eroticism, Vietnamese humor can assume an almost surrealistic character, as in the butterfly scene in *The 17th Parallel*, discussed below.

Some purely visual aspects of Vietnamese cinema can be related to their long art tradition. Unusually handsome black-and-white camera work is widespread in both documentaries and feature films and argues for a basically aesthetic approach (color is much less developed artistically). Night scenes can be remarkable, with whites glowing against a black background much as in lacquer work, a Vietnamese specialty. The sinuous lines and atmospheric effects of many outdoor scenes recall ink paintings on silk—as do many of the subjects chosen: the boy on a buffalo in *A Quiet Little Town* is a motif of both high and folk art.

The very popular Vietnamese dance drama has left its mark on cinema: negatively in some melodrama and stock characters, and positively in an emphasis on body language and graceful and appropriate pacing. Camera movements (except for over-zooming) can be subtle and expressive. Music tends to be Western and overly lush; much more could be done with traditional native instruments.

The danger of the Vietnamese emphasis on emotions is of course that it can encourage overacting, a problem in many older Vietnamese movies and in some newer ones as well. I have in fact watched a director urging an actress to broaden her style (since sound is mixed later, a director can give continual instructions, as in silent movie-making); and the People's Artist Tra Giang—a humorous and energetic woman—is too often called upon to mist over her eyes. But the acting in the better Vietnamese movies is remarkably understated and effective, and the emotional climaxes can be powerful. Moreover the acting style seems more Western than the Asian of the stereotype, which is a definite help for an occidental audience.

The cinema language is also generally international. From the earliest film I have seen, *The Golden Bird*, the better Vietnamese directors have been able to use that language in a quiet, subtle, and assured manner, in which all elements are carefully integrated and interrelated. For instance, in *When the Tenth Month Comes*, the heroine leaves the stage when she breaks down; the male opera singer turns to his right toward her to continue singing and is confused when she is not there. In the audience, the school teacher has been watching the opera with his quasi-girlfriend. He leaves to follow the heroine. His girlfriend turns to her right to speak to him and finds he has left. Because of the direction of the camera, the actor and the girlfriend have turned to opposite sides of the screen, creating a lovely visual effect. The sequence has, however, more than a visual interest. The quiet parallelism expresses the film's theme that contemporary experience is a repetition of the past, a later chapter in the long Vietnamese tradition of war and loss.

Similarly, in *The Abandoned Field*, a long shot shows the wife pushing off in the family dugout to harvest flowers. Almost unnoticed, her husband drops a cloth into the boat as she leaves. Later, when she is attacked by a helicopter, she puts the cloth over her head as camouflage (a practice followed by the guerrillas in other scenes). That is, her having the cloth was a matter of life or death. The point is made very quietly, but it is one of many such that create the mood of the film: the family is living in constant danger and will in fact suffer tragedy. Such reminders render poignant the scenes of normal family life. The effort at maintaining a kind of normalcy despite the war is, as stated above, a theme of Vietnamese movies. Dang Nhat Minh said that the Vietnam war was different from World War II, in which all normal life was suspended for four to six years. The Vietnam war lasted from 1945 to 1975, and the Vietnamese had to try as much as possible to carry on their lives.

The Western viewer must therefore be aware of specific cultural differences that may be masked by the apparent accessibility of the cinematic language. The husband and wife in *The Abandoned Field* seemed too saintly to some Hawaii viewers. But the Vietnamese filmmaker Bui Dinh Hac mentioned in discussion that the wife had to suffer not only through the war but from the "brutality" of her husband; he slapped her once. Hitting someone on the head is in fact a major offence in Vietnam, but the American audience did not realize this. The wife was slapped because, through her negligence, their baby had fallen into the water and almost drowned. The Vietnamese audience would consider this also a major failing. The film had, therefore, provided a much rounder characterization of the couple than the American audience perceived.

Feature Films and Directors

While visiting Vietnam, I was naturally shown films considered outstanding, so I cannot comment on the general quality of Vietnamese cinema. Nevertheless, levels were easily noticeable, and the weaknesses of middling films permit a more accurate appreciation of the better ones. For instance, *When Mother Is Away* has long scenes of the heroine's five children disporting themselves, an obvious delight to the Vietnamese audience; these scenes helped me understand that the passages in *The Abandoned Field* of the liaison couple playing with their child were both especially appealing to the local audience and much more controlled than those in the former film.[32]

A number of films are stagey: the camera remains more or less fixed and the actors move before it, reciting their lines as if in a play. This practice is found especially in older films, such as sections of *We Will Meet Again*, but has continued in such films as *Once Upon a Time in Vu Dai Village* by the historically important director Pham Van Khoa.[33] Many Vietnamese films, like ones from other Asian countries, tend to melodrama. *The Peal of the Orange Bell* treats the interesting topic of Agent Orange, but turns it into a collection of antiquated plot turns rendered with a slowness of action unusual in Vietnamese movies. Similarly, *The Last Crime* takes up the interesting theme of the social reintegration of the prostitutes and gangsters prominent in South Vietnamese society, but the heroine's few facial expressions are all appeals to an easy pity.

The Vietnamese now criticize much of their early work as propagandist. The only such recent feature film I have seen is *The River of Aspiration*, the story of an honest manager trying to raise production at an electric plant. The heavy-handed socialist realism and old-fashioned narrative style of the film may be due to its being the department's offering on the occasion of a party congress.

None of the above films is totally without interest. *The Last Crime* features the fine acting of Tran Quang as a menacing but attractive gangster. The children of *When Mother Is Away* seem unaware of the camera (Vietnamese films generally use children very well). In *The River of Aspiration*, a number of scenes are injected with humor; for instance, a workers' representative quotes Marxism to argue against working too hard.

Occasionally, what should be a merely workmanlike production rises to a higher level. *When Grandmother Is Away* was the directorial debut of Nguyen Anh Thai and intended as a low-budget film for children. The story is a clear temptation to sentimentality: tension in the family leads a grandmother to leave the apartment and make her living in the streets; her grandson, suffering greatly from her absence, tries to find her. The film is carried off without a trace of sentimentality, but with a good deal of realistic emotion. Modern family problems are described very frankly—an important theme in this very family-centered society—as are those of the urban poor in Haiphong. The ending is not the grandmother's return, but the boy's accident as he catches a glimpse of her and jumps out of a bus window into the street. In the hospital he has a dream that leaves everything beautifully unresolved. *When Grandmother Is Away* is a small and unexpected masterpiece.

An unevenness can be found in the work of certain directors, such as that of the prolific, pioneering Tran Vu.[34] His graduation project, *The Golden Bird* (1962), a short fiction film, is a masterful exercise in international cinema language expressing Vietnamese content. The narration is well-paced and concise; the photography is poetic and expressive; a wide but not showy array of camera angles, movements, and techniques is used; the acting is expressive and unstrained; the background music enhances the mood without distracting from it; and the emotional effects are realized. Details are used well throughout; the fact that the Frenchman and his Vietnamese underlings are not the peasants they are disguised to be is seen from the fact that they roll their cigarettes with paper instead of leaves. One putative peasant looks very funny with his dark glasses, another with the whiteness of his legs when he rolls up his pants. The story is told more in such images than in words. *The Golden Bird* is the creation of an artist educated and at ease in his art form. Apart from its expert documentary passages and a few good dramatic scenes, Tran Vu's later *We Will Meet Again* (1972) is a step backward. The camera is fixed before a room in which the melodramatic villain stomps and expostulates. A clump of embarrassed peasants trots along a marked path waving rakes and hoes, supposedly in insurrection. However, in his last film, *Brothers and Relations* (1986), Tran Vu recovers his earlier form. The story of a veteran returning to Hanoi to find an indifferent society is told with an economy and understatement that express only more effectively the strong personalities, emotions, and philosophical differences involved. Each scene is interesting in itself and contributes unfailingly to the whole. *Brothers and Relations* achieves a quiet perfection in its genre.

Similarly uneven, but on a lower level, is the work of Vietnam's best known woman director, Bach Diep.[35] Apart from its heavy overuse of the zoom lens, *Punishment* (1984) is an interesting character study of a South Vietnamese Army officer during the chaos of the 1975 fall of Hue. Despite some extraneous material, the basic story of his demoralization, his escape from society and the consequences of his action, and his final decision to return, is told clearly in terms of his relation to his family and fellow soldiers and to the North Vietnamese officers. The destruction of his career and family is a reflection or symptom of that of the South Vietnamese army and society, preparatory to its reconstruction on another basis. Unusual for Vietnamese films, the narration does not move sequentially in time, but—perhaps influenced by Dang Nhat Minh's *City Under the Fist*—plays with chronology to reveal itself gradually. There are a number of nice touches: a young North Vietnamese soldier does a little imitation of a macho SVA officer to amuse a little boy. Bach Diep's later *Legend of a Mother* (1987) is a retrogression to staginess and melodrama. This is particularly regrettable because the interesting story of a woman who adopted children during the war and returned them afterwards to their families did inspire some good scenes of Vietnamese women interacting among themselves and taking care of the very physical needs of infants. But the villainous men are ludicrously broad (one pours knockout powder into the whiskey he offers his secretary), and a dream sequence is crude enough to be funny. The two films are distant enough in style to make them unrecognizable as the work of a single director. Neil Gibson reports that Bach Diep's latest film, *A Small Alley*, an examination of the personal consequences of poverty in contemporary Vietnam, is stylistically much more accomplished.

The director Hai Ninh has long been a pillar of Vietnamese cinema, entrusted with some of its major projects and now Director of the Feature Film Studio in Hanoi.[36] He completed a number of productions during the war under difficult conditions. The bombings of Hanoi played havoc with the work on the sound track for *The 17th Parallel—Day and Night*, but gave him the idea for his film *The Girl of Hanoi*. His work illustrates some of the strengths and weaknesses of the industry. Hai Ninh has the Vietnamese capacity for self-criticism. He finds his early films often too slow, the movements and action too long. The propaganda content seems very high to him now, which makes them seem old-fashioned especially to the younger Vietnamese audience. "Nobody wants to listen to propaganda now," one young person told me. Even Ninh's latest film, *Shipwreck Beach*, is an argument in favor of the Vietnamese position on the boat people: they were deluded with false promises by criminals.

Hai Ninh's movies are often melodramatic, with cardboard heroes and villains and devices like the drugging of the heroine's drink to have sex with her. In *First Love*, a seemingly benevolent American adviser is in fact stealing Vietnamese children to send them as orphans to the U.S. where they will be trained as spies to be slipped back later into Vietnam. Hai Ninh regularly twists realism to make an ideological point. For instance, in *The Girl of Hanoi*, the young heroine climbs into a one-person bomb shelter, a few bombs fall, and she emerges smiling.[37] In *First Love*, the scene of a protest demonstration begins well—with an aerial view of the plaza as citizens and police square off in a geometric pattern—but then degenerates as the *students* start shoving the *police* around. The unreality of this is revealed in the next scenes, which show the police chasing people through the city at night. At the end of *The 17th Parallel*, the villain has finally cornered the heroine, but he wants to hear her communist propaganda just one more time before he kills her. She reads a paper so eloquently that the South Vietnamese soldiers revolt, are joined by a crowd of women, and kill the villain.

The plots of Hai Ninh's films often seem to go in circles rather than spirals. For instance, *The 17th Parallel* comprises two feature-length sections; the second starts off with the same characters in basically the same situation as the first. Even the main villain, whom we thought we saw killed, appears with a large scar on his face. As a result, Hai Ninh's films often lack a sense of forward momentum.

For all these faults, his work has undeniable good points. He encourages the fine, often sensuous camera work that is characteristic of the best Vietnamese films, both features and documentaries. He can achieve striking images, such as some of the close-ups in *The 17th Parallel* and the almost surrealist flotsam and jetsam of American artifacts in Saigon. He can narrate some sections through mainly visual means, such as several flashbacks in *First Love* and the heroine's search for her family in the bombed ruins in *The Girl of Hanoi*. Some scenes are strikingly original, like that of revolutionaries conferring while sitting in round basket boats on a river in *The 17th Parallel*. In the same movie can be found one of the funniest and strangest scenes in all Vietnamese cinema. A South Vietnamese Army troop is receiving a tall, lanky CIA agent and his obligatory Vietnamese mistress. The troop makes a formal path before the agent by lining up double-file facing each other. Suddenly he turns to his right, raises his arms in an odd way and starts pacing away from the reception ceremony in long, slow, spidery steps. The Vietnamese officer at the other end of the line raises his arms and starts moving in the same way toward the American. They continue this strange dance toward each other, gradually sinking lower and lower on their haunches and lowering their arms forward until their slowly waving hands come together on the ground over a butterfly. The CIA officer was just using his cover as a lepidopterist.

One of Hai Ninh's most interesting achievements is his depiction of Duy, the male protagonist in *First Love*. By no means a cardboard character, he is the subject of an almost existentialist analysis of alienation. When Duy loses his first love, he loses hope and then "life becomes irrational." He cannot believe in the Americans, but cannot join the resistance. In his aimlessness and thus listlessness, he becomes the perfect victim of the corruption of war-time Saigon, where "life belongs to the prostitutes and the Americans." Having left his place in society, he turns against it and his family. This theme of the need for a moral, hopeful purpose in life is major in Vietnamese cinema and also in their conception of the war. Hai Ninh's works are in fact a key to our understanding of many of the themes treated in Vietnamese films, such as that of reconciliation. Hai Ninh can also be recognized as a pioneer in the opening of the industry to new subjects. The nudity and sexuality in *Shipwreck Beach* were unprecedented. In *The Girl of Hanoi*, the child is told the story of the Vietnamese hero's receiving the magic sword to smite the invaders and has a sort of vision of the event, told through animation—an anticipation of later expressions of the "metaphysical" in life.

In contrast to Hai Ninh's productivity, Pham Ky Nam is famous for one feature film, *The Young Woman of Sao Beach* (1963), but it is one of the most interesting ever made in Vietnam.[38] Despite occasional weak points—some melodrama and sentimentality, some overlong scenes, and soupy music—the film is bursting with originality. The lustrous black-and-white camera work is unusually expressive even for Vietnamese cinema, with interesting angles, camera movements, and lighting. In one night scene, a baby is being born while a battle is sounding outside; inside the room, the lone ceiling lamp is set swinging, causing a variety of light effects. Scenes of actual combat—rare in Vietnamese films—are handled expertly. The complicated and interesting narrative is told in very bold scenes. In one plot line, the heroine meets a South Vietnamese officer she once knew. He tries to rape her, but is interrupted by a French officer who enters the hut, sees the heroine's anguished face, and—saying, "What a beautiful expression!"—photographs it. He then shoos the South Vietnamese out the door and rapes the heroine himself. The scenes of her posttrauma suffering, her husband's reactions, and the effect the rape has on their relation to each other are described with unusual fullness. In a final, long, silent scene, the two reach a qualified understanding. The husband is soon killed in battle. Later in the movie, Viet Minh commandos attack the French officer. He has returned to his room, put a record on the machine, and is settling back to relax. They burst in, and the violent—and most interestingly photographed—struggle is carried on to *le jazz hot*.[39] Created so early in Vietnamese film history, *The Young Woman of Sao Beach* must have had a very positive effect on its future development. Even today, an artist like Dang Nhat Minh can look back to it for inspiration and even validation.

Hong Sen is recognized as having produced the modern breakthrough film for Vietnamese cinema, *The Abandoned Field—Free Fire Zone*.[40] Hong Sen's other works are considered less successful. *Left Alone*, which I have not seen, has an original subject: a downed American flyer is offered refuge by a woman from an ethnic minority. The film's exoticism has attracted foreign viewers, but the Vietnamese found it less interesting, and aesthetic objections were raised by other film artists. According to Neil Gibson, the climactic scene of the woman breastfeeding the American was judged to need reshooting and the film has never been released generally in Vietnam. Hong Sen is now finishing a new production.

The greatest talent of the next generation of Vietnamese filmmakers is Dang Nhat Minh, whose *When the Tenth Month Comes* is worthy to rank as a classic of world cinema.[41] I have discussed that film elsewhere and will concentrate here on the films produced immediately before and after that work. *City Under the Fist* is the most experimental feature film made in Vietnam. Going much further than earlier flashback techniques used by Pham Ky Nam and others, the complicated story is told through a chronological kaleidoscope, the narrative jumping between at least four different periods through visual and thematic connections. Interjected are imaginary scenes expressing the protagonist's fears or speculation as to what might have happened. All this complication has a definite expressive purpose: the film is describing the protagonist's almost feverish rethinking process stimulated by an historic event; he is being forced to reshape his views of history, society, and his own past actions. Moreover, that event had provoked the same thought process in the government and the society as a whole, so the mental effort of the audience to follow the narrative is a personal recreation of their own experience as well as that of the protagonist and a reliving of the historical moment described.

The protagonist's story is embedded in that historical event or—perhaps more accurately—in the now generally accepted interpretation of that event, which I will need to describe in detail. After 1975, the North Vietnamese went through a period of ideological enthusiasm. The government decided that, with the end of the war, they could move rapidly to restructure society in a scientific, socialist form. To do this, they banned folk practices, such as the song festival of Bac Ninh, and made efforts to purge untrustworthy people. In the general atmosphere of suspicion and repression, an individual could be judged not only on his or her own actions but on those of relatives as well (the correction of this bad practice continues today). The atmosphere of recrimination caused a good deal of unhappiness and unrest in the country.

This ideological movement was a product of the conservative wing of the Vietnamese Communist party, which is generally identified with the high party official Truong Chinh. Truong Chinh was in turn identified with the faction of the party that leaned toward the Chinese as opposed to the Russians. Further complicating factors were the deteriorating relations with the People's Republic of China and tensions within Vietnam between the ethnic Vietnamese and the ethnic Chinese minority, many of whom had to leave the country as boat people. The final shock came with the Chinese invasion across the northern border "to teach the Vietnamese a lesson." A connection was made between the invasion, the local Chinese considered disloyal or at least divided in their loyalties, and the earlier repressive atmosphere, now blamed on Chinese influence. Interestingly, a very similar sequence of events had occurred after the defeat of the French. In 1955–56, the Vietnamese began an ideological land reform so severe that it provoked a peasant revolt that was savagely repressed. The government later issued an apology and blamed Truong Chinh and Chinese advisers.[42]

Some historians, including Vietnamese, disagree with the above interpretation of events. My only concern here is how it is used in *City Under the Fist*. Told *sequentially*, the story is about a young man who abandons his fiancée because her family has come under suspicion and he does not want to jeopardize his career in journalism. The suspicion has been cast on the family by a local Chinese who is actually a spy and tries to recruit the protagonist to Maoism. At the invasion, the journalist is sent north to inspect the ruins of a town destroyed by the Chinese, the town in which he used to visit his fiancée. There he rethinks his past and confronts the external and internal negative influence of Chinese-style ideology. He realizes that out of fear and ambition, he has acted in a way that is unworthy of a human being. His suspected fiancée is now married to a heroic Vietnamese army officer. Told *cinematically*, the story is a marvel of visual poetry, photographed with a peculiar texture and following the leaps of the protagonist's mind as he works his way with anguish toward a new way of thinking. The director writes, "The film is an act of repentance for many Vietnamese who for a long time allowed a simplistic ideological orthodoxy to destroy their feelings."[43] Similarly, a scholar from China stated in 1987, "After the excesses of the Cultural Revolution, we don't ask so much about the ideology of an idea or a policy, but whether it's human or inhuman."

This search for the authentically human is a characteristic of Vietnamese cinema today and a theme of Minh's latest film *The Young Woman on the Perfumed River*, based on a true story: a prostitute helped a revolutionary who then tried to ignore her after the country was reunited and he was appointed to a government post. The film was controversial because of its sex scenes and its contrast of the official to a faithful South Vietnamese Army veteran. The social criticism of the film is sharp, for instance, about the suppression of journal articles by government officials. One journalist decides to quit because she doesn't want to continue writing the "phony" articles her editors demand. The film is thus important evidence of Vietnamese *glasnost*. The use of a prostitute as personifying the problems of reconciliation and social reconstruction in the country is found in a number of movies and will be discussed below. The film is Dang Nhat Minh's first in color, and he clearly enjoyed some of the effects he was able to produce. His creative use of symbolism is also evident, for instance, in the shot of the prostitute's tiny boat being towed away by a large armored military river vessel. The film does not, however, have the artistic unity so characteristic of Minh's two earlier films. Visually, it is divided between the lush, moody, romantic photography of the first third—the life of the prostitute on the river—and the very flat, at times overlit photography of the later sections. Similarly, in his narration, Minh seems to waver between a reportorial style and a romantic, pictorial one. The acting of the two principals tends to the melodramatic and sentimental, and some of the background music is clumsy. Minh seems to have been stretching his work in new directions in this film, directions that will undoubtedly find a more skillful expression in later works.

Dang Nhat Minh's contemporary Nguyen Xuan Son made his debut with the remarkable feature film *The Last Distance Between Us* (1981).[44] The title refers to the need for reconciliation between former enemies in the North and South. In a 1988 interview, Xuan Son told me, "The greatest distance is that between people. In my film, I wanted to say that we had to settle the distance between former Saigon soldiers and ourselves. That distance is very large." The story describes the life of a low-level, undercover resistance worker living among his neighbors in the South: an older, alcoholic veteran of the South Vietnamese Army and the widow of a veteran. As they live together, they become ever closer and more sympathetic to each other. The life of the revolutionary is told in a very practical, undramatic way. He has small jobs but big worries. He is torn between his duties as an agent and as an only parent to his young daughter. When his comrades suspect the veteran of informing on him, the agent says he will vouch for him, because he feels sorry that the veteran's life seems so futile. When he feels the police closing in, he hints to the widow that she might have to take care of his child. The arrest scene is masterfully understated, one of the best pieces of editing I have ever seen. The revolutionary looks a second longer than usual at the widow as he goes out the door. The people become so real, so ordinary, that the brief scene of the widow being tortured by the police is shocking.

A strong point of the film is the casting—the actors seem to be living their roles rather than playing them. The father's role is filled by a very ordinary-looking Saigon stage actor. For the veteran, Xuan Son chose a former Saigon documentary maker who had studied in Japan. "I could see vividly the feelings I wanted existing in his soul. When I asked him to play the role, he was surprised and suggested I look at his films. But I told him, 'I don't want your films. I want you.' " The camera work is as quiet and careful as the other aspects of the movie. The effects seem more beautiful because they call no attention to themselves. Few films are so convincing.

Son's later film, *Fairy Tale for 17-Year Olds*, is quite different. Perhaps under the influence of *When the Tenth Month Comes*, it emphasizes overtly poetic camera work to express the romantic fantasies of a young girl. Despite its strong points, which I have described in an earlier article,[45] it does not always achieve a unity in its depiction of different dimensions of reality and suffers from some over-acting. Like his contemporary Minh, Xuan Son seemed to be stretching his art in new directions in the film and was remarkably successful in passages.

The older directors of the Vietnam Cinema Department are very proud of their younger colleagues and give them a good deal of encouragement and, more important, the opportunity to work. Since the reduction of production money, however, one case of a senior director using his position to obtain preference has been reported.

A most impressive young director is Le Duc Tien, whose second film, *A*

Quiet Little Town, is a very original comedy.[46] With an unusually deft and witty script, the movie satirizes officious party functionaries, the bureaucratization of life, and small-town pretensions, provincialisms, and ambitions. A curious plot twist at the end permits the audience to test itself on its own class prejudices or "feudalism," as it is called in Vietnamese Marxist terms. The movie, however, goes beyond the normal expectations of the genre. It creates a very accurate and affectionate—though unromanticized—picture of a small, provincial town. An unusually large number and variety of characters are portrayed with seeming effortlessness, and in the end, each retains his sympathy and dignity. The very funny jokes are separated by quiet actions and views, so that the mood is tempered into a gentle, almost elegiac vision. The narrative is framed and punctuated by a boy riding a water buffalo, a common view in the countryside, a motif in folk art, and a happy childhood memory of many. The director seems to be evoking the roots of the culture as a criticism of and a refuge from many of the problems of contemporary society.

Le Duc Tien's next movie, *Bom the Bumpkin*, is the first to base itself on folk stories, songs, jokes, and motifs, much as Dang Nhat Minh's *When the Tenth Month Comes* based itself on the poetic tradition. The film is the product of a conscious effort to develop a distinctive, national cinema and reveals the affection contemporary Vietnamese feel for their cultural past and the inspiration they draw from it. The national content includes the self-portrait of the Vietnamese. Hai Ninh states, "In *Bom*, we are making fun of ourselves. We are using irony and humor about our own character. We are more frank and open now about our good and bad sides. The filmmakers wanted to show people how they should live in this society." The film is also a big-budget historical pageant, filmed in color, and using classical dance troupes and many of the most successful actors in the industry. The project was, in all likelihood, a film to test the international market. The colorful costumes establish a festive, dreamlike mood, supported by stylized movements and gestures based on folk opera (the camera work is sometimes a little flat for such a film). The clusters of dramatized stories concern Bom's proverbial stupidity, the credulity that makes him an easy mark (he is sold a flock of wild geese in a field), and the way he misunderstands all the instructions intended to form him into a cultured scholar. These story clusters are framed by fantasy sequences based on a folk song about Bom: he is offered increasingly greater riches by a landlord in trade for his fan, but is too much the poor booby to accept them. By the end of the film, the characters have acquired an endearing reality, and the recurring motif a curious depth.

Do Minh Tuan is the youngest director whose work I have seen. He graduated from the University of Hanoi in philology and then from the Cinema School. *The Lamp in the Dream* is his debut film. In it, he tells the story of a young teenager, Trung, who is a product and a manifestation of the postwar society of

Vietnam. In a private 1988 paper on the film, the director writes, "Fourie[r] said: from women and children we can understand a nation." For Trung, the war is a childhood memory colored with celebrations of victory. He is typically Vietnamese, living in poverty, but open to his society and his moment in history and easily caught up in his "dream world." The society he lives in is a troubled one, marked by separations and losses in the war. To these are added modern problems. His parents are long divorced, and his father has disappeared. His stepfather was brutal, and Trung needed to be protected by his older brother. Now Trung is living alone in a room. His mother comes to visit him, but—in an unusual scene for the Vietnamese—he refuses to open the door through which she is entreating him. The boy's older brother is involved in petty crime (typically stealing bicycles), and their relation has become ambivalent. Trung has worked at a little restaurant, but quits because he has had enough. His job at a lacquer factory comes to an end when his hand is burned in an accident. He is gradually being alienated from his family and society and is suffering the emotional consequences of loneliness and anxiety, which are threatening to deform his character. At one point, he uses his slingshot to break his stepfather's ceramic pots. He gives himself his own birthday party, putting up a sign, "Birthday Party for Mr. Trung." He dreams of a happy folk holiday for children and elders. "This is a Society full of paradox, misery, but full of charity," the director writes. Trung's teacher—who has felt his sadness in one of his class essays—and schoolmates notice his distress and make efforts to help him. The teacher's boyfriend tries to befriend the boy. An old calligrapher encourages his interest in art and promises to do a hanging scroll for him with the words "A light that never dies." "The important thing," he tells Trung, "is to be moral, to be able to live with yourself."

But the negative forces in society work against Trung. His older brother's stealing gets Trung in trouble with the police. The father of a schoolmate who wants to help him objects to her seeing such a disreputable boy. The old calligrapher dies before he can finish the scroll. Trung is progressively thrown back on himself as, one after another, the normal social attachments cannot provide adequate support. But while thrown back on his isolation and suffering, he comes also to his own resources. There is indeed a lamp in the surrounding darkness, a point of light by which he can read; a play on the saying, "When a man reads a book, his eyes are bright for a thousand years." The film ends with an image of Trung alone, mounted on a horse, certainly a symbolic, not a realistic image. Placed between the wounding and the supportive forces of society, between temptations to crime and encouragement to morality, Trung is realizing himself as an independent person, responsible for his own journey through life.

The complicated story is told with the utmost delicacy and tact and with compassion for all concerned. Little touches describe the characters perfectly.

The girl in Trung's class takes the lead in helping him because "I'm a monitor." Her father puts on his army uniform when he has something serious to discuss with the family. *The Lamp in the Dream* and *When Grandmother Is Away*, with their respectful and original analysis of the problems of young people, compare favorably with such films as Luis Buñuel's *Los Olvidados* and François Truffaut's *The 400 Blows*.

Themes of Vietnamese Cinema

The justice of the Vietnamese cause in the wars against the French and the Americans is so taken for granted that no time is spent offering the kinds of reasons for involvement that are so prominent in American pro-war films like *The Green Berets*.[47] Significantly, such reasons are provided in films on Vietnam's involvement in Kampuchea, as in the documentary *The Day of Return*.

Mourning is naturally a major theme in Vietnamese cinema. It is central in *When the Tenth Month Comes* and *Fairy Tale for 17-Year Olds*. The framework of *The Last Distance Between Us* is the return of the grown-up daughter to visit the graves of her parents. Mourning is also an important plot element in other stories; the final section of *Brothers and Relations* involves the search for the remains of a relative who has fallen in the war. Such films can be compared profitably to American works on the same subject. In fact, after a screening of *When the Tenth Month Comes* on Kauai, an American woman rose to say that she had suffered terribly in the war and that Minh's film was the only one she had ever seen that expressed what she had undergone. Minh was flabbergasted.

Like all civil wars, the Vietnam conflict left many resentments, and members of groups considered hostile or disloyal—former South Vietnamese government and army personnel, Roman Catholics, ethnic Chinese, and so on—have suffered in varying degrees. Vietnamese cinema, however, has emphasized the need for reconciliation, as seen in *The Last Distance Between Us*. At the end of Hai Ninh's documentary, *City at Dawn*, the voice-over states: "The Vietnamese family is now reunited." Hai Ninh discussed the problem in an interview:

> After liberation, we needed to create the harmony of a single people in a united country. We needed unification of soul as well as of politics. To do this, we have to get down to human nature—charity, generosity—to unify ourselves on the basis of equality.

Reconciliation extends even to American soldiers. They are shown acting humanely in *Legend of a Mother*, and their portrayal in *The Abandoned Field*, for all its faults, attempts to give them sympathetic traits: camaraderie and family affection.

A common symbol of this problem of reconciliation is the prostitute, who during the war symbolized the corruption of the South Vietnamese regime and American influence. After the war, many were sent into reeducation camps and then offered menial jobs. Their reception by society was generally nonsupportive, and even negative, as described in *The Last Crime* and *The Young Woman on the Perfumed River*. In Hai Ninh's *Shipwreck Beach*, the conventional boyfriend rejects his fiancée when he discovers her past. Speaking of the film, Hai Ninh says:

> There were lots of prostitutes after the war. People didn't want to compromise themselves. But the prostitutes were victims of the war like any other. They had to be helped to normalize their lives. Revolutionaries should have charity for such people, should give them confidence and hope. So stories of prostitutes have a broader reference. On the one hand, they committed mistakes because of the historical and social situation they were in, so they were like others who committed crimes during the war. On the other hand, society can be judged by the way they are helped and reintegrated.

Criticism of society and government is in fact widespread in Vietnamese films, ranging from making fun of party zealots who figure as minor characters, to films in which criticism is the central theme. Human failings of officials can be targeted—such as vanity and bureaucratic bossiness—but also large social trends and whole government policy directions, albeit past ones, as in *City Under the Fist*. An important basis for criticism seems to be a traditional view of social relations. In *The Last Crime*, the young woman became a prostitute after her mother's divorce. Family tensions—caused by the father's concentration on his government job and desire to get ahead—begin to destroy the family in *When Grandmother Is Away*. Parental problems are the initial cause of the young boy's alienation in *The Lamp in the Dream*. Significantly, the director of that film stated that he was using the boy as a symbol of society. The fact that Vietnamese filmmakers take children so seriously—*When Grandmother Is Away* was in fact made as a children's film!—may be one reason why they use them so well.

An even deeper theme than social and family relations is a general humanism, an emphasis on being authentically human rather than a deformation by whatever cause—for instance, ideological excess and fear in *City Under the Fist*. The ending of *A Quiet Little Town* shows a young married couple standing on the high point of an arched bridge, while the older functionaries, party officials, doctors, and so on, run in place toward them, unable to rid themselves of their old ideas and attitudes and become simply human. Tran Van Thuy's *Report on Humaneness* uses this theme overtly as a criticism of government and society. Humanism implies morality, a sense of hope and purpose in life, without which all is futility and vanity. As the father in *The Last Distance Between Us* tells the alcoholic veteran, "It is easy to die; it is hard to do something."

The importance of these themes for Vietnamese society can be seen from their central place in literature as well as cinema. They have also—just as do the aesthetics of Vietnamese films—a universal significance and appeal.

Vietnamese Films Discussed in This Article

As much information is provided as is available.

The Abandoned Field—Free Fire Zone [Canh dong hoang], 1979, dir. Nguyen Hong Sen.

Arriving at the Steps of the Bridge [Den Voi Nhung Nhip Cau], 1983.

Battleground Along the Route, 1970 (this may possibly be *The Road Battle*, 1971, dir. Nguyen Kha).

Bom the Bumpkin [Thang Bom], 1987, dir. Le Duc Tien.

Brothers and Relations [Ahn va em], 1986, dir. Tran Vu and Nguyen Huu Luyen.

The Citadel Vinh Linh, 1970, dir. Ngoc Quynh.

The City at Dawn, 1975, dir. Hai Ninh and Nguyen Khanh Du.

City Under the Fist [Thi Xa Trong Tam Tay], 1982, dir. Dang Nhat Minh.

The Class for Compassion's Sake.

The Conical Hat [Nom Que].

The Day of Return [Ngay Ve], 1979.

Dien Bien Phu, 1954, dir. Nguyen Tien Loi.

Dong Ho Painting Village [Lang Tranh Dong Ho].

The Electric Line to the Song Da Construction Site [Duong Day Len Song Da], 1981, dir. Le Manh Thich.

The Evil and the Punishment, 1973.

Fairy Tale for 17-Year Olds [Chuyen Co Tich Cho Tuoi 17], 1986, dir. Nguyen Xuan Son.

First Love, 1977, dir. Hai Ninh.

The Forest of Cuc Phuong.

The Girl of Hanoi [Em Be Hanoi], 1974, dir. Hai Ninh.

The Goddess Quan Am [Quan Am Thi Kinh].

The Golden Bird [Con Chun Vanh Khuyen], 1962, dir. Tran Vu.

Hanoi, an Epic Poem, 1973, dir. Phan Quang Dinh.

Hanoi Through Whose Eyes [Hanoi—Trong Mat Ai], 1983, dir. Tran Van Thuy.

Ho Chi Minh City, May 1978, 1978.

Independence Day 1945 [Ngay Doc-Lap], 1975.

Lacquer Painting [Son Mai], 1982, dir. Luong Duc.

The Lamp in the Dream [Ngon Den Trong Mo], 1987, dir. Do Minh Tuan.

The Last Crime [Toi Loi Cuoi Cung], 1979, dir. Tran Phuong.

The Last Distance Between Us [Khoang Cach Con Lai], 1981, dir. Nguyen
   Xuan Son.
Left Alone [Con Lai Mot Minh], 1984, dir. Hong Sen.
Legend of a Mother [Chuyen Thoai Ve Nguoi Me], 1987, dir. Bach Diep.
Love Duets of Bac Ninh, 1987, dir. Thanh An.
Luu Binh and Duong Le [Luu Binh Duong Le], 1987, dir. Pham Thu.
Nguyen Ai Quoc—Ho Chi Minh, dir. Pham Ky Nam.
On the Crest of the Waves, Facing the Storm [Dau Song Ngong Gio], 1967,
   dir. Ngoc Quynh.
On the Same River, 1959, dir. Nguyen Hong Nghi and Pham Hieu Dan.
Once Upon a Time in Vu Dai Village [Lang Vu Dai Ngay Ay], 1982, dir.
   Pham Van Khoa.
1/50th of a Second in a Lifetime [Mot Phan Nam Muoi Giay Cuoc Doi], 1984,
   dir. Dao Trong Khanh.
The Peal of the Orange Bell [Hoi Chuong Mau Da Cam], 1983, dir. Nguyen
   Ngoc Trung.
Punishment [Trung Phat], 1984, dir. Bach Diep.
A Quiet Little Town [Thi Tran Yen Tinh], 1986, dir. Le Duc Tien.
The Red Cochineal [Canh Kien Do], 1987, dir. Vu Le My.
Report on Humaneness [Chuyen Tu Te], 1986, Tran Van Thuy.
Return to Dien Bien Phu—The Hope.
The River of Aspiration [Dong Song Khat Vong], 1986, dir. Nguyen Ngoc
   Trung.
*The Secret of the Statue of the Dau Pagoda [Dieu Bi An Trong Pho Tuong Chua
   Dau]*, 1987, dir. Phung Ty et al.
The 17th Parallel—Day and Night [Vi Tuyen 17 Ngay Va Dem], 1972, dir.
   Hai Ninh.
Shipwreck Beach [Bai bien doi nguoi], 1983, dir. Hai Ninh.
A Small Alley, 1988 or 1989, dir. Bach Diep.
Unforgotten Days and Nights.
Victory at Dien Bien Phu [Chien Than Dien Bien Phu], 1964, dir. Tran Viet.
We Will Meet Again, 1974, dir. Tran Vu.
When Grandmother Is Away [Khi Vang Ba], 1985, dir. Nguyen Anh Thai.
When Mother Is Away [Khi Me Vang Nha], 1979, dir. Nguyen Khanh Du.
When the Birds Return, 1984, dir. Khanh Du and Anh Thai.
When the Tenth Month Comes [Bao gio cho den thang muoi], 1984, dir. Dang
   Nhat Minh.
The Young Woman of Sao Beach [Chi Tu Hau Bai Sao], 1963, dir. Pham Ky
   Nam.
The Young Woman on the Perfumed River [Co Gai Tren Song], 1987, dir.
   Dang Nhat Minh.

Notes

1. In 1983, selections of Vietnamese films were shown at the Mostra International del Cine Nuevo at Pesaro and in Algiers. In 1984, a selection was shown at a conference in Spain to commemorate the 10th anniversary of the end of the Vietnam war. The American cinematographer Haskell Wexler and the Vietnamese director Bui Dinh Hac attended this conference. That same year, a week-long series of Vietnamese films was shown in Paris. A few Vietnamese films have also been screened at the Festival of Three Continents at Nantes.

2. This was followed by *Once Upon a Time in Vu Dai Village* the next year. In 1987, *Fairy Tale for 17-Year Olds* was shown along with the documentary *1/50th of a Second in a Lifetime*. Through connections made at the festival, the former film was shown widely in the United States and then at São Paolo and the Berlin Film Festival. A showing of *When the Tenth Month Comes* was also arranged at the 1988 Hong Kong International Film Festival.

3. Members of the consortium included Nguyen Thu, Geoffrey D. Gilmore of the UCLA Film and Television Archive, L. Somi Roy of the Asia Society, Victor Kobayashi of the University of Hawaii Summer Session, Emily Laskin of the American Film Institute, Stephen O'Harrow of the U.S. Committee for Scientific Cooperation with Vietnam, and myself. The project began with the screening of five films at the 1988 Hawaii International Film Festival and the participation of two filmmakers and a film critic from Vietnam. The panel discussions with Vietnamese and American filmmakers at that festival were, to my knowledge, the first public bilateral discussions of the war to be held in the United States. An American tour of those five selected films and others is now in progress, including an estimated thirty-five sites.

A number of international contacts for Vietnamese cinema were made through the Festival as well. For a major example, Neil Gibson and Leslie Gould founded the Campaign for Vietnam Cinema in England, which has shipped more than a container load of equipment to Vietnam, has organized in 1990 a Season of Vietnamese Films at the National Film Theatre in London, and has arranged for the sale of five features and two documentaries to Channel 4. Gibson's documentary *Vietnam Cinema* (1960) is an important historical record.

4. I would make special mention of Vice Minister of Culture Nguyen Dinh Quang (both visits and 1988 festival), the General Director of the Vietnam Cinema Department Nguyen Thu (second visit and 1987 festival), the Deputy General Director Bui Dinh Hac (second visit and 1988 festival), and the directors Nguyen Xuan Son (1987 festival) and Dang Nhat Minh (1988 festival), who spent two months in Hawaii as Filmmaker-in-Residence at the Institute of Culture and Communication, East-West Center. Also very helpful were Nguyen Van Tinh, Pham Ngoc Diep, and Duong Manh Hien, who cared for me in Hanoi.

On those visits and festivals, see, e.g., Anonymous, "Day La Lan Dau Tien Toi Duoc Gap Ke Thu . . . ," *Tuoi Tre Chu Nhat* (15 January 1989): 9; P. B., "Giua Viet Nam Va My," *Saigon Giai Phong* (15 January 1989); Ethel Greenfield Booth, "The Vietnam War: De-Rambo-ized by the Vietnamese," *Los Angeles Times/Calendar* (19 March 1989): 65; Burl Burlingame, "Festival offers insight on Vietnam," *Honolulu Star-Bulletin* (29 November 1988): B-1; John Charlot, "Vietnam, The Strangers Meet: The Vietnam Film Project," in *The East-West Center Presents the Hawai'i International Film Festival, November 27–December 3, 1988* (Honolulu: The East-West Center, 1988): 44–49; "Vietnamese Cinema: The Power of the Past," *Journal of American Folklore* 102, No. 406 (October–December 1989): 442–52; "Victims of a Common Tragedy," *The Los Angeles Times*, Calendar Part II: Festival '90 (26

August 1990): 5, 19; Tran Dac, "Suy Nghi Bau Dau Cua Mot Nha Nghien Cien My Ve Phim Truyen Viet Nam [Initial Thoughts of an American Researcher on Vietnamese Feature Films]," *Nghe Thuat dien anh*, No. 2 (1987): 55f.; Roger Ebert, "Hawaiian fest promotes East-West understanding," *Chicago Sun-Times* (12 December 1987); "How the other side views Vietnam: Hollywood images trigger festival fire," *Chicago Sun-Times* (11 December 1988): 3, 6; Janice Fuhrman, "In film, U.S., Vietnam making peace: Emotions run high as film festival presents both sides of a common tragedy," *The Japan Times* (9 December 1988): 15; Barry Hampe, "Vietnamese gov't preps docu series," *The Hollywood Reporter* (10 November 1987): 1, 4; "Vietnam seeks co-prod'n deals," *The Hollywood Reporter* (3 December 1987): 1, 18; Eric Herter, "Antidote to Hollywood: Vietnamese Films Show The Human Face of War," *East West* 8, No. 3 (Spring 1989): 12, 14; Karen Jaehne, "Cinema in Vietnam: When the Shooting Stopped . . . and the Filming Began," *Cineaste* 17, No. 2 (1989): 32–37; Victor Kobayashi, "Vietnam cinema flourishes without war stories," *Honolulu Star-Bulletin* (19 May 1988): A-23; Dang Nhat Minh, "Phim Vietnam o Ha-oai," *Nhan Dan/Chu Nhat* (12 March 1989): 4; Stephen O'Harrow, "Vu Dai Village in Those Days," in *The Hawaii International Film Festival, November 30–December 6, 1986* (Honolulu: The East-West Center, 1986): 50; Jay Scott, "Comparing images of a shared wound: Filmmakers on both sides look at Vietnam War," *The Globe and Mail*, Toronto (9 December 1988): C1; A. A. Smyser, "Spotlighting movies made in Vietnam," *Honolulu Star-Bulletin* (29 March 1988): A-3; Xuan Son, "Gap Go O Ha-oai [Meeting in Hawaii]," *Nhan Dan* (16 January 1988): 3; Charles Turner, "Vietnamese filmmaker says 'our art does reflect life'," *Centerviews*, The East-West Center (January-February 1989): 5; Bob Welch, "Just like the movies: Her turkey dinner helped bring opposing nations together," *Journal-American*, Seattle (28 December 1988): A3. The American tour of Vietnamese films has occasioned a large number of articles.

I have since received letters with news from Vietnam and have had the opportunity of updating my information in long conversations with Neil Gibson at the 1990 Hawaii International Film Festival, after he had spent six months in Hanoi. I am grateful also for the observations of the non-Vietnamese with whom I discussed Vietnamese films. Due to communication difficulties with Vietnam, my information is still incomplete on a number of points and references and I was unable to double-check others.

More information can be found in the publications of the Vietnam Cinema Department and other Vietnamese organizations in English, French, and Vietnamese: Anonymous, *Dang Muc Phim Viet Nam 1980–1982: List of Vietnamese Films* (Hanoi (?): The Viet Nam Film Archives, 1983); Anonymous, *Vietnamese Feature Films, Films de Fiction Vietnamiens: Catalogue 1972–1984* (Ho Chi Minh City: Magazine "Dien Anh" [The Cinema], 1985); Trinh Mai Diem, *30 Years of Vietnam's Cinema Art* (Hanoi: The Vietnam Cinema Archives, 1983); Banh Bao and Huu Ngoc, *L'Itinéraire du Film de Fiction Vietnamien: Expériences vietnamiennes* (Hanoi: Éditions des Langues Étrangères, 1984); Ngo Manh Lan, "Cinema of Viet Nam on the Way of Approaching Life" (Typescript, n.d.), and "Looking Inwards: Vietnamese Cinema in the Eighties," *Cinemaya*, No. 2 (January-March 1988–89): 6–14; Nguyen Duy Can, ed., *Lich Su Dien Anh Cach Mang Viet Nam* (Hanoi: Cuc Dien Anh, 1983); also to be consulted are the Vietnamese-language film magazine *Dien Anh* and the English-language *Film Vietnam*. Vinafim regularly publishes mimeographed information sheets on new films.

5. This film was the product of a Vietnamese team that included the work of the cameraman Nguyen Thu, now the General Director of the Vietnam Cinema Department. A separate film was made by the distinguished Russian director Roman Karmen, *Vietnam on the Road to Victory*, working with the script writer Nguyen Dinh Thi and the director Pham Van Khoa. On the prior history of cinema in Vietnam, see Bao and Ngoc, "L'Itinéraire": 3ff. I am unable to discuss pre-1975 South Vietnamese films. The majority of

these were reportedly entertainment movies, often including music. Dang Nhat Minh told me that the one artistic film he knew was *Xin Chon Noi Nay Lam Que Huong*. After 1975, the South Vietnamese industry was reorganized by Northerners, and a number of North Vietnamese directed movies at the Ho Chi Minh City studio, such as Hai Ninh with *First Love* and Hong Sen with *The Abandoned Field*. All but a few of the post-1975 films I have seen were produced in North Vietnam.

6. For details see Diem, "30 Years": 33–41.

7. In the late 1980s, a typical budget approximated forty million dong; the exchange rate with the U.S. dollar varied from 380 dong to 4000 (monetary reform has since stabilized the situation). The necessary money is loaned from a bank and must be repaid from funds generated by selling the film to the distributor, who now has the right to refuse to accept a film. Recent competition from television has depleted financing, resulting in even lower budgets and shorter shooting schedules. The earlier distributing agency has now been divided into Fafim for internal distribution and Vinafim for external. External distribution has until recently been limited mainly to East Bloc countries.

8. All purchases were apparently being made from East Bloc countries. The film, all 35-mm., was usually the East German (Orwo NT55 Firma negative, Orwo PF2 Firma stock), although the Vietnamese would have preferred the more expensive Kodak. Orwo black and white is passable, but the color film has proved so unstable that the department cancelled its plans to start filming most features in color (they wanted to make colorful, historical films for the international market). The Campaign for Vietnam Cinema has now provided a 35-mm. hot processing negative machine that can handle Fuji and Kodak, but because of the expense of those stocks, the first purchases are reportedly being made of the West German Agfa.

German, Soviet, and American cameras are used (Arriflex 2-B is mentioned), but they are practically antique. Some lenses have lost their sharpness in depth-of-field focus, and filters are few. A great deal of time is lost adjusting lights that are too old and too few. The indoor studio in Hanoi is an old, dusty, barnlike structure without heat or air-conditioning. Little work is done in video because of the lack of equipment, but more video and television work is projected. The latest work of the director Dang Nhat Minh was in video. Recent donations of equipment by the Campaign for Vietnam Cinema should improve the situation markedly.

Filmmaking—as other enterprises in Vietnam—is complicated by the government's policy of guaranteed employment. The shoot I witnessed was burdened by a work group of fifty people, when twenty-five would have sufficed. The superfluous ones simply got in the way and watched. Government policy—as well as more personal reasons—can encourage the department to spread its few funds as widely as possible rather than concentrating them on the very best filmmakers.

9. Lan, "Looking Inwards": 10.

10. Webster K. Nolan, "Vietnam *glasnost*: 'Socialist formulas don't work'," *The Honolulu Advertiser* (12 August 1988): A-27.

11. See Paul Clark, *Chinese Cinema: Culture and Politics since 1949* (Cambridge: Cambridge University Press, 1987), pp. 41f., 44, 61, 69–82, 156–60.

12. I was unable to obtain an exact definition of the credit line *Bien Tap* "Script Approval," an office of the Ministry of Culture (Neil Gibson, personal communication), or to discover the function of a woman I met who was checking a new print of a film that had already been released (possibly another make-work position).

13. The only film that I was told had been suppressed after completion is Hai Ninh's *Shipwreck Beach* of 1984, which was withdrawn after its showing at that year's national film festival. Reports vary widely on the reasons for this action. Apparently *not* a factor was the nudity in the film—more than in any other Vietnamese film to date and earlier

by three years than Minh's *The Young Woman on the Perfumed River*. When the film was first shown, one government official objected to the scene in which the very evil villain describes living in Vietnam as being in a prison; the official called this "a slap in the face of the government." Others say the film was not released because of its aesthetic failings, a real possibility.

14. Born in Hanoi in 1934, Nguyen Thu started work as a cameraman in 1952, contributing footage to more than ten documentaries, including the first version of *Dien Bien Phu* (1954). While working on that film, Thu lost a leg while moving in a mine field to get a better camera angle. From 1960 to 1964, he studied at the Faculty of Feature Films Direction of the All-Union-States Institute of Cinema in the USSR. After further work as a scriptwriter and director, he became in 1978 the Deputy General Director of the Vietnam Cinema Department and Director of the Feature Films Studio in Hanoi. In 1984, he became the General Director of the department and a member of the National Assembly (and member of the Culture and Education Commission of the VIIth and VIIIth Legislatures of the Assembly).

15. Diem, "30 Years": 21.

16. On Russian teachers in China, see Clark, "Chinese Cinema": 40f. The Vietnam Film Archives and the Cinema Technique Institute were founded in 1979, Diem, "30 Years": 37–40.

17. For instance, the directors Hong Sen and Dang Nhat Minh studied in Bulgaria; Nguyen Thu, Nguyen Xuan Son, Le Duc Tien, and Do Minh Tuan in the Soviet Union; and Luu Trong Hong, Chief of the Technical Section of the Hanoi Feature Film Studio, and his chief engineer Nguyen Kim Cuong, in East Germany. Pham Ky Nam and Dang Nhat Minh studied in France.

18. I was told of a 1975 coproduction with the Soviet Union on the bombing of Haiphong, *Coordinates of Death*. In 1987, the department collaborated with the German Democratic Republic on *Life in the Forest*, the story of a German fighting with the French army who defected to the Viet Minh.

19. Diem, "30 Years": 22.

20. Susan Manuel, "Vietnam's view: The other side of the picture: Vietnam's filmmakers depict war in human terms," *Honolulu Star-Bulletin* (November 1988): B-1, 4:4.

21. Dang Nhat Minh, "In the Realm of Darkness and Light," *Cinemaya*, No. 7 (April-June 1990): 12.

22. For the history of the Central Studios of Documentary and Scientific Films, Hanoi, see Diem, "30 Years": 34f. In 1985 Luu Xuan Thu was appointed director of the studio. Born in 1932, he began his career as an actor and became a famous cinematographer for both documentaries and feature films. He is still active as a director of documentaries. He has recently been appointed director of Secofilm, described above.

23. Dang Nhat Minh, "So That Different Peoples May Come Together," in *The East-West Center Presents the Hawai'i International Film Festival, November 27–December 3, 1988* (Honolulu: The East-West Center, 1988): 40–43: 40. Hong Sen began as an army cameraman and turned to features only after the war, using his experiences as a basis for *The Abandoned Field*. The development of feature films from documentaries parallels the earlier one of prose novels from journalism. In Vietnamese literature, prose was used mostly for government reports and short folktales, while "novels" were in verse. Twentieth-century journalism influenced the creation of modern Vietnamese language and new genres, especially the prose novel, which could be romantic, but was more often realistic; e.g., Nguyen Khac Vien and Huu Ngoc, *Anthologie de la Littérature Vietnamienne*, Volume 3, *Deuxième Moitié du XIXe Siècle—1945* (Hanoi: Éditions des Langues Étrangères, 1975), pp. 54f., 369.

24. Diem, "30 Years": 15f.

25. *Arriving at the Steps of the Bridge,* on a Vietnamese-Soviet construction project, is influenced by *Electric Line,* but less successful. A number of documentaries are undoubtedly bland, if informative on the many interesting aspects of Vietnamese culture—such as *Lacquer Painting, The Secret of the Statue of the Dau Pagoda,* and *The Conical Hat.* A number of other works can be categorized as "newsreel documentaries," often with a heavy ideological slant. *Ho Chi Minh City, May 1978* describes the city three years after the 1975 takeover, reporting on the efforts at social reform. *The Class for Compassion's Sake* describes efforts to care for disabled or homeless children in the city. *The Day of Return [Ngay Ve],* the first documentary to be made in Kampuchea after the invasion by the Vietnamese, combines moving interviews with Kampuchean displaced persons and victims of the Pol Pot regime with unfortunate footage of a staged victory parade and rally. I have described a number of documentaries in John Charlot, "Fairy Tale for 17-Year Olds," "Vietnamese Documentary Films," in *The 1987 Hawai'i International Film Festival, November 29–December 5, 1987* (Honolulu: The East-West Center, 1987), pp. 65f., 67–70: 67–70.

26. I have not seen the sequel, which carries the biography beyond 1945, but have been told it is equally successful.

27. An interesting aspect of this effort at completeness is the attention paid in war documentaries to *all* those involved in the war effort, especially those whose work is usually unnoticed. For instance, *Battleground Along the Route* describes the activities of those charged with keeping the supply routes open, from the dangerous work—such as exploding antipersonnel mines—to the ordinary but necessary, like tending gardens. The film can be compared to the French 1952 documentary *Avec la Rafale* (directed by Kowal) about armored trains. Keeping the routes open is a subject of segments of other French documentaries of the time. The possible influence on Vietnamese cinema of documentaries made by the French army on the Indochina war should be explored.

28. *Return to Dien Bien Phu—The Hope* is the record of an anniversary celebration of the battle, which shows the current state of the site. The hope for peace is personified by the ethnic people of the region, who have suffered for centuries from living in such a border and battle zone. They can now enjoy peace and unity with their neighbors, as symbolized in their circular dance of welcome into which the visitors are drawn.

29. Diem, "30 Years": 11, 16. Also Nolan, "Vietnam *glasnost.*" Compare Clark, "Chinese Cinema": 44f.

30. Diem, "30 Years": 27. For China, compare Clark, "Chinese Cinema": 56ff., 63ff., 101, 117f., 125f., 133–37, 166, 180.

31. Minh, "So That Different Peoples": 43. Charlot, "Power of the Past": 448–51.

32. Anonymous, "Vietnamese Feature Films": 33. *When Mother Is Away* was a popular success, but was heavily criticized by the army, which protested that it would never let a mother of five children—or even two!—leave them alone to go on a mission. Such a mother would not be asked to serve except in a support capacity, and if she absolutely had to leave, her children would be placed in the care of others. The Vietnam Cinema Department replied that it was taking artistic license to tell a good story.

33. In that film, the director reportedly left his actors largely to their own devices. On Pham Van Khoa, see Diem, "30 Years": 23, 26, 56, 58; Hoang Quy, "Veteran Film Director Pham Van Khoa: People's Artist," *Film Vietnam,* No. 2 (1984): 14ff.; Anonymous, "Vietnamese Feature Films": 39, 73; on the film, O'Harrow, "Vu Dai."

34. Diem, "30 Years": 23, 24, 26, 55, 57ff.; Anonymous, "Vietnamese Feature Films": 11, 19, 31; Charlot, "Vietnam, The Strangers Meet": 47f.

35. Diem, "30 Years": 26, 57f., 60; Anonymous, "Vietnamese Feature Films": 13, 25.

36. Diem, "30 Years": 23f., 26, 44, 56, 58ff.; Anonymous, "Vietnamese Feature Films": 5, 9, 17, 35. During my second visit to Hanoi, Hai Ninh received Geoffrey Gilmore and

me graciously at the studio and accorded us four interviews, which I have used in this article.

37. A Vietnamese who lived through the bombing told me that fear and some panic were the normal reactions. In contrast, in Hai Ninh's *The 17th Parallel*, the children are horrified rather than edified by the burning of an old villager who has worked for the resistance.

38. Diem, "30 Years": 23, 51, 55ff., 60; Anonymous, "Vietnamese Feature Films": 21.

39. Earlier, the officer has been shown looking at the photograph he took of the heroine while he listens to some piano playing. When the husband attacked the South Vietnamese officer, a needle stuck in the groove of the record being played. Curiously, a French army documentary of 1952, *Aviation de Chasse en Indochine* (directed by Kowal), uses jazzy piano playing as background music to a scene of the fighter plane approaching and attacking the target.

40. Diem, "30 Years": 26, 54f., 59, 61; Van Hac, "Hong Sen and his Works," *Film Vietnam*, No. 1 (1984): 10f.; Anonymous, "Vietnamese Feature Films": 23, 27, 45, 55; Charlot, "Vietnam, The Strangers Meet": 45f.

41. Anonymous, "Vietnamese Feature Films": 51, 61; John Charlot, "When the Tenth Month Comes . . . ," in *The Hawai'i International Film Festival, November 26–December 8, 1985* (Honolulu: The East-West Center, 1985), p. 48; "Vietnam, The Strangers Meet": 46f.; Minh, "Phim Vietnam," "In the Realm," which contains an autobiography and filmography, and should be compared with the following information from different sources. Dang Nhat Minh's documentaries (director and script writer) include *On the Trails of Geologists [Theo Chan Nguoi Dia Chat]*, 1968; *Ha Bac—My Native Land [Ha Bac—Que Huong]*, 1969; *The Faces of May [Thang 5 Nhung Guong Mat]*, 1975; *Nguyen Trai—Great Vietnamese Poet of the 18th Century [Nguyen Trai]*, 1980; *Hanoi—City of Flying Dragons [Hanoi—Thanh Pho Rong Bay]* (video), 1986. Feature films: *Nhung, a Young Woman of Saigon [Chi Nhung]*, 1970; *Stars on the Sea [Nhung Ngoi Sao Bien]*, 1973; *A Rainy Day at the End of the Year [Ngay Mua Cuoi Nam]*, 1978; *City Under the Fist [Thi Xa Trong Tam Tay]*, 1982; *When the Tenth Month Comes [Bao Gio Cho Den Thang 10]*, 1984; *The Young Woman on the Perfumed River [Co Gai Tren Song]*, 1987; [the following item is from Minh's 1990 filmography] *A Man Alone [Chi Mot Nguoi Con Song]* (video), 1989. On the three before the last item, Minh was scriptwriter as well as director; I have no further information on *A Man Alone*.

Minh was born in 1938 in Hanoi, the son of a prominent doctor. He studied at the *lycée* at Hue and, when his parents joined the resistance, in the forests of Tuyen Quang Province, graduating in 1954. He studied later at the Institute of Russian Language and Literature, Moscow, graduating in 1959. He worked as a Russian translator at the Vietnam Cinema Department until he was asked to direct a documentary. He received six months training in Bulgaria in 1976 and eight months in Paris in 1985. He has published award-winning short stories and film criticism. He was elected General Secretary of the Vietnam Cinematography Association in 1989.

42. Stanley Karnow, *Vietnam: A History* (New York: Penguin Books, 1984), pp. 225f.

43. Minh, "Phim Vietnam": 40.

44. Nguyen Xuan Son was born in 1938 and studied directing at the Vietnam Cinema School from 1965 to 1968, where he then worked as a lecturer until 1972. From 1972 to 1979, he studied feature film direction at the All-Union-States Institute of Cinema in Moscow. Besides the two films discussed, Nguyen Xuan Son has directed *A Blunder*, 1983; *Looking for the Land*, 1984; and *The River Mouth* (documentary), 1985. Anonymous, "Vietnamese Feature Films": 69.

45. Charlot, "Fairy Tale for 17-Year Olds": 65f.

46. Le Duc Tien was born in 1949. From 1967 to 1972, he worked as a war reporter for the military studio and from 1975 to 1979 studied film directing at the Soviet Univer-

sity of Cinema. Le Duc Tien's professors were A. Xtolpier and N. Ozerop. In 1982, he was assistant director on *The Case of the Aimless Bullet* and in 1983 on *The Mistake*. In 1985, he directed *The Sound of the Peace Bomb*. Charlot, "Vietnam, The Strangers Meet": 48f.

47. *The Green Berets* seems to have exercised an important influence on later films. Its training sessions are echoed in *Full Metal Jacket,* and the famous "birth" scene in *Platoon* of soldiers deplaning in Vietnam seems to have been taken directly from the parallel scene in *The Green Berets*. Dang Nhat Minh viewed a large number of American films on the war while he was Filmmaker-in-Residence at The East-West Center; his diplomatic response when asked to evaluate a film he disliked was, "It's better than *The Green Berets*."

Important and unrecognized has been the influence on American films of Pierre Schoendoerffer's *La 317ᵉ Section [Platoon 317]* (1965) and *The Anderson Platoon* (1967). Schoendoerffer is now coordinating a feature film on Dien Bien Phu to be filmed in Vietnam. He was the French army documentary cameraman for that battle and was captured at the fall of the fortress.

8 | Cinema and Nation
Dilemmas of Representation in Thailand

Annette Hamilton

WALTER BENJAMIN, IN "The Work of Art in the Age of Mechanical Reproduction" (1936), drew attention to the extraordinary changes in the concept of "art" and "artist" consequent upon the development of new technological processes. Reproductions of art works substitute a plurality of copies for a unique existence and permit art forms to meet the beholder in his or her own particular situation. According to Benjamin, "These two processes lead to a tremendous shattering of tradition.... Both processes are intimately connected with the contemporary mass movements. Their most powerful agent is the film" (Benjamin 1969, 221). The most important effects of film arise from its technical capabilities:

> By close-ups of the things around us, by focusing on hidden details of familiar objects, by exploring commonplace milieus under the ingenious guidance of the camera, the film ... extends our comprehension of the necessities which rule our lives.... With the close-up, space expands: with slow motion, movement is extended.... Evidently a different nature opens itself to the camera than opens to the naked eye.... The camera introduces us to unconscious optics as does psychoanalysis to unconscious impulses. (Benjamin 1969, 236–37)

From the point of view of a "pure" art form, "the necessities that rule our lives" are predominantly those deriving from space, time, and perception. Film and cinema, however, can only exist within social, economic, and cultural parameters: film is expensive and must find its sustenance and support in a broader audience than other forms of "pure art"; film, once created, can circulate and recirculate at rates far beyond the capacities of any forms other than photographic images; film indeed does so today through television, cable, and satellite technologies hardly imaginable in Benjamin's day, although these are still aspects of the same technological processes, the replication and circulation of images.

Film production and reception necessarily involve a series of complex relations between cultural forms and structures, economic relations within an industrial-commercial matrix, and the socio-political realities within which production and circulation take place. Today, the potential conflicts between sites of production and globalized circulation are emergent as never before, as the full impact of new technologies begins to be understood by national governments. This is most particularly apparent in Asia, as competing commercial interests introduce satellite services capable of transcending national cultural and social boundaries and offer programming defined by the interests of global modernity and transnational capitalism, which cut across national interests and extremely limited local concepts of appropriate viewing for the mass audiences. Here I do not intend to take up this issue directly, but rather to look at the way the relation among nation-state, political struggle, and cultural expression has created a specific context for film in Thailand, which exemplifies the dilemmas of a national cinema required to survive on a solely commercial basis while being subject to direct political intervention. The result is a schismogenesis: filmmakers of an educated and often elite background are forced to make films for a popular audience which other members of the elite and educated sectors ignore or despise; a popular audience is molded by performative and narrative traditions often alien to the elite and educated filmmakers; an "international" context emerges for certain kinds of Thai films, and thus co-exists a dual context for "success," where success in one context seldom equates with success in the other.

This analytic perspective is hardly novel. Wimal Dissanayake has focused our attention on the situation of serious filmmakers in Asia, whom he sees as among the "sensitive instruments" of society (Dissanayake 1988). Christine Fugate has described the situation of Thai filmmakers as one involving three audiences: the Bangkokians, the provincial viewers, and the international or foreign audience. She correctly points out that the films most popular with Thai critics and popular audiences do only limited business in Bangkok and even less in the provinces, citing the instance of Euthana Mukdasnit's film *Butterfly and Flower*, which received the East-West Center Award at the 1986 Hawaii International Film Festival but made only 5 million *baht* in Thai circulation, most of that in Bangkok (Fugate 1990, 7).

Anyone interested in Thai film, professionally or academically, is only too aware of the situation described here: the purpose of this chapter is to explore the role of the Thai state directly and indirectly in the film industry from the point of view of both makers and audience. I will suggest that the Thai power elites' concepts of the role of film derive directly from an attempt to assert and maintain a curious repressive-modernist control over the political/social consciousness of a society plunged headlong into a postmodernist global economy.

Thailand of course is not alone in this situation: the neighboring capitalist states of Southeast Asia all manifest to a greater or lesser extent the same pattern, but Thailand is particularly powerfully affected precisely because Thailand "modernized" so early and so thoroughly at the level of communicative infrastructure and education (see Hamilton 1987). It is important to recognize that around 90 percent of the population has access to centrally supplied electricity, and around 80 percent is effectively or substantially literate (including women). Wherever there is electricity, people have access to television. My own research among rural dwellers in a south-central province showed that television was the first consumption item families would invest in after they were linked to electrification services, and VCRs were also in demand among the more affluent. Villagers in one nonelectrified region I worked in said they constantly requested electrical service in order to be able to watch television.

Cinema too is available to virtually everyone. Every provincial town of any size has a cinema (or, in some towns such as Nakhorn Sri Thammarat, scores of them). These cinemas show "double" programs of films that have already had their first run in Bangkok; entry is around 10–20 *baht* (fifty cents to one dollar) and here is where most movie financial returns are made. But even remote villages still have access to cinema, through the *nang reua*, mobile cinemas, which move from village to village and sometimes between provinces with a program of films. Mobile cinemas appear at every important temple festival or public holiday and occupy open ground where temporary screens are erected. Three films will be shown: one Chinese, one Thai, one *farang* (foreign), usually in that order. The Chinese film will be one of three genres: a comedy, a "historical" drama, or an "action" film with gangsters or martial artists. This will be followed by a Thai film, usually a drama *(nang chiwit)* or a comedy (depending on which was shown in the "Chinese" segment). Finally, there will be a foreign film, which could be a horror film or a love story. Some people say the last film shown in remote areas is a straight pornographic feature, although I have never seen this myself. The program doesn't usually begin until 9:00 p.m. or later, and hence this "last feature" will not begin until well after midnight. Certainly there was a very high demand for Western pornographic films at video stores in provincial towns, at least until the "video crackdown" in 1989 (see Hamilton forthcoming), and the association of foreigners with pornography is well entrenched in mass consciousness.

There is, thus, an extremely high level of availability and exposure to cinematic and televised images in Thailand. In spite of this, however, Thailand is not a society that knows itself through cinema and television. Although societies such as that of contemporary America may exist and reproduce through the images and meanings that flow from cinema and television, Thailand has not become the kind of video, visual culture where "[r]epresentations of the real have become stand-ins for actual, lived experience" (Denzin 1991, x). Nevertheless, in many respects Thailand is an example of a dramaturgical society; but its dramaturgical principles are not based on a postmodern imaginary created through a commercialized visual culture, but rather on varying structures of recognizable narrative and performance, some of which are based on much older forms and others of which are a product of more recent political events.

Film, for the masses of people in Thailand, is still heavily interpreted through older narrative traditions. Even the common word for movie, *nang*, derives directly from the traditional performative genre of the shadow play. *Nang* is the word for "hide" or "skin"; *nang yai* and *nang talung* are two forms of entertainment using stretched hides to make "puppets" similar to those used in the shadow-play of Indonesia and elsewhere. *Nang yai* is based solely on the traditional epic, Ramayana, while *nang talung* is less formal and rests on the puppeteers' use of puns and jokes around current issues during the performance of simple, familiar stories. Exactly the same process takes place with the dubbing of non-Thai films for showing to rural audiences today: the dubbed versions may have little to do with the original scripts of the films and insert instead references, jokes, and allusions to current events which can be derived from the narrative and which correspond to the interpretive traditions of the audience. The more formal word, *pab-payont*, means literally "moving image" and is used in all formal contexts in Thailand, such as award ceremonies and so on.

The "deep structure" underlying the conflicts of the Thai film industry derives from the existence of three social segments, two of which are engaged in a bitter struggle over "national representation," often in the context of the third. These can be understood as:

(1) the pseudo-traditionalized conservative power elite, including some elements of the bourgeois commercial classes and military groups;

(2) the younger, educated, Western-oriented bourgeoisie, anxious for social change and pushing at the boundaries of possibility in the current deeply conflicted political environment;

(3) the rural and provincial people, many of whom are still engaged in agriculture but who are being incorporated in multiple and little-understood ways into global capitalism both as producers and consumers. This group also contains the marginalized elements in Thai society: the ethnic and religious minorities (hill tribes, Muslims); the urban poor; those supported directly by the sex industry; beggars and drug addicts; and a variety of others who are, from the dominant segment's perspective, not supposed to exist.

The critical point here is that there is singularly little mutual comprehension among these three groups. People do not move from one social context into another on similar terms. As in other Asian societies, hierarchy and patronage structure all social relationships. Social mobility is possible, particularly at a material level, but once achieved it cuts people off to a considerable extent from others. Particularly in the context of the hyper-rapid social and economic changes of the past decade, there is singularly little understanding of the respective world views between the segments. Forces within the first segment control the media environment, both formally (through censorship) and informally (through funding, taxes, and other indirect means); the writers, filmmakers, and producers come from the second segment; the third largely constitutes the paying audience. This of course is something of an oversimplification: educated children of the first segment frequently share the ideological positions of the second, while many members of the second segment come from a provincial small-town background. Nevertheless it provides a working model through which to understand the complex factors coming into play in cultural reproduction in Thailand.[1]

The struggle over representation in Thailand is a struggle between the interests and ideological perspectives of these three segments, of which the third provides the constituent focus for the other two, but in very different positions. For the elite, the actual life conditions of people in rural and provincial areas are generally still comprehended through images of the old farmer toiling away with his buffalo in the rice field. Country and rural life is seen as necessary but moronic, something the urban elite wish to have nothing to do with beyond looking at the lovely green of new rice fields on the way to their golfers' condominium in their Mercedes. Slum-dwellers and other "worthy" unfortunates should be supported by charitable activities and donations to temples; the "unworthy" do not deserve notice except when they can be of service, including pleasure services. For people in this segment, Thailand still is a "two-group" society, elite Bangkokians and everybody else (*Khon Muang Luang* and *Khon Baan Nork*).

For the educated urban intelligentsia, the rural villagers and other marginalized groups provide a focus for their own sense of injustice in society. This group includes many ex-students formed by the events of 1973 and many Western-educated people, as well as others in a wide variety of public-service sector positions (education and administration particularly) who are profoundly aware of the disjunctions between the booming Thai economy and the political and social forms, which derive from earlier times. The continued domination by and struggles between various factions of the military, the unscrupulousness and greed of sectors of the commercial classes, the role of middle-men (characteristically identified as "Chinese") in the extraction of surplus from the rural sectors, the depressed conditions in some areas in particular, the prominence of the sex industry and exploitation of female and child labor: above all, the refusal by arms and agencies of the state to permit the free flow of information through the mass media has created an oppositional sense that focuses on specific injustices to the rural and poor sectors as symbols of everything that is wrong in modern Thailand. These foci have now been joined by environmental issues, which, since the floods of 1988, have come into greater prominence and which can be seen to encapsulate all of the socially meaningful issues touched on above.

Thus, for many of those concerned with cultural reproduction, their main contribution to a "worthy" society emerges from a focus on the marginalized, suppressed, and disadvantaged. Unable to reflect society as it is, filmmakers and writers focus on suffering and injustice at the "edges," which seldom appeals to the mass audience. In part, this is because the filmmakers and writers themselves may have little direct experience of the marginal areas they are focusing on, especially in the context of the last five to ten years, and the "masses" may not readily identify themselves in such films. But in part also the unpopularity of social realist films reflects both the maintenance of a popular narrative and performative tradition that molds popular taste and can been seen reflected in many of the "successful" films and the expectation of audiences that they will see the lives of the wealthy and successful, rather than the poor and suffering, on film. Furthermore, Thai audiences profoundly expect a happy ending: that justice finally is done, that conflicts end harmoniously, that husbands and wives, or parents and children, finally achieve a good understanding of one another, that life includes hope as well as pain. This happy ending is hardly consonant with the message of the social realist film, since it would negate its impact.

The dialectic between elite and masses film was apparent from the earliest introduction of film to Thailand. The very first film ever shown in Thailand was brought by S. G. Machovsky and his French troupe and consisted of some items from the Lumière Brothers series, including "Boxers" and "Aquanaut." They were shown exclusively to members of the Bangkok elite at a theater belonging to Prince Alangkard in 1897 (Dome 1982; Somchart 1990). This stimulated the interest of the upper classes in film, which was reflected in the production of short documentaries, most notably films about the modernizing activities of King Rama V (King Chulalongkorn), especially the introduction of the railway system. The didactic intent of these productions was to show Thailand as a modern state under the leadership of a modern monarch. From that time forward, one aspect of Thai filmmaking has been the representation of state-sanctioned and ideologically impelled versions of reality.

Film for general entertainment, however, also entered the kingdom at an early date. The first commercial productions were Japanese, and Japanese investors provided the first commercial cinema in Bangkok in 1905. By the 1920s, cinemas were constructed in the main provincial towns, and by 1927 there were more than ten in Bangkok. (See Hamilton 1992 for a fuller account of the introduction of commercial film and its relation to literacy and foreign fictional genres in Thailand.)

A steady flow of foreign films entered the kingdom and increasingly circulated to the provinces and countryside as the commercial possibilities of film were seized upon by small-scale entrepreneurs. The most popular sources of these films have varied in different periods: before 1960 most films came from the United States, Taiwan, the United Kingdom, Japan, and India. Today, the most popular foreign films come overwhelmingly from the United States, Taiwan, and Hong Kong.

Nevertheless, a Thai film industry was founded early and has continued ever since, side by side with foreign imports. The first Thai feature film, *Nang Sao Suwan*, was made in 1922, although the production was under the direction of Henry A. Macrae and Universal Pictures, U.S.A. (Songyot 1990).[2] In 1927 an all-Thai company produced *Chok Song Chan (Double Luck)* by Manit Wasuwat. The industry grew slowly, however: in the 1950s an average of 25 films were made per year, in 1961–1976 an average of 70, with 609 films being made between 1979 and 1983. In 1983, seventy Thai firms made films for 823 theaters, of which ninety-five, with seating for 81,038, are in Bangkok (Setaporn et al. 1985). Some 254 foreign films were shown (against 109 Thai films) to a total audience of 86,190,000 viewers (Stamps and Facilities Division, 1984).

While in some periods the state has attempted to support the Thai film industry by taxation of imports, the relation between state and film is more profoundly reflected in the use made of film by various arms of the state for specifically "national" ends. There is no space here for more than a brief survey, but it is important to illustrate the way in which the state has historically perceived the role of film in order to understand the contemporary dilemmas of film production. It is of particular interest to me that the Thai state has never perceived its role as having to do with the circulation of images to an "outside" world; its preoccupations have always been focused on internal issues and the fissures and splits that recur within the competing power factions of the national elite and the concomitant necessity of controlling the behavior and perceptions of the people. This use of film represents the creation of reality, a process that is familiar enough in propaganda but that is both more far-reaching and less explicit in Thailand.

A few examples of this process will illustrate the point. In the events surrounding the overthrow of the absolute monarchy in 1932 by the military, which represented largely the interests of an emergent middle class, the king himself insisted that the ceremony whereby the first Thai constitution was presented should be filmed. In the filmic presentation, the implications were ambiguous: from the viewpoint of the military, the leaders of the revolutionary group submitted the constitution to the king for signature, but from the viewpoint of the film, the king could be seen as having conferred the constitution to the revolutionary group and thus maintained ultimate authority (Songyot 1990). During the 1930s and 1940s, the new government used film extensively to promote nationalism, military idealism, and a hyper-idealized view of the life of the peasantry. Among the many feature films appearing at this time was *Leurd Taharn Thai (The Blood of the Thai Soldier)*, commissioned by the Ministry of Defense to demonstrate the modernity of the Thai army after the doubling of the military budget in 1934. In 1940 Dr. Pridi Bannomyong, one of the prominent political leaders of the 1932 coup, produced a film called *The King of the White Elephant*, in English, which was simultaneously shown in Bangkok, New York, and Singapore. Dr. Pridi's intention, it seems, was to ensure him nomination for the Nobel Peace Prize, but the Thai military government of the time led the country into World War II on the side of the Japanese instead. In 1942 *Baan Rai Na Rao (Farm and Paddy: Our Beloved Home)* demonstrated the modern methods now used by the Thai farmers, while *Nam Tuam Dee Kwa Fon Laeng (Flood Is Better than Drought)* was meant to cheer up the farmers after the disastrous floods of the same year. In 1943 the Royal Thai Air Force produced *Nak Bin Klang Kuen (Night Pilot)* to demonstrate the heroic performance of the air force in fighting against the Western allies. With the exception of Dr. Pridi's film, which seems to have been directed towards an external goal, all these films were designed to manipulate images of the state in a national context.

In the postwar period, up to 1957, when the authoritarian military regime of Field Marshal Sarit took over government, both film production and venues for film showing increased. Social circumstances of the time, however, were still largely under military control, in a context of labor activism, economic difficulties, the rise of armed "bandits" and gangster groups in the countryside, and the question of communism. Several film-production companies were established, some under the control of aristocrats such as Prince Sukornwannadit Dissakul and others that specialized in producing anticommunist feature films. American influence was felt with the foundation of film agencies importing films for the Bangkok audience in particular. New film venues proliferated: Sala Chalerm Krung, built under the patronage of King Rama VII in 1930 was joined by Rong Pabpayont Kings, Rong Pabpayont Queens, Chalerm Khetra, and the Empire. Many of the films made at this time touched on themes that had never before been represented in Thai films: a few examples are *Suparb Booroos Sua Thai (Sua Thai the Gentleman-Villain)*, *Santi Weena* (the story of a countryside love affair), and *Botaan*, a love story concerning a Chinese girl and a boy belonging to a noble family, an event normally considered impossible in society.

Social and economic conditions under the hyper-authoritarian Sarit regime saw rapid changes, as industrial development began, the military were able to control Chinese-held mercantile capital, labor migration increased, and U.S. influence expanded. At this time virtually all film showings included U.S. Information Service documentaries, news, and American cartoons, while Thai films were subjected to more rigid censorship than ever before and filmmakers were forbidden to make any form of comment or reflection on the king, the military, the police, or the bureaucracy. Films of this period supported state ideology in every respect, and "action" films emphasizing the peril and bravery of crime fighters against Chinese, who were portrayed as underground gangsters and Communists, became very popular. These fighters were always depicted as private citizens or self-motivated individuals, although the police always appeared in the last episode when all the fighting was over.

The dramatic end of Sarit's regime on October 14, 1973, ushered in a new period of film-state relations which has remained significant right up to the present. The rise of the bourgeoisie, the increased level of education of the people, the struggles between mercantile capital, and the dominant military and bureaucrats indicated that fissures in the state could no longer be suppressed. The quest for political freedom and democracy and the demand for better conditions for workers, for land justice in the countryside, and for the maintenance of decent returns in the agricultural sector produced an atmosphere of total polarization within the society, something that even the events of 1932 had failed to produce. Censorship, however, remained important, and those controlling the capital needed for filmmaking were not necessarily willing to permit this new atmosphere to be reflected in film. Nevertheless, from among the intellectuals and students emerged a new class of film director, some of whom remain active today. Prince Chatri-Chalerm Yukala, Permpol Chuay-Arun, Euthana Mukdasnit, Chana Kraprayoon, Manop Udomdej, and Somboonsuk Niyomsiri ("Piak Poster") are among this group. In films of the 1970s, and indeed into the 1980s, these producers raised issues that never before had been canvassed in any form of mass media in Thailand and introduced the "marginal" into the mainstream of their work. Such issues included the situation of women and workers (*Thep Thida Rong Raem [Factory Angel]*) and *Thep Thida Bar 21 [The Angel of Bar 21]*, both by Euthana Mukdasnit), of peasants *(Tong Pan, Pracha Chon Nork, Luuk Isaan)*, of intellectuals and educated people living and working in the provinces *(Kroo Baan Nork [The Provincial Teacher], Nong Ma Wor [Nong Ma Wor Village])*, the elderly *(Wai Tok Kra)*, and the hill-tribe people *(Khon Poo Khao)*. While these are only a few examples among a great many other films, and while they did not directly or overtly challenge the forbidden arenas of state power, they came into existence significantly as ideological statements in reaction against the dominant forms consequent on the collaboration between filmmakers and state apparatus.

The contemporary dilemmas of Thai filmmakers spring from several sources, one of the most important of which is the organization of the film industry itself. As already mentioned, there is no direct state subsidy or support for Thai filmmakers and film must reach a commercially viable market. Film production companies are organized on a "stable" model, with a continuing group of producer, director, technicians, and actors. Each "stable" (although "family" would better describe the way Thais see these groups) usually concentrates on film genres and styles that are especially attractive to the paying audience. These can change in relatively short periods of time. During the 1980s, for example, the most popular films were of the *nang chiwit*, or "drama" type, which appealed particularly to young women and focused on family, love, and money in the context of issues around tradition and modernity (see Hamilton 1992 for a detailed discussion of Thai "melodramas" of this kind). In the mid 1980s a number of films in this genre were made by filmmakers identified with the

1970s "new wave" and displayed novel approaches to hitherto repressed social issues. A good example of this kind is *Ya Pror Me Chu (The Accusation)*, directed by Manop Udomdej and released in 1985. This film was based, as so many are, on a real-life story concerning the wife of an army major who was sued by her husband for divorce on the grounds of her adultery with five army privates. Aided by a talented woman barrister, she fights back against the charges and exposes the horrible realities of her relations with her husband and his own sordid sexual life. This film, widely admired by younger educated and intellectual people, nevertheless caused a major scandal by its sexual frankness and by the implication that a senior military figure could be guilty of socially inadmissible practices. Another example is Panthewanop Thewakun's film, *Chang man, chan mai care*, starring the very popular Likhit Ekmongkol. This too was an extraordinary story, broaching the subject of male prostitution and middle-class Thai women. The particular punch of this story, apart from its depiction of low life in Bangkok, was provided by the fact that the woman concerned had been a member of the young radicals in the 1970s. A third well-known example is Euthana Mukdasnit's film, *Nampoo* (1984), again based on the real-life story of a teenage heroin addict, neglected by his separated middle-class parents. Each of these films was praised by critics, academics, and intellectuals and was at least moderately successful with the Bangkok audience. It is films such as these which have moved out into the international film circuit and achieved the only representation of Thai film outside the country. But they are certainly not in any sense representative of the Thai film industry, or of the films that form the continuing basis of the industry as a whole.

Far more commercially successful in the 1980s were gangster films modeled on the immensely popular Hong Kong genre. Although there are significant differences between the Chinese and the Thai versions of this genre, both are immensely popular among provincial and urban working-class males. At the center of these films is always a vast amount of gunplay and dramatic scenes of machine-gun massacre and general mayhem. While the film censorship rules ought to prevent the making and showing of such films, until recently at least there seemed to be no interference with them provided they did not depict police or other officials.

Towards the end of the 1980s, however, and into the 1990s, the predominate form of popular film has been oriented towards the teenage market. Again, there are numerous Hong Kong imports of a comparable type. Urban youth has provided a large and expanding audience, and with the rising affluence of the urban bourgeoisie as Thailand rushes headlong into its capitalist revolution this provides a lucrative source of support for the industry. In Thai the term *nang nam nao*, or "polluted water film," is used to describe these popular forms.

While certain of the intellectual educated classes, particularly those who retain social perspectives derived from the events of the 1970s, praise the "social message" films of the kind mentioned above, the great majority of the Thai elite actually despise Thai film altogether. For many, the idea of actually watching Thai film strikes them as absurd, an activity fit only for low-class people and rural nobodies.

Digressing a moment, it was this aspect of the attitude of the majority of "educated" Thai people to Thai film which most amazed me when I began research in Thailand. Apart from those sharing the perspectives of the more radical intelligentsia, and consequently praising certain of the social realist films, virtually everybody decried Thai film with the familiar term *nam nao*. The notion that someone like myself would want to watch and study Thai film struck most of them as absurd. I can see now that my fascination with the subject came from my interest in the role of film in Australia. I was deeply impressed at the liveliness and vitality of the Thai film industry, considering the odds against it; but more than anything I was impressed that there was a Thai film industry at all. Accustomed to the common Western view that all "developing societies" are saturated with American film and television in the latest form of cultural colonialism, as Australia itself had been, it seemed it should be a matter of congratulation that Thailand had such a long and full history of self-representation in film.

In Australia the relation between cinema and nation has been determined by issues of cultural nationalism. Against the onslaught of American and British product (which, being in English, is so readily transferred and accepted) state interventions in the Australian film industry have been designed to foster Australian film for Australian audiences, to make Australians visible to themselves, to define their own cultural identity against the plethora of foreign images. Yet, for Australian filmmakers with a small home market, the overseas view is equally important. And for Australians generally, it seems to be a matter of great pride when Australian films are shown overseas, even more so when they are hailed as international successes. It is the kind of confirmation of identity and self-worth that would seem typical of colonial situations.

But Thailand was not colonized. Hence the idea of being confirmed in the eyes of an Other has never loomed large,[3] while the linguistic relic of colonialism, namely, some level of basic familiarity with a European language, has also been absent, at least until the present, when English is beginning to spread much more widely than ever before as a result of international tourism. Again, only in the context of late global modernity has the possibility of Thai film being received internationally occurred to some "serious" filmmakers, and an internal market of fifty-four million people is quite sufficient to support the kind of low-scale, low-budget filmmaking that occupies most of the commercial ground.

It may prove useful here to look at some of the views of people from different social segments of Thai society about film and its role in Thailand. The first example comes from a brief article written by M. L. Kukrit Pramoj, one of the most prominent political and cultural figures in recent Thai history. Kukrit was a close adviser to the king at the time of the 1976 coup and became prime minister in 1975. By no means an extreme rightist, he nonetheless represents a traditionalist conservatism in cultural policies. He contributed an article to a book concerning traditional Thai drama during the reign of King Rama II, in which he tells of going to see a movie called *Khao Chue Karanta (A Man Called Karn)*. The film concerns a young doctor who left Bangkok in order to aid the struggling ill in the countryside. He finds out in the end that the core of the problem lies in the state itself. M. L. Kukrit had heard that this was an unconventional film that lifted the standard of Thai movies from *nam nao*. Kukrit expresses extreme contempt for the film, arguing that throughout history Thai movies have basically used the structure of Thai traditional dramas. Such narratives always involve a situation where the leading actor and actress come from different classes or backgrounds, or where the leading partners were separated by forces beyond themselves (for example, winds or giants), or where a female giant disguised as a beautiful woman intervenes in the relationship. As in traditional dramas, the lead actress always wears a lot of jewelry, no matter how poor she is supposed to be. A clown always follows the leading actor, and the leading lady has to have a maid of honor. (All these characteristics are indeed remarkably true even of movies made in the mid to late 1980s.) Kukrit argues that movies should continue to follow these traditional formats. He says:

> People of this generation think that all the old formula movies are "unreal," that the leading actor and actress should dress according to reality. . . . The movie *The Man Called Karn* actually threw away all the main characters of the Thai drama mentioned above, so, therefore, I can agree with many people that it is an unconventional movie, and it "comes out of polluted water." (Kukrit Pramoj 1979, 70–71)

Kukrit thus rejects Thai films that deviate from the traditional narrative structures of the Thai drama and classifies those films that deviate as *nam nao*, thus reversing the intellectuals' classification.

As an example of the views of a filmmaker, a long interview with Manop Udomdej was published in 1988.[4] Manop made the film *The Accusation*, mentioned above. His own history and background indicate the kinds of settings from which the "new" directors come and the way they become involved in film. Manop began his career as an art teacher in a small primary school in an obscure province in Isaan (one of the most impoverished areas of the country), where he described his role as that of a "national sculptor"—that is, his task was to mold ideologically and socially the pupils in his charge. He left this job and went to work as a scriptwriter and radio announcer for a Catholic church agency. He was sent to take special lessons in film production by the church and then became a film producer with the Catholic Council for Development of

Thailand. From this position he produced the film *On the Fringe of Society*, as writer, director, and producer. The film cost only 1.4 million *baht* (around $70,000). It was first shown in the theater at Thammasat University,[5] where it was a great success. A representative from the London Film Festival selected his film for showing in London, and tickets were sold out two weeks before the screening. The film moved into the international festival circuit and was shown in Australia in 1988. He says, "In fact, it is a slight film, but it shows some things which people were interested in during that period but nobody dared to produce the film. This is how I joined the film production business."

Following the film's success, Manop became head of the extension and broadcasting section of the Catholic Council for Development. Here he worked in rural areas and tried to teach people about politics, economics, and culture. He resigned after four years, was unemployed for three years, during which time he struggled mightily, and then made contact with another famous filmmaker, Piak Poster, and met Somdej Santipracha, the proprietor of Poonsap Production Company. He gave them an outline proposal for *The Accusation*, which was accepted more or less at once and produced "some reasonable financial return." He subsequently produced *Once Is Enough* in 1987 for the same production company. Clearly Manop is a good example of the filmmaker whose work comes from a concern with social justice and whose connection with rural and deprived sectors has molded his approach to filmmaking.

An example of a film review gives a clear summary of the way in which "serious" films are received by most critics in the popular print media. In mid 1987 the final touches were being put on a Thai film, made in Bangkok, which was the object of much enthusiasm and praise among foreigners in Thailand and some Thai intellectuals, who had been invited to various private screenings.[6] The film was called *Baan*, meaning "home," and depicts life in the urban slums of Bangkok with all its suffering and hardship. What the foreigners liked about it was precisely its "truth" quality: it was believed to show things in Bangkok as they were for a large proportion of the population, accurately and tragically.

Early in 1988, after the film's commercial release, a long review of it appeared in the *Siam Rath* weekly magazine, which regularly publishes film reviews with starred ratings. The writer begins by observing that many people believe Thai stories are not suitable for film production. He disagrees and says the problem is to find someone who reads and can choose good stories. However, the reviewer does not praise *Baan*. He says it is too "heavy." Everything looks cruel, serious, full of suffering and bitterness, from the beginning to the end. Everyone in the story suffers from an unkind fate. Not a smile or a laugh is permitted to the audience. He argues that the film errs in failing to emphasize that the problems of the whole family stem from its leader only. It is wrong, he says, to imply that everyone must suffer from one fate when the problem of merit is the problem of the family's leader only. He admires the courage of the filmmaker, who did not want to make it softer for the audience. Yet it is hardly surprising, he says, that the film is making no money, considering the condition of the Thai movie audience at present, especially on account of the life-style of the Thai people under a government that likes only singing (referring to the preference of the present prime minister for films with plenty of singing and dancing). He suggests that the condition of much of the Thai audience is not so different from the condition of the characters in *Baan*, and no matter who people are, they all have problems. The film audience is largely poorer people on farms and factories outside Bangkok. These people do not like to see films where people are poor. Instead, they like to be happy and laugh and to see people living a rich life, living in a way ordinary people would like to live but cannot hope for themselves (translation of part of this review provided by Parnee Stoddart, June 8, 1988).

With the democratization of the late 1980s, under the first elected government for many years, the issues around filmmaking emerged into national prominence. Filmmakers, like others in the arena of cultural production, were chafing at the limitations placed on their freedom of representation. There were signs of a new liberalization, really a new spirit, in the mass media, with lively current affairs programs and high-profile newsreaders such as Dr. Somkiat Omnivol bringing a fresh new perspective to politics and society of a kind never before seen. In a sense, the postmodern media world was slipping through the barriers, with numbers of new foreign films, the spread of video outlets and cable television, international tourism, new liberalized rules around television viewing, and other factors that seemed to indicate the possibility of a new relation between nation-state and culture.

In this context, a National Seminar on the Future of the Thai Film Industry was held in late 1988 under the auspices of the Faculty of Communication Arts at Chulalongkorn University. Most of the more than one hundred people attending were from the film industry, academics, and representatives from the Public Relations Department, which controls various aspects of media in Thailand. The prime minister himself opened the seminar, indicating at least the possibility of high-level support for the film industry. He commented that films play an important role in the development of the country and can support education, arts, and culture. He made a clear statement of the "cultural nationalist" type: the flood of foreign films coming into the country was disadvantaging and spoiling "good Thai culture." He mentioned that the government had to try to find solutions to this as they had done in some of the developed countries.

Permpol Chuay-Arun, a director, began the seminar by describing the frustrations of the filmmaker when the audience's perceptions are so narrow. He asked if the government had considered cultivating an audience to have an analytical mind in viewing films. He suggested film should be included in the school curriculum. His own experience making a "serious" film that failed utterly at the box office *(Muang Nai Mag)* had shown him he had no option but to produce *nam nao* films to please the audience.

A well-known and popular star, Sorapong Chatree, described a different relation between film and government. She pointed out that film stars are constantly being called upon by the government to appear free at special occasions, to sing and help raise funds at charity occasions and so on, and even to grace private parties for prominent people. They receive no remuneration, however, for this and as soon as they cease to be popular they lose their living altogether. She suggested that the Thai film industry is like a family system in which all involved feel sympathy for each other, which results in very slow development of the industry.

Chaiwat Taweewongsongtong is a booking agent for Five Star Productions and secretary of the Thai Film Makers Association. He described the way small films have to be "packaged" through an agency such as his, and the problem is that "good" films are rejected by the audience and this can cost the agent a great deal. An example was the film *Duey Klao*, produced to commemorate the king on the occasion of the longest reign celebrations. Although the film received many awards, no distributors would take it. He suggested cash incentives should be given to producers of "good" films. Furthermore, the censorship system leads to a standstill in the movie industry. Anyone who produces "outside their frame" will be "ordered to re-adjust." This view was supported strongly by Santi Sawetwimol, a columnist, who added that television also destroys the quality of Thai films (because they have to be cut to fit the time available on the stations).

Piak Poster, the famous director, pointed out that although the prime minister's office had set up a Film Promotion Board to support and advise the film industry, many of the board members actually detested Thai films. Apichart Halamchiag, an ex-film star and now parliamentary representative of the Social Action Party, added to the view that there needed to be government support for the industry, while a member of the Censorship Committee, Acharn Cha-Oom Prasertkul, put forward the view that if films simply reflected society there would be no need for them to be censored. But if films are viewed as having great influence over people's behavior, then censorship is absolutely necessary. He remarked that Thai people are easily persuaded: for them seeing is believing, especially rural people. The Censorship Bill, first issued in 1930, set out the principles that film should build understanding and good behavior in society. The main problem with the Censorship Board is that the police and military are overrepresented, and these people tend to think rather rigidly and have little artistic spirit. (In fact, seventeen out of eighteen members come from these two groups.)[7]

The possible liberalization and support suggested by the holding of this seminar, however, was overtaken by the rapid changes in the political scene, which culminated in the military coup that overthrew the elected government of Chartchai Choonhavan and ushered in yet another period of confusion and uncertainty. Any moves toward further liberalization of cultural expression have gone on hold, if not backward. The censorship provisions provide abundant mechanisms for intervention in media by the new government.

The provisions are based on The Cinema Act of 1930, modified in 1932, 1962, and 1971, which controls film production at all stages. The law permits the banning of a production or the confiscation of a film if it is believed to be harmful to the general public. Before showing, each film must be submitted to the censorship committee. A film said to be contrary to public order may be confiscated during its showing. The guidelines issued by the Ministry of the Interior forbid the following:

1. Plots insulting sacred images or places, or that lead to an unfavorable attitude towards the national religion;

2. Unusual methods used by criminals which may promote more such crimes;

3. History of notorious criminals;

4. Cold-blooded murder or execution;

5. Cruel torture to animals or human beings;

6. All that is sexually obscene;

7. Stories harmful to good understanding among countries or nations;

8. Films showing acts of lèse majesté;

9. Films on politics which may discredit the present government system or stir up violence;

10. Films showing immoral behavior;

11. Plots insulting or leading to an unfavorable attitude towards royalty.

Additional rules are set by the army and the Ministry of Education. Army regulations ban films on demonstrations or protest marches, films portraying government officials as criminals, films in which actors dress up as monks or novices in the Buddhist religion, and films supporting communism. The Ministry of Education lays down an additional twenty-one rules relating to sexual relations, behavior detrimental to juveniles and students, films depicting gangsters, drug addicts, or criminals in a favorable light (Setaporn 1985, 52–66).

Some of these restrictions are observed rigidly while others are more or less ignored. It is possible to see scenes of incredibly vivid bloodshed and violence any day in Thailand notwithstanding provision 4, above. On the other hand, the censors use the scissors on any explicitly sexual scene, including nudity, in Western films, or may just black out the offending body parts with a pen. The effects of censorship go much further, however; the *sai nang*, film distributors, who put up the capital for films, constantly make judgments in terms of what will be permitted and what may not be. Anyone who tries to step too far out of line may suffer not only financial losses but direct or indirect use of force against themselves or their premises: everyone knows the way in which influential, highly placed figures use hired guns and gangsters to enforce their views. The domination of the Censorship Board by the police and military ensures that the interpretation of "politics," forbidden in film under the common interpretation of provision 9, is extraordinarily wide. Anything at all which might be conceived of as criticizing the existing state mechanisms and organizations is forbidden. Bribery and corruption of some elements of the police, an everyday event for many people, is not permitted to appear on screen. Neither can it be suggested that public officials might connive to smuggle or exploit the rural farmers; nor is it possible to depict the impotence of police in fighting crime. Those few films that really do make such suggestions become underground films, shown only in special private circumstances. *Tong Pan* (1976) is an example; the film criticized the failures of the bureaucratic system in the context of rural development. Other films survive with some of their criticisms intact: *Prachachorn Nork* (*On the Fringe of Society*, 1981) had to be rewritten again and again by order of the censor, while *Muen Puen* (*Gunmen*, 1983) perhaps gained a little leeway by being directed by Prince Chatri-Chalerm Yukala.

It is obvious, therefore, that the kind of issues that serious filmmakers feel obliged to tackle are those that touch on this forbidden dimension of Thai society. The contempt for the common people, evident in the statement by the censor quoted earlier, is replaced for the intelligentsia by a kind of pitying superiority that inevitably casts "the common man" as victim. The Association of Thai Film Makers, many of its members being from among the "serious" group, select "good" films for the international film contests and thus determine the cinematic representations of Thailand that circulate through the global art-movie circuit. Although many Westerners might enjoy and find much to praise in these films, the sense of pressure and danger associated with them in Thailand cannot be understood. After all, any number of Western movies depict crooked cops and evil government agents, so the frisson of the forbidden associated with making discreet references to the role of the state in such films is entirely lost on the Western audience. The program notes that go with such films seldom bring these issues out, concentrating instead either on the depiction of personal tragedy or the artistic quality of the films themselves.

Another recent case in point is the film, *The Elephant Keeper*, the most recent film of Prince Chatri. This film focuses on the ecological and social disasters in marginal rural zones, the destruction of the forests and of the way of life of traditional foresters, the indifference and corruption of police, the evil machinations of Chinese businessmen, and the helplessness of the simple people, as well as the animals, caught up in this nightmare struggle.

The Elephant Keeper has come to prominence not just because it touches on these normally hidden and deeply contentious issues, but also because during the filming in Northeast Thailand local gangsters, presumably working for illegal logging interests, attacked the film crew, one member of which was killed. Thus art and life were intertwined as is so often the case in Thailand. This film, too, failed utterly at the box office, losing around seven million *baht* (around $350,000). Its release into Western circuits, however, highlights the difficulties involved in the crossover. For the Australian audience, at least, cultural incomprehension immediately comes into play: merely providing sketchy subtitles does nothing to really resolve this. For example, in *The Elephant Keeper* a critical aspect of the story focuses on the different social and "class" positions of the main protagonists: the earnest, naive, tertiary-educated junior ranger, the evil exploitive Chinese timber merchant, the corrupt police chief, and the good-hearted but helpless and desperate "local people." To a Western audience these characters are likely to be undifferentiated: just "Thais." The "hidden" but constantly circulating rumors about police corruption and business practices at every level of Thai society are reflected in the film but may not be "read" by a Western audience. The "Chineseness" of the timber merchant is a critical aspect of the film: non-Thais, however, would not necessarily even recognize him to be Chinese. Nor would the long history of debate around the Chinese control over business in Thailand have any resonance to Westerners, even though this is one of the most profound and daring assertions in the film.

The stylistic qualities of *The Elephant Keeper* conform to what Westerners might expect of an "underdeveloped" film industry (which Thailand's is not). The film work is technically basic, slow, and loosely paced. The editing is adequate, but plain. The quality of the film is hazy, with much filming in shade and forests and indoors, with inadequate lighting. While the development of the plot, set as a lengthy and unmediated flashback, is clear enough, the subtitles eliminate much of the subtlety of dialogue concerning the interplay between individuals of different class positions and backgrounds, which is essential to the film's meaning. Apart from the fact that it deals with a currently fashionable and ideologically correct issue, there is little to recommend it to an uninformed or "cold" Western audience, whether film buff or otherwise.

Nevertheless, this situation can be understood by an analysis that places the Thai film industry within its local context. Thai films are seldom if ever made with the eye of an alien Other in mind. They exist in a strange interstitial space, mirroring the social and cultural conditions in Thailand itself, and are part of a continuing power struggle over the cultural reproduction of imagery as powerful elements determined to retain control attempt to pull back from the implications of a postmodern world order and a global cultural field. Thus, for Thailand, the issue is not so much a question of difference between nations as of the possibility of expression of differences within.

Notes

1. I have explored some aspects of media and national identity elsewhere (Hamilton 1992a) but have not yet published the bulk of the data on media, culture, and communication obtained in recent fieldwork in Bangkok, Hua Hin, and in a number of rural villages in Prachuab Khiri Khan Province. Fieldwork was supported by Macquarie University research grants and the Australian Research Council and has been carried out at various times between 1985 and 1990.

2. Much of the historical information in this section comes from an unpublished paper by Dr. Songyot Whaewongse of the Faculty of Social Sciences, Silpakorn University, Nakhon Pathom. I would like to express here my deep gratitude for his lively interest in and support of my research and for his stimulating insights into Thai films which he has so generously shared. His historical account in turn relies on two papers by Somchart Bangchaeng (1987, 1990) as well as the earlier account by Dome Sukvongse (1982). Excellent though these sources are, it would be fair to say that there is still no full-length comprehensive study of the genesis and evolution of Thai film. Boonrak Boonyaketmala, however, has recently published an article that details many aspects of the history and recent organization of the Thai film industry (Boonrak 1992), while a dissertation in French by Gerard Fouquet examines the period 1970–88. The difficulties of a thorough investigation are magnified by the huge losses of early film material, in part consequent on the bombing of Bangkok during World War II, in part also on the lack of interest in and awareness of the importance of conserving national film heritage.

3. Although the delirious rapture with which the Thai people and media greeted the crowning of Porntip Nakhirunkanok as Miss Universe suggests some desire for international recognition: symbolically, perhaps, in the field of feminine beauty.

4. There is no identification of the author of this article. It appeared in a popular film magazine in 1988.

5. Thammasat University is the second major university in Bangkok, the other being Chulalongkorn University. Thammasat is associated with "radicalism" and Chulalongkorn is seen as more "conservative." Thammasat became the focus of the leftist movement in the period 1973–76 and hence was the target for rightist attacks and the site of the massacre of students on October 6, 1976. This resulted in a military coup and the ousting of parliamentary government. The impact of this event on educated young Bangkokians, especially students, was immense. Thai soldiers, pledged to defend the nation, were firing on their own young people with M-16 rifles, M-79 grenade launchers, and carbines. Some students were burned alive or lynched. Official reports acknowledged forty-six dead but there were probably many more. Thirteen hundred students were arrested and taken off. Many others fled, some to other countries and others to the jungles and border areas where a variety of "rebel" groups were based. In many respects the massacre of students in Thailand in 1976 resembled the massacres in Burma in 1988 and in China in 1989, even though the historical conditions appear quite different and the level of popular support for the "radicals" was far greater in Burma than in Thailand. The long-lasting aftereffects of "October 76" are still being played out in a variety of contexts in Thailand, of which the struggle over cultural reproduction is only one. See Morell and Chai-Anan (1981) for a full account of the 1973–76 period and some aspects of the aftermath. The events of May 1992 can be seen as a continuation of the struggles, although today the protesters are middle-class professionals, many of whom were students in 1976.

6. A long-time Australian resident of Bangkok, Laurie Maund (now of Chiangmai), who is frequently called upon to take small parts as a *farang* in Thai films, attended one of these meetings and told me about the great respect and admiration for the film which those attending expressed.

7. My research assistant in 1988–89, Patchara Kiatuntavimon, from the Faculty of Communication Arts at Chulalongkorn University, attended the seminar in Bangkok and made notes on the various speakers' contributions. I would like to thank her for her diligence and patience, and also thank Dr. Darunee Hirunrak, dean of the faculty, who assisted and supported my research in a variety of ways.

Bibliography

Benjamin, Walter.

    1969   "The Work of Art in the Age of Mechanical Reproduction" (1936), in *Illuminations*. New York: Schocken Books.

Boonrak Boonyaketmala.

    1992   "The Rise and Fall of the Film Industry in Thailand, 1897–1992," *East-West Film Journal*, 6,2:62–98.

Denzin, Norman K.

    1991   *Images of Postmodern Society*. London: Sage Publications.

Dissanayake, Wimal, ed.

    1988   *Cinema and Cultural Identity: Reflections on Film from Japan, India, and China*. Lanham, Maryland: University Press of America.

Dome Sukvongse.

    1982   "Paetsip ha pii pab-payont nai Prathet Thai" [Eighty-five Years of Movies in Thailand], *Silpa Wattanatham*, 3, 8 (June).

Fouquet, Gerard.

    1988   "Le Cinema Thai Contemporain (1970–1988)." Ph.D. diss., Université Paris VII, Paris.

Fugate, Christine.

    1990   "Hit or Flop? Thai Film's Success Vary with Audience," *Centerviews*, November-December, p. 7.

Hamilton, Annette.

    1987   "Mass Media and National Development in Thailand." Proceedings of the International Conference on Thai Studies, Australian National University, Canberra, vol. 2.

    1991   "Rumours, Foul Calumnies and the Safety of the State: Mass Media and National Identity in Thailand," in *National Identity and Its Defenders 1939–1989*, ed. Craig Reynolds. Melbourne: Monash University.

    1992   "Family Dramas: Film and Modernity in Thailand," *Screen* (Glasgow) 33:3.

    1993   "Video Crackdown, or, the Sacrificial Pirate." *Public Culture*, vol. 5 no. 3.

Kukrit Pramoj, M. L.

    1979   "The Structure of Thai Drama and Thai Movies at Present," in *Commun Bang Plakarn Kieoukap Lakhorn Nork lae Bot Lakhorn Nork Nai Rama 2* [Some Information on Lakhon Nork and the Text of the Drama by King Rama II], ed. Kochai Sarikbut. Bangkok.

Morell, David, and Chai-Anan Samudavanija.

    1981   *Political Conflict in Thailand.* Cambridge, Massachusetts: Oelgeschlager, Gunn and Hain.

Setaporn Cusripituck, Silpachai Bijayendrodhin, and Theerawuti Kongpricha.

    1985   Communications Policy in Thailand: A Study Report. Submitted to UNESCO, Bangkok.

Somchart Bangchaen.

    1987   *A Deet Pab-payont Thai* [History of Thai Film]. Handbook of the 7th Suparnahong Thong Kham.

    1990   "Hoksip jet pii Pab Payont Thai 2466–2533" [Sixty-seven Years of Thai Film, 1923–1990). Bangkok: National Film Association.

Songyot Whaewongse.

    1990   "Thai Sociological and Political Aspects of Thai Film: An Overview." Unpublished ms.

Thailand. Stamps and Facilities Division. Revenue Department.

    1985   Statistics. Bangkok.

9 | National Cinema, National Culture
The Indonesian Case
Karl G. Heider

O<small>FF THE COAST</small> of mainland Southeast Asia live more than two hundred million people on countless islands. The cultural and linguistic diversity of these peoples is legendary. The larger islands, and even many of the smaller ones, are home to more than one language and culture. The peoples of the islands are divided by their mutually unintelligible languages and their different cultures. For over a century now, the central government has been faced with a persistent problem: the Dutch colonial administration and its successor, the Republic of Indonesia, have tried to fuse some of these various peoples into some sort of manageable entity. Far more progress has been made toward this goal in the political, administrative, and military spheres than in the cultural sphere. There is a centralized governmental organization, and there is a national army, and there are no significant rebel or secession movements. But in cultural terms, regionalization is still strong.

Here I want to look at the cultural issues involved and to consider the construction of a national Indonesian culture. Particularly I want to look at the ways in which Indonesian cinema has been a vehicle—perhaps the major vehicle—of this development. (This continues the argument advanced in Heider 1991.)

Although here I want to consider only Indonesian cinema, it is in fact just one part of the whole. Even taking seriously the notion of constructing a national culture on screen eventually demands that we look at the entire range of images which bombard Indonesians, including the various Indonesian-produced dramas made for the national television channel, and besides the films made in Indonesia, those films imported from abroad and shown in theaters, on television, and rented through videocassette shops. There are few Indonesians, no matter how isolated or how poor, who are not at least occasionally within sight of some of this visual onslaught.

Eventually we must pull it all together—movies, television, and the still-lively varieties of more traditional Indonesian theater and dance forms. Ulf Hannerz, the Norwegian anthropologist, has used the term "macroanthropology" for a conceptual position which looks at cultural phenomena, the sharing of meanings, and cutting across community lines. Hannerz offers this analogy to "the linguistics of contact" described by Mary Louise Pratt. He is trying to go beyond simple center-periphery thinking, whether it be the Wallerstein world system theory, and imperial model in which the center controls but allows cultural diversity in the periphery, or a "radical diffusionism" in which "the center mostly speaks, and the periphery mostly listens, without talking back" (1989:206). This seems to be similar to the understanding which Pico Iyer develops in his picaresque Asian travelogue, "Video Nights in Kathmandu" (1988). The central question then focuses not so much on the economic or political relations of center to periphery as on the cultural question: what sort of emergent cultural form is being created and purveyed to the people? And, of course, here the concern is with an emergent national, not world, culture.

In his influential essay on nationalism, Benedict Anderson talks about nations as "imagined communities." By this he means to focus on the fact that a nation's commonality is not the result of face-to-face interaction but is in important ways an imagined construction. And he discusses in some detail the impact of the printing press, and how "print-capitalism . . . made it possible for rapidly growing numbers of people to think about themselves, and to relate themselves to others, in profoundly new ways" (1983:40).

But the effects of widely available printed materials in vernacular languages since the fifteenth century are very similar to the effects of widely screened movies in national languages since the 1920s. We can profitably reword Anderson's claim thus: image-capitalism, or commercial movies, . . . make it possible for people to think about themselves, and relate themselves to others, in profoundly new ways.

Indeed, Anderson elsewhere (1979/1990) has written about the importance of post-revolutionary monuments in Indonesia as a type of communication. The most important of these material symbols of nationhood stand in public places in Jakarta and are not experienced by most Indonesians except as their images are projected across the nation. As important as books, magazines, and newspapers are in this highly literate society of Indonesia, it is the cinema which has played a major role in the imagining, or constructing, of an Indonesian culture. Neither Anderson nor, in a recent review article, Robert Foster (1991) have paid attention to the importance of national cinema in the construction of national culture. But by virtue of its immense popularity, cinema is important, for these imagined communities are to an important degree *imaged* communities. And, as Anderson, the political scientist, spoke anthropologically about nationalism, here an anthropologist addresses emergent nationalism as an imaging of national culture.

The diversity of Indonesia is well known, for it has been witnessed, even exaggerated in the anthropological literature. Virtually all anthropological writing on the area has examined specific, unique, local cultural phenomena.

There is a tremendous gap between our focused tribe, village, and ethnic group studies and the ways in which political scientists and others comfortably think on the national level as they discuss things "Indonesian." As early as 1963 Hildred Geertz had begun to talk about an emerging "Indonesian metropolitan superculture." However, Edward Bruner, at the same period, flatly stated that "no distinctively national Indonesian culture or society has yet developed" (1961:520). And two decades later, Bruner still insisted that "we are deluding ourselves if we believe that there is a fixed thing floating over the Archipelago labeled 'modern Indonesian culture' just waiting to be discovered and described, with the implication that it is everywhere the same 'thing,' interpreted the same way by members of the various regional cultures" (1979:300). But surprisingly, when one thinks about it, Indonesian films come close to fitting Bruner's description! For each film is a "fixed thing," a finished product, its duplicated copies sent out to *bioskops* across the country, offering identical images of this national culture to all audiences. But of course, Bruner raises the crucial question: how the different audiences understand and transform this message for their own uses. This is surely one of the most important next steps in the study of Indonesian cinema.

Of all cultural phenomena on the national level, it is language which is most obviously "Indonesian" in the sense that the national language has been recognized, politicized, debated, and analyzed. No one could possibly doubt that there is an "Indonesian language." But the rest of culture is more problematic. Even when the nationalistic students swore their famous Youth Pledge on October 28, 1928 (today a national holiday), they proclaimed one land, one people, and one language, but *not* "one culture."

So despite the great emphasis on language as a unifying common element, there has been much more ambivalence about the rest of culture. The status of regional culture in Indonesian thought is complex. On the one hand it is celebrated with regional cultural institutes—of Javanologi, Baliologi, etc., but I think that this is a sort of folklorization, for it serves to push regional cultures out of ordinary life and to mummify and trivialize these cultures in museums, tourist performances, souvenir dolls, special regional gift shops, and, as the embodiment supreme, there is the Beautiful Indonesia Mini Park near Jakarta, a sort of Disneyland with samples of traditional *adat* houses from each major Indonesian region. But in another sense there is an overall formal denial of ethnicity. For example, in conversation there is often mention that an acquaintance or a public figure is of a particular ethnic group—Orang Batak, Orang Java, etc., but in published biographical sketches this is almost never done and people are, in this formal context, defined by their place of birth. But of course, this can be misleading, since for all sorts of reasons, a person born in Padang may not be an Orang Padang.

And even using the name of the city, Padang, to designate the ethnic group,

Minangkabau, embodies this denial of ethnicity. For Padang is the new capital of West Sumatra, a coastal city lying outside the traditional Minangkabau heartland. After the unsuccessful war of secession in the late 1950s, the Jakarta government moved the capital of the province from Bukittinggi, in the heartland, to the coast, the *rantau*, or the outside. Now there are Minangkabau living throughout Indonesia, and Minangkabau restaurants flourish everywhere (even in Wamena, among the Grand Valley Dani of Irian Jaya!) But it is now the custom to call the people Padang People (Orang Padang) and their cuisine Padang Food (Masakan or Makanan Padang.) I have a feeling that this submerging of ethnicity has progressed farther with the Minangkabau than with most other ethnic groups, but it is symptomatic of the general trend.

Let us turn to the movies. The first Indonesian film was made in (about) 1926 (see the social history of Indonesian cinema by Salim Said, newly translated into English [1991]). Through the 1930s the growing local film industry turned out films based on Indonesian oral traditions—legends, myths, etc., and it also drew on other local theater traditions. The films were all in the Indonesian language but were produced and directed by Europeans or Chinese, with Indonesian or Eurasian performers.

After an almost complete hiatus in the 1940s, during the Japanese occupation and the Struggle for Independence, filmmaking resumed with a flourish: 1950, the first year of peace, saw 23 Indonesian feature films (only one of which survives). Production waxed and waned after that, but for the last decade, it seems to have settled in to a steady 60 or 70 feature films per year. This is modest compared with other Southeast Asian countries, and accounts for less than half the films shown in Indonesian *bioskops* or available in videocassette rental shops across the nation. Imports from the Chinese countries, the USA, India, and Europe make up the majority of films available in Indonesia.

James Peacock, in his study (1986) of the *ludruk* proletarian drama in the Surabaya region of East Java in the early 1960s, argued that these stories functioned to show people from rural areas how to adjust to urban modernity. Embedded in coarse humorous formulaic plots were models for their new behavior. (It may be that Nigerian television performs a similar function of satirical familiarization—see Hannerz 1989 and Ugboajah 1985.) Indonesian movies also perform that function; both by what they show and what they do not show, they provide a model for modern, pan-Indonesian culture.

From the beginning, Indonesian movies have been made in the Indonesian language. There are no regional language movies, not even Javanese (although the population of Javanese-speakers alone is larger—100 million people—than that of any other Southeast Asian country). A few distinctive words in a regional language may be tossed into the script, and the Indonesian may be spoken with a regional accent but even when scenes are set in remote villages, the people speak to each other in good Indonesian, not the local language which would be appropriate to the setting. There are few exceptions, such as comedies which use Jakarta slang. The most celebrated film of 1988, *Djut Nya Dien*, about the Acenese heroine of the resistance against the Dutch, was the most striking exception—much of its dialogue was actually in Acenese with Indonesian subtitles. But it does not seem to have started a trend towards regionalization.

Many films are set outside Jakarta, but only a few aspects of a locality are depicted: famous views of landscapes, distinctive regional house forms, and ceremonies. The extensive genre of sentimental films specializes in ceremonies: wedding ceremonies especially, but also ceremonies for circumcision, funerals, harvests, and bridge openings. These are shown with ethnographic fidelity. One could make quite an acceptable compilation film on Javanese Ritual or Weddings of Indonesia by assembling clips from these feature films. But the authentic nuggets are found edited into stories which otherwise show no sign of regional culture. They are used indexically to say "these people are truly Batak, or Minangkabau, or Javanese" while at the same time the entire weight of the film is saying "these Batak, or Minangkabau, or Javanese actually speak, act, even dress like Indonesians everywhere."

Salah Asuhan: The Minangkabau Who Are Not Minangkabau

Salah Asuhan is a movie which was made in 1973 from one of the first, and still one of the most famous Indonesian novels, a Dutch period melodrama, published in 1928 (de Queljoe 1974). Both the author of the book and the director of the film were Minangkabau and the story is mainly about Minangkabau. Much of the film was shot on location in West Sumatra and we see Minangkabau Great Houses, pony carts, and famous landscapes. The first wedding scene looks completely authentic and was probably done entirely by local experts, and the final shots of the Tabut ceremony on the beach at Pariaman were surely shot at the ceremony itself.

But although Minangkabau has a famously matrilineal clan organization (see Kato 1982), what is presented in the film could just as well be cognatic Java or even a strongly patrilineal society. We see the hero, his mother, his mother's brother, and his mother's brother's daughter, whom he marries, but no sign at all of any other members of either clan involved. It is especially unlikely that no clanmates of the mother's brother's daughter support her when the hero abuses and deserts her.

When I raised this issue with the director, he objected to my reading, saying that it was typically Minangkabau to send the young man abroad for schooling. But it would have been done by the boy's clan and his uncle would have been only the manager and agent of the clan. Stretching matters, one could contend that the film allows such Minangkabau-ness to be inferred, but in fact, nothing in the film makes any of it explicit, and the boy's obligation is clearly shown to be to the uncle, not the clan.

Putri Giok: The Chinese Indonesian Who Are Not Chinese

Another more elaborate example of this flattening of ethnicity is *Putri Giok*, one of the only Indonesian films to deal in any way with social tension between Indonesians and Indonesian Chinese. This film is vaguely reminiscent of *Romeo and Juliet*: an Indonesian Chinese brother and sister (she is Putri Giok, The Jade Princess), are both dating pribumi Indonesians. Their father, an authoritarian real estate developer, breaks up both relationships, egged on by his wily business partner, who is worried about the effect of ethnic mixing on the business. (Interestingly enough, this partner, the agent of disorder in the film, is cast as and played by, a South Asian, not an Indonesian of any sort.)

The entire film is an argument for harmony through assimilation to the pan-Indonesian culture. None of the Indonesians have any recognizable ethnicity, and the main activity of the youth centers around a girls' softball team—softball being a decidedly un-Indonesian sport. The film's message is that Indonesian Chinese are to be accepted as Indonesian, not as Chinese. The Chinese family is in fact already quite assimilated culturally. Only a few signs point to their Chinese origin: their names, their faces, and a single Chinese wall scroll.

It is especially interesting how the film handles religion. It could have ignored religion, as do most Indonesian films. But it could not have generalized—there is no common national religion, as there is a national language which cuts across parochial boundaries. So, improbably, the mother is Buddhist, the daughter Catholic, and the son Moslem.

Yet in another sense, there is a national religion. The appeals to understanding and acceptance of the Chinese as Indonesians are formulated in a particularly religious manner but to the symbols of the Republic: through the national anthem, through an Independence Day speech by the wife of the Vice-President, and, especially, by the large wall ornament of the Garuda holding the symbols of the Pancasila, the Five Principles of the Republic. At the moment of sudden conversion of the agent of disorder, the South Asian, he turns to the Garuda hanging on the wall above him, and stands at attention as voices of reason echo in his mind and a heavenly choir sings. No Indonesian would suggest that patriotism is a substitute for religion, glossed as "belief in One God," but that is certainly how it appears in the film's setting.

At the end of the movie the father and his partner have the sudden conversions typical of Indonesian melodrama, the two couples are reunited with blessings all around, and the different gene pools are united in a single national culture. (There is a very curious sly twist at the very end of the film: Giok, now reunited with her Herman, is applauded by the guests at the party, as she wears

a Chinese silk dress. This is a little subversive touch which denies the assimilation message of the rest of the film.)

But it is actually the long opening scene of the film which is the most ele-
gant statement of assimilation into the national culture. There is a great chorus
of youths singing "Indonesia Raya," the very European national anthem, accompanied by a European-style brass band (no traditional tune, no gamelan or-
chestra here). The camera pans first across rows of singers wearing black and
white school uniforms, those obligatory pan-Indonesian costumes which are
literally uniform for school children through high school, and whose uniform-
ity is especially striking in this country which has—or recently had—the
world's richest variety of local textiles. Soon the camera moves to more singers,
now each in a different, readily recognizable regional ceremonial costume. And
of course, they are singing the patriotic hymn in unison. One thinks, again, of
Benedict Anderson's words:

> ... there is a special kind of contemporaneous community which language
> alone suggests—above all in the form of poetry and songs. Take national an-
> thems, for example, sung on national holidays. No matter how banal the words
> and mediocre the tunes, there is in this singing an experience of simultaneity.
> At precisely such moments, people wholly unknown to each other utter the
> same verses to the same melody. The image: unisonance. (1983:132)

Again we have regionalism used indexically to say that we are all one. Regional
differences are toned down and regional cultural distinctiveness is reduced to
a few standard motifs which are used to deny regionalism.

The sorts of settings, behaviors, and social relations which are presented
constitute a generalized national culture. And this is a generalized successful
middle-class culture. Lower-class life, even generalized poverty, is rarely shown.
(Krishna Sen [1989] has discussed some films which do deal with poverty, but
these are rare exceptions.) And social conflict—that is, problems arising from
intrinsic structural incompatibilities such as race, ethnicity, economic differences, or especially political positions—is rare indeed on film.

Of course, from the standpoint of the economics of the film industry, each
film should have as wide an audience as possible. One way to appeal to audiences across the archipelago is to make films of overwhelming spectacle. Here,
Indonesian filmmakers draw on the Central Javanese 15th Century kingdom of
Madjapahit. I was surprised to see the most successful (and expensive) of these,
Saur Sepuh, playing in Irian Jaya in 1988. Is it possible that in addition to the
common Indonesian culture which films are creating for present and future,
the historical spectaculars are delivering a specific (Majapahit) past to all Indonesians? (Relatively few Americans were ever actually engaged in pushing forward or resisting the Western frontier, yet, thanks in part to Hollywood, the

Western dominated our shared history.) To some extent, this reanimation of past Madjapahit glories through cinema does function to provide a common past in the way that archaeology does in many countries.

By discovering the traces of forgotten, prehistoric cultures, and by establishing continuity between these past cultures and the present, archaeologists provided an added prestigious temporal depth to the claims of nationalism. This was true for European powers as well as for minority, third world, or colonized peoples. Bruce G. Trigger describes the close relationship between archaeology and nationalism since the mid-nineteenth century:

> Like nationalist history, to which it is usually closely linked, the culture-historical approach can be used to bolster the pride and morale of nations or ethnic groups. It is most often used for this purpose among peoples who feel thwarted, threatened, or deprived of their collective rights by more powerful nations or in countries where appeals are being made to counteract serious internal divisions. Nationalist archaeology tends to emphasize the more recent past rather than the Palaeolithic period and draws attention to the political and cultural achievements of indigenous ancient civilizations. (1989:174)

This describes nicely the *Madjapahit* movies. With perhaps the difference that while the historical Madjapahit was mainly limited to Java, the movie *Madjapahit* implicitly becomes the ancestral state for all of Indonesia. It would be instructive to examine Indonesian archaeology in this light. (Trigger discusses most other majors world areas but ignores Indonesia.) Although the central government has been active in restoring the great Hindu and Buddhist temples of a millenium ago (Borobudur is the most famous), I suspect that on the whole, Indonesian archaeology is not as effective in this way as is archaeology in other, comparable countries, and that cinema has taken on the burden of providing an imagined past.

But most Indonesian films construct a pan-Indonesian culture in modern form. These plots and settings are probably driven more by economics than by some central political planning of the Jakarta government. The government interest in encouraging, censoring, and occasionally sponsoring films seems to focus more on protecting and enhancing the images of specific events or individuals, and not on broader social planning. (See Sen's discussion of censorship [1988].) *Desa Di Kaki Bukit* (The Village at the Foot of the Hills [1980]), by Asrul Sani, is a rare exception: its unacknowledged sponsor was the national family planning program, and its plot shows how conservative village resistance to family planning clinics and other sorts of modernization is overcome by determined patriotism and love (see Heider 1991:81–86). Similarly, Lutze attributes the "catholicity" or "all-Indianness" of Hindi films primarily to economic motivations (1985:5).

Many Indonesians, while acknowledging the absence of regional ethnographic verisimilitude, feel that Indonesian films have become Americanized under the impact of all the Hollywood imports. I would agree that in a few rather superficial ways, particularly concerning sexuality, this is true: kissing, handholding, and form-revealing clothing, have become almost routine in the films of the last decade. The artifacts of upper-class Westernized Jakarta Indonesians, from dining tables to automobiles, are shown constantly. And in this respect, these dramas and melodramatic films do present a model for Western style domestic life. They show people how to live a middle-class, non-ethnic life in Indonesia today. It would be interesting to learn just how the imports, especially American domestic dramas, fit into this picture. I suspect that the American contributions are generally seen as totally unrealistic models for any Indonesian behavior (indeed, many Americans feel the same way), while the Indonesian versions are the more accessible models, presenting a possible future, giving instructions in the new national culture. In this sense, the Indonesian films really do convey a strong Americanization of world culture.

But if one goes beyond the settings to consider the basic motivations of the actors and the central conflicts of the plots, it appears that these Indonesian films have become more Indonesian, not less. I would identify the two most important features of Indonesian-ness as 1) emphasis on social groups rather than autonomous individuals and 2) emphasis on conflict between order and disorder rather than between good and evil. Films of the 1950s, made by men trained in Western cinema, are more Western, less Indonesian, in these particulars, than are films made in the 1970s and 1980s (see the extended argument to this effect in Heider 1991). Asrul Sani, one of the grand older men of Indonesian cinema, who began his career in the 1950s and is still productive today, exemplifies this shift in the landmark films of his own career.

Finally, I would like to look briefly at those who were responsible for making Indonesian films, those who were the constructors of this national culture on the screen. We find an irony: they were, at first, overwhelmingly from abroad—from Europe and from China, but later they were Indonesian Chinese and Minangkabau. In various respects, then, they were from the outside or from the periphery, and certainly not the core, of Indonesian society. People who could not be players in the classic *wayang* of Java found opportunities in the new niche of cinema. And, in many respects like the Jews who invented Hollywood (to use Neal Gabler's phrase) these outsiders were responsible for creating the image of the common Indonesian culture.

Gabler also suggests that the Jews of Hollywood

> had a special compatibility with the industry, one that gave them certain advantages over their competitors. For one thing, having come primarily from fashion and retail, they understood public taste and were masters at gauging

market swings, at merchandising, at pirating away customers and beating the competition. (1988:5)

Again, this suggests the Minangkabau, famous for their small business skills across the country, and even more, the Chinese Indonesians, who had long concentrated in business (e.g., Peacock 1973:46).

And the parallel goes further: in America, by the late 1930s, virulent anti-Semitism allied with rabid anti-communism found the cinema industry Jews an irresistible target. Ironically, this was in the name of the very all-American culture which these same men had done so much to create (Gabler 1988:311–86).

In Indonesia there have been sharp but cryptic attacks on "non-Indonesian" influences within the film industry which subverted the true Indonesian cinema. It is specifically "Indonesian Chinese filmmakers who are being attacked . . . the non-native producers who still dominate the domestic film industry . . . " (Said 1982:10, 1991:9). Even the appearance of Eurasian actors has been criticized:

> Any domination, if it could be called that, of Eurasian faces in Indonesia occurs only in films. And it was this relatively frequent appearance of Eurasian faces in films that gave rise some time ago to controversy among observers of the world of film. (Depari 1990:78)

But for all that critics may deplore the commercialization and the "non-native" influence on Indonesian films, it is just these two factors which have been most influential in producing national culture in a national cinema which can be sold and viewed across the archipelago. There is an emergent national Indonesian culture. It is not localized—there are no "Indonesian villages"—but it is being imagined and modeled and developed in the national cinema.

Bibliography

Anderson, Benedict.

1983   *Imagined Communities. Reflections on the Origins and Spread of Nationalism.* London: Verso.

1990   *Language and Power. Exploring Political Cultures in Indonesia.* Ithaca: Cornell University Press.

Bruner, Edward M.

1961   "Urbanization and Ethnic Identity in North Sumatra." *American Anthropologist* 63:508–21.

1979   "Comments: Modern? Indonesian? Culture?" in Gloria Davis, ed., *What Is Modern Indonesian Culture?* Athens: Ohio University, Center for International Studies.

Depari, Eduard.

    1990   "Eurasian Faces in Indonesian Films" pp. 77–79 in Salim Said, ed., *Indone-sian Film Festival 1990*. Jakarta: Foreign Relations Division, The Indonesian Film Festival Permanent Committee.

de Queljoe, David.

    1974   *Marginal Man in a Colonial Society. Abdoel Moeis' Salah Asuhan*. Papers in In-ternational Studies—Southeast Asia Series, no. 22. Athens: Ohio University, Center for International Studies.

Foster, Robert J.

    1991   "Making National Culture in the Global Ecumene." *Annual Review of An-thropology* 20:235–60.

Gabler, Neal.

    1988   *An Empire of Their Own. How The Jews Invented Hollywood*. New York: Crown Publishers.

Geertz, Hildred.

    1963   "Indonesian Cultures and Communities," in Ruth McVey, ed., *Indonesia*. New Haven: HRAF Press.

Hannerz, Ulf.

    1989   "Culture between Center and Periphery: Towards a Macroanthropology." *Ethos* 54.3–4:200–16.

Heider, Karl G.

    1991   *Indonesian Cinema. National Culture on Screen*. Honolulu: University of Ha-waii Press.

Iyer, Pico.

    1988   *Video Nights in Kathmandu: And Other Reports from the Not-So-Far East*. New York: Random House.

Kato, Tsuyoshi.

    1982   *Matriliny and Migration: Evolving Minangkabau Traditions in Indonesia*. Ithaca: Cornell University Press.

Lutze, Lothar.

    1985   "From Bharata to Bombay: Change and Continuity in Hindi Film Aesthet-ics," pp. 3–15 in Pfleiderer and Lutze.

Peacock, James L.

    1973   *Indonesia: An Anthropological Perspective*. Pacific Palisades, California: Goodyear Publishing Company.

    1987   *Rites of Modernization: Symbolic and Social Aspects of Indonesian Proletarian Drama*. Chicago: University of Chicago Press.

Pfleiderer, Beatrix, and Lothar Lutze, eds.

    1985   *The Hindi Film. Agent and Re-agent of Cultural Change*. New Delhi: Manohar.

Said, Salim.

    1982   *Profil Dunia Film Indonesia*. Jakarta: Grafitipers. (1991 English translation by

Toenggoel P. Siagian as *Shadows on the Silver Screen: A Social History of Indonesian Film*. Jakarta: The Lontar Foundation.)

Sen, Krishna.
    1988   "Filming 'History' under the New Order," in Krishna Sen, ed., *Histories and Stories: Cinema in New Order Indonesia*. Clayton: Monash University.
    1989   "Power and Poverty in New Order Cinema: Conflicts on Screen," pp. 1–20 in Paul Alexander, ed., *Creating Indonesian Cultures*. Sydney: Oceania Publications.

Trigger, Bruce G.
    1989   *A History of Archaeological Thought*. Cambridge: Cambridge University Press.

Ugboajah, Frank Okwu, ed.
    1985   *Mass Communication, Culture and Society in West Africa*. Munich: Hans Zall/K. G. Saur.

10 | The Representation of Colonialism in Satyajit Ray's *The Chess Players*

Darius Cooper

WHEN COLONIZED ARTISTS respond to forces of colonialism and racism, they try to, in Franz Fanon's words, "mold the national consciousness, giving it form and contours and flinging open before it new and boundless horizons."[1] Whether disseminated through literature, cinema, or any other art form, this vision becomes "combative" because "it assumes" what Fanon calls "responsibility," since "it is the will to liberty expressed in terms of time and space."[2]

These forms and contours are precisely what Indian filmmaker Satyajit Ray discovered in the two very nationalistic and combative short stories of the eminent Hindi writer Munshi Premchand—*Shatranj-Ke-Khilari* (*The Chess Players*), written in 1924 and *Sadgati* (*Deliverance*), written in 1931. Ray completed the adaptation of the former in 1977 and the latter for Indian television in 1981.

In their roles as colonized artists (Premchand writing in a pre-independent India and Ray filming in a post-independent India),[3] both exhibit the same compulsion to show how colonialism and racism are structures which promote what Edward Said so eloquently defines as "the difference between the familiar 'us' and the strange 'them.' "[4] Under their colonized gaze, the "us" stands for the Occidental and the British in colonial terms and the three upper Hindu castes in racial terms. Similarly, the "them" stands for the Oriental and the Indian in colonial terms, the outcast and untouchable Hindu castes in racial terms, and how when "a certain freedom of discourse is permitted," it always belongs to the stronger culture or the dominant caste because only "they" can give shape and meaning to this vast mystery and struggle and the problems involved therein. Both Ray and Premchand want to, through their respective texts, expose "the constricted vocabulary of such a privilege and the comparative limitations of such a vision."[5]

In this essay I shall examine the different narrative discourses employed by Ray in his critical and historical look at a colonized India's past in *The Chess Players* and how he tries to define Indian nationalism, in the words of the "subaltern" Indian historian Ranajit Guha, "primarily as a function of stimulus and response. Based on a narrowly behaviourist approach this represents nationalism as the sum of activities and ideas by which the Indian elite reponded to the institutions, the opportunities resources, etc., generated by colonialism."[6] Although Ray's approach would be considered "narrow" by historians like Guha, Ray's complicated and interesting narrative treatment of his text is not without its uses. To Premchand's original story in which only the two Lakhnavi chess-besotted jagirdars or landlords figure as reciprocating their "responses" to the overriding "stimulus" of chess offered by the British, Ray adds the two important historical figures of Wajid Ali Shah, the ruler of Oudh, and General Outram, the British Resident (dispatched by the then Governor General Lord Dalhousie), to whom Wajid is ordered to surrender his crown. The narrative moves of the two chess players functioning in Premchand's story are put in a particularized historical context by Ray. The complex problems that emerge out of their own mutual oppositions on the chessboard are paralleled in Ray's text by the complicated contradictions arising in the power play that develops between the two elites, Wajid and Outram, as they struggle for control over Oudh. Guha's grudging acknowledgment of this elitist historiography of "stimulus and response" can very pointedly be extended to Ray's film as well since it

> . . . helps us to know more of the structure of the colonial state, the operation of the various organs in certain historical circumstances, the nature of the alignment of the classes which sustained it; of some aspects of the ideology of the elite as the dominant ideology of the period; of the contradictions between the two elites and the complexities of their mutual oppositions and coalitions; of the role of some of the more important British and Indian personalities and elite organizations.[7]

In the Preface to the published script of *The Chess Players*, Ray defines three primary reasons that drew him to Premchand's short story: "My interest in chess, the Raj period, and the city of Lucknow itself."[8] Since chess already figured in Premchand's story, Ray's research in the other two areas revealed interesting facts about the deposed King Wajid and the British resident Outram. The former, according to Ray

> was an extraordinary character. Outram describes him as a worthless King, which he probably was, but this was compensated for by a genuine gift for music. He was a composer, singer, poet, and dancer. He also wrote and produced plays on Hindu themes (he was a Muslim himself) in which he acted the main part. All this made the King a figure worthy of film treatment. As for the character of Outram, I was struck by the fact that he had qualms about the task he had been asked to perform. This was revealed in a couple of Dalhousie letters. Thus both the King and Outram were complex three dimensional characters.[9]

It is important to catalogue here the principal sources Ray consulted while preparing for the film. Many of them were cited by Ray in the December 31, 1978 issue of *The Illustrated Weekly of India* when an Indian critic, in an October 22, 1978 issue of the same magazine, attacked Ray for displaying a very Orientalist approach in his depiction of Wajid Ali Shah as a weak, ineffectual, and effeminate monarch. Defending his position, Ray listed in detail the following historical sources he referred to in order to authenticate his creation of these two actual historical figures. I have taken them from Andrew Robinson's introduction in the published script where they have been properly cited. The remarks and comments are Ray's. I am not citing all but only those relevant to this essay:

1. *Blue Book on Oude* . . . It contains, among other things, a verbatim account of Outram's last interview with Wajid, and describes Wajid's taking off his turban and handing it to Outram as a parting gesture.
2. *Abdul Halim Sharar's Guzesta Lucknow* (translated into English by E. S. Harcourt and Fakhir Hussain as *Lucknow: The Last Phase of an Oriental Culture*) . . . Sharar provided most of the socio-cultural details, as well as a fairly extended portrait of Wajid both in Lucknow and his Calcutta periods.
3. The Indian Histories of Mill and Beveridge, both critical of the Annexation.
4. *The Letters of Lord Dalhousie:* One of these letters provided the information that Outram grumbled about the new treaty and apprehended that Wajid would refuse to sign it.
5. The biographies of Outram by Trotter and by Goldschmid.
6. *The Indian Mutiny Diary* by Howard Russell . . . who was on the spot when the British troops ransacked the Kaiserbaugh Palace. He gives the only description of the interior of the palace I have come across.
7. The young Wajid's personal diary *Mahal Khana Shahi*. This turned out to be the unending account of his amours.
8. The text of Wajid Ali Shah's *Rahas* (where he plays Krishna).
9. *Umarao Jan Ada* (*A Courtesan of Pleasure*) which gives a fascinating and authentic picture of Lucknow in Wajid's time.
10. All English and Bengali newspapers and journals of the period preserved in The National Library in Calcutta.
11. I was also closely in touch with Professor Kaukabh of Aligarh University. He happens to be a great grandson of Wajid Ali Shah and is considered one of the best authorities in India on Wajid.[10]

The reason for such a historical immersion on Ray's part becomes very clear in the film's prologue itself. Before entering the narrative proper, Ray sets up the historical frame within which his filmic text is going to operate. He does this "to educate," in Andrew Robinson's terms, "the (Indian as well as the Western) audience's widespread ignorance of the facts of the relationship between the British and Oudh in the century leading to the Annexation—in India as much as elsewhere: to which the film's ten minute prologue seemed the only solution."[11] An exposition of this kind of film narrative is traditionally undertaken in the summary mode. And since "the cinema," according to Seymour Chatman, "has trouble with summary, directors often resort to gadgetry."[12] Ray, however, avoids many of these gadgetry pitfalls ennumerated by Chatman as "the montage sequence, peeling calendars, dates written as legend on the screen etc . . . "[13] in his prologue. While an invisible narrator in a voice-over paints for us the historical background against which the fictive narrative scenes will stand out, the prologue provides in Genettian terms an interesting "connective tissue . . . whose fundamental rhythm is defined"[14] by (a): a presentation of the two chess players absorbed in their game followed by (b): several characteristic vignettes of Wajid Ali Shah. This is completed by (c): a cartoon section sketching the British takeover of Oudh as a large "cake" swallowed by the Governor General Lord Dalhousie.

Ray begins his historical exposé with a close-up of a chessboard. From the right side of the frame a hand enters, hovers over the pieces, and moves a white Bishop. From the left side of the frame another hand enters, moves a Black Knight in response and captures a White Pawn. In a voice-over the prologue's invisible narrator synecdochically tells us to

> Look at the hands of the mighty generals deploying their troops on the battlefield. We do not know if these hands ever held real weapons. But this is not a real battle where blood is shed and the fate of empire decided—

The camera pulls back and we now see the two Lakhnavi landlords Meer Roshan Ali and Mirza Sajjad Ali (hereafter referred to as Mir and Mirza). As Ray's camera fixes the two friends playing chess with rapt concentration, the narrator intones:

> It has been like this ever since the day the two friends discovered this noble game. You may ask: have they no work to do? Of course not! Whoever heard of the landed gentry working? These are noblemen of the capital of Oudh or Lucknow.

A close-up of a Mughal arch follows. The camera slowly pulls back and images of domes and minarets rapidly accumulate on the screen. A group of noblemen from a nearby rooftop are now shown watching pigeons wheeling in the sky along with gaily colored paper kites fighting duels with each other in the sky. Such innocent pastimes are next juxtaposed beside a more cruel one where a brutal and insensitive crowd is shown in feverish animation at a cockfight. Then Ray inserts a close-up of a throne. The camera pulls back to reveal that it is empty. In steps the narrator to inform us in mocking tones: "This is the throne of King Wajid, who ruled over Oudh. But the King had other interests too." Now Ray introduces us to Wajid playing the Hindu god Krishna in his play *Rahas* where he is surrounded by an adoring female conglomerate of the proverbial goopiyaas or Krishna's consorts. The accompanying song we hear is a love song composed by Wajid himself. More vignettes of the protean Wajid follow: First, a Muslim Wajid, surrounded by a crowd, plays the Tasha (drum) at the grand Islamic festival of Mohurrum. Then we see him at night reclining in his harem with his favorite concubines. Next comes a close-up of Wajid. As the camera pulls back, we see him finally sitting on his throne. The irony, of course, is not lost on the narrator who informs us: "Nevertheless, there were times when the King sat on the throne."

Such an introduction skillfully summarizes the sad but inevitable cruel part played by the aristocratic class of landlord and King in facilitating Oudh's annexation by the colonial rulers. Their blinkered absorption in games and the arts and their ensuing neglect of state affairs created not only a native political impotence but also gave the imperialist aggressor the justification to step in and set things right. This is indicated by the final portion of the prologue in which the British colonizer makes his appearance. This portion of the prologue begins with Wajid sitting in his durbar (court). The camera moves in toward the crown on his head. The narrator, on cue, informs us:

> If he was not overfond of ruling, he was certainly proud of his crown. Only five years ago, in 1851, he had sent it to London to be displayed at the Great Exhibition. But listen to what an Englishman had to say about it.

A close-up of a letter written by Lord Dalhousie is now accompanied by an English voice reading from the letter:

> The wretch in Lucknow who has sent his crown to the Exhibition would have done his people and us a great service if he had sent his head in it—and he would never have missed it. That is a cherry which will drop into our mouths one day.

An animation follows showing cherries and their crowns being knocked off by Dalhousie. And as the last cherry is swallowed up, the narrator informs us in historical tones what Indian states each of those swallowed cherries signified:

> Punjab, Burma, Nagpur, Satara, Jhansi. The only one left is the cherry of Oudh whose friendship with Britain goes back to the reign of Nawab Siraj-ud-Daula. Nawab Shiya had been unwise to pit his forces against the British. No wonder he was defeated. But the British did not dethrone him. All that they did was to make him sign a treaty pledging eternal friendship and five million rupees compensation. Ever since, the Nawabs of Oudh have maintained this friendship. When British campaigns needed money, the Nawabs opened their coffers.

The animated section that follows illustrates this process. We see a Nawab asleep on the throne. Next to him is a cake with OUDH written over it. In struts the Governor General, who taps the sleeping Nawab on the shoulder. The Nawab wakes and hangs his head in shame and the GG points angrily at

OUDH. The Nawab takes out a knife and slices off a piece of OUDH and hands it to the GG who gulps it down and struts away. Concludes our narrator: "Poor Wajid! If only you knew what was in the mind of the Resident of Lucknow, General Outram." Herein ends the prologue.

The grand doctrine of British "efficiency" that Joseph Conrad so severely castigated in the opening pages of *The Heart of Darkness* and which the British so often used to justify their "takeovers" of those Indian states ruled by inefficient monarchs like Wajid was nurtured, as Ray's prologue so accurately indicates, by the very lassitude of its natives—men like the two chess players and their ruler Wajid. The prologue thus sets up the tone and the direction which Ray's film is going to take. The characters in this animated strip critically comment on the caricatured figures of the two chess players portrayed in the rest of the film. In addition, the stylization represented in the prologue is in keeping with the stylized tone and setting of the film itself. It reflects the film's accurately revealed vision of a Lakhnavi elitist culture where aesthetics, calligraphy, dance, games, music, poetry, role-playing, decorum, manners, style of dress and mode of address, customs and costumes, all took precedence over history's realpolitik trends. The mocking commentary and the lush visuals constitutes a cultural attack on Oudh's elite itself.

In addition to the prologue Ray adds to his filmic text three crucial scenes, none of which figure in Premchand's original short story. The first is the scene between the chess players and the city's garrulous and gracious Hindu Munshi, a character created by Ray to establish the harmony that existed between the Muslims and the Hindus in Wajid's Oudh; the second is the scene where Wajid, in a long monologue, accepts before his ministers the hopelessness of his political position; and the third scene occurs in the study of the British Resident, where General Outram, in a long monologue, contrasts the ideologies of someone like Wajid with his own master's political ambitions.

The chess players are about to commence their game one day, when the city's Munshi arrives to see them. Annoyed by this intrusion, but in keeping with the nawabi code of hospitality, they receive him in their "hall of audience" most graciously. In the conversation that ensues between them, the two main topics discussed are "chess" and "the British." The Munshi, at first, elaborates on the "rumors" he has heard of the "British" speculating some sort of "a takeover" of Oudh. But finding the two nawabs casting wistful glances at the chessboard, and realizing his own untimely intrusion, he very skillfully steers his remaining remarks to "the history of chess" to capture their bored and straying attention. Wanting to retain the "British" in his conversation, however, the Munshi now cleverly proceeds to teach them the rudiments of playing chess "the British way," its main contribution lying in the "Englishman's ability to produce quick decisions" in the game. Reacting strongly to this, the nawabs, who play chess at a more leisurely and languid pace, launch a mighty tirade against other, similar, British qualities, which they detest. These include the British obsession with "speed," "communications," and "actions"; their insatiable "desire for wealth," and their "confounded efficiency" in administration. So animated does Mir become, at one moment, that he snatches an ancient cutlass from the wall and brags about the martial eminence of his ancestors. Since Mir has never handled a weapon before, he cuts a very clumsy figure, ventilating empty rhetoric with this ancient relic in his unaccustomed hands.

The inclusion of this scene is crucial for two reasons. In the first instance, it points to similar actions which will be performed by *both* nawabs at the end of the film. Second, it allows Ray to presage the irony and hollowness of what they profess, as will become apparent in the end of the film. Mir's inability to handle a hereditary weapon when confronted by mere *notions* of British "efficiency" is reflected at the film's end by Mir's clumsy firing from *his* ancient gun on being labeled a cuckold. The martial eminence of ancestors rings hollow when Mir fires at Mirza instead of aiming his weapon against his real enemies—the *gori palton* (white troops) of the British. Although these two nawabs rave and rant against the efficiency ethics of the British, it is here they meet their own downfall. In fact, their willingness to "now play chess according to British rules" in the film's last shot exposes their mock-heroic attitudes as prefaced earlier in this pivotal scene with the Munshi. "Whatever happens, the British can't stop us playing chess," is Mir's parting shot delivered to the departing Munshi.

In his enlightening section "Point of view and its relation to Narrative Voice," Seymour Chatman points out that:

> Though it's true that preconceptions of various sorts affect our physiological vision . . . there remains an essential difference between perceptions and conceptions. . . . The narrator's is second-order or heterodiegetic conceptualizing *about* the story—as opposed to the first-order conceptualizing of a character within the story. These distinctions most clearly emerge where the two conflict, where the narrator is operating under a clearly different set of attitudes than those of the character. Then the narrator's conceptual point of view . . . tends to override the character's, despite the fact that the latter maintains the center of interest and consciousness.[15]

Throughout the film, Ray as narrator is very unsympathetic to the characters of the two Lakhnavi chess players. Their conceptual point of view is constantly undermined by Ray's presentation of the narrative in which they figure or by other characters inhabiting the chess players' mise-en-scène. This enables Ray to exhibit their characteristic blindness to everything around them because of their obsession with chess. Let me cite the marvellously orchestrated connubial scene between the Mirza and his begum (wife) Khurshid who has become the unfortunate victim of her husband's cruel neglect of her at all times.

When Mir makes the remark that "whatever happens, the British can't stop us playing chess," Mirza retaliates, "We are talking of war and he thinks only of chess." The fact that Mirza is infected with the same chess-virus is indicated by Ray in the scene that follows between Mirza and his begum Khurshid. Mirza's conceptual view of chess is repeatedly undermined by Khurshid, who as it were, becomes the spokeswoman for Ray. In addition, Ray undermines Mirza, both on the level of his script and through the mise-en-scène and camera movements as well. The scene opens in Khurshid's bedroom where we see her feigning a migraine headache so that Mirza is forced to abandon his chess game with Mir and hurry to her zenana (bedroom) where she will try to seduce him. As he ministers to her, she snaps out at "that stupid game" which keeps him so preoccupied. Mirza's response is characteristic: "why it's the king of games. Ever since I started to play chess . . . my power of thinking has grown a hundredfold." But Mirza's thinking *outside* the realm of the chess game has *not* grown at all! It has, in fact, *narrowed* to such an extent that in Khurshid's undermining retort the game only makes him "sit hunched over that stupid piece of cloth and jiggle around those stupid ivory pieces." Khurshid further indicates the dangers of such an obsession which has forced his friend's (that is, Mir's) wife to take a lover. "All Lucknow knows that his wife is carrying on with another man. Only you and your friend don't know." Having surprised him on the verbal level, Khurshid, in a stunning reversal of sexually appropriated roles, orders her husband to lie down on the bed. When he meekly complies, she boldly sits above him.

In this mise-en-scène, Ray shows the woman defiantly taking the man's position in activating the sexual process, while the man lies in the customary passive female position. Khurshid wants him, "especially your eyes, red from staring at those stupid chess pieces" to look "at me," as his flesh and blood wife and not just those ivory representations of women he literally fingers and paws on the chessboard. She is objectifying herself sexually, using all her feminine wiles to arouse his dormant/absent passion. In metonymic terms, she is becoming the royal begum or queen of this chess besotted haveli or household. As this game begins and she pulls a coverlet over them, Ray cuts to the drawing-room where Mir wonders about the prolonged absence of his friend. He tiptoes to the door, listens, then tiptoes back. A reverse traveling shot follows. As the foreground of the mise-en-scène is darkened by the two ends of a curtain drawn together, Mir's hand suddenly appears in the middle, and with a deft but casual movement, he shifts one of his pawns to a more advantageous position on the chessboard.

Ray cuts back to the Mirza/Khurshid sexual site in their bedroom where Khurshid's failure to achieve Mirza's arousal and the uncomfortable silence between the two is further accentuated in the mise-en-scène by the distant barking of dogs and passing of carriages on the road in the night outside. Khurshid finally releases him and sits on the edge of the bed looking away. Ray's mise-en-scène makes it very clear that while her sexual game has failed, Mirza's responses are to the contrary. He is agitated, not so much by his masculine lack, but by his prolonged absence from the chessboard. He is anxious to get back to his abandoned chess game and excuses his lack of sexual zeal by stating to his begum that "my mind was elsewhere. It was with Mir waiting and the game half-finished." He is completely oblivious to his wife's perpetual waiting and *her* half-finished or never-satiated games of passion. Ray has him sing a love song to cover up his awkwardness, but the intrusion of his song at such a delicate moment ironically deflates the poised masculine role of the lover he is trying to assume in his wife's presence. As he hurriedly exits, like a betrayed scheherazade, Khurshid angrily calls for her faithful old maidservant and demands that "you tell me a story. I want to stay awake all night."

Ray cuts to the drawing-room. Mirza slowly walks in and assumes a solemn air. Mir guessing by his dishevelled appearance at what must have transpired, solicitously inquires about the begum:

Mir: A bad headache?
Mirza: Very bad.
Mir: Tch. Tch. (Sighs ostentatiously, then moves a piece). Check!

Ray's narration, as I have tried to show, is very ironic in relation to the two chess players, because they are, in E. M. Forster's celebrated definition, "flat characters endowed with a single trait"—their consuming obsession for chess.[16] Because of this, their behavior in any situation is highly predictable. Having witnessed Mirza's behavior in a domestic situation, we can certainly anticipate what his (as well as his friend's) actions will amount to when they are finally confronted with the alarming political changes taking place around them in Oudh.

"Round characters," to continue Forster's definition, are on the other end of the spectrum. In Chatman's accurate description, "they possess a variety of traits, some of them conflicting or even contradictory; their behaviour is not predictable—they are capable of changing, of surprising us. They inspire a strong sense of intimacy."[17] We see this intimacy very clearly established between Ray and his historical character of Wajid Ali Shah. Wajid's character is presented by Ray in ways that are always capable of surprising not only the British resident General Outram with his limited and fixed notions of Occidental masculinity, but Ray's narration also creates in us the strong anticipatory need "to demand the possibilities of discovering new and unsuspected traits" in Wajid. Ray very skillfully modulates Wajid's functions "as open constructs, susceptible to further insights." He becomes for us, and for Ray, "virtually inexhaustible . . . for contemplation."[18]

Before Wajid Ali Shah actually *speaks* his monologue, Ray depicts the monarch's characteristics through purely *visual* images. In a visual resumé, we see Wajid adopting several *roles* and expressing several *abhinayas* (gestures). Ray frames him first as Lord Krishna, playing the flute and assuming the stance of the eternal lover. Then, we see him leading a Mohurrum procession, dressed resplendently as a Muslim prophet. This is followed by a shot of Wajid, stroking his cat, in a style very reminiscent of a James Bond villain, while enjoying the sensuous glances of the kathak dancer at a lavishly performed *jalsa* (dance performance). Next, we see Wajid composing a poem and reciting it loudly to his court during a trial when he is expected to render a judicial verdict. These expressions of Wajid's eccentric personality are crucial indices of his effort to transcend his position as ruler/king by adopting all these different roles of dancer/flute-player, prophet, lover, and poet. His confidence in himself is fueled by his imaginative life, in which all this role-playing enhances the traditional, royal picture. Furthermore, his ministers, his courtiers, and even the ordinary citizens of Oudh, accept this. So, when Wajid comes out with a poem instead of a judicial verdict at a trial, they are not in the least surprised.

This peculiarity of Wajid, which Ray cites here, has an analogous and similar moment in Forster's *A Passage to India*. This happens when Aziz (also a Muslim, like Wajid, who is lying ill in bed and has some quarrelsome Muslim friends visit him) suddenly decides to recite a poem. Immediately, all squabbling in that narrow, dirty room stops, and a moment of transcendence in achieved. The imaginative life, celebrated in the poem, casts its spell over the speaker and the listeners, and the day-to-day existence with its dullness and squalor is overwhelmed:

[The poem] had no connection with anything that had gone before, but it came from his heart and spoke to theirs. . . . The squalid bedroom grew quiet; the silly intrigues, the gossip, the shallow discontent were stilled, while words accepted as immortal filled the air. . . . The poem had done no "good" to anyone, but it was a passing reminder, a breath from the divine lips of beauty, a nightingale between two worlds of dust.[19]

Similarly, Wajid's recitation, though having no connection with the trial, is an unspoken appeal for acceptance, first as a poet and then as a lawgiver and king. The poem, though of no practical value, forces the audience to experience the imaginative life and poetic words over merely mortal issues and verdicts. At the end of the kathak recital, when Wajid learns from his weeping Prime Minister, Ali Naqui, that the British Resident General Outram is due to arrive and ask for Wajid's peaceful surrender to the British Government, Wajid's first reaction is to upbraid Ali Naqui for such "unmanly" display of emotion in public. "Only poetry and music should bring tears to a man's eyes," he tells him eloquently. Even with his fate sealed, Wajid clings to his unique claim to kingship. In the monologue that follows, he demands with amazing rhetoric (from his ministers) the answer (if there could be one) to the following syllogism: If the British think that he is unfit to rule, could they produce a single English monarch from among them who could compose poetry and music of a high order like Wajid

Ali Shah? "The common people sing my songs," he declares, "and they love my poetry because of its candor."

It is precisely this bewildering aspect of Wajid's personality that intrigues General Outram. Outram tries to deconstruct Wajid from a mental framework of Western thought, in which Wajid emerges (and here I am applying Edward Said's categories) as "irrational, depraved (fallen), childlike, and different."[20] In Outram's dominating framework, Wajid is "contained and represented" as a ruler completely lacking in masculinity. Instead of ruling like a man, Wajid loves to dance. Instead of admininistering and rendering verdicts, Wajid composes poetry and songs. These are unkingly, decadent, and unmanly qualities for a ruler to possess. The scene where Wajid is deconstructed by General Outram for the benefit of Captain Weston, one of his assistants, is played out very skillfully in two specific discourses designed by Ray (and here I am applying Ranajit Guha's categories): the "primary discourse" of Outram and the "secondary discourse" of Weston. The first is denunciatory and official and the second is complimentary and insurgent.

We are in Outram's study. As we come into the scene, Ray shows Outram reading aloud to Weston from an official document that gives "an hour by hour account of the King's (Wajid's) activities, dated the 24th of January." What we get from this primary discourse is the official description of Wajid. In Ranajit Guha's accurate description, "it (is) official in so far as it (is) meant primarily for administration use—for the information of government (Outram as British resident), for action on his part, and for the determination of his policy."[21] Weston's responses, however, are that of the insurgent or in Guha's terminology "emanating from the other side."[22] They offer resistance and opposition to the damaging portrait of Wajid that Outram's discourse is trying to build.

Ray works out this dialectic like a chess game with appropriate moves and countermoves, adding a richness to Premchand's original story in which only one chess game is displayed. In addition, Ray's examination of the components of both these discourses is designated along two "functions" sought by Outram's colonial way of thinking—what Guha accurately refers to as the "indicative" and the "interpretative." Both have to, in Guha's definition, "interpenetrate and sustain each other in order to give (the offical discourse) its (intended) meaning."[23] Since Outram has not confronted Wajid as Weston has, Outram will provide, as the official British resident, the indicative function from the details provided by that offical document. He hopes that Weston will provide the appropriate and substantiating interpretation enabling Outram to fix Wajid as a King unfit to rule or govern Oudh. This will then enable Outram to act accordingly in taking away Wajid's kingdom from him.

"Did you know," Outram informs Weston at the outset, "that the King prayed five times a day?" The indicative intent here is that instead of ruling and administering Wajid is more interested in trivial and non-monarchical activities like "praying." Weston's insurgent response to this is "Five is the number prescribed by the Koran, sir." This immediately affirms Outram's ignorance of Islamic religion and culture through which he is now asked to interpret Wajid and *not* through the colonial one of the British. Acknowledging Weston's move, Outram tries another colonial approach. Dipping into the official document, Outram comes up with the following damaging fissures in Wajid's personality:

> "His Majesty listened to a new singer Mushtrari Bai, and afterwards amused himself by flying kites on the palace roof." That's at 4PM. Then the King goes to sleep for an hour but he's up in time for the third prayer at 5PM. And then in the evening—now where is it?—"His Majesty recited a new poem on the loves of the bulbul" (a Persian nightingale).

Since the official report leaves out the appropriate indices, Outram expects Weston to come up with the damaging adjectives and epithets to typify Wajid as the inappropriate ruler. "Tell me Weston.... What kind of poet is the King? Is he any good, or is it simply because he is the King they say he is good?" Every effort is made by Outram in his discourse to shift the "accomplished" qualities of the King to the "terrible."

But Weston will not allow that shift to take place. Using his own authority—for Weston knows the Urdu language and the people and culture of Oudh firsthand—he informs Outram that as a poet, "I think [Wajid] is rather good." To prove this he not only recites a Wajid poem in translation but also interprets it for him. To Outram's closed militaristic British mind, the poem "doesn't amount to much." And when he informs Weston about it, the latter quickly counters by indicating that the poem "doesn't translate very well, sir." Checkmated again, Outram's next gambit is to target the perplexing image cast by Wajid's bizarre masculinity itself. The nonviolent Wajid challenges not only Outram's concept of the virile, masculine ruler, but also what Ashish Nandy observes in his brilliant review of the film: "the dominant concept of kingship in Indian Islam as well as the Hindu Kshatriya or soldier tradition."[24] We can see very clearly here why that Indian critic was so upset about Ray's "effeminate portrait" of Wajid.

When Weston insists that Wajid is "really gifted" as a composer of songs and poems, *and* as a dancer, Outram's colonial ire rises. "Yes, so I understand," he fires back at Weston, "with bells on his feet, like naked nautch girls." We see very clearly here the indicative colonial intent in operation: how can you call Wajid a King, when in addition to wearing a crown on his head he also wears bells on his feet? Arriving rapidly at his conclusion, Outram demands: "And what kind of King do you think that all this makes him, Weston? All these various accomplishments?" When the insurgent Weston slyly responds: "Rather a special kind, sir," Outram stops pacing, stiffens, and erupts very sharply to Weston. "Special? I would have used a much stronger word than that, Weston.

I would have said a bad King. A frivolous, effeminate, irresponsible, worthless King." And when Weston tries to protest, Outram, using his official rank as British Resident, warns Weston that "any suspicion that you hold a brief for the King" would ruin Weston's chance for any future promotions "once we take over" Oudh. It is a lamentable victory on Outram's part, but the struggle between the two men and the imposition of the two discourses by Ray bring out brilliantly the working out of the colonial intent and execution of British administrative policy. It adds an important narrativized layer completely missed by Premchand in his otherwise excellent short story.

While the above scene shows Outram in his official garb, Ray in a later scene humanizes him by showing him as a victim of his own government's policies as well. On this level Ray shows Outram privately expressing his anger at the British government for endorsing Oudh's annexation without any justification. In this scene, Outram interestingly offers his doubts to Dr. Joseph Fayrer, a young residency physician, who unlike Weston is not Outram's inferior. Outram tells him that "we have even less justification for confiscation here. . . . The administration here is execrable. I don't like our fat King either. But a treaty is a treaty." This refers to the early treaty Wajid has signed with Outram's predecessor where the British government had insisted that Wajid disband his army and turn over most admininstrative problems to the British forces that would hereby guard his borders and maintain law and order in his kingdom. When that treaty was conveniently abrogated in 1937, Wajid, in Outram's words "was not informed." In giving expression to his doubts and ire, Ray makes Outram a scapegoat of history and real-politik as well. As a servant of Her Majesty's Government, "the soldier" Outram has to obey the wishes of the Crown: "I'm called upon to do my damnedest to get him to sign and abdicate." Outram feels uneasy to face Wajid and dishonor him a second time. When the treaty was abrogated without Wajid's knowledge or consent, it was administratively broken. Now to appropriate his kingdom without his consent again is to commit administrative treachery! The fate that he had spelled out for Weston would have embraced Outram himself if he had failed to carry out his duties. And although Ray shows him ultimately obeying "the soldier" in him, it is a very reluctant Outram who finally emerges as the winner in this duel for Oudh and Wajid's surrender of his crown.

Another significant departure on the narrative level lies in the completely new and different ending worked out by Ray to bring his study of colonialism to a satisfying end. But before taking a critical look at it, let us work out the ramifications found in Premchand's original narrative closure. His ending is, in Chatman's words, "the traditional narrative of resolution . . . which in Barthesian terms articulates in various ways a question, its response . . . which can either formulate the question or delay its answer."[25] In Premchand's text, the hermeneutic question posed is: what will ultimately happen to these two chess players who are so ignorant about the changes taking place all around them?

With cloaked faces, Premchand shows our two noblemen playing their game. "Check" and "checkmate" are the only words that escape their lips. So engrossed are they in their moves that they fail to see their city visibly collapsing on the other side of the river. Their vision does not stray beyond the rigid square of their chessboard. The historical process which they fail to notice is in fact filled in by the voice of the author:

> In the meantime, (Premchand writes) the country is collapsing. The soldiers of The East Indian Company march on Oudh. Commotion and panic everywhere.... But our two good friends, the chess players, remain blissfully unaffected.... Their one fear is they will be spotted and reported by an official retainer.[26]

Each of them subsequently *does* express fear, but here again, the nawabs are made to empathize with Oudh's sad fate only when each one finds himself at a losing end on the chessboard itself.

When Mirza repeatedly "checkmates" Mir, the defeated Mir corroborates his humiliation by offering a continuous and alarming historical commentary of Oudh itself being checkmated by the superior forces of the British army. He hysterically yelps at Mirza that there must be at least five thousand soldiers coming, and they are all young, strapping specimens with pink, baboon faces. Mirza shows no interest, whatsoever, in what Mir is saying. (The fact that there is also a youthful, strapping soldier, enjoying his wife at home, reaffirms Mir's emasculation for a third time in the story.) When they resume another game, it is Mirza who takes over as historical commentator as he is on the losing end of the chessboard. Mir, on the other hand, has relapsed into his normal indifference again:

> "My God," says Mirza-ji, "you *are* heartless." [They've taken our Nawab Sahib prisoner]. "If such a calamity doesn't move you, what will?" to which the Mir replies: "First save your king, then think of the Nawab Sahib. Checkmate! I win."[27]

Their sense of responsibility does not extend to their own ruler or their feudal lands, which have brought them thousands of rupees, the favors of patronage, and all kinds of luxury and comfort every year. Their patriotism, in fact, is a fiction evoked during losses and gains at the chessboard. Thus it is appropriate that their final quarrel, which results in each killing the other, erupts from the game of chess itself.

The last section of the story begins with Mirza accusing Mir of "cheating." Tempers flare up, and wild words are exchanged. Most of the insults, embedded in these wild words, refer to each man's pedigree. Each reviles the other's most ancient Muslim ancestors. In a typically racial, reductive pattern, Mirza's ancestors are reduced to "farmers who all cut grass" and the Mir's to "the original cooks . . . in the house of Gazi-uddin-Hyder."[28] Both men insult their ancestors using each's past family tree as a convenient scapegoat to gloss over their own impotence and inadequacy in the present. And when they eventually kill each other, we feel no sympathy for their death. They have died defending the (fictitious) honor of their *chess viziers* instead of really defending their sovereign Wajid Ali Shah against a foreign invader. They have, in fact, invited their own doom and the collapse of their beloved city by displaying a completely futile and reckless whim of aristocratic excess. And the foreign power whose work is facilitated by such internal rot has only to enter the fray and drag away what Premchand describes with resounding irony in his last line: the two chess players' "compassionate corpses." In the final analysis, such an end befits this pair— as useless in their deaths as they were in their lives.

Ray's ending, in Chatman's words, is more "revelatory." Its emphasis is not on resolution at all. "The function of (his) discourse is not to answer that (hermeneutic) question nor even to pose it . . . but rather that a state of affairs be revealed."[29] Finding the peace of Oudh threatened by the military presence of the British, the two chess players decide, in the penultimate stages of the film, to play chess "outdoors" for a change. Mir finds a deserted mosque in the countryside where we see them resume their games. Into this sylvan setting, Ray introduces the character of Kaloo, a young and impressionable Hindu boy. He is the only villager who has stayed behind to see the colorful and impressive uniforms of the British troops moving into Oudh. As a child, he is obviously fascinated by the pomp of the pageant, but he clearly has an important, referential role to perform as well.

While he goes to fetch food, the nawabs start squabbling. At the precise moment when Mir points an ancient gun at Mirza, Kaloo rushes in, loudly announcing the arrival of the "gori palton" (white troops). Unnerved by this, the Mir fires the gun, and Ray crosscuts from shots of the majestic British troops to the stunned faces of the two nawabs. For the first time, the awesome intention of the British to annex their kingdom finally dawns on them. When Kaloo chooses this moment to ask his all-important question: "Why is nobody fighting the Angrez (British)?" he becomes, very appropriately, the historical spokesman of the Indian Nationalist Movement itself, which ninety years later would successfully drive out the British from India on August 15, 1947.

While pointing thus to India's political future through the figure of Kaloo, Ray, at the same time, shows the two nawabs finally understanding their own cowardly collaboration with the enemy. This is a vast improvement over Premchand's ending, where the two nawabs kill each other. Ray's masterful irony is indicated by making them immediately adopt the British style of playing chess (which the Munshi had instructed them on) now that Oudh has a "gora" or "white" ruler on its throne. Ray's trenchant criticism of such a betrayal is firmly underlined by the film's last shot in which these two silly caricatures (for that is how he wants history to always "fix" them) are seen swatting mosquitoes and bursting into roars of laughter as they begin their first chess game according to their colonial masters' "new rules." Ray's narrative discourse, in a historical as well as fictive sense, succeeds in transforming Premchand's textual material to "a (penetrating) study of the *historic failure of an entire Indian (province) to come to its own*; a failure due to the inadequacy of the (Lakhnavi) bourgeoisie to lead it to a decisive victory over colonialism."[30]

Notes

1. Franz Fanon, *The Wretched of the Earth* (New York: Grove Press, 1968), p. 240.
2. Fanon, p. 240.
3. India gained its independence from the British on August 15, 1947.
4. Edward W. Said, *The Word, the Text, & the Critic* (Cambridge: Harvard University Press, 1983), pp. 43–44.
5. Said, pp. 43–44.
6. Ranajit Guha, *Selected Subaltern Studies* (New York: Oxford University Press, 1988), pp. 38–39.
7. Guha, pp. 38–39.
8. Andrew Robinson, *The Chess Players and Other Stories* (London: Faber & Faber, 1989), p. vii.
9. Robinson, p. vii.
10. Robinson, p. 6.
11. Robinson, p. 7.
12. Seymour Chatman, *Story and Discourse* (Ithaca: Cornell University Press, 1983), p. 69.
13. Chatman, p. 69.
14. Gerard Gennette, *Narrative Discourse* (Ithaca: Cornell University Press, 1980), p. 97.
15. Chatman, pp. 155–56.
16. Chatman, p. 132.
17. Chatman, p. 132.
18. Chatman, pp. 132–33.
19. E. M. Forster, *A Passage to India* (New York: Harcourt Brace & World, 1952), p. 195.
20. Said, p. 40.
21. Guha, p. 47.
22. Guha, p. 47.
23. Guha, p. 53.
24. Ashis Nandy, "Beyond Orientalism Despotism: Politics and Femininity in Satyajit Ray," *Sunday*, 1981, pp. 56–58.
25. Chatman, p. 48.
26. Munshi Premchand, *24 Stories from Premchand* (New Delhi: Vikas Publishing House, 1980), p. 83.
27. Premchand, p. 84.
28. Premchand, p. 84.
29. Premchand, p. 84.
30. Guha, p. 43.

11 | Cinema, Nationhood, and Cultural Discourse in Sri Lanka

Wimal Dissanayake

THE THREE MAIN languages spoken in Sri Lanka are Sinhalese, Tamil, and English. Although very occasionally films get made in Tamil (*Ponmani, Vaadai Kaattu*) and English (*Rampage*), there is hardly a Tamil or English-language film industry in Sri Lanka of any consequence that merits discussion. Hence in this chapter I shall be focusing exclusively on Sinhalese cinema.

The first Sinhalese film, *Broken Promise* (*Kadavunu Poronduva*) was released on January 21, 1947. In 1965 *The Changing Countryside* (*Gam Peraliya*) ushered in the new artistic cinema in Sri Lanka. The objective of this chapter is to examine the birth of serious cinema in Sri Lanka in relation to the wider circumambient cultural discourse without which a proper understanding of the event is not possible. Before examining the content, style, and impact of Lester James Peries's *The Changing Countryside*, we need to pay attention to the diverse historical and social forces that inflect the discursive space opened up by a film culture and the diverse configurations of power and ideology that are inscribed in it.

It is very important to bear in mind the fact that films are cultural practices that grow out of specific materialities, historicities, and temporalities. Films are generally examined as works of art, instances of mass entertainment, illustrations of technological innovations, or projections of social visions with inadequate attention being paid to the fact that they are cultural practices in which the artistic, entertainment, industrial, technological, economic, and political dimensions are closely intertwined and mutually implicated. As a consequence of our unwillingness to recognize the importance of this fact and the usual tendency to examine films as art or entertainment or industry without seeking to investigate the interlinkages, we have, by and large, been unsuccessful in assessing their true import and consequences.

As a result of the works of modern film scholars it is gradually dawning on more and more people that films need to be appreciated as significant social products and cultural practices; hence the complex ways in which social meanings are generated through films have been thrust to the fore of discussion. Films have become one of the most important and powerful media of entertainment in the modern world and we need to map out the ways in which they have become a means of pleasure and significance to so many diverse people. This means that it is imperative that we pay ever-increasing attention to the idea of film as cultural practice and the complex interrelationships that subsist between art and entertainment, industry and audience, image and power, narrative and culture, technology and social vision.

Films are cultural events; but they are not autonomous in that their meanings and significances are derived in large measure from the cultural matrix in which they operate as well as their relationships to other cultural narratives. This point is crucial. The term intertextuality commonly used by cultural analysts denotes the significant relationship that exists between a given film and other filmic texts and cultural narratives that have been produced before in terms of meaning. As Janet Staiger remarks, "intertextuality is not simply a moment in a text or some relation between two texts but rather a central continuing relational activity. It involves the remote determinations of processing a filmic narrative by repeatedly referring to other texts. It can best be comprehended as an ongoing circulation textuality."[1]

In order to understand the full significance of film one has to situate it in the wider cultural discourse and cultural narratives. This is particularly important in the case of countries like Sri Lanka which can lay claim to rich and vibrant traditions of art and literature extending over a period of nearly fifteen centuries. The semioticized space occupied by cinema in such countries derives its meaning and definition in large measure from the codes and conventions associated with other art forms.

In 1901, at a private screening for the then Governor West Ridgeway and the prisoners of the Boer War, the very first film was shown in Sri Lanka, then called Ceylon. It was a documentary dealing with the victory in the Boer War, the funeral of Queen Victoria, and the coronation of Edward VII. Naturally, the early screenings attracted the British living in the island and the Anglicized Ceylonese. However, before long, cinema attained the status of a mass entertainment in large part due to the efforts of Warwick Major, a venturesome Britisher who introduced what was then usually referred to as "bioscope" showings. Films were shown in the open air or in makeshift tents. Film showings in Sri Lanka took on a more stable form with the construction of permanent theatres for their screening. In 1903, Madan Theatres, which had established a chain of theatres in India, expanded its operations to include Sri Lanka. Madan Theatres began to show Indian films which became extremely popular, and very soon a rival company, Olympia, followed suit.

It is generally believed that the first feature film to be made in Sri Lanka was *Royal Adventure* (1925). Interestingly, the lead role in this film was played by Dr. N. M. Perera who was later to become a powerful politician and a Minister of Finance. Although the film was shown in India and Singapore, for some unexplained reason, it does not seem to have been released in Sri Lanka.

As with most other countries during the 1920s and 1930s, films associated with the names of Charlie Chaplin, Greta Garbo, John Barrymore, Rudolph Valentino, and Douglas Fairbanks, Jr., were extremely popular in the island. The two films *The Sheikh* and *The Thief of Baghdad*, it is reported, enjoyed phenomenal popularity. However, by the 1930s, it was the Indian popular film, more than English films, that began to attract greater attention of the masses. For example, the film *Bilwa Mangal*, a musical, became an instant record-breaking success at the box-office. That Indian films began to enjoy such a massive popularity should come as no surprise in view of the fact that linguistically and culturally India shares much in common with Sri Lanka.

On January 21, 1947, the first Sinhalese feature film was released, *Broken Promise* (*Kadavunu Poronduva*). It was based on a popular stage play by the same name and directed by B. A. W. Jayamanne. An actor and actress who were to dominate the Sinhalese screen for many years to come, Eddie Jayamanne and Rukmani Devi, were associated with the film. *Broken Promise* was a great success; local audiences were thrilled to hear Sinhalese being spoken for the first time on screen. The film was a melodrama, meretricious and sentimental, and did not reflect any serious grasp of the medium of cinema. However, based as it was on South Indian models, it set the pattern for popular films that were to follow, all of which were set to a pre-structured formula which combined action, humor, music, dance, and spectacle. Siri Gunasinghe is right when he said that *Broken Promise* is important not merely because it was the first Sinhalese film but because it set the trend which unfortunately for a long time to come held up the growth of the film as an independent medium. *Broken Promise* was no more than a stage play reproduced in moving pictures; little or no attention was paid to the tremendous possibilities of the camera or the basic art of editing; the only basic requirement was for the actors to go through their paces, declaiming, crying, singing, and dancing.[2]

The genre of cinema inaugurated by B. A. W. Jayamanne drew heavily on the existing traditions of stage plays and Indian popular cinema. Interestingly, both these forms of cultural narrative were greatly indebted to the Parsi theatre which was developed in India in the nineteenth century. The Parsis, who were generally rich, gifted, and versatile, in part because of the absence of a deep-seated cultural tradition of their own in the Indian soil, took up drama in both Gujarati and Hindustani. During the nineteenth century the Parsis had earned a wide reputation as skillful playwrights and adroit technicians, influencing the theatre of both North and South India. There were a number of Parsi theatrical companies touring the country and performing before crowded audiences; some of them, for example, the Elphinstone Dramatic Company of Bombay, visited neighboring countries including Sri Lanka and played to overflowing and admiring audiences. Indeed, the modern theatrical revival in Sri Lanka is directly attributable to the Parsi theatre. These dramatists had a practical cast of mind and were more interested in commercial success than artistic achievement. The Parsi theatre excelled in both social and historical plays. Stylistically, they displayed a curious amalgam of realism and fantasy, music and dance, narrative and spectacle, lively dialogue and stage ingenuity all welded within the framework of melodrama. These plays with their melodious songs, crude humor, bon mots, sensationalism, and dazzling stage craft were designed to appeal to the broad mass of people, and they did. The normal adjectives used by scholars of drama and theatre to categorize these dramas are "hybrid," "vulgar," and "sensational." The Parsi theatre drew on both Western and Indian modalities of entertainment, representing an attempt to appeal to the lowest common denominator.[3] Thus, we notice that these plays bear an uncanny resemblance to the generality of popular Indian films and by extension to popular Sinhalese films as well. If the folk-dramas were based on rural areas and presented the vocabulary of traditionally inherited theatrical expression, the Parsi plays signified an urban theatre exposed to Western styles, sensibilities, and semiotics of entertainment. A structural and discursive analysis of the Parsi theatre and the early popular Sinhalese films would bring to light remarkable correspondences and affinities in terms of thematics, textualization, and styles of presentation.

The second important stage in the evolution of Sinhalese cinema is signified by the work of Sirisena Wimalaweera. He sought to locate his experiences in a cinematic space inflected by history, tradition, and cultural nationalism. His first film was *Mother* (*Amma*, 1950), and his second was *Woman of Grace* (*Seedevi*, 1951). Unlike Jayamanne, he made an attempt to invest his work with a local sensibility grounded in history and tradition. His other films include *Siri Sangabo* (1952), *Village Damsel* (*Pitisara Kella*, 1953), *Sardiel* (1954), *Asoka* (1955), and *Younger Son* (*Podi Putha*, 1956).

Sirisena Wimalaweera served to advance the cause of Sinhalese cinema by grounding it in local history and sensibility; his desire to connect cinema with history and tradition and indigenous cultural discourse constituted a significant step forward. However, in terms of style and technique he occupied the same cultural space occupied by the Jayamanne films. His filmic texts were inscribed by a desire to combine the power of the new medium of cinema and its apparatus with a calculated recuperation of the past. Hence, in terms of serious artistic cinema many discerning critics of the time found Wimalaweera's films wanting.

The next major event in the evolution of Sinhalese cinema took place in 1956 when Lester James Peries made his film *The Line of Destiny* (*Rekhava*). This film constituted a decisive rejection of the existing genre of filmmaking in Sri Lanka. Peries repudiated the then prevalent style of filmmaking by discarding the formula to which cinema was wedded. Instead of shooting his film inside the studios, as was the common practice then, he shot his entire film on location; sound was also recorded on location. He rejected the highly theatrical style of acting and the declamatory mode of delivery in favor of a more realistic form of acting. He displayed a commendable grasp of the medium—the use of camera, editing, framing etc.—that was conspicuously absent in the Sinhalese films made until then. All in all, *The Line of Destiny* signified a new and consequential departure for Sinhalese cinema.

The story of *The Line of Destiny* is set in rural Sri Lanka. The film opens with a stilt-walker-*cum*-musician arriving in the village of Siriyala. He has with him a monkey who performs various antics for the amusement of his audiences. Two thugs from the village try to rob him, and Sena, a boy from the village, prevents the robbery. In gratitude, the stilt-walker, who is also an accomplished palm-reader, volunteers to read the boy's palm and predict the future. He tells Sena that he will become a famous healer and bring honor to the village. It so happens that one day when Sena and his friend Anula are flying a kite, she suddenly loses her eyesight. The village physician who attends her is unable to restore it. Anula recalls the words of the stilt-walker. Sena touches her eyes, and miraculously Anula regains her vision. Consequently, Sena now acquires a reputation in the village as the boy with the magic touch. His father, however, is a felon, and together with the notorious money-lender in the village seeks to exploit this situation for his own monetary gain. They organize a healing campaign to impress the villagers. A rich land owner brings his son for treatment, but unfortunately the boy dies. The villagers are outraged and are convinced that it is Sena's fault. To make matters worse, the village begins to experience a serious drought. The villages who are compelled to endure severe hardships are of the opinion that Sena is possessed by some evil supernatural power. The villagers under the guidance of the land owner organize an exorcising of the evil spirit, but the devil dancers believe that the boy is innocent. The rich land owner, in a fit of anger, tries to strangle Sena. However, the monsoon rains arrive and once again peace and tranquility return to the village of Siriyala.

This, in essence, is the story of *The Line of Destiny*. Clearly, it is a story that is a little naïve in its conception. However, the director succeeded in presenting it filmically and with a certain measure of restraint. Many Westernized critics in Sri Lanka found this film to be a moving experience and a great work of art. It gained wide critical recognition internationally, winning high praise at some of the most prestigious film festivals, including Cannes, Edinburgh, and Karlovy Vary. However, the local intelligentsia, the generality of Sinhalese film critics, while applauding Lester James Peries's attempt to make a serious film, found the central experience highly contrived and lacking in credibility. It displayed an inadequate and uncertain grasp of Sinhalese culture.

The next significant landmark in the growth of Sinhalese cinema is Lester James Peries's film *The Changing Countryside*, made in 1965. Based on the celebrated novel with the same name by the leading novelist in the country, Martin Wickremasinghe, this film marked a turning point. It was an unqualified critical success, equally appreciated by the Westernized and local intelligentsia, and a serious tradition of filmmaking was born. *The Changing Countryside* won the

Grand Prix at the Critics Award at the Indian International Film Festival held in New Delhi in 1965. The Jury of the Indian International Film Festival, which included Lindsay Anderson, Andrej Wajda, Georges Sadoul, and Satyajit Ray, commended it for the "poetry and sensitivity with which it explores and illuminates personal relations." Local movie-goers were no less enthralled by it and felt a justifiable pride. *The Changing Countryside* signified the opening of a cultural and representational space that was authentic and artistic.

The film deals through vividly realized characters with the collapse of the feudal social order and the emergence of the middle class. This is indeed an experience that is fraught with great meaning for those countries emerging from the shadows of feudalism to encounter a newer set of social, political, and economic realities. Kaisaruvatte Muhandiram and Matara Hamine are husband and wife and represent the decaying social order. Nanda is their daughter. Clearly, the family has seen better days. Piyal is a young and attractive teacher of English who gives lessons to Nanda. However, he is regarded as belonging to an inferior social class. Although Nanda is emotionally attracted to Piyal, marriage is out of the question because of the wide social gap that exists between them. Instead Nanda marries Jinadasa, a man approved by her parents. Her married life is full of hardships, but being a loyal and devoted wife, she endures it all. As their economic situation deteriorates, Jinadasa decides to leave home and search for gainful employment. In the initial few months she receives letters from him; after that nothing is heard from him. Meanwhile Piyal does well and becomes a successful businessman. It is learned that Jinadasa had died in a hospital in the provinces, miserable and penniless. After a while Piyal and Nanda marry. One day when Piyal is on a business trip, Nanda receives a telegram informing her that her husband is deeply ill in a remote hospital. Nanda, understandably perturbed, rushes to see him. There much to her surprise she realizes that the man who is dead is not Piyal, but Jinadasa. Later Piyal and Nanda come together achieving a depth of understanding and attachment having critically engaged the past.

When Martin Wickremasinghe published his celebrated novel, *The Changing Countryside*, in 1945, it was greeted—and justifiably so—as a landmark in Sinhalese fiction. Ediriweera Sarachchandra, the most eminent literary critic of the time, praised the novel for its authentic portrayal of peasant society in Sri Lanka and the sureness with which the imported art form of the novel was allowed to develop along indigenous modes of sensibility. He valorized the novel for capturing effectively the inward life of its characters and the complex ways in which social forces overdetermine character.

When Lester James Peries's film, based on Martin Wickremasinghe's novel, was released in 1965, it was instantly recognized as a superior work of cinematic art that persuasively captured a slice of Sri Lankan reality. The anglicized classes that had been greatly impressed by Peries's early films felt that in this film the director had not only displayed once again his mastery of the medium, but also had gone even further in consolidating his strengths. The local intelligentsia that was appreciative of Peries's earlier attempts to create a meaningful and authentic Sinhalese cinema, but were somewhat disappointed by the artificiality and contrivedness of *The Line of Destiny*, found in *The Changing Countryside* a wonderfully honest work of art that touched the lives of the people in interesting and complex ways. Martin Wickremasinghe and Ediriweera Sarachchandra were unstinting in their praise of the film. The more discriminating of the Sinhalese movie-going public, who had been disenchanted with the puerile melodramas that were served up as works of cinema, found in *The Changing Countryside* the cornerstone of a new and significant cinema. Hundreds of thousands of readers who had over the past two decades read Wickremasinghe's novel saw in the film a wonderful transcoding of it.

With *The Changing Countryside* serious cinema had arrived in Sri Lanka. This birth of a cinema was vitally connected with the notion of cinema as a cultural practice and the cultural production of nationhood. At the beginning of this chapter I stressed the need to perceive cinema as a cultural practice because it has great implications for the question of nationhood and national cinema. National cinema can be understood at a number of different levels of apprehension. First, it can be examined in terms of economics where questions of industry, film culture, and nationhood acquire a significance of meaning. Second, it can be analyzed in terms of textuality, that is in terms of content and style and cultural formations. Here the important issues that merit detailed probing are the authenticity of the experience that is presented and the ways in which the idea of nationhood is inscribed in it, the cultural embeddedness of the styles of presentation, and the instrumentalities by which films as cultural texts relate to the larger cultural discourse. Third, the concept of national cinema can be investigated in terms of the self/other binary; the operative question here is the uniqueness of the cinema vis-à-vis other cinemas that impinge on the given culture. For example in the case of Sri Lanka, the South Indian cinema was from the very beginning a formidable force to contend with, and so Sinhalese filmmakers who were bent on creating a national cinema always sought to define their creations in opposition to the main body of South Indian films. Fourth, national cinema needs to be explored in terms of other highly legitimated and long-standing modes of symbolic expression like art, poetry, fiction, and drama. When seen within the discursivities of these different dimensions, *The Changing Countryside* understandably enough signified the birth of a national cinema.

In order to understand the true dimensions of national cinema, one has to relate it to and anchor it in the wider cultural discourse shaping the lives of the people. Questions of history, tradition, cultural formation, social change, and ideologies of nationhood figure very prominently in this endeavor. The ways in which cinema inserts itself into the existing and interlocking cultural practices and the ways in which it produces the idea of nationhood become extremely important in this regard.

When Lester James Peries's *The Changing Countryside* was made in 1965, Sri Lankan society was undergoing a transformation that had deep and far-reaching implications for the lives of the people. The year 1956 marked an important watershed in the development of Sri Lankan society. S. W. R. D. Bandaranaike was swept into power in a populist wave that was determined to do away with the remnants of colonial power structures. He put in place an administration that made Sinhalese the official language of the country and the language of higher education. The Westernized elite that had dominated Sri Lankan society had given way to an indigenous elite that was securely rooted in the traditional culture. More and more people from the rural areas were securing important jobs in upper echelons of administration and the institutes of higher learning. Theirs was a newfound interest and pride in what was native and indigenous. Moreover, as a consequence of these changes and transformations Sinhala arts and letters began to flourish with a renewed vigor and sense of purpose. Thanks to the efforts of writers such as Martin Wickremasinghe, Gunadasa Amarasekara, K. Jayatilake, and Siri Gunasinghe, Sinhalese fiction was making rapid headway as a medium of creative expression that sought to explore complex aspects of Sri Lankan reality, while Sinhalese poetry was entering into new and uncharted terrains with a great measure of self-assurance. With the production of Sarachcahandra's *Maname* in 1956, modern Sinhalese drama had entered a period of unprecedented vitality and creative growth. Literary critics were exuberantly productive as they sought to combine the best conceptualities of the East and the West. All these changes in cognition and consciousness, the extensions of the discursive boundaries, and societal transformations served to create an ever-expanding and critically discriminating public for arts and letters. *The Changing Countryside* connected well with these changes, enabling discerning audiences to construct their cultural identity in relation to it; this was indeed a vital step in the establishment of a national cinema.

In 1979 I interviewed several people who represented a cross-section of the Sinhalese movie-going public regarding their response to *The Changing Countryside*. In my interviews, terms such as "artistic," "authentic," "serious," "meaningful," and "national" surfaced again and again as attributes of positive valorization and legitimization. The film was constantly evaluated in terms of the larger cultural discourse in which it was embedded. The question of meaning-making in relation to a film is an interesting one in view of the fact that it is not something found in the film but made by the viewer. Meaning-making is an active process where an attempt is being made by the viewer to position his or her self in relation to the filmic text. It is also a political activity, broadly defined, where the power of the state, the authority of the past, and issues of race, religion, gender, etc., find articulation directly or indirectly.

Many of the interviewees discussed the film in relation to the concepts of cultural identity and nationhood. It is evident that when we talk of nationhood, in most cases, national identity is fashioned into a coherent and unified entity by ignoring various internal differences and tensions relating to race, religion, language, gender, class, and so forth. The discursive formations of nationhood seek to occlude certain discontinuities and elide contradictory phenomena. This became evident in my interviews too. When my interviewees talked about questions of nationhood, they very rarely referred to the fact that Sri Lanka is a multiracial and multireligious society and that there are other races living in the island besides the Sinhalese. Homi Bhabha says that it is through the "syntax of forgetting" that the problematic identification of a national people becomes manifest.[4] The relationship between the part and whole, past and present is cut across by the impulse to forget.

Lester James Peries's *The Changing Countryside* is indeed a very significant film that signalized the birth of a serious and artistic cinema in Sri Lanka. Reading the film as well as the wider cultural discourse to which it is vitally connected, we can attain a better understanding of the complex relationship that exists among film, cultural identity, and nationhood.

Inspired by the work of Lester James Peries and sensing the possibilities of cinema as an important site of cultural production and contestation of cultural meaning, a number of newer filmmakers made their appearance on the local scene. Among them D. B. Nihal Sinha, G. D. L. Perera, Titus Thotawatte, Sugathapala Senerath Yapa, Vasantha Obeyesekere, Amaranath Jayatilake, Dharmasena Pathiraja, Sumithra Peries, Vijaya Dharma Sri, and Tissa Abeysekera deserve special mention. They in their different ways and with varying degrees of success sought to enrich the Sinhala cinematic tradition and widen its representational practices and discursive boundaries. Among these filmmakers, I will single out Dharmasena Pathiraja, who in my judgment is the most talented and has succeeded in investing Sinhalese cinema with a greater measure of social commitment and exemplifying the power and the multivalence of the cinematic image.

So far Pathiraja has made six feature films, most of which, with the possible exception of *Eya Dan Loku Lamayek* (1977), generated a great deal of critical attention and commentary. I would like to comment briefly on four of them in view of the fact that they represent a widening of the cultural discourse surrounding Sinhalese cinema and engage in newer and more troubling issues imbricated with the question of nationhood.

When Dharmasena Pathiraja entered the world of cinema the artistic and intellectual landscape of Sri Lanka was in a state of confusion, with many anxiously searching for alternate pathways to social progress and social understanding through creative art. The so-called Peradeniya school which had exercised a formative and decisive influence on arts and letters and inflected the thinking of bilingual intelligentsia in the 1950s and 1960s was on the wane; some of the leading members of this school like Gunadasa Amarasekera had begun to voice certain misgivings regarding the self-understanding and theoretical directions. There was a social revolution underway. More and more students who were securely rooted in the indigenous modes of thought and lifeways were entering the universities and higher seats of learning and had begun to make their presence felt. Newer and more compellingly powerful questions were raised in relation to questions of nationhood, imperialism, post-coloniality, bilingual intelligentsia, localism and globalism, marginality, and so on. It is against this background, and fully aware of its implications that Dharmasena Pathiraja emerged as a film director.

Pathiraja's first feature film was *Ahas Gavva* (1974). He had made a short film called *Sathuro* earlier. He has always evinced an interest in textualizing the lives, the problems, and the predicaments of urban youth—something that had not been accomplished with much conviction in earlier Sinhalese films. *Ahas Gavva* explores the unemployment among youth that had assumed menacing proportions by the mid 1960s. This film captures sensitively and honestly their aspirations, misgivings, and fears against a backdrop of social uncertainty and confusion. In this film, as indeed in all his films, Pathiraja sought to move away from the representational practices much valorized at the time, especially as manifested in the work of Lester James Peries, and to reshape the signifying systems by inflecting them with a critical humanistic desire through distanciation and rupturing of the identificatory mechanisms. In comparison with his later films, *Ahas Gavva* appears to be a little superficial in its cinematic interrogation of the chosen issues and their social import; nonetheless we perceive the creativity that was to manifest itself more fully and cogently in the later films.

His next film, *Bambaru Avith* (*Wasps Have Come*, 1978), once again displays Pathiraja's dedication to fashioning a cinema that is socially committed and one that does not shy away from interrogating the much valorized bourgeois individualism that undergirded many of the earlier Sinhalese films. A sense of freedom and a ludic spirit pervade this film which has the effect of subverting some of the cherished beliefs of society. The story is set in a fishing village. Anton Aiya, despite the fact that he acts and behaves like the rest of the fishermen, is an exploiter. He thrives on the efforts of other fishermen. Into this setting arrive the representatives of the young urban entrepreneurial youth. They are attuned to Western culture; they dress so; they prefer Western music. A clash ensues between Anton Aiya and Baby Mahattaya (Victor), who represents urban youth, and the latter wins. Weerasena, a middle-class leftist, also belongs to this urban youth group. The arrival of these youths from the city has clearly precipitated a social crisis that demands a solution, and all that Weerasena can do is to stand up on a parapet and make a speech which, interestingly, no one listens to. He goes back to the city. In this film Dharmasena Pathiraja examines with remarkable candor the plight of the poor, the exploitative nature of society, cultural confusions, and the lack of political will and direction needed to ameliorate the situation.

In his next film, *Para Dige* (*Along the Road*, 1980), Pathiraja sought to open up a representational space in which the plight of the young who migrate to the city from rural areas and deracinate themselves culturally in the process could be textualized. Urban chaos, dehumanization, the pernicious impact of urbanization, and industrialization are all semioticized in the film in a way that foregrounds an acute contemporary problem. Chandare migrates from his native village to the city. He earns a living by living off those who fail to pay their mortgage on their cars. His girlfriend is a stenographer and they live in a boarding house. She gets pregnant by him, and they seek an abortion. The doctor demands 3000 rupees, and the filmic digesis is concerned with the frantic efforts they make to find the requisite sum of money. In *Para Dige* the director has honestly and sympathetically portrayed their predicament, metaphorizing them as victims of urbanization and capitalist exploitation.

The fourth film of Dharmasena Pathiraja that I wish to discuss briefly is *Soldadu Unnahe* (*The Old Soldier*, 1981). The film deals with four characters who are distinctly marginalized in society: an old soldier who is a veteran of World War II, a prostitute, a man compelled by force of circumstances to end up as an alcoholic, and a pick-pocket. The story is confined to three days: Independence Day and the day preceding and following it. Through a series of flashbacks, the characters' miserable lives and how they have been socially produced are narrativized in a way that calls attention to the nature of social oppression in capitalist societies. The idea of nationhood is central to the thematics of this film. Independence Day is celebrated with the customary pomp and pageantry and the politicians exult in the newly won freedom. At the same time, the director contrapuntally shows the lives of his four chosen characters in all their degradation to enforce the point that independence and freedom have no meaning in terms of their being in the world and their lived reality. The disturbed and disturbing state of mind of the old soldier emblematizes the contradictions and disparities inscribed by capitalism in society. In this film, Pathiraja raises serious questions related to the constructed narratives of nationhood and highlights some of the occluded faultlines.

What Dharmasena Pathiraja has attempted to do is to focus on the contradictions and inequities of capitalist societies and to foreground the predicaments of youth caught in the competing discourses of tradition and modernity, localism and globalism. He has felt that this segment of society needs to be examined sympathetically as a way of understanding some of the pressing problems affecting the nation. Unlike earlier Sinhalese filmmakers, Pathiraja has sought to locate the experiences, predicaments, and privations of his chosen characters in the wider social and economic discourse to which they are infrangibly linked. Culture is a terrain on which contestation of meaning takes place incessantly, and where economic and personal issues are imbricated in complex ways. His films reconfigure the experience of modern youth in a way that highlights the inscription of economic forces on culture as well as on personal lives. Using urban chaos as a privileged trope Dharmasena Pathiraja has sought to interrogate the idea of nationhood and its surrounding cultural discourse as found in Sinhalese cinema. The vocabulary of filiation is central to the construction of nationhood and what Pathiraja has sought to do is to problematize it by probing into the troubled lives of youth and to question the logic and coherence of some of the received categories of nationhood and culture.

Notes

1. Janet Staiger, "Securing the Fictional Narrative as a Tale of the Historical Real," *Southern Atlantic Quarterly* 88, 2:393–413.

2. Siri Gunasinghe, "Sinhala Cinema," *Ceylon Today*, Feb.–April 1968.

3. Wimal Dissanayake and Malti Sahai, *Sholay—A Cultural Reading* (New Delhi: Wiley Easter, 1992).

4. Homi Bhabha, *Nation and Narration* (London: Routledge, 1990).

12 | The End of the National Project?
Australian Cinema in the 1990s

Graeme Turner

THE 1970S REVIVAL of an Australian cinema was accomplished through a range of industrial and policy initiatives directed toward the development of Australian film as the cultural flagship of the nation. Australian cinema in the 1990s, however, is notable for a gradual dissociation of the industry, its legitimating discourses, and its products from any explicit participation in nation formation. This dissociation is evident within a number of key locations: within policy documents aimed at securing a continuation of government support; within shifts in the character of the texts the industry produces; and within Australian cultural and film criticism. This chapter examines what amounts to a disarticulation of the Australian cinema from "the Australian nation," before considering some general questions about cinema and nationhood within postcolonial societies.

The revival of the Australian cinema was not only an economic intervention to subsidize a local culture industry; it also represented a semi-official project of nation formation. In 1969 there were many economic and industrial factors which encouraged the Australian government to establish an institutional infrastructure for the production of Australian features, but one could argue that the single most important factor was the opportunity to directly participate in the construction of the national culture. Certainly it is clear that, at the end of the 1960s, a developing "nationalist mythology" in Australia had come "to recognise film as the most desirable medium for projecting an image of the new confidence and maturity seen to mark contemporary Australian culture and society" (Turner, 1989, 101). The consequent establishment of a film school and a number of state-run film funding bodies was the achievement of a long campaign for government support, a campaign explicitly framed around a sense of the importance of filming "our own stories," "our own daydreams," and on using film to mythologize our own land and cityscapes. (See Weir, 1987.)

Throughout the seventies and most of the eighties, the cultural importance of the local film industry was widely, even unproblematically, understood. Australian film established its local and international audience, while Australian dramas and mini-series on television became ratings winners. Bipartisan support at the party-political level indicated that there was little disagreement with the enabling arguments: these included the notion that our cultural specificity needed to be preserved and defended against the influence of other, imperializing, cultures (usually those of America or Britain); and the sense that this cultural specificity was textually grounded in a way of seeing the world that was distinctive, and that would be at risk if exposed to the normal workings of the market. While some of these nationalist positions were advanced by way of relatively simple chauvinistic arguments, there were also many quite sophisticated justifications for a state-funded film industry. Certainly, those arguments which addressed Australia's postcolonial status were careful to highlight the varying interests served by the idea of the nation within different historical circumstances. While "the nation" in Britain, for instance, might be a discursive formation which has been more or less captured by a conservative establishment, within Australia and other postcolonial societies the idea of the nation retains a progressive potential as a point of resistance to domination from outside, a point at which local interests may be expressed and defended against the logics of internationalization. Furthermore, within such formulations, Australian film retains the capacity to rewrite imperial histories, to appropriate American generic forms, and to operate as a critical, if marginalized, body of representations within mainstream Western cinema.

If we are to understand the Australian revival as a success, it has to be in these cultural nationalist terms. Success in such terms, though, is difficult to demonstrate; cultural achievements are not as easily quantifiable as economic achievements. When we view it primarily from the economic perspective, as the following remarks reveal, the "success" of the industry seems highly questionable:

> In 1989, 12% of the nearly 300 films released [in Australia] were Australian. They took 5% of the box office. At the end of 1990, 91 of the all time top hundred gross film rentals in Australia had been foreign—only the *Crocodile Dundees*, *The Man from Snowy River*, and *Mad Max* films and *Phar Lap*, *Gallipoli*, and *Young Einstein* make the top hundred. 2% of the movies screened on prime time television during ratings periods are Australian. In the six years to 1990, Sydney commercial television stations each showed an average of one Australian film every two months in prime time during ratings periods. (Australian Film Commission, 1991, 3)

One can easily demonstrate the deceptiveness of such apparently objective measurements by choosing different items and different relationships. For instance, another way of encapsulating the market penetration of Australian films might be to point out that the two biggest box-office successes ever released in Australia were *Crocodile Dundee* and *Crocodile Dundee 2*. Nevertheless, the more positive constructions have their limits; it is hard to deny the fact that the Australian film industry has provided very little financial return for the taxpayers' investment over the last two decades.

Such a problem is now concerning the Federal Parliament's Inquiry into the film industry—the House of Representatives Standing Committee on Environment, Recreation, and the Arts Inquiry into the Performance of Australian film, or "The Moving Pictures Inquiry." This Inquiry is examining the economic performance of the industry, so although its brief does not categorically exclude cultural factors, they are regarded as ancillary rather than primary considerations. Indeed, the Inquiry can be seen as a marker of a change in the official attitude to the industry, a change which may well authorize different kinds of assessment to those which have been preferred in the past. At the very least, the Inquiry marks a point at which the present government's ideological investment in its cultural flagship is being reconsidered.

The Moving Pictures Inquiry coincides with a pervasive rhetoric of economic rationalism within Australian politics, and thus can be situated within a more generalized, explicitly "responsible," scrutiny of public expenditure. The GATT negotiations over industrial protection are of relevance here, too. In most areas of trade, the Australian government has been lobbying for the abolition of protective barriers, such as those which keep its primary commodity producers out of the EEC. American film industry representatives have called Australia's bluff by nominating the Australian film industry as a site where subsidies and local content quotas operate as barriers to free trade between American film producers and their second largest foreign market. As a result, the internationalist and deregulatory rhetoric employed by Australian representatives in the GATT talks has already leaked into arguments around the regulation and control of the culture industries at home; over the last two years, the issues of ownership and of local content within the Australian media have been radically affected by this leakage.

It is increasingly the case that any defense of the industry which privileges its participation within the construction of nationhood over its contribution to a free market economy looks like an anachronism. In a wide variety of contexts, the cultural importance of the film industry is being challenged. The primary object of these challenges is the protected status the film industry and cultural industries generally have enjoyed within debates about state intervention in the economy. The strategy employed is to disconnect "the industry" from "the nation," thus exposing the industry to the conventional economic modes of evaluation. It is a strategy that is meeting with some success. In the rest of this chapter I want to examine three locations where the change in the status of Australian film is apparent, before going on to draw some conclusions from these developments.

The first location is "The Moving Pictures Inquiry," specifically the draft submission addressed to this Inquiry from the Australian Film Commission (AFC, 1991). This submission addresses the performance of Australian films through reference to their profits and losses; the various material forms assumed by their audiences (box office receipts, television ratings, reviews, "word of mouth," and so on); the financial returns to the state for its investment; the performance of non-Australian films in Australia; and through comparisons with other Australian cultural industries. The AFC sounds numerous warnings about the misleading "objectivity" of such analyses of performance; for instance, in its assessment of the adequacy of the performance of Australian films, the submission points out that "adequacy" is itself a complex issue to address without stipulating exactly what measuring mechanisms are to be used. Even "success" and "failure" "can occur in complicated and contradictory ways" (AFC, 1991, 4). Routinely, the document contests the power of the figures to support unambiguous conclusions. Nevertheless, even while it explicitly queries the terms of reference within which it has to work, the document implicitly accepts the economic rationalism within which it must make its sense. For the most part, its interrogation of the Inquiry's framing assumptions is muted and cautious; the vast bulk of the argument remains quantitative, statistical, and thus, apparently, value-free. It is only in the concluding section that cultural, "subjective," arguments are mounted—and then with a resigned sense of their own powerlessness:

> Success can be defined in many ways. Films can "succeed" by reaching large audiences, by breaking box office records, by making profits, by receiving praise from critics, by stimulating new ways of thinking and seeing or simply by delivering pleasure to audiences of any size.
> Our expectations of the performances of our films are high. We seek to compare the performance of our films with those from larger countries with more established film industries. We demand that our films find consistently bigger first release audiences in Australia than our musicians or our fiction writers before we judge their commercial success comparable. Disappointments are exaggerated by the scale of the occasional extraordinary success. (AFC, 1991, 71)

All important qualifiers, of course, but not offered with any hope of prevailing. What is most notable about this document is that while it advances vigorous arguments in favor of continued government protection, the connection between the Australian cinema and the national culture is never explicitly made. The AFC submission seems to accept that the national cultural project has become an industrial enterprise. It is tempting to see this shift in the supporting rhetoric, the removal of what had been a central plank within most arguments for the industry, as more than strategic; indeed, as a sign of the end of the "national project." In my second location, where I will consider shifts in the character of the films produced over the last decade, this view is reinforced. The films of the seventies were relentless in their reproduction of Australian histories and in their explicit attempts to capture an Australian national character on film; the films of the late eighties and nineties tend not to be moved by such preoccupations. What they *are* moved by is less easy to describe since we are not looking at anything like a unitary movement. While there have been a number of shifts in the generic frames and thematics of film texts from this period, it is possible to locate within each of them a common element: a rejection of the explicit rhetorics of nation and nationality that so dominated the first decade of the revival.

The point can be made by reviewing some of these textual shifts and by outlining significant changes in the industrial structures—changes that produce textual effects. I would not be the first to notice the migration from the "quality" European influenced art film typified by *Picnic at Hanging Rock* toward more commercial and more generic projects. It is widely accepted that the Australian film industry has used the last ten years very differently to the preceding ten. While the critical successes of the seventies were low-key period dramas, doggedly resistant to the narrative codes of Hollywood genres—*Picnic at Hanging Rock*, *Sunday Too Far Away*, and *My Brilliant Career*—the successes of the eighties were genre films—*The Man from Snowy River 1 and 2*, *Crocodile Dundee 1 and 2*, the *Mad Max* films, and *Young Einstein*. There have been few subsequent blockbusters to emulate the scale of such films, but there are numerous examples of locally produced projects achieving high production values, winning popular audiences, and working comfortably within the generic frames of mainstream transnational cinema. Examples would include thrillers such as *Ground Zero*, *Dead Calm*, and *Grievous Bodily Harm*, or the Tass-Parker low-budget comedies such as *Malcolm* or *The Big Steal*.

Critics have largely accepted this move into the mainstream. Some have applauded the *Mad Max* films for "outdoing" Hollywood on its own territory, and *The Man from Snowy River* or *Starstruck* as successful approprations of Hollywood forms (Cunningham, 1985). Where once the Australian cinema was in hot pursuit of originality, an Australian look, the late eighties is the moment of Meaghan Morris's "positive unoriginality" (Morris, 1988). She examines this quality in *Crocodile Dundee* where "positive unoriginality" enables the survival of cultural specificity through "the revision of American codes by Australian texts, in a play which can be beheld quite differently by various audiences" (Morris, 1988, 247). In *Crocodile Dundee*, this "cultural strategy is scarcely concealed," she says; the film's "borrowings are as clearly displayed as Dundee's outback costume, with its comic mishmash of cowboy/western, bushman/jungle shreds—originating and imitating nothing . . . " (248). The result is the combination of "economic pragmatism with cultural assertion" so that "positive unoriginality" ends up serving nationalist objectives.

There are many levels of appreciation and irony in Morris's account of the representational strategy that works so well in *Crocodile Dundee*. Other accounts of the "Australianizing" of American genres are much less ambivalent about the national service being performed. Stuart Cunningham and Tom O'Regan both insist that this acceptance of commercial genres has not meant an abandonment of the representation of the specificity of Australian culture (Cunningham, 1985; O'Regan, 1989). Indeed, within our most recent films, the foregrounding of a representative "Australian-ness" so clear in the films of the seventies gives way to a more precise interest in the local or the regional. *Death in Brunswick* offers a rich social context for its personal stories, unselfconsciously drawing on the specificities of Greek-Australian immigrant communities in inner-city Melbourne. The teen movie *The Big Steal* locates itself within an equally rich suburban subculture that is undramatically recognizable. In another adjustment which seems to explicitly reject the dominant paradigms of the seventies, the movement from the national to the local is matched by a temporal relocation, from the past to the present. The films showing in Australia now—*Proof, Death in Brunswick, The Nirvana Street Murders*—are all contemporary dramas dealing with highly detailed local environments. Where once the mythologies of the past were mobilized as a means of refracting propositions about the nature of the Australian present, the current crop of films is directly interested in the richness and diversity of contemporary Australian society.

The decade has also witnessed the gradual erosion of the dominance of male film-makers and masculine concerns—the bush, mateship, war—in Australian cinema. Gillian Armstrong's tenure as the token female Australian director has now come to an end; the work of Ann Turner (*Celia*), Jane Campion (*Sweetie, Angel at My Table*), Tracy Moffatt (*Nice Coloured Girls, Night Cries*), and most recently Jocelyn Moorhouse (*Proof*) has dominated recent accounts of Australian cinema. While their work does not constitute a complete break with what has gone before, they have certainly multiplied the angles of inspection from which Australian experiences have been surveyed. A beneficiary of this has of course been the experience of women, but there has also been a greater degree of formal experimentation, an impatience with "safe" generic options, and a greater investment in the understanding of the relation between the subjects and their social context.

These generalized textual histories are further complicated when we consider the conception of the audience implicit in the production and promotion of genre films, and in the big blockbusters supported by the 10BA tax concessions of the 1980s. Tom O'Regan describes a change in the "mindset" of the producers, toward "meeting rather than inventing the audience": the result was a "differentiated cinema audience" rather than a monolithic "Australian public" (O'Regan, 1989, 120). This reinforced the trend for films to situate themselves within transnational generic fashions:

> Film-making sought its relation, its publicity profile, in relation to contemporary cycles of cinema. In so doing it defined itself rather less than its . . . predecessors had in terms of the public discourses, the marks of Australianness, the registers of discussions of society and its shape. In the process a different kind

of intertextuality was posed: not one in a privileged relation to the discourses of Australians and Australian society but one in relation to conformity and difference within genre cinema. (O'Regan, 1989, 130)

Within the industry, there was great division about what was seen as internationalization, but there were other structural changes which made commercial logic almost irresistible. Initially, television productions had been ineligible for support from the film funding institutions, but this prohibition was removed in the 1980s. The resulting convergence of the two sectors of the industry affected all levels, from financing to the production personnel. As the privatization of the industry grew, so did the relative importance of pre-sales; this made television the most reliable revenue source for producers. The production of television drama and miniseries became part of the "film industry"; in many cases, projects intended for cinema release were downscaled in response to shortfalls in financial backing and produced for television. Now, the scale of the convergence is such that one could argue the film and television industry in Australia predominantly addresses a mainstream television audience rather than a mainstream cinema audience.

It is important to stress that the 1980s were years of dramatic structural change for the film and television industry. Oscillations of government policy saw funding based on a system of tax concessions for investors give way to an eighteen-month hiatus when there was no institutional structure at all. In the current model (the Film Finance Corporation, or film bank), the government has reverted to a state-funded central body which operates, despite its purpose of ameliorating market conditions, very much on commercial principles. This is a structural contradiction in the remit of the Film Finance Corporation. The uncertainties this contradiction produces were evident in its earliest funding decisions: supporting a wartime period drama starring Bryan Brown and a period melodrama starring Australian pop star Kylie Minogue and the minor American actor Charlie Schlatter. Both decisions invoke principles now widely held to be inappropriate to the industry: the local audience for the Australian period drama has long gone and there is no evidence that importing a minor American star has any positive effect on the audience or sales of the finished film. Casting Kylie Minogue in *The Delinquents* would seem shrewd were it not for its effect on the point of the story (it necessitated changing the lead character from a racially marginalized Eurasian to a delinquent WASP), and its irrelevance to a film whose censorship classification excluded Minogue's major market. On the other hand, *Blood Oath* is in fact a very adventurous film for contemporary Australia, and its use of Bryan Brown is anything but predictable.

All of these developments—textual and structural—signify a withdrawal from the national project, from an industry committed to the almost programmatic discovery of a visual vocabulary for Australian material to an industry which no longer sees itself as the product of cultural policy.

Not everybody finds this an acceptable situation. Significantly, those critics who most approved the directions of 1970s Australian cinema and who applauded such films as *Gallipoli* and *Newsfront* are uncomfortable with these new directions. I have noted elsewhere how *The Man from Snowy River* exposed a division between audiences and critics; while the critics were scathing in their condemnation of the film, audiences responded with pleasure and affection (Turner, 1986). While this was a sign that Australian cinema had located its popular audience, the schism had worrying consequences; Australian films had alienated some of their most influential supporters, thus disconnecting themselves from the discourses of national culture so often deployed in the industry's defense. Tom O'Regan suggests that among the consequences of this were a decline in "the importance of the general feature film to cultural definitions" and a "profound sense of disenchantment" which ran against the grain of what looked, from other points of view, like a flourishing industry (O'Regan, 1989, 125).

This brings me to my third location. The disenchantment has now spread among cultural critics who were initially quite comfortable with many of the new agendas set by the industry in the 1980s. Many have been supporters of the industry, sources of intellectual weight for industry submissions, or key players within the lobbying game which has kept the industry on government agendas. These critics are not yearning for lost aesthetic values, for the decorousness of the early period dramas; nor are they entirely opposed to the commercialism of the privatized industry. Their discontents are potentially more profound because they are provoked by a lapse in faith in the whole idea of a national cinema and, in particular, the political desirability of the cultural project of nation formation.

For such a position to articulate itself, it has to question the intervention of the state in cultural production and the discourses of nationhood which legitimate such interventions. John Docker's argument for the removal of Australian content requirements from domestic television poses such questions (Docker, 1991). Docker opposes any role for the state in determining broadcasting content and rejects claims that Australian television's cultural specificity would be obliterated in a free market. His analysis rests on a populist faith in the Australian audience continuing to demand Australian texts without the system of subsidies and regulation currently in place. While Docker's position has been vigorously challenged and is largely discredited now (see Bennett, 1991; Craik, 1991; Cunningham, 1991; Hunter, 1991; Turner, 1992), it is a sign of change in the orientation of the cultural critique of the Australian film and television industry. The widening gap between cultural critique and cultural policy is also noted in

Elizabeth Jacka's contribution to the same debate, the inquiry into Australian content on television.

Jacka's work, and her collaboration with Susan Dermody, has been fundamental in its provision of critical support to a diverse and adventurous Australian film industry. Without ever being in any sense a nationalist document, Dermody and Jacka's *Screening of Australia* (1987 and 1988) is an exemplary account of the development of a national cinema. Yet, Jacka's article "Australian Cinema: An Anachronism in the 80s?" (1988) discloses a deep disquiet about the positions with which her support for the national industry inevitably aligns her. She advances the proposition that, given the globalization of Western cinema and given the consensual and thus oppressive ideological rhythms nationalism so often sets up, the pursuit of a national cinema is an entirely anachronistic endeavor. Indeed, the idea of the nation as an independent entity is itself anachronistic in "the present phase of multinational capitalism":

> It denies the reality of the way social life is organised in the last half of the 20th century. Multinational capitalism, presently reinforced by the deregulationist impulses of Australian and other advanced capitalist governments, is *dissolving* national boundaries, and we are increasingly positioned in a world whose economic, cultural and informational organisation is transnational, not national. It is only at a formal political level that nation-states retain some identity. (Jacka, 122)

Jacka admits that the alternative to nationalism—internationalism—has its problems too; she quotes Boris Frankel's remark that it is far from "radical to be in favour of the break up of nations": "the main beneficiaries" of such a break-up, says Frankel, "are the large transnational corporations, and the bureaucrats eager to rationalise whole communities, regions and industries away" (122). As a result of such reservations, Jacka's argument is somewhat modified by the article's end, but the original proposition has been influential; it connects with a range of rhetorics within cultural criticism generally and about Australian cinema specifically which express an accelerating skepticism about the industry and its cultural function.

Jacka's article reflects her impatience with the strategic and theoretical difficulties inherent in defending the national cinema, an impatience shared by many. To support any form of cultural production simply because of its "Australian-ness" is to find oneself aligned with some extremely conservative and chauvinistic points of view. In Australian history, nationalism has served to legitimate racism, a rampant cultural masculinism, and neo-imperialist views of nationhood that conceive of it through metaphors of maturation and personal growth. To defend the idea of the nation in Australia can involve those on the progressive left of cultural politics in a series of double binds: the dialectic or, more accurately, the permanently contradictory relations between dependence and independence that mark the condition of the postcolonial; the need to resist the consensualizing erasure of internal differences accomplished through discourses of nationhood, while recognizing the necessity of these discourses in order to produce the shared acknowledgment of community. Australian cultural criticism has also to deal with its specific history of cultural nationalism. Offering one's views on the national often means risking accusations of essentialism, of xenophobia, or of ascribing to unitary definitions of an organic and immutable "national identity." Defending the idea of the nation requires us to continually differentiate what we mean by such a term from the more conventional, naturalized, meanings of Australian nationalism, the so-called radical nationalism of the conservative Left. As always, the national is highly contested territory and not everybody enters it in order to preserve rather than to eradicate differences.

If Jacka's article speaks of the weariness of maintaining one's support for a national cinema within such a theoretical and ideological climate, it also speaks directly of the difficulty of maintaining such support in the face of the kinds of texts the Australian industry has produced. It is a conservative body of films, on the whole, preoccupied with male bonding and a radical nationalist version of Australian identity, offering little in the way of formal challenges to dominant genres or modes of film-making. Jacka argues that the dominant codes employed in representing Australia through our films may have sharpened the definition of the nation but that this definition is still too unitary, too narrow, and too anachronistic to be worth defending. She sees a clear link between the construction of the nation in our films and earlier, regressive, versions of cultural nationalism:

> Older versions of cultural nationalism . . . embody an essentialist notion of the Australianness that is to be exhibited in the indigenous cultural works that the policy will foster; this can be a populist version that identifies Australia with various supposed egalitarian qualities that are said to characterise its people, or other versions which, for example, identify Australia with certain qualities of its landscape or even, much more confusedly, with aspects from its traditional vanishing past, as is now the danger with some deployments in white culture of traditional Aboriginal art and artefacts. (1988, 123)

According to Jacka, Australian cinema has done little to interrogate such assumptions or to move beyond them; certainly, the revival has demonstrated little interest in "contemporary social and political issues or circumstances."

While I am sympathetic to this, and to a number of other arguments Jacka makes, I do not share her view of the idea of the nation, nor of the way in which film may participate in the process of constructing such an idea. Jacka's version of nationalism is curiously Eurocentric in that it sees nationalism's political potential largely in accordance with a history of modern European nationalisms;

that is, as oppressive and anti-democratic, a weapon in the suppression of difference. The extreme version of this position is found in Tom Nairn's much quoted remark:

> "Nationalism" is the pathology of modern developmental history, as inescapable as "neurosis" in the individual, with much the same essential ambiguity attaching to it, a similar built-in capacity for descent into dementia, rooted in the dilemmas of helplessness thrust upon most of the world . . . and largely incurable. (Nairn, 1977, 359)

As Benedict Anderson demonstrates, it is not that simple. Certainly, postcolonial uses of nationalism have enabled silenced voices to be heard and have countered the effects of an imperializing nationalism on those it has subordinated. Anderson offers a much more historically contingent view of nationalisms which accents their ability to operate as if they are "modular," "capable of being transplanted, with varying degrees of self-consciousness, to a great variety of social terrains, to merge and be merged with a correspondingly wide variety of political and ideological constellations" (14).

Nationhood is of course historically, not naturally, produced—or, even, invented. Jacka implies that nationhood is therefore especially compromised, inauthentic. Her resistance to the political project of nation formation is a resistance to its "constructedness," as a fictionalized sense of community which is laid over more natural and authentic social formations. Again, Anderson offers a useful reminder that *all* communities "larger than primordial villages or face-to-face contact . . . are imagined. Communities are to be distinguished, not by their falsity/genuineness, but by the style in which they are imagined" (15). It is this last point I want to foreground; that a proper critique of the national cinema should approach it *precisely in terms of* its invention of the nation, through the interrogation of its representations and the uses to which they are put.

Understandably, Jacka experiences difficulty in proposing alternatives to the national as bases upon which to mount a cultural critique of the Australian cinema. Her suggestion of "the local" as another way of thinking about the industry depends on the very same notions of cultural specificity which have undergirded the discourses of nationalism. The "local" does provide new opportunities, however, in that while the national sets up consensual rhythms that work to minimize differences, the local works to privilege differences:

> . . . what is presented as the local is recognisable as applying to a particular and specific set of circumstances and forces that operate at any given time and place, be they signs of place, accent, and idiom, or more diffuse but no less vivid ways of hooking into the social unconscious or social "imaginary" of a particular subculture. (126)

While this is true, the ways in which this can be hitched up to national cultural policy are limited:

> However, clearly the local in this sense cannot be legislated for; it will erupt unpredictably if spaces are created for it, and this is where regulation for *Australian* content re-enters the picture. For there is little chance of the local appearing in a situation where economic pressures make cultural production impossible, and once again because of the ways national economies and regulation are organised, it is only by preserving the Australian nature of the production process that one can create space for the local. (127)

At this point, Jacka comes full circle; after canvassing other options we return to a national system of regulation and control, justified in terms of its ability to preserve the local, the diverse formations of culture within the nation state. The argument, then, stops well short of offering an alternative to the idea of the national cinema; but it also stops well short of reconfirming support for the cultural remit of the Australian film industry.

The implications of this position, given the extent to which it has been taken up, are profound. It undermines the authority of the cultural arguments for a national cinema and thus places the industry in a very dangerous position. When we consider the climate of deregulation and economic rationalism currently existing in Australia, the international campaign against subsidies and protection, the changes within the industry's structure, and the formal and thematic trends within the film texts I have outlined, the dangers multiply. This is an industry which will disappear if solely economic considerations are allowed to prevail. Once its license to represent the nation is withdrawn—and that seems to be happening—it is likely to lose its license to operate at all.

Without its culture industries—be they ever so compromised by the texts they produce—the postcolonial society is extremely vulnerable. Whatever reservations one might have about its validity, to surrender the category of the nation as not worth interrogating is at least strategically unwise. It falls into a trap set for the new world by the old world in that it implicitly questions the legitimacy of the invented new nations through a comparison with the timeless authenticity of the old nations. One has to accept that the idea of the nation in postcolonial cultures is inevitably riddled with contradictions, its deployment necessarily flexible and contingent:

> Postcoloniality means living with contradictions, occupying positions that can be shown to be less than consistent. The postcolonial intellectual may feel compromised when criticising their own culture, because their criticism tends to align them with the coloniser; alternatively, uncritical defense of their culture aligns them with the automatic nationalism so widely and variously used as a mechanism for generating consensus on a delimited definition of the nation.

> The postcolonial must take on the tricky task of operating differently in different contexts. . . . (Turner, 1991)

Nationalism has proved to be something of a problem in contemporary screen and cultural theory. We don't deal with this by dispensing with the category—not while we can still contest it and its constitutive discourses. We should not assume that the battles for the discourses of the nation are over, or that the product of these discourses has been in some way finalized. Iain Chambers has recently reminded us that "the nation" "as a heterogeneous cultural and linguistic unit is not a closed history, something that has already been achieved." Rather it is "an open framework, continually in the making." Writing from Britain, where the "framework" looks perhaps the least open, Chambers can still suggest that it is possible to "move out of the mythological tempo of 'tradition' into the more fragmented and open discontinuities of histories" (Chambers, 1991, 47). Without underestimating the difficulty in cracking open the specific codes of nationalism within any contemporary historical conjuncture, this is a timely reminder of the need to resist the temptation to move the struggle onto less contested territory.

The preceding remarks suggest, perhaps, an undue pragmatism, an overstated sense of the strategic in my defense of the idea of the nation. To counter that impression as I conclude, it is worth restating the contention that a nation's narratives—be they in film or prose—do participate fundamentally in that culture's explanations of the world, in the production of what Jameson called "the political unconscious." Some of my earlier work has outlined what this entails in Australian film and fiction, locating an Australian accent in our narratives that is, while not necessarily unique, "audible and distinctive" when placed in relation to that of other English speakers (Turner, 1986). Jacka, in fact, rejects this metaphor as essentialist, but I want to defend it. An accent is not an essentializing sign of an overriding, singular difference; rather it is a socially produced marker of differences which speaks generically and variously of locality, of region, and of nation. When a national cinema can be said to reproduce an accent, or group of accents, within its narratives, it is serving an important cultural function: a function that is empowering for the voices speaking through the cinema and for those who listen and recognize in those voices something of themselves. It is possible to demonstrate that the Australian cinema, with all its shortcomings and inadequacies, does have its national accents; indeed, among the reasons why the industry is so difficult to institutionalize, and so easily absorbed as culture, is that it can speak with many, simultaneously harmonic and discordant, voices. From within the bureaucracies which run the Australian industry now, this may well be something of a worry; from outside, the discordant/harmonic chorus signifies the richness of the cultural source.

The trends I have described in this chapter are not all worrying; the discovery of a popular audience evident in the current crop of confidently Australian genre films marks a welcome movement away from an elitist and colonialist aesthetic, and the arrival of a feminine voice is welcome too. But most of the developments I have described implicitly deny the importance of the cultural source. It seems to me far too early to jettison the idea of a national culture, and to call off the attempt to make movies that actually come from somewhere. The alternative is to try to speak from everywhere, which may turn out to be nowhere at all.

Bibliography

Anderson, Benedict (1983). *Imagined Communities: Reflections on the Origin and Spread of Nationalism*. London: Verso.

Australian Film Commission (1991). "Analysis of the Performance of Australian Films since 1980." Draft submission to the House of Representatives Standing Committee on Environment, Recreation and the Arts Inquiry into the Performance of Australian Film.

Bennett, Tony (1991). "Political and Theoretical Digressions." *Media Information Australia*, 59.

Chambers, Iain (1990). *Border Dialogues: Journeys in Postmodernity*. London: Routledge.

Craik, Jennifer (1991). "Popular, Commercial and National Imperatives of Australian Broadcasting." *Media Information Australia*, 59.

Cunningham, Stuart (1985). "Hollywood Genres, Australian Movies." In Albert Moran and Tom O'Regan, eds., *An Australian Film Reader*. Sydney: Currency.

—— (1991). "Docker: Criticism, History and Policy." *Media Information Australia*, 59.

Dermody, Susan, and Elizabeth Jacka (1987 and 1988). *The Screening of Australia*. Vols. 1 and 2. Sydney: Currency.

Docker, John (1991). "Popular Culture versus the State: An Argument against Australian Content Regulations on Television." *Media Information Australia*, 59.

Hunter, Ian (1991). "Governing Culture." *Media Information Australia*, 59.

Jacka, Elizabeth (1988). "Australian Cinema: An Anachronism in the '80s?" In Susan Dermody and Elizabeth Jacka, eds., *The Imaginary Industry: Australian Film in the Late 80s*. Sydney: AFTRS Publications.

Morris, Meaghan (1988). *The Pirate's Fiancée: Feminism, Reading, Postmodernism*. London: Verso.

Nairn, Tom (1977). *The Break-Up of Britain*. London: New Left Books.

O'Regan, Tom (1989). "The Enchantment with Cinema: Film in the 1980s." In Albert Moran and Tom O'Regan, eds., *The Australian Screen*. Melbourne: Penguin.

Turner, Graeme (1986). *National Fictions: Literature, Film and the Construction of Australian Narrative*. Sydney: Allen and Unwin.

—— (1989). "Art-Directing History: The Period Film." In Albert Moran and Tom O'Regan, eds., *The Australian Screen*. Melbourne: Penguin.

—— (1991). "Of Rocks and Hard Places: The Colonised, the National, and Australian Cultural Studies." Unpublished keynote address. Dismantle Fremantle, Murdoch University.

—— (1992). "It Works for Me: British Cultural Studies, Australian Cultural Studies, and

Australian Film." In Lawrence Grossberg et al., eds., *Cultural Studies*. London: Routledge.
Weir, Tom (1985). "No Daydreams of Our Own: The Film as National Self-Expression."
In Albert Moran and Tom O'Regan, eds., *An Australian Film Reader*. Sydney: Currency.

Contributors

Chris Berry is a scholar of Chinese cinema who teaches at La Trobe University, Melbourne, Australia. He edited the book *Perspectives on Chinese Cinema*.

John Charlot teaches in the Department of Religion at the University of Hawaii and is the author of several books. He curated sections on Vietnamese cinema for the Hawaii International Film Festival.

Darius Cooper is a professor in literature and film studies at San Diego Mesa College. His book on Satyajit Ray's films will be published shortly.

Wimal Dissanayake is a senior fellow at the East-West Center, Hawaii, and the author of several books. He edits the *East-West Film Journal*.

Annette Hamilton is a professor of anthropology and comparative sociology at Macquarie University. One of her main areas of scholarly interest is media in Thailand.

Karl G. Heider is a professor of anthropology at the University of South Carolina. He is a scholar of Indonesian cinema and the author of the book *Indonesian Cinema*.

Patricia Lee Masters holds a Ph.D. from the University of Hawaii. She is the director of the Mutual Assistance Association and a scholar of Japanese culture.

Marie Thorsten Morimoto is a Ph.D. candidate at the University of Hawaii. She is writing a dissertation on issues of national identity in Japanese education.

Isolde Standish is a research student in the School of Oriental and African Studies, University of London, and is interested in Korean and Japanese popular culture.

Graeme Turner is a professor of English at the University of Queensland, Australia, and the author of *Cinema as Social Practice*.

Rob Wilson is a professor of English at the University of Hawaii. He is a scholar and poet and the author of *American Sublime*.

Yingjin Zhang is an assistant professor of Chinese at Indiana University. His book on the configurations of the city in Chinese film and literature will be published shortly.

Index

Ab Dilli Dur Nahin, xvi
The Abandoned Field—Free Fire Zone (Canh dong hoang), 112, 119–20, 124, 136n5, 137n23; American soldiers in, 130; patriotism of, 116; symbolism in, 117; tenderness in, 118
Abeysekera, Tissa, 198
The Accusation (Ya Pror Me Chu), 150, 152, 153
Ah Cheng, 38
Ahas Gavva, 199
Ahmad, Aijaz, 101, 103n19
Ahn Byung-Sup, 96, 97, 99–100
Alam Ara, xv
Along the Road (Para Dige), 200
Amarasekara, Gunadasa, 197, 199
Anderson, Benedict, x, xi–xii, xiv, 12, 50–51, 163, 168, 212
Anderson, Lindsay, 195
Angel at My Table, 207
The Angel of Bar 21 (Thep Thida Bar 21), 149
Apocalypse Now, xxiii, 112
Armes, Roy, 39
Armstrong, Gillian, 207; *My Brilliant Career*, 206; *Starstruck*, 206
Arriving at the Steps of the Bridge (Den Voi Nhung Nhip Cau), 138n25
Ashby, Hal: *Coming Home*, xxiii, 112
Asoka, 193
Avec la Rafale, 138n27

Baan, 153–54
Bach Diep, 111; *Legend of a Mother*, 116, 122, 130; *Punishment*, 121–22
Bae Chang-Ho, 91, 97–98, 103n16
The Baise Uprising (Baise Qifa), 45
Bakhtin, Mikhail, xxvii, 32–33, 37, 38
Bao gio cho den thang muoi. See *When the Tenth Month Comes*
Barthes, Roland, 80, 99
A Baseball Team of Strangers, 92
Bat 21, 117

Battleground Along the Route, 138n27
Bayan Ko: Kapit sa Patalim (My Country: Clutching the Knife), xvii
Benjamin, Walter, 141
Bernal, Ishmael, xxviii
Berry, Chris, 39
Bhabha, Homi, xvii, 43, 51, 52, 55; and *DissemiNation*, xxvii, 53; on forgetting, 46, 59, 198
The Big Steal, 206, 207
Bilwa Mangal, 192
The Birth of New China (Kaiguo dadian), 45
The Black Cannon Incident (Heipao shijian), 53, 54, 97
The Black Republic, 82–83, 92
Blood Oath, 208
The Blood of the Thai Soldier (Leurd Taharn Thai), 147
Bom the Bumpkin (Thang Bom), 116, 128
Boonrak Boonyaketmala, 159n2
Bordwell, David, 65
Born on the Fourth of July, xxiii
Botaan, 148
A Brighter Summer Day (Gulingjie shaonian sharen shijian), 60, 62n11
Brocka, Lino, xvii, xxviii
Broken Promise (Kadavunu Poronduva), 190, 192
Brothers and Relations (Ahn va em), 117, 118, 121, 130
Brothers and Sisters of the Toda Family, 17
Brown, Bryan, 208
Bruner, Edward M., 164
Bui Dinh Hac, 109, 119, 134n1
Buñuel, Luis, 130
Burch, Noël, 20
Butterfly and Flower (Peesua Lae Dokmai), xix–xx, 142

Campion, Jane, 207
Canby, Vincent, 31

Canh dong hoang. See *The Abandoned Field—Free Fire Zone*
Celia, 207
Certeau, Michel de, xxi
Chakrabarty, Dipesh, 51
Chambers, Iain, 214
Chang man, chan mai care, 150
The Changing Countryside (Gam Peraliya), 190, 194–96, 197–98
Chatman, Seymour, 177, 180, 182, 188
Chatree, Sorapong, 155
Chatri-Chalerm Yukala, Prince, 149, 157–58
Chatterjee, Partha, xii
Chayu puin (The Free Woman), 70
Chayu puin 90, 70
Che i sŏng (The Second Sex), 70
Chen Jialin, 45
Chen Kaige, xxii–xxiii, 53; *Yellow Earth,* 37, 38, 39, 54, 97, 99
The Chess Players (Shatranj-Ke-Khilari), xxviii, 179–86, 188–89; making of, 174–76; prologue, 176–79
Chilsu and Mansu (Ch'il-su wa Man-su), 81–82, 92, 100
Chow, Rey, 42
Chuay-Arun, Permpol, 149, 154–55
Chun, Allen, xxv
Chun Doo Hwan (Chon Tu-hwan), 65, 68, 93, 94, 95, 101; student uprisings against, 70–72, 77
Ch'un hyang-chŏn (The Story of Ch'un hyang), 67–68, 72
Chuyen Co Tich Cho Tuoi 17. See *Fairy Tale for 17-Year Olds*
Chuyen Tu Te (Report on Humaneness), 109, 115, 131
Citizen Kane, 112
City at Dawn, 113, 130
A City of Sadness (Beiqing chengshi), xxv–xxvi, 56, 58–59, 60
City Under the Fist (Thi Xa Trong Tam Tay), 116, 122, 125, 126, 131
The Class for Compassion's Sake, 138n25
Come, Come, Come Upward (Aje aje bara aje), 96
Coming Home, xxiii, 112
The Conical Hat (Nom Que), 138n25
Conrad, Joseph, 179
Coppola, Francis Ford: *Apocalypse Now,* xxiii, 112
Cosmatos, George P.: *Rambo: First Blood II,* xxiii, 96, 112
The Cranes are Flying, 112

The Creation of A World (Kaitian pidi), 45
Crichton, Michael, 14
Crocodile Dundee, 203, 206
Cunningham, Stuart, 206–207

Dang Nhat Minh, 106, 113, 124–26, 136n5, 137n17, 139n41, 140n47; *City Under the Fist,* 116, 122, 125, 126, 131; *When the Tenth Month Comes,* 105, 108, 110, 111, 112, 116, 117, 119, 124–25, 127, 128, 130, 134n2; *The Young Woman on the Perfumed River,* 109, 118, 126, 131, 137n13
Daoma zei (Horse Thief), 37, 38, 39, 53, 54
The Day of Return (Ngay Ve), 130, 138n25
Dead Calm, 206
Death by Hanging (Koshikei), xviii, xix
Death in Brunswick, 207
The Decisive Engagements (Dajuezhan), 45–47, 50
Deep Blue Night, 97–98, 103n16
The Deer Hunter, xxiii
The Delinquents, 208
Denzin, Norman K., 143
Depari, Eduard, 171
Dermody, Susan, 210
Derrida, Jacques, 52
Devdas, xv
Devi, Rukmani, 192
Diem, Trinh Mai, 111, 113, 116
Dien Bien Phu, 106, 115, 137n14
Ding Yinnan, 45
Dirks, Nicholas B., xi
Dissakul, Prince Sukornwannadit, 148
Dissanayake, Wimal, 142
Djarot, Eros, xxviii
Djut Nya Dien, 166
Do Minh Tuan, 137n17; *The Lamp in the Dream,* 106, 117, 128–30, 131
Docker, John, 209
Dome Sukvongse, 159n2
Dong Ho Painting Village (Lang Tranh Dong Ho), 113
Dong Zhaoqi, 44
Don't Cry for Salim the Lame (Salim Langde Pe Mat Ro), xix
Double Luck (Chok Song Chan), 147
Dower, John, 15, 16, 17, 26
Duey Klao, 155

Eastwood, Clint, 21
Eckert, Carter J., 66–67, 69, 71
Eisenstein, Sergei, 111, 112
Ekmongkol, Likhit, 150

The Electric Line to the Song Da Construction Site (Duong Day Len Song Da), 113, 138n25
The Elephant Keeper, 157–58
Elshtain, Jean Bethke, 28
The Emperor's Naked Army Marches On (Yuki Yukite Shingun), xxvii, 1, 7–10
The Evil and the Punishment, 114
Eya Dan Loku Lamayek, 198

Factory Angel (Thep Thida Rong Raem), 149
Faiman, Peter: *Crocodile Dundee*, 203, 206
Fairy Tale for 17-Year Olds (Chuyen Co Tich Cho Tuoi 17), 116, 117, 127, 130, 134n2
Fanon, Franz, 52, 174
Farm and Paddy: Our Beloved Home (Baan Rai Na Rao), 148
Fires on the Plain (Nobi), xxvii, 1, 4–7
First Love, 112, 113, 122, 123, 136n5
First Son (Changnam), 98, 99
A Fistful of Dollars, 21
Flood Is Better than Drought (Nam Tuam Dee Kwa Fon Laeng), 148
The Forest of Cuc Phuong, 114
Forster, E. M., 182
Foster, Robert J., 163
Foucault, Michel, 14
Fouquet, Gerard, 159n2
Frankel, Boris, 210
Freud, Sigmund, 19, 46
Fugate, Christine, 142
Full Metal Jacket, xxiii, 140n47

Gabler, Neal, 170–71
Gabriel, Teshome, 38–39
Gallipoli, 203, 209
Geertz, Hildred, 164
Gellner, Ernest, xii
Genroku Chushingura, 15–16
Getino, Octavio, 38
Gibson, Neil, 107, 110, 124, 134n3, 135n4
Giddens, Anthony, xii
Gilmore, Geoffrey D., 134n3, 138n36
The Girl of Hanoi (Em Be Hanoi), 122, 123, 124
The Goddess Quan Am (Quan Am Thi Kinh), 113
The Golden Bird (Con Chun Vanh Khuyen), 111, 119, 121
Gould, Leslie, 134n3
The Green Berets, 130, 140n47
Grievous Bodily Harm, 206
Ground Zero, 206
Guha, Ranajit, 174–75, 184
Gunasinghe, Siri, 192, 197
Gunmen (Muen Puen), 157

Hagen Koo, 95
Hai Ninh, 107, 111, 115–16, 128, 138n36; *City at Dawn*, 113, 130; *First Love*, 112, 113, 122, 123, 136n5; *The Girl of Hanoi*, 122, 123, 124; *The 17th Parallel—Day and Night*, 112, 118, 122, 123, 139n37; *Shipwreck Beach*, 118, 122, 124, 131, 136n13
Hak Kyung Cha, Theresa, 90
Halamchiag, Apichart, 155
Han Hyong-mo, 70
Hannerz, Ulf, 162–63
Hanoi, an Epic Poem, 114
Hanoi Through Whose Eyes (Hanoi—Trong Mat Ai), 109, 115
Hao Guang, 45
Hara Kazuo, xxvi; *The Emperor's Naked Army Marches On*, xvii, 1, 7–10
Harvey, David, xiv
Herman, Dianne, 16
Hibiscus Town (Furongzhen), 44
Ho Chi Minh City, May 1978, 138n25
Hoan Tich Chi, 106
Hobsbawm, Eric, xii
The Home and the World (Ghare Baire), xxi–xxii
Hong Sen, 113, 137n17; *The Abandoned Field—Free Fire Zone*, 112, 116, 117, 118, 119–20, 124, 130, 136n5, 137n23; *Left Alone*, 124
Horse Thief (Daoma zei), 37, 38, 39, 53, 54
Hot Winds (Garam Hava), xxiv–xxv
Hou Xiaoxian, xxv–xxvi, 56–59, 60–61, 62n10
Hu Yaobang, 61
Huang Jianxin, 53, 54, 97
Huang Mingchuan, 60, 62n12
Hwang Chiu, 94–95

Ibraghimov, Ajdai, 111
Im Kwon-Taek, 87n5, 90, 91–92, 96, 97, 99
Independence Day 1945 (Ngay Doc-Lap), 114
In'gan sijang 1, 87n4
In'gan sijang 2, 68
In'gan sijang 89, 87n4
Ishihara Shintaro, 14
Iyer, Pico, 163

Jacka, Elizabeth, 209–214
The Jade Princess (Puteri Giok), xvi, 167–68
Jameson, Fredric, xxvii, 30, 36, 38, 39, 40n4, 97, 102n10
A Japanese Tragedy, 12, 19–20, 28
Jayamanne, B. A. W.: *Broken Promise*, 190, 192
Jayamanne, Eddie, 192
Jayatilake, Amaranath, 198
Jayatilake, K., 197
Jeffords, Susan, 45

Jing Mukui, 45
Joffe, Mark: *Grievous Bodily Harm*, 206

Kalatozov, Mikhail: *The Cranes Are Flying*, 112
Kapoor, Raj, xvi
Karmen, Roman, 111, 135*n*5
Ke Yizheng, 59–60
Kedourie, Elie, xii
Khon Poo Khao, 149
Kidlat Tahimak, 102*n*10
King of the Children (Haizi wang), xxii–xxiii, 53, 54
The King of the White Elephant, 147–48
Kinoshita Keisuke, 12, 19–20, 28
Kobayashi, Victor, 134*n*3
Kotcheff, Ted: *Uncommon Valor*, xxiii
Kozaburo Yoshimura, 2
Kraprayoon, Chana, 149
Kristeva, Julia, 52
Kubrick, Stanley: *Full Metal Jacket*, xxiii, 140*n*47
Kŭdŭlto urich'ŏrŏm, 81
Kukrit Pramoj, M. L., 151–52
Kumai Kei, xxiii
The Kunlun Column (Weiwei kunlun), 45
Kuro arirang, 70, 78–81
Kurosawa Akira, 12, 20–23, 27, 28, 91
Kyôgoku Jun'ichi, 23–24

Lacan, Jacques, 46
Lacquer Painting (Son Mai), 138*n*25
The Lamp in the Dream (Ngon Den Trong Mo), 106, 117, 128–30, 131
Laskin, Emily, 134*n*3
The Last Crime (Toi Loi Cuoi Cung), 110, 120, 131
The Last Distance Between Us (Khoang Cach Con Lai), 110, 117, 127, 130, 131
Le Duc Tien, 127–28, 137*n*17, 139*n*46; *Bom the Bumpkin*, 116, 128; *A Quiet Little Town*, 118, 128, 131
Lee Doo-Yong, 90, 91, 92, 94, 101*n*3; *First Son*, 98, 99; *Spinning Wheel*, 95–96, 97, 98–99
Lee Jang-ho, 92
Lee Kyu-hwan, 67–68, 72
Lee, Peter, 95
Left Alone (Con Lai Mot Minh), 124
Legend of a Mother (Chuyen Thoai Ve Nguoi Me), 116, 122, 130
Lei Feng, 44
Leone, Sergio, 21
Lévi-Strauss, Claude, 3
Li Jun, 45–47, 50

Li Qiankuan, 45
Li Ruihuan, 44–45
Li Xiepu, 45
The Line of Destiny (Rekhava), 193–94, 196
Liu Xiaoqing, 46
Liu Zaifu, 37
Long Yun and Chiang Kai-Shek, 45
Love Duets of Bac Ninh, 114
Lutze, Lothar, 169
Luu Binh and Duong Le, 113
Luu Trong Hong, 137*n*17
Luu Xuan Thu, 111, 137*n*22
Luuk Isaan, 149

MacArthur's Children (Setouchi Shonen Yaku Dan), xxv
Machovsky, S. G., 146
Macrae, Henry A., 147
Mad Max, 203, 206
Malcolm, 206
Maltby, R., 75
A Man Called Karn (Khao Chue Karanta), 152
Man from Island West (Xibu lai de ren), 60, 62*n*12
The Man from Snowy River, 203, 206, 209
The Man with Three Coffins, 92
Maname, 197
Mandala, 91–92, 99
Maple Viewing, xv
Markle, Peter, 117
Maruyama Masao, 13–14, 21
Maund, Laurie, 159*n*6
Medhurst, A., 85
Mellen, Joan, 15, 20
Miller, George: *Mad Max*, 203, 206; *Man from Snowy River*, 203, 206, 209
Minh, Dang Nhat. *See* Dang Nhat Minh
Minogue, Kylie, 208
Mirza, Saeed Akhtar, xix, xxvi
Missing in Action, xxiii
Mizoguchi Kenji, 15–16, 17, 19
Mo Yan, 36
Moffatt, Tracy, 207
Moorhouse, Jocelyn, 207
Mother (Amma), 193
Muang Nai Mag, 155
Mukdasnit, Euthana, xix–xx, xxviii, 142, 149, 150
Mul-wirŭl kinnŭn yŏja, 70
The Mulberry Leaves (Pong), 98
My Brilliant Career, 206

Nairn, Tom, 212
Namja sijang (The Male Market), 68

Nampoo, 150
Nang Sao Suwan, 147
Neale, Stephen, 72
Nehru, Jawaharlal, xvi
Newsfront, 209
Nguyen Ai Quoc—Ho Chi Minh, 113
Nguyen Anh Thai: *When Grandmother is Away*, 118, 120–21, 130, 131
Nguyen Dinh Quang, 108
Nguyen Kim Cuong, 137*n*17
Nguyen Thu, 105, 110–11, 116, 134*n*3, 137*n*14, 137*n*17
Nguyen Van Linh, 110
Nguyen Xuan Son, 137*n*17, 139*n*44; *Fairy Tale for 17-Year Olds*, 116, 117, 127, 130, 134*n*42; *The Last Distance Between Us*, 110, 117, 127, 130, 131
Nice Coloured Girls, 207
Nietzsche, Friedrich, xxvii, 34, 38
Night Cries, 207
Night Pilot (*Nak Bin Klang Kuen*), 148
The Nirvana Street Murders, 207
Niyomsiri, Somboonsuk, 149
Nong Ma Wor Village, 149
Noyce, Phillip: *Dead Calm*, 206; *Newsfront*, 209

Obeyesekere, Vasantha, 198
Oguri Kohei, 12, 16, 23–28
The Old Soldier (*Soldadu Unnahe*), 200
Old Well, 37, 38
On the Fringe of Society (*Pracha Chon Nork*), 149, 153
On The Hunting Ground (*Liechang zhasa*), 54
On the Same River, 106
Once Is Enough, 153
Once Upon a Time in Vu Dai Village (*Lang Vu Dai Ngay Ay*), 120, 134*n*2, 138*n*33
1/50th of a Second in a Lifetime (*Mot Phan Nam Muoi Giay Cuoc Doi*), 113, 134*n*2
Onŭl yŏja (*Today's Woman*), 70
O'Regan, Tom, 206–208, 209
Oshima Nagisa, xviii
Our Sweet Days of Youth, 98
Ozu Yasujirô, 17

P'ae Yong-kyun, 71
Pak Chong-wŏn: *Kuro arirang*, 70, 78–81
Pak Kwang-su, 71, 81–84, 85, 90, 91, 92, 100
Pandey, Gyanendra, xxvii
Park Chung Hee (Pak Chŏng-hŭi), 67, 68–69, 70, 77, 81; film policy of, 72–75
Park Ho-tae, 70
Pathiraja, Dharmasena, 198–201

Pattinson, Michael: *Ground Zero*, 206
Peacock, James, 165
The Peal of the Orange Bell, 120
People in a Slum, 98
Perera, G. D. L., 198
The Perfumed Nightmare, 102*n*10
Peries, Lester James, 190, 193–96, 197–98, 199; *The Line of Destiny*, 193–94, 196
Peries, Sumithra, 198
Phalke, D. G., xv
Pham Ky Nam, 113, 124, 125, 137*n*17, 139*n*39
Pham Van Khoa, 120, 134*n*2, 138*n*33
Phar Lap, 203
Picnic at Hanging Rock, 206
Platoon, xxiii, 112, 140*n*47
Ponmani, 190
Poster, Piak, 153, 155
Ppong, 68
Pracha Chon Nork, 149, 153
Pratt, Mary Louise, 163
Premchand, Munshi, 174, 175, 186–87, 189
Pridi Bannomyong, 147–48
Proof, 207
The Provincial Teacher (*Kroo Baan Nork*), 149
Punishment (*Trung Phat*), 121–22

A Quiet Little Town (*Thi Tran Yen Tinh*), 118, 128, 131

Raja Harishchandra, xv
Rambo: First Blood II, xxiii, 96, 112
Ray Jiing, 62*n*6
Ray, Satyajit, xxi–xxii, xxvi, xxviii, 179–86, 188–89, 195; *The Chess Players* prologue, 176–79; making *The Chess Players*, 174–76
The Red Cochineal, 114
Red Sorghum, xxvii, 30–31, 38–40, 40*n*9, 41*n*20; human body in, 31–32, 33, 37, 38; narrative style of, 35–37; wine image in, 33–35
Ren Pengyuan, 45
Renan, Ernest, 50, 59
Report on Humaneness (*Chuyen Tu Te*), 109, 115, 131
Resnais, Alain, 112
Return to Dien Bien Phu—The Hope, 138*n*28
Rhapsody in August, 27
Rhee, Syngman (Yi Sŭng-man), 66–67
The River of Aspiration (*Dong Song Khat Vong*), 118, 120
Robinson, Andrew, 176
Roh Tae Woo (No T'ae-u), 65, 72
Rouge (*Yanzhi*), 59

Roy, L. Somi, 134n3
Royal Adventure, 191

Sacrificed Youth (Qingchun Ji), xviii–xix, 54
Sadoul, Georges, 195
Said, Edward W., ix, 14–15, 100, 103n20, 174
Said, Salim, 165, 171
Salah Asuhan, 166–67
Sanger, David, 22
Sani, Asrul, 169, 170
Santi Weena, 148
Sarachchandra, Ediriweera, 195, 196, 197
Sardiel, 193
Sarit, Field Marshal, 148
Sasse, W., 86n1, 87n3
Sathu, M. S., xxiv–xxv
Sathuro, 199
Saur Sepuh, 168
Sawetwimol, Santi, 155
Schlatter, Charlie, 208
Schoendoerffer, Pierre, 111, 140n47
The Sea and Poison (Umi to dokuyaku), xxiii
The Secret of the Statue of the Day Pagoda (Dieu Bi An Trong Pho tuong chua Dau), 138n25
Serious, Yahoo: *Young Einstein*, 203, 206
The 17th Parallel—Day and Night (Vi Tuyen 17 Ngay Va Dem), 112, 118, 122, 123, 139n37
Shapiro, M., 87n3
Shatranj-Ke-Khilari. See *The Chess Players*
The Sheikh, 192
Shimpa stories, xv
Shinoda Masahiro, xxv, 11, 12, 17–19
Shipwreck Beach (Bai bien doi nguoi), 118, 122, 124, 131, 136n13
Sinha, D. B. Nihal, 198
Siri Sangabo, 193
The Sisters of Gion, 19
A Small Alley, 122
Solanas, Fernando, 38
Somchart, Bangchaeng, 159n2
The Song of Lei Feng, 44
Songyot Whaewongse, 159n2
Spinning Wheel (Mulleya Mulleya), 95–96, 97, 98, 99
Spivak, Gayatri Chakravorty, 52
Sri, Vijaya Dharma, 198
Staiger, Janet, 191
Starstruck, 206
The Sting of Death, 12, 16, 23–28
Stone, Oliver: *Born on the Fourth of July*, xxiii; *Platoon*, xxiii, 112, 140n47
The Story of Tank Commander Nishizumi, 2
Strike, 112

Sua Thai the Gentleman-Villain (Suparb Booroos Sua Thai), 148
Suh Nam-dong, 87n3
Sunday Too Far Away, 206
Sut'ak (The Rooster), 84, 85
Sweetie, 207
Sykes, Richard, 118

Tadao Sato, 2
Tadashi, Imai, 27
Takeshi: Childhood Days, 12, 17–19, 21, 28
Tass, Nadia, 206
Taweewongsongtong, Chaiwat, 155
Terkel, Studs, 3
There was a Father, 17
Thewakun, Panthewanop, 150
Thi Xa Trong Tam Tay. See *City Under the Fist*
The Thief of Baghdad, 192
Thompson, E. P., xxvi
Thomson, Chris: *The Delinquents*, 208
Thotawatte, Titus, 198
Thu, Nguyen. See *Nguyen Thu*
Tian Zhuangzhuang: *Horse Thief*, 37, 38, 39, 53, 54; *On the Hunting Ground*, 54
Tik'et (Ticket), 87n5
A Time to Live and a Time to Die (Tongnian wangshi), 57–58
Todorov, Tzvetan, 76, 79, 80
Toi Loi Cuoi Cung (The Last Crime), 110, 120, 131
Tong Pan, 149, 157
Tra Giang, 107
Tran Dac, 109
Tran Quang, 120
Tran Van Thuy, 109, 115, 131
Tran Vu: *Brothers and Relations*, 117, 118, 121, 130; *the Golden Bird*, 111, 119, 121; *We Will Meet Again*, 113, 114, 120, 121
Trigger, Bruce G., 169
Trinh Mai Diem, 111, 113, 116
Truffaut, François, 130
Turner, Ann, 207

U-chang Kim, 95
Udomdej, Manop, 149, 150, 152–53
Umukpaemi ŭi sarang (Love in Umukpaemi), 84
Uncommon Valor, xxiii
Unforgotten Days and Nights, 114

Vaadai Kaattu, 190
Victory at Dien Bien Phu (Chien Than Dien Bien Phu), 115
Vietnam on the Road to Victory, 135n5

The Village at the Foot of the Hills (*Desa Di Kaki Bukit*), 169
Village Damsel (*Pitisara Kella*), 193
Virilio, Paul, 1

Wai Tok Kra, 149
Wajda, Andrej, 195
Waking In Seoul, 100–101
Wan Ren, 59
Wang Shaoyan, 44
War and Youth, 27
Wasps Have Come (*Bambaru Avith*), 199–200
Wasuwat, Manit, 147
Wawa, 59–60
Wayne, John: *The Green Berets*, 130, 140n47
We Will Meet Again, 113, 114, 120, 121
Weir, Peter: *Gallipoli*, 203, 209; *Picnic at Hanging Rock*, 206
Welles, Orson: *Citizen Kane*, 112
When Grandmother Is Away (*Khi Vang Ba*), 118, 120–21, 130, 131
When Mother Is Away (*Khi Me Vang Nha*), 118, 120, 138n32
When the Birds Return, 113
When the Tenth Month Comes (*Bao gio cho den thang muoi*), 112, 119, 124–25, 127, 128; making of, 110; mourning in, 130; poetry in, 116, 117, 128; religious aspects of, 108, 111; United States debut of, 105, 134n2
White, Hayden, xi

Wickremasinghe, Martin, 195, 196, 197
Williams, Raymond, 76–77, 80
Wilson, Rob, 103n17
Wimalaweera, Sirisena, 193
Wincer, Simon: *Phar Lap*, 203
Woman of Grace (*Seedevi*), 193

Xiao Guiyun, 45
Xie Jin, 44
Xin Chon Noi Nay Lam Que Huong, 136n5

Yang, Edward (Yang Dechang), 60, 62n11
Yapa, Sugathapala Senerath, 198
Yau, Esther C. M., 96–97
Yellow Earth (*Huang tudi*), 37, 38, 39, 54, 97, 99
Yi Myŏng-se, 71
Yojimbo, 12, 20–23, 28
Young Einstein, 203, 206
The Young Woman of Sao Beach (*Chi Tu Hau Bai Sao*), 124, 139n39
The Young Woman on the Perfumed River (*Co Gai Tren Song*), 109, 118, 126, 131, 137n13
Younger Son (*Podi Putha*), 193
Yun Tong-ju, 93–94

Zhang Nuanxin, xviii–xix, 54
Zhang Yimou, xxvii, 30–31, 36, 38, 39, 41n29
Zhong Chengxiang, 40n9
Zhou Enlai, 45